Feminist
Organizations

IN THE SERIES

Women in the Political Economy

EDITED BY RONNIE J. STEINBERG

FEMINIST ORGANIZATIONS

Harvest of the New Women's Movement

EDITED BY

Myra Marx Ferree
and Patricia Yancey Martin

Temple University Press
Philadelphia

Temple University Press, Philadelphia 19122
Copyright © 1995 by Temple University (except Chapter 5,
copyright © Hester Eisenstein, and Chapter 25, copyright
© Jo Freeman). All rights reserved
Published 1995
Printed in the United States of America

Library of Congress Cataloging-in-Publication Data

Feminist organizations : harvest of the new women's movement / edited
by Myra Marx Ferree and Patricia Yancey Martin.
    p.   cm. — (Women in the political economy)
    Includes bibliographical references (p.   ) and index.
    ISBN 1-56639-228-4 (CL : alk. paper). — ISBN 1-56639-229-2 (PB :
alk. paper)
    1. Feminism—United States—Societies, etc.   2. Women—United
States—Societies and clubs.   I. Ferree, Myra Marx.   II. Martin,
Patricia Yancey.   III. Series.
HQ1426.F4727   1995
035.42′06′073—dc20

                                                    94-2718

Illustration on pages iii, 1, 25, 135, 221, 261, 337, 395, and
409 by Estelle Carol and the Women's Graphics Collective.
Women's Graphics Collective, Chicago. Special Collections
Department, Northwestern University Library.

Contents

Acknowledgments

The story of this book is somewhat surreal; it feels more as if the book chose us than the reverse. The process began in March 1990 at the Eastern Sociological Society meetings, when Patricia Yancey Martin, Myra Marx Ferree, and Robin Leidner found themselves in the hallway between sessions deploring the scarcity of research on feminist organizations, comparing notes on who was doing what, and fantasizing about the possibility of bringing these researchers from different disciplines and specialties into contact with one another. On the spot, Pat and Myra recklessly decided to apply for funding for a working group conference. We guessed that six—if we were lucky, perhaps a dozen—other scholars might be interested. We were under the illusion that few researchers were working on feminist organizations as such. We were, as subsequent events happily revealed, wrong.

We sent invitations to ten scholars, chosen to represent a mix of disciplines and all career stages, from pre-dissertation to the most established reputation. Every single one agreed to participate. As word of mouth spread, others *asked* to be included. We had received start-up funding from the American Sociological Association's "problems in the discipline" small-grant program, funded by the National Science Foundation. Even the minimum expenses of our growing conference could not be met by this grant, and our universities (the University of Connecticut and Florida State University) generously provided matching funds. We are grateful for all the financial support we received, but even so, most of the conference costs were paid by the attendees.

All told, forty-three scholars came, representing eight different fields —political science, history, anthropology, American studies, women's studies, social work, organizational behavior, and sociology—and including three from Great Britain and one from Canada. We are very grateful for all the help we had in making this unexpectedly large but shoestring-budget conference come to pass. Janet Astner of the American Sociological Association provided her expertise and helped us find a convenient and reasonable Washington hotel. Our friend and colleague in sociology at George Washington University, Ruth Wallace, recruited two very capable graduate students, Rachelle Cummins and Gail Hanson, who did all the hard work of handling local arrangements.

The conference itself was a watershed event. The intensity and intelligence of the discussion were memorable, as was the fact that everyone truly managed to participate. As editors we owe a great debt to the conference attendees, who raised issues, challenged assumptions, and shaped the discussion in ways we could never have foreseen. We particularly thank those who offered so much and yet for various reasons do not have a paper in this volume: Rebecca Bordt, Helen Brown, Steve Buechler, Esther Chow, Celia Davies, Jennifer Frost, Heidi Gottlieb, Vivien Hart, Robin Leidner, Sharon Maxwell, Beth Reed, Joyce Rothschild, Barbara Ryan, Deborah Schwartz, Carmen Sirianni, Ronnie Steinberg, and Penny Weiss.

The gap between conference and book is a long one, and many others supported us in making that leap. We especially thank University of Connecticut graduate students Diane Schaal, for her tireless efforts on the seemingly endless clerical and bibliographic chores, and Rachel Levy, Lance Hannon, and Stephane Baldi, whose help at various stages was critical; thanks are owed as well to Christine Mowery at the University of Delaware and Marlene Powell at Florida State University. Friends and colleagues also came through with assistance, often at short notice. Our warmest gratitude is extended to Judith Lorber and Beth Hess, who helped out when we needed it most—just when we thought we would lose our minds if we read yet another revision! Their brilliant editing helped several of our authors to sharpen and focus their arguments better than we had been able to do. Susan Hartmann and Ronnie Steinberg also read and offered valuable comments on the manuscript, including desperately needed help in finding an organizational structure.

We thank the contributing authors, all twenty-five of them, who undertook to provide an original essay for an edited collection—like editing itself, an undervalued task in academia. Appreciation is due to some for bearing with us through the many drafts we demanded of them and for the hard work they invested in revising and revising again, and to others who spared all of us by turning in such polished and elegant drafts.

Editing is always more work than one imagines when one plunges into a task such as this. Why else would any sane person do it? But this project has also brought more pleasure than we could have guessed. In addition to the remarkable experience of the conference itself, we have truly enjoyed the opportunity to come to know the authors in this book as we worked with them, and to get to know each other much better as well. Having e-mail to speed our thinking back and forth, we have really worked *together*. Getting this book out, finally, means we will now have to find other ex-cuses to team up, but we look forward to our continued collaboration as yet another reason to be thankful that this book found us.

PART I

Introduction

CHAPTER I

Doing the Work of the Movement: Feminist Organizations

■

MYRA MARX FERREE
AND PATRICIA YANCEY MARTIN

Among the most fundamental developments in American society in the past thirty years is the reemergence of feminism as a significant, though controversial, force. The political visibility of feminist ideas ranges from A(nita Hill) to Z(oe Baird). Indeed, Jo Freeman argues that the primary political parties in the United States are engaged in nothing less than a polarized culture war over the place of feminism in American society: "The two political parties have now completely polarized around feminism and the reaction to it. . . . On feminist issues and concerns the parties are not following the traditional pattern of presenting different versions of the same thing. . . . They are presenting two different and conflicting visions of how Americans should engage in everyday life" (1993, 21). In families and workplaces around the country, feminism is invoked to explain conflict and justify change as well as to attack proponents and decry efforts to challenge the status quo. The very centrality of feminism to American social and political debates, however, suggests that the women's movement has successfully called into question many taken-for-granted ideas about male dominance and institutionalized privilege based on gender.

Feminism's impact is evident on many fronts. When a judge in New York scolds attorneys for their attempt to depict a rape victim as a "loose woman," this reflects a change in consciousness, one outcome of twenty years of work by rape crisis centers. When the Association of American Colleges makes inclusion of scholarship on women a criterion for acceptable liberal arts curricula, credit must be given to the decades of work by women's studies programs, women's research centers, and women's caucuses in the academic disciplines. When citizens by the hundreds of thousands take to the streets of Washington to press for a Congressional guarantee of women's reproductive rights, their mobilization represents the grassroots organizing done by hundreds of local chapters of national feminist organizations and community-based programs.

As these examples attest, the movement's impact can be attributed in large part to the activities of feminist organizations that have worked for change—in the law, the courts, universities, corporations, local communities and individual women's lives. Few people have remained untouched, directly or indirectly, by these organizing efforts. The cultural changes they have triggered are one important indicator of their success. A second measure of the effectiveness of feminist organizations is the vehemence of the countermovements they have generated, evident in the mobilization of anti-feminist organizations such as Eagle Forum, the National Association of Scholars, and Operation Rescue.

A third measure is the sheer number of feminist groups. Literally thousands of organizations—including rape crisis centers, battered women's shelters, women's studies programs, women's health clinics, and women's bookstores, restaurants, theater groups, credit unions, and other profit and nonprofit organizations—were founded during the past three decades. Many have survived, some have prospered, and most have had a profound impact on the lives of women they touched. The women's movement exists because feminists founded and staffed these organizations to do the movement's work. Some are as tentative as volunteer-run hotlines, others as intense as illegal abortion collectives, still others as massive as the nation-wide National Organization for Women. All these organizations sustain women and are sustained by them. They are tangible evidence of the movement in many feminists' lives and in the social and political life of the nation. But few of them have been studied in the depth and detail they deserve.

Despite dramatic growth in the number of feminist organizations in this generation, feminism itself is not new. Its roots go back well over a hundred years (Flexner 1959; Buechler 1990b), even though the term "feminist" came into common use only at the turn of the century (Cott 1987). To be sure, when scholars spoke of feminism before the late 1960s, they were referring to the remnant of early twentieth-century feminism that persisted on a small and declining scale through the 1950s (Rupp and Taylor 1987). But in the 1960s a new type of women's movement emerged as a clarion call to millions of women to rethink their priorities and question the social arrangments that defined them as second-class citizens. Many long-institutionalized organizations of the earlier feminists, such as the National Women's Party, the League of Women Voters, and the American Association of University Women, provided organizational resources and a sense of history to the nascent movement and were themselves revitalized by the new mobilization. The women's liberation groups that grew out of the student left and new women's rights organizations such as the National Organization for Women gradually defined themselves as part of a single larger movement that they came to call feminism. The term feminism thus was expanded and rejuvenated, to cover a multitude of movements: among them, efforts for reproductive rights, employment and pay equity, and the political representation of women at all levels; against battering, rape, and other forms of violence against women, to name a few.

Some of the activists involved claimed to have invented a unique type of organization, a *feminist* organization, which they defined as embracing collectivist decision-making, member empowerment, and a political agenda of ending women's oppression. Working with women, for women, they encountered tensions and problems in their inevitable collisions and collaborations with what they called "the male-stream." For some, the tension between separatist culture and mainstream political change proved unmanageable, but a large number of rape crisis centers, feminist women's health centers, shelters for battered women, women's studies programs and research institutes, bookstores, art galleries, and theater collectives did survive. As chapters in this volume demonstrate, the organizations that did not collapse changed, though not necessarily in the direction of stultifying bureaucracy and displaced goals predicted by Robert Michel's "Iron Law of Oligarchy."[1] Although often classified as a social movement "of the 1960s," the second wave of the women's movement has organizationally outlived many of its contemporaries. This book addresses the fundamental questions of how and why so many feminist organizations managed to endure. What price did they pay? What effects have they had? What promise do they hold?

A Story of Survival and Effectiveness

Feminism is not dead, we believe, largely because of the number and variety of organizations it generated, nurtured, and influenced. Indeed, feminism can no longer be easily classified into bureaucratic or collectivist forms, if it ever could (Ferree and Hess 1985, 1994). Contemporary feminist organizations mix both elements in their structures, practices, and goals as they work to survive and to transform society. We see four aspects to the picture of survival and effectiveness drawn by the essays in this collection.

First is the issue of *institutionalization*. By institutionalization we mean the development of regular and routinized relationships with other organizations. Many feminist organizations founded in the decade 1965 to 1975 are celebrating their twentieth or twenty-fifth anniversaries. Their survival provides evidence that they became institutionalized in at least some respects. While organizations that would not or could not institutionalize folded, they served an important purpose nevertheless, as chapters in this volume by Strobel, Whittier, and Staggenborg attest. The important, and largely unasked, question about feminist organizations that survived is what their institutionalization means for feminism. Such organizations were surely co-opted in some ways, but did they abandon their feminist goals, practices, and agendas? To invoke a standard of feminist purity, as some have done (Ahrens 1980), obscures awareness of the ways in which organizations continue to seek and sometimes achieve significant change. The articles in this volume illustrate how feminist organizations question authority, produce new elites, call into question dominant societal values, claim resources on behalf of women, and provide space and resources for feminists to live out altered visions of their lives.

A rape crisis counselor, no matter how institutionalized her relationships with the police may become, is unlikely to feel indifferent about rape. Caring deeply about it, in her own life and in the lives of other women, she may work hard and long to combat it. It may be a central issue for her long after she stops working in a center. The personal passage through a feminist organization by feminist activists has been and remains transforming for many (Remington 1990, 1991). Organizational experiences can shape world views, politics, and a sense of self in relation to society, as many women can testify. It is important not merely to see individuals as resources used by organizations (as much social movement theory does) but to consider how individuals use the organizations they found or join, and how they employ the lessons learned in one group when they move to another. The empirical evidence gathered by Spalter-Roth and Schreiber, Reinelt, Eisenstein, Matthews, and Katzenstein challenges the claim that institutionalization necessarily leads to deradicalization. Chapters by Strobel, Barnett, Whittier, and Christiansen-Ruffman raise further questions about the political learning that goes on within movement organizations. In evaluating any feminist organization, we think it appropriate to ask: Were any of the activists or women on whose behalf they worked transformed? Did society change at all as a result of their efforts? Do the organizations continue to make a difference?

Second is the issue of *the relationship of feminist organizations to the movement*. We argue that the women's movement exists in a dynamic and reciprocal relation with its organizations, giving them their broad purpose, specific agenda, and supply of activists, while drawing from them a set of practices, political and material resources, and a supportive context within which activists can carry on their lives while struggling for change. This is a relationship that Mansbridge's chapter calls "accountability," and it exists as both an individual and a collective tension in the movement (see also Leidner 1993). Although social movements cannot be reduced to their formal organizations, such institutions are vital. The resource mobilization perspective on social movements has often severed the study of social movement organizations from the study of the movement as a fundamental challenge to the status quo, as if survival and institutionalization were the *goals* rather than the *means* of movements. Scholars are only now recognizing what activists have long known: the transformative intent and impact of feminist organizations (see Leidner 1991; Blanchard 1992; Martin et al. 1992). We think it appropriate to ask, as Staggenborg does in this volume: How does organizational survival help or hinder the accomplishment of the movement's broader agenda? What are the short- and long-term effects on policy, mobilization potential, and the surrounding culture?

Third is the issue of the *tensions arising from the multidimensionality of feminist politics*. The feminist movement is not coherent, singular, or unified. It does not and cannot pursue a single strategic course. It is a multifaceted mobilization that has taken different forms at different times, in different areas of the country, in different socioeconomic and political contexts, and among women of diverse racial, ethnic, class, and age groups, as chapters by Christiansen-Ruffman, Whittier, and Arnold particularly demonstrate. It is possible to appreciate this variety most when we look at movement organizations, for they vary in scale, scope, intent, form, and practice in amazingly rich and multiple ways. This diverse movement is constantly engaged in internal political relations: that is, in negotiations among participants that allow decisions to be made and work to be done (see Melucci 1989). This process is evident in women's movement organizations and their practices. The vitality and tensions of these organizations must be seen in the context of the social movement they represent.

Feminist organizations are an amalgam, a blend of institutionalized and social movement practices. They have changed over time in response to their own needs, the needs of the women they serve, and the demands of their environment (see Schmitt 1994). In the position of *outsider*, they pursue a feminist agenda that has barely begun to alter the social arrangements that disempower and victimize women. Yet as *insiders*, many have achieved a measure of respect and acceptance from the mainstream, becoming so familiar as to be no longer newsworthy, becoming so successful as to arouse resentments, angry reactions, and sometimes violent attacks. A movement organization is not a contradiction in terms, but it is, by definition, in tension. It is always a compromise between the ideals by which it judges itself and the realities of its daily practices, as the essays by Farrell, Morgen, Matthews, Pardo, Tom, Arnold, Spalter-Roth and Schreiber, Mueller, and Acker bear witness. To understand the tensions intrinsic to feminist politics, we need to ask: What compromises are made, and at whose expense? Which groups of women set the agenda for the practical politics done in and by the organization, and on whose behalf? How are the day-to-day negotiations for survival carried out and with what effect?

Fourth, feminist organizations are the outcome of *situationally and historically specific processes*. In each time and place, feminism reflects its history and prior developments as well as present opportunities and constraints, as shown particularly in chapters by Gelb, Barnett, Pardo, Eisenstein, Simonds, and Christiansen-Ruffman (see also Katzenstein and Mueller 1987; Gelb 1989). The global women's movement consists of many diverse movements that coexist and often are quite dissimilar. The specific shape and nature of the women's movements in the United States in the 1990s reflects distinctive features of American history: for example, the relative weakness of a socialist tradition, the continuing significance of race, a decade of an antifeminist national administration. In addition, American feminism has been shaped by distinctive political practices and opportunities such as the prominence of lobbying groups, grassroots voluntary organizations, and a tradition of nonprofit community services to supplement a weak welfare state, as well as by the exceptionally active mobilization from the right, which has both attacked and borrowed from feminism, as we see in the chapters by Marshall, Hyde, and Simonds. These factors contribute to the plenitude of women's movement organizations of all sizes, shapes, and orientations. As Gelb's chapter points out, no other nation-state has as large and diverse a set of feminist organizations as the United States. American feminists work through these organizations to influence organizations of many other types—political, educational, religious, and commercial. Appreciation of the variety of their forms, practices, goals, ideologies, and effects will increase understanding of second-wave feminism's survival and its varying, albeit partial, successes. In evaluating a feminist organization we should ask: How are its options expanded or limited by the features of the legal, political, or economic situations with which it has to deal? by the specific generational, economic, or racial/ethnic experiences and identities of its members? by its history?

Activists' experiences within feminist organizations provide a rich and largely unmined source of data for the development of social theory. The editors come from two areas of sociology—namely, political sociology (Ferree) and the sociology of organizations (Martin)—that have not taken much theoretical account of these developments. In considering why this is so, we hope to encourage this pattern to change.

Why Have Feminist Organizations Been Ignored?

Despite a quarter-century of successful organization, feminist groups have largely been ignored by organizational scholars. Most sociologists of organizations, and their favored theories, have focused on large corporations, state bureaucracies, and labor unions that presume men to be their primary members and that relegate women, and women's life circumstances and experiences, to the margins (Acker 1990). Concern with big-budget, politically powerful organizations is consistent with the sociopolitical standpoint of men who have many qualities in common with the similarly (or more) privileged men who run large business and state organizations. These sociologists are unlikely to perceive small, grassroots, social movement organizations founded by feminists as interesting or important. If the dominant models and norms that guide organizational theory, research, and publication view such low-budget, high-commitment, women-run organizations as uninteresting, women scholars (who have low status within the discipline, the academy, and the subspeciality of organizational research) may be reluctant or unable to challenge them. Biases toward managerial needs and rational-technical control in large public and private organizations strongly encourage women organizational scholars to attend to similar issues.

To change this situation, a critical mass of feminist scholars in many disciplines must cooperatively develop new theory and discourse about feminist organizations. Such theory should have practical value for feminist activists who work in organizations to produce social transformations that benefit women. The felt need for such study can be seen in efforts of activists themselves to take stock of where they are and where they are going (see esp. Remington 1990, 1991). We have assembled this book as the first scholarly step in that direction.

We intend this volume also to challenge the preconceptions in feminist theory. Until recently, much of the women's studies perspective and research on feminist organizations reflected ideological judgments more than systematic observation of their forms, practices, and effects (as Ryan [1992] argues; see Ferguson 1984). In "Rethinking Feminist Organizations," Martin (1990b) sets an agenda within sociology for research on feminist organizations that focuses on their concrete forms and practices and on the dilemmas and effects their participants experience. Several popular claims are questioned, including the assumption that bureaucracy is inherently antithetical to feminism, and its corollary, that institutionalized feminist organizations cannot be agents of change. Martin calls for a more open-ended approach to the study of feminist organizations and a focus on what they do, how they work, and their transformative impact on members, other women, and all of society. Ferree and Hess (1985, 1994) have also argued against prejudging one type of feminist organizational strategy as more central or effective than another; rather, different organizational forms (such as grassroots and participatory service-delivery, mass-membership mobilization for lobbying or demonstrations, expertise-centered educational efforts, and identity-oriented, culture-building work) all play important and distinctive roles in the movement of which they are a part. Staggenborg (in this volume) proposes that outcomes that count as successes can be found in policy, organizational, and cultural arenas, and that all three are important. This book will, we hope, move the scholarly agenda toward a more balanced accounting of the successes and failures of feminist organizations and of feminist protest, organizing, and activity from within other organizations.

Biases in theories of gender and social change have also led scholars away from the study of feminist organizations. Theoretical models such as the old sex role paradigm led to countless studies of attitude change about women's roles but neglected feminist efforts for structural and political change. For example, although many studies of attitudes about rape were conducted, few asked whether or not changes in rape-processing laws or procedures affected women's experience of sexual assault and, either way, how and why so? On the one hand, within social movement theory, those who define themselves as working on new social movements (e.g., Melucci 1989; Rucht 1988) have singled out some types of feminist activism for attention (especially the identity-centered small groups) but discounted those organizations that cooperate with the mainstream as co-opted or inconsequential. On the other hand, many political scientists and sociologists who work within the resource mobilization paradigm have focused almost exclusively on mass-membership organizations such as the National Organization for Women, taking institutionalization for granted, and ignoring grassroots organizations where membership is difficult to define and where formal structures and survival dilemmas are difficult to see. The chapters by Barnett, Christiansen-Ruffman, Taylor, and Staggenborg further develop this critique.

In sum, a number of theoretical biases and limitations have contributed to pervasive inattention to feminist organizations. As submerged networks of actual and potential mobilizers, the women's movement is sustained by the organizations it has produced, and these *less than totally institutionalized* organizations may be more challenging and disturbing to the status quo than some critics seem to think (Martin 1994). The police may, for example, think rape crisis staffers are *raving feminists* who demand immediate, profound change; and college administrators may view their *radical* women's studies programs with alarm, with little regard for how conforming and mainstream such organizations try to appear and, indeed, in many ways are (see Martin 1994). What if the police and college administrators are correct, and movement scholars who focus on the failures of rape crisis centers and women's studies programs to be "truly" radical are wrong? Social movement researchers who deplore the ideological and procedural imperfections of feminist organizations may be underappreciating these groups' practical situations and their role in producing fundamental political and social change (as critiques by Marshall, Reinelt, Katzenstein, and Eisenstein in this volume suggest).

Feminist organizations are, we argue, a form of movement mobilization in the present and a resource for feminist mobilization in the future. Indeed, the most important outcome of any wave of social movement mobilization may be the institutionalized resources it provides for future mobilizations (Tarrow 1983; Mueller 1992). Organizations reach across individual life spans, connect generations, and transmit their members' memories, hard-earned wisdom, and unrealized hopes. Organizations define boundaries between insiders and outsiders, establish hierarchies, garner resources, provide a home base for activists, and institutionalize mistakes as well as successes. Thus the women's movement of the future will, for better or worse, reflect today's feminist organizations, just as these organizations reflect a movement with an extensive, complex, and contradictory past.

In recent years, research on feminist organizations has increased (e.g., Morgen 1986; Sealander and Smith 1986; Tudiver 1986; Gelb 1989; Staggenborg 1989, 1991; Leidner 1991, 1993; Solomon 1991) and an outpouring of case study material on women's protest activities has appeared (e.g., Mansbridge 1986; Bookman and Morgen 1988; Echols 1989; Blumberg and West 1990; Mathews and DeHart 1990). These scholars have begun to ask about what a range of feminist organizations are doing, why they are making the choices they make, and what effects they are having on their members and society. When we learned of the number of individual scholars struggling with these questions, we thought the time was ripe to bring them together into a broader discussion of feminist organizations.

The tie that binds us in this book, and many of the pioneers who studied feminist organizations before us, is feminism, not our disciplines or specialities within disciplines. The scholars confronting these questions are diverse in discipline, and many do not define their specialities as either social movements or formal organizations. Some are interested in women's politics, some in women's history, some in feminist practice, some in social change, and only a few in feminist organizations per se. With this book we collectively attempt to legitimate a new field of interdisciplinary study and to share the insights and questions that we have discovered we hold in common.

The Background of This Book

This volume arose from a form of feminist organization. Martin had organized a session on feminist critiques of bureaucracy at the 1987 American Sociological Association annual meeting. Both Ferree and Martin had found themselves as commentators on panels of papers (at the 1990 Berkshire Conference on the History of Women and at the American Sociological Association) that demonstrated strong interest in this topic but showed little connection to theories of either social movements or social organization. We saw virtually no networking among scholars and little theorizing about the significance of individual feminist organizations for the movement as a whole. To address these concerns, in February 1992 we organized a conference on the topic "Feminist Organizations: Harvest of the New Women's Movement" in Washington, D.C., with funding from a Problems of the Discipline grant (from the National Science Foundation and American Sociological Association) and our home institutions. Where we initially expected a dozen or so researchers to participate, even our limited effort to begin networking turned up more than three times as many. Ultimately, forty-three scholars, a mix of established researchers and recent and pending Ph.D.s from a range of disciplines, reported on their empirical research and discussed theoretical questions about feminist organizations. We aimed for a wide range of participants and a broad perspective to create a basis for the development of comprehensive, useful, and practical theory. Our goal was and is to develop theory not only *of* the women's movement but *for* the movement (a phrase we owe to Steve Buechler, one of the conference participants), ideas that work not only for scholars but for the countless activists and organizations that do feminist work "in the street" (Mansbridge, this volume).

This collection is the result of the conference. We include many essays first presented there as working drafts and others unearthed by the networks formed there. We regretfully excluded some excellent papers that did not quite fit or get finished on time. Grounded in the specifics of concrete cases, our book contributes to theory through analytical essays that will, we hope, help future scholars investigate the richly diverse feminist organizational landscape. The chapters by Mansbridge, Gelb, Acker, Taylor, Mueller, Staggenborg, and Freeman particularly fall in this category. The others focus, variously, on feminist efforts to reshape an organizational context from the inside; on the experiences of members in creating, sustaining, or working within feminist organizations; and on the diversity of organizational practices that produce transformative changes in individuals and society. The authors represent a range of fields within the social sciences: political science, history, anthropology, Chicano studies, American studies, women's studies, social work, education, and sociology.

By titling the book "feminist organizations," we direct attention to the intersection of feminism as a social movement with organizations as entities that mobilize and coordinate collective action. We do not view feminist organizations either as organizational subtypes or as ideal types. *We define feminist organizations as the places in which and the means through which the work of the women's movement is done.* Despite the variety of cases examined here, had we included the full range and variety of feminist organizational types and forms, the volume would be still thicker. We direct attention to existing studies of feminist theater groups (Solomon 1991), feminist art galleries (Quinney 1990), women's studies journals (Blanchard

1992), the National Women's Studies Association (Leidner 1991, 1993), and political networks at the international (Tudiver 1986), national (Gelb and Palley 1987), and local (Boles 1991) levels; to additional research on feminist organizations providing health care (Morgen 1986; Thomas 1993), rape crisis services (Burt, Gornick, and Pittman 1984; Gornick, Burt, and Pittman 1985; Matthews 1989; Byington et al. 1991; Koss and Harvey 1991; Martin et al. 1992) and shelter for battered women (Schechter 1982; Rodriguez 1988); to feminist organizing among women of color (Giddings 1984; Chow 1987; Garcia 1989); in unions (Gabin 1990; Blum 1991), and on behalf of specific issues such as the ERA (Mansbridge 1986; Mathews and DeHart 1990). We note the existence of many other types of feminist organizations and issues that cry out for more detailed organizational study: for-profit organizations such as presses, bookstores, and record companies; nonprofit groups with a dual focus on women of color and a specific feminist issue, such as the National Black Women's Health Network; political groups ranging from nonpartisan state Commissions on the Status of Women through the partisan fund raisers (Democratic) EMILY's List or (Republican) WISH List; the organizational forms taken by women's studies programs or departments on different campuses and the variety of resources and objectives they hold; the networks built between informal lesbian communities and formal membership organizations working on feminist issues; the structure of both long-lived organizations such as the Women's Bureau of the Department of Labor and ephemeral ones such as R2N2 (Reproductive Rights National Network); the differences among the fifty states in the organizational structures and effectiveness of feminist policy networks.

To what extent does the term *feminist organizations* capture the content in ou book? It works well in most respects but falls short of our ideals in others. For example, we wish we could better capture the *processual* aspect of feminist organizing that is the focus of many chapters. Thus the title may not seem to apply as well to the organizing that consciously expresses feminist resistance from within the mainstream, discussed particularly by Eisenstein, Katzenstein, and Reinelt. Still, no feminist organizations are wholly set apart from male-dominated institutions, and all are engaged in a process of organizational change. We do not wish to suggest that feminist organizations are a static outcome of mobilization efforts rather than a continuing process of organizing to produce social transformations that benefit women (see Acker, this volume).

Broad as it is, our book is limited in other ways also, particularly in regard to country, race, and time. Whereas our title may suggest a universal claim, our accomplishment is intentionally more modest. Our chapters chiefly concern feminist organizations in the United States, although we do include some offerings from Canada and Australia as sister nations, to help us reflect on issues in feminist organizing across societies. Our selections focus primarily on those organizations staffed mostly by White middle-class feminists, although chapters on organizing women of color deliberately challenge conventional thinking about the boundaries and meanings of feminist organizations in general. Our collection concentrates on issues and organizations mostly from the 1980s, but some selections reach back to the 1960s and 1970s to provide historical points of reference against which these current concerns and patterns can be assessed.

We think it crucial for the book to include non-U.S., non-White, and non-1980s organizations, because these studies draw attention to feminism of different types and forms and prevent an overly parochial definition of feminism. Yet we do no see it as a shortcoming that this volume focuses on the efforts and situations of predominantly White women in the United States in the 1980s who were struggling to practice feminism in organizational contexts, because their experiences are still seriously underresearched. The contrasts provided by our wider comparisons highlight the invisible background of their self-described feminist practice. Moreover, several studies address common misconceptions. Strobel, for example, notes the struggles to be race- and class-inclusive that formed the practice of the Chicago Women's Liberation Union in the early 1970s, and Barnett notes that mainstream White women's organizations saw race as more important than gender in the 1950s. Such studies raise the important question of how (some) White feminists learn to recognize and critique racial (and class and ethnic) bias. Chapters by Katzenstein, Tom, Eisenstein, and Mueller offer insights on this question.

The Current Context of Feminist Activism

The largely invisible field of action in which the women's movement was, and is, moving and developing has fed the claims of some that the feminist movement is declining if not dead already (cf. Faludi 1991). These widely circulating and frequently accepted claims are given credence, even in feminist circles, because the localized efforts of grassroots feminists have been undocumented, unanalyzed, and unacknowledged. How, in the presence of the tremendous variety and impact of feminist organizations that this book documents, is it possible for activists to believe that the women's movement is dead or that a postfeminist period has arrived?

We think there are many reasons. The very ubiquity of some types of feminist organizations has tended to make them unremarkable. Many people, ourselves included, take them for granted. Feminist organizations are no longer news; thus they rarely draw media attention. Or, if the media do report on them, they rarely acknowledge the organizations' feminism. A newspaper may feature a story on battered women's shelters, focusing on the women and the shelter's efforts to help them, but never mention that this organizational response to violence against women arose from and remains rooted in feminism as a social movement, or that activists continue to critique battering as a form of male domination. Younger women are often shocked to realize how recently the many organizations where they study, work, volunteer, or turn for services were founded; they assume that women's studies programs, rape crisis centers, battered women's shelters, abortion providers and birthing centers, feminist bookstores, women's concerts, and the like have always been available.

If the women's movement disappears from the pages of the press, we should not be surprised if readers infer that the movement is "gone," especially if some elements of the media are actively telling them so. This is, we believe, a pernicious myth. In quantitative terms, the number of women who participate in feminist organizations—whether as occasional volunteers, committed contributors, employees, advocates, or students—is surely much greater today than it was in the heyday of the consciousness-raising group. While the public may be aware of local feminist organizations, such as health clinics, bookstores, hotlines, or shelters, the radical challenges such groups pose may be obscured by their pervasiveness and taken-for-granted nature. In Washington the women's policy network, including such obviously feminist organizations as the National Organization for Women, continues to raise fundamental issues as well as negotiating for more modest but essential short-term victories. These feminist organizations are *seen but unseen* and rarely acknowledged as successful mobilizations of a movement that continues to press for change (Spalter-Roth and Schreiber, this volume).

A more accurate measure of the health of the contemporary women's movement can be made by taking stock of feminist organizations. We believe the strengths and weaknesses of the movement are revealed in feminist organizational dynamics. This includes the ability to withstand an onslaught of antifeminist mobilization, actively encouraged by the federal administration in the 1980s. The chapters by Marshall, Simonds, and Hyde portray this countermobilization most graphically. Not only are abortion providers under physical siege (as Hyde and Simonds show), but other feminist organizations too have become targets of the New Right's fury. Women's studies programs are under attack from right-wing ideologues (see the statement of principles of the National Association of Scholars); battered women's shelters are denounced as feminist enclaves set on destroying the family and male authority (see testimony in the *Congressional Record* by opponents of federal funding).

This paradoxical situation, in which feminist organizations are invisible to many yet vehemently attacked by the New Right, is a consequence of feminist institutionalization. Implications of institutionalization on internal movement dynamics also cry out for study. Judy Remington, a feminist activist and journalist in Minneapolis, suggests that feminist organizations have struggled to survive but have rarely considered what it would take to achieve more than the minimum, to prosper rather than just hang on (1991). While acknowledging the tremendous obstacles to mere survival, she challenges feminists to imagine more than this, to think through what a more mature and institutionalized movement might seek, and to have the courage to consider the limits feminists have placed on their own organizations. Remington argues, for example, that the concept of empowerment is self-limiting: What can feminist organizations do for women who are already powerful and strong besides make them feel guilty about the power they hold and punish them for their strength and leadership? She recounts the example of one leader who minimized her authority by writing her title as small as possible ("Exec. Dir.") and describes many cases where the drive for egalitarianism drove out the best and the brightest. If we do not acknowledge the power women have, how can powerful women exercise it responsibly? Chapters by Reinelt and Eisenstein argue for an expanded and more constructive understanding of power, including ways to avoid what Remington (1990) calls "running with the brakes on" by limiting women's willingness to be powerful.

Harnessing the abilities of all and encouraging women to work to the fullest extent of their potential requires feminist organizations and activists to confront the issues of institutionalization more squarely. In the 1990s we are discovering that being a social movement and being an organization with social and political power are not mutually contradictory alternatives but complexly interrelated processes, which we have barely begun to study.

In sum, we submit that the U.S. women's movement of the 1990s is manifested in many issue-focused movements and diverse feminist organizations. The movements for reproductive rights, against battering, and so on have produced innovative organizations that continue to offer feminist critique and organizational resources for political change, with or without the echo of protest activities on the streets. Neither ignorance of their origins nor counterattack by their opponents has extinguished their spark. Many so-called institutionalized organizations continue to engage in protest and pursue a radical social change agenda from within the mainstream. Activists wander back and forth between organizational expressions of feminism: They attend a women's studies class in the morning, volunteer in a clinic defense group in the afternoon, attend a women's music concert in the evening. In its penetration of and connection with the realities of women's daily lives, the contemporary women's movement differs from the feminist movements that preceded it and from many other late twentieth-century social movements (students' rights, antinuclear, peace) as well. It is to the specifics of its organizations that we now turn.

Overview of the Parts and Chapters

We have grouped the selections to represent the particular challenges that feminist organizational practice poses to established social theory and to the political status quo. Following this introduction (Part I), we have placed in Part II those essays that particularly explore the implications of doing feminist work from within a mainstream context. Jane Mansbridge (Chapter 2) offers a guide for such work: Does it represent accountability to a feminist community or constituency? Such accountability can rarely be exercised by formal political mechanisms but is commonly felt by activists as a moral demand, sometimes as the call of an individual conscience formed by feminist principles, sometimes as a collective critique by groups that legitimately express feminist concerns. This "feminist community" to which, Mansbridge argues, activists feel accountable is constituted through processes of writing and discussion, activities she combines in the term "discourse." Mary Fainsod Katzenstein (Chapter 3) also looks at the power of discourse, examining what she calls "discursive politics" within a specific institutional arena, the Catholic Church. She surveys the myriad feminist organizations that have sprung up within its borders and points out that in this case the inability of feminist organizations to produce changes in formal policies has gone hand in hand with an increasingly radical critique of the institution's practices.

Amy Farrell (Chapter 4) offers a concrete example of accountability:

the balancing act that the editors of *Ms.* magazine performed between the demands of the readership, perceived as the legitimate expression of a feminist community, and the demands of the advertisers, who wielded institutional power in the form of money. Eventually, advertiser pressure killed the magazine. Yet *Ms.* was almost immediately reborn in a new form—without advertising, and accountable to its readership directly. To categorize this outcome as either the "death" or the "continuity" of the magazine emphasizes only one side of what could be understood as a victory both for the commitment of the readers and for the control of the advertisers. Hester Eisenstein (Chapter 5) examines the case of Australian "femocrats," their perceptions of feminist accountability, and their responses to it in practice. While they are formally responsible to the government in power and take this responsibility seriously, they balance these demands against their sense of obligation to women as a constituency. Whether they are as uncorrupted by power as they believe matters less than the insights they offer into the tensions of dual loyalties and the practical experience of being both "mandarins" and "missionaries."

Claire Reinelt (Chapter 6) analyzes the search for and exercise of institutional power by a feminist coalition of battered women's shelters in Texas. This group had to mediate between the government agency that funded it and the local shelters that it in turn funded. Reinelt indicates that the coalition used its power to increase feminist perspectives in the individual shelters as well as to stabilize their funding, thus radicalizing and institutionalizing them simultaneously. Roberta Spalter-Roth and Ronnee Schreiber (Chapter 7) pursue this problem of bringing radically feminist ideas (outsider issues) into the established political system (insider tactics) by examining the policies and practices of multiple groups in the Washington, D.C., women's policy network. They find that tensions between the issues and the tactics may lead to recasting concerns in more palatable language, seeking to expand diversity but in limited ways, and muting criticism while working to change policies. They conclude that accommodation to the establishment was not equivalent to co-optation of feminist principles, and point to limited but significant successes in swimming against the conservative tide. Joyce Gelb (Chapter 8) concludes the section by pointing out how this sort of organizing is a particularly American phenomenon. She notes that feminist lobbying draws upon features of both American political systems and American political expectations for its considerable effectiveness and suggests the need for more comparative research.

In Part III we focus on the internal dynamics of feminist organizations, in particular, the transformations brought about in the course of activist struggles. Joan Acker (Chapter 9) presents a theoretical overview of these issues, stressing the ongoing processes that organizing entails and the dynamics of race and class. Her essay highlights the incredible difficulties any feminist organization faces in seeking to survive. Margaret Strobel (Chapter 10) provides a concrete illustration of organizing as process in the history of the Chicago Women's Liberation Union (CWLU). She describes the means that the CWLU developed for learning from the mistakes of Students for a Democratic Society (SDS) and other organizations in the New Left with which its activists had experience, and from its own successes and mistakes. She stresses the lessons that its members carried forward into their future roles as leaders and members of other feminist groups, long after the CWLU fell apart. Allison Tom (Chapter 11) explores the learning process that was structured into a training program in a Canadian feminist bank in the early 1980s. Like many American feminist service providers that relied on CETA-funded staff in the 1970s (see also Matthews), this bank struggled with the issues of difference arising from using paid trainees who came with class-specific experiences and expectations into an organization they did not control. When trainers defined the trainees as "like them" but "not as developed," their identification with the women they were "helping" created obstacles to less hierarchical and more effective learning processes on both sides.

These learning processes transformed both organizations and their individual members. Nancy Whittier (Chapter 12) demonstrates that experiences in grassroots feminist organizations depend on the broader political context in which they are situated. She identifies shifts in the identities and practices of feminists in a midwestern city over a twenty-five-year period and provides a framework within which to understand broader shifts in movement organizations as reflecting generational changes. The transition she examines throws new light on the stronger role that lesbian identity played in defining the feminist politics of later cohorts. Bernice McNair Barnett (Chapter 13) argues for the significance of individual and collective learning processes as part of feminist transformative politics. She looks at African American women's organizing in the 1950s as part of both the feminist movement and the civil rights movement, and points out that White feminist organizations owe an unacknowledged debt to the collectivist innovations of Black women's organizing practices. Her broader definition of leadership as innovation and strategic example, as much as formal position and speechmaking, shows how both class and gender dynamics shaped the contributions of African American women's groups.

In Part IV we address the emotional aspects of work in feminist organizations. Verta Taylor (Chapter 14) argues that conventional understandings of social movements have severed reason from emotion in a dualistic model; even when the values attached to each extreme are reversed, the separation is maintained. She shows that no movement, the women's movement particularly, can be understood unless the interplay of reason and emotion are acknowledged. Sandra Morgen (Chapter 15) demonstrates this approach in her study of four feminist health care providers. In the struggle for feminist change, organizational conditions are intertwined with participants' subjective experience of both the joys of self-realization and transformation and the crushing force of burnout. Morgen points particularly to the emotional hazards that personalizing structural conflict may pose, and the influence of emotions on the specific ways in which organizational issues are framed. Wendy Simonds (Chapter 16) analyzes the emotions of abortion clinic workers engaged in defending themselves, and their clients, from the attacks of Operation Rescue. Members' internal negotiations around allowing themselves to feel shame or anger, and to speak out or remain silent about aspects of the abortion process, illustrate graphically Taylor's point that reasoning and emotion are intertwined.

Next, we focus in Part V on the diversity of strategies that social movement organizations can and do use. Whether resolving internal conflicts, challenging the state, reacting to attacks, or setting goals and priorities, organizations have multiple paths to follow, each of which carries costs and benefits. Carol Mueller (Chapter 17) highlights the differences between organizational types in the strengths and weaknesses of their characteristic responses to internal and external conflict. She particularly points to the challenges facing movements that are flooded with new members, which, she reminds us, has frequently been an issue for feminist groups. Gretchen Arnold (Chapter 18) studies coalition formation among battered women's advocacy groups in St. Louis. Symbolic issues regularly threatened to wreck their coalition despite a consensus on practical political goals. Arnold uses this example to show the possibilities and limits of the coalition form, where deep commitment to ideological principles is not assumed. Nancy Matthews (Chapter 19) explores the different tactics adopted by six rape crisis centers (RCCs) in California to deal with the impact of state funding on their internal practices, goals, and structures. She argues that in addition to straightforward confrontation or accommodation, a third path of engagement with the state was sometimes chosen as groups struggled to make the state more responsive to their wishes. Cheryl Hyde (Chapter 20) analyzes the diverse responses of nine feminist organizations across the United

States to attacks by the New Right during the 1980s. The strength of the attacks as well as the previous self-conception and social networks of each group contributed to the variety of transformations that the organizations underwent. While feminist organizations responded to the New Right, the New Right also responded to feminism, as Susan Marshall (Chapter 21) shows. She demonstrates that although on some issues they chose to argue directly against feminism, antifeminist groups selectively appropriated elements of feminist discourse for nonfeminist ends. The antifeminists she studied paid close attention to feminist groups and activities in search of co-optable themes and for signs of weakness and vulnerability. As a group, the papers in Part V demonstrate the variety of strategies available to feminist organizations for addressing both their internal conflicts about identities, goals, and priorities and their external conflicts with their publics, communities, and funders. These essays also indicate the significance of ideological commitments in shaping the range of strategies and resources that are actually utilized in any particular situation.

Part VI provides a range of challenges to conventional thinking about feminist organizing and its accomplishments. By pushing the boundaries of what is defined as political or feminist, these authors encourage a re-examination of conventional concepts of social change. Suzanne Staggenborg (Chapter 22) draws from her extensive work on the reproductive rights movement to argue that social movement successes take the form of organization building and cultural transformation as well as more familiar changes in law and policy. Her framework allows us to see interconnections between different types of organizing activities, including those that are sometimes dismissed as "mere" organizational maintenance or community building rather than political change. Mary Pardo (Chapter 23) highlights the significance of organization building as a personally transformative experience with feminist meaning by studying social class differences in two Chicana women's organizations, one in the inner city and one in a middle-class suburb. The community organizing she examines in the 1980s—like that which Strobel recounted for White feminist organizers in the 1960s and Barnett described for African American community organizers in the 1950s—suggests a basis for an emergent feminist consciousness among Chicana women in the 1990s. Linda Christiansen-Ruffman (Chapter 24) provides a theoretical framework for seeing all these experiences as part of what Staggenborg would call a cultural success of feminism: namely, the emergence of a specific women's political consciousness from the "closet" of male definitions of what counts as politics. On the basis of three quite different examples (a working-class mothers' housing coalition, an ethnically based women's group, and a self-consciously feminist newspaper), she argues that practical feminism guides women's community-building activities and transforms their thinking about politics. The empowerment of women, a central goal of much feminist organizing, occurs not apart from women's race and class experiences but in close interaction with them, as Christiansen-Ruffman demonstrates.

We close with Part VII, a commentary by Jo Freeman, who is arguably the founding mother of the study of feminist organizations. Her pioneering work on the differences between the feminist organizations of the "older" and "younger" branches of the movement (1975) and her daring critique of the internal dynamics of feminist collectives, "The Tyranny of Structurelessness" (1972), guided many feminist researchers over the years. In her afterword (Chapter 25) Freeman shows how the content and context of research on feminist organizations have changed over the course of twenty-five years.

In collecting the recent work that moves forward from Freeman's original insights, we pay tribute to the commitment she showed to rigorous intellectual examination of the movement, with all its flaws, as well as to the ultimate good of the movement that such critique advances. With a similar dedication to the proposition that honest self-examination is a tonic and stimulus to healthy growth and continued vitality, we offer these studies of feminist organizations to the scholars and activists of the women's movement. We hope to spur scholars and activists to reflect on their experiences, expand their vision of feminist organization, develop and support effective strategies, and discard practices that are ineffective. We encourage the millions of women and girls for whom feminist organizations and organizing are an enduring and unquestioned presence in their lives to consider the energies and struggles that sustain these groups and the potential for social change that they offer. This book is dedicated to the prospect of their ultimate success.

Note

1. Robert Michels (1959) in his classic study of the Social Democratic Party in Germany (first published in 1915) argued that social movements that institutionalize gradually replace their goal of changing society with a desire to survive organizationally, as the leaders find it more important to preserve the positions they have won than to represent their constituents' interests. Michels thought it absolutely inevitable that leaders would look out first for themselves and sacrifice their members' interests to that end: hence the name "Iron Law."

PART II

The Politics of Engagement:
Challenging the Mainstream

CHAPTER 2

What Is the Feminist Movement?

■

JANE MANSBRIDGE

Most politically active feminists in any country work in occupations, from homemaker to chief executive officer, whose primary goal is not to advance feminism. When their work affects women, these feminists often turn for conscious inspiration to the "women's movement." They also, I argue, often feel internally accountable to that movement. The entity—"women's movement" or "feminist movement"—to which they feel accountable is neither an aggregation of organizations nor an aggregation of individual members but a discourse. It is a set of changing, contested aspirations and understandings that provide conscious goals, cognitive backing, and emotional support for each individual's evolving feminist identity.

To understand this kind of internal accountability, one cannot define the feminist movement only through the formal organizations that facilitate and direct its activities in any country or set of countries. This common way of understanding any social movement has the advantage of providing concrete entities to study. But few feminists feel accountable to particular organizations for their actions. The movement that inspires them and can ask sacrifices from them is far broader than that.

Nor, to understand accountability, can one define the feminist movement only as composed of those individuals who claim allegiance to it. If an interviewer from a national survey organization phones and asks the question, "Do you consider yourself to be a feminist?" from a quarter to a third of American women these days answer "yes." This percentage is not much smaller than the percentage who consider themselves Democrats or the percentage who consider themselves Republicans. Nor does it seem to vary dramatically by race or class. In 1989, when a survey asked a representative sample of women in the United States, "Do you consider yourself to be a feminist?" 42 percent of Black women said "yes," compared with 31 percent of White women. As many working-class women as middle-class women said "yes."[1] The next year, when another survey gave women in the United States a list of adjectives, including the label "feminist," and asked them to rate themselves on each from 1 to 10 (that is, from "totally wrong for you" to "perfect for you"), 28 percent of Black women and 11 percent of White women said that "feminist" was a "perfect" description for themselves. More than half (52 percent) of these women rated themselves at 6 or above, putting them to some degree in the feminist camp rather than against it.[2] If we were to define the movement through the declared allegiance of these individuals, we would include a large number of women who answer that they are "feminists" on a survey but have never called themselves "feminists" to themselves, acted politically as feminists, or, probably, felt any degree of accountability to the feminist movement.

One could plausibly define the movement as meaning only the "active" feminists, ranging from, say, the more than 10 percent of American women who in 1990 said the label "feminist" was "perfect" for them to a far smaller number who would say that almost all of their identity was bound up with being a feminist. The activists undoubtedly constitute much of what feminists mean when they speak of the movement as "we." Yet even the aggregate of activists does not fully constitute the movement, which has a life and meaning beyond a sum of individuals.

The discursively created movement is what the people in the movement say it is, what is taken up and held to be feminism. The discourse that creates the movement is not top-down. It works by what is of use. Although few people now remember the name of Carol Hainisch (1970), who first said in print that "the personal is political," early in the movement those words helped many women make sense of their lives. Then others took up the words to explain (among other things) the ways that formal politics had kept off its agenda so much that was important to women.

Key texts and phrases by feminist writers have often framed certain issues, such as Betty Friedan's (1963) "the problem that has no name," Jane O'Reilly's (1972) "click" in the first volume of *Ms.* magazine, or Audre Lorde's (1984) pithy conclusion, "The master's tools will never dismantle the master's house." But the discursive process is always collective. Producers of words choose their words by what they think will make sense to others. An author's anticipation of her audience already shapes the earliest version of what she says. The movement then sifts and either discards or keeps and cherishes her words. The "movement" is made up of women figuring out and telling one another what they think makes sense, and what they think can explain and help crack the gender domination that they feel and are beginning to understand.

I argue that this discursively created movement is the entity that inspires movement activists and is the entity to which they feel accountable. It is changing, open to new insights and interpretations, but consistent at its core: the commitment to ending male domination. We can think of it as "street theory," as opposed to the feminist theory taught in the academy. It is the fluid and continually evolving body of meanings that feminists think of when they ask themselves, "Am I a feminist?" If they don't agree with some political stands or interpretations that cluster at the core of this discourse, they may say, "I guess I'm not a feminist," or "Maybe that makes me not a feminist." Feminists can be held accountable to this "movement" by someone (mostly a someone in their own heads) saying, "That wasn't a very feminist way to act."

This kind of accountability is an accountability through identity. It differs from "descriptive representation," one way that ordinary politicians are sometimes accountable to their constituents. In descriptive representation, representatives act in ways their constituents want them to act because they themselves resemble their constituents (they come from a farming family, or are liberals, or rednecks). Acting in their own self-interest or according to their own ideals leads them automatically to act the way their constituents would in the same situation. Accountability through identity, on the other hand, requires thinking of the collective as a worthy entity and oneself as part of that entity (in a way that would lead representatives, say, to vote for farm subsidies in order not to *let down* the "farmer" in themselves, or the "liberal," or the "redneck").

Feminist identities are usually achieved, not given, particularly in the first generation of the second wave. Many feminists who are now activists have gone through a powerful personal transformative experience in which over some period of time they "became" feminists. Their identities changed as they saw that the explanations in feminist "street theory" explained their lives, as they made the ideals of that theory their own, and as they took risks and bore costs to advance those ideals in the world in which they lived. Today, feminist identities are created and reinforced when feminists get together, act together, and read what other feminists have written. Talking and acting creates street theory and gives it meaning. Reading keeps one in touch and continues to make one think. Both experiences, of personal transformation and continuing interaction, make feminists "internally accountable" to the feminist movement.

As state bureaucracies, universities, privately supported social services, magazines, and other organizations begin to provide jobs so that some

feminists can put their political principles to work in an activity that gives
them an income, such employment almost inevitably makes some demands
that divert energy and sometimes commitment from what might otherwise have been a purely feminist agenda. In the midst of such pressures,
including accountability to one's funders and one's clients, it is often internal accountability to the feminist movement that provides resistance to
"co-optation."

In cases such as that of the Australian "femocrats" which Eisenstein
describes (Chapter 5), the country's elites have been few enough that the
active members of the feminist movement could monitor the actions of
those in "feminist" jobs and rally in public protest if they saw accountability flagging. Alternatively, those in feminist jobs could use such rallies
as part of a "Mutt and Jeff act," telling their superiors, their parliamentary
allies, or anyone who wanted stability, "You must give me the careful, sensible, moderate reforms I'm asking, or *they* will riot in the streets." At the
same time, those rallies and the knowledge of more radical interpretations,
more confrontative versions of "street theory," could keep those who were
tempted by co-optation "honest": that is, more keenly accountable to the
discursive movement that was part of their identities.

When the new staff in a battered women's shelter enter with an individual therapeutic rather than a collective perspective, when the shelters
themselves become more dependent on the state, when advertisers make it
clear that survival as a relatively inexpensive newsstand-distributed magazine requires giving up feminist principles, and when new bureaucrats have
no internal commitment to feminism, the power of the discursive movement is put to the test (see Chapters 18, 19, 4, and 5 by Arnold, Matthews,
Farrell, and Eisenstein). If the new entrants have never had a personal transformation that gives them an internal commitment to feminism, getting
together with other women and with more committed feminists to talk
and act is often the only potential source of change. If one's choice must
be to compromise, or even forgo completely the chance to make a feminist
impact, only talking together will give collective support to a difficult or
bitter choice (see Spalter-Roth and Schreiber, Chapter 7). In some contexts,
such as the Roman Catholic Church, coming together to talk, and to act
through talking, may be the only feasible source (and a powerful source)
of change, as Katzenstein demonstrates (Chapter 3).

Feminists creating a presence within the mainstream ("boring from
within") are most subject to pressures for co-optation. The conditions for
success or even continued existence often undermine feminist goals and

processes, as with the advertisers' demands on *Ms.* (Farrell, Chapter 4). In these circumstances, accountability to the feminist movement, as a practice enacted through discourse, helps make resistance possible. The evolving discourse enunciates feminist values, serves as an arena for contest over those values, and reveals how others have applied feminist analyses to their lives. That evolving discourse takes place in feminist and mainstream books, magazines, television, movies, and other media, and it takes place through talk. It gives those who take part in it emotional inspiration and cognitive tools. It enables actions that come out of this talk to be "feminist" actions, and allows decisions to be collective even when they have ostensibly been taken by only one individual.

Each individual's application of feminist analysis to her daily life and each establishment of a feminist presence within a mainstream organization contributes to the feminist movement. The location is less important than the action. Indeed, many feminist actions may seem infinitesimal or symbolic, often better characterized as negotiations or "micronegotiations" than as "resistance," because they explicitly or implicitly recognize the context of power in which they take place.

These actions are supported by ongoing feminist discourse, and that discourse in turn is supported by organizations—often within mainstream organizational forms (Katzenstein 1990)—that bring feminists together, allowing them to articulate face to face their evolving thoughts, conflicts, and commonalities and to give shape to their actions. Just as organizations shape discourse and discourse shapes organizations, so feminists take support from the ongoing feminist movement, as embodied in organizations and in discourse, and, through what they say and do, give support back. The relation between individuals, organizations, and discourse is mutually reinforcing. It can wither in concert as well. Particularly those feminists most isolated in their daily lives from the organizational manifestations of the movement most need contact with its discourse. The demise of the newsstand version (and the cheap subscription version) of *Ms.* magazine ended a vital ongoing contact with the discourse for many women in the United States. The spread of a feminist organizational presence within mainstream organizations maintains such contact for many others.

As the organizations connected in one way or another with the feminist movement become more diverse (for example, as shelters for battered women come to include some affiliated with the Catholic Church), and as women from many backgrounds come to work in feminist organizations, the power and flexibility of the discursive movement is tested further.

Locally based, working-class Latina or Black women often have different personal goals and feel comfortable in structures different from those that appeal to cosmopolitan, mobile, young, White, middle-class feminists. The forms of sexism that different groups of women have to face, the options open to them in dealing with that sexism, and the costs they have to pay often differ greatly from one group to another. Despite the efforts of individual Black and Latina and Asian women to influence their mostly White organizations, and their standing up at conferences to present their points of view, it was not until a significant literature by women of color appeared that the larger feminist movement began to learn significantly from those differences and be transformed. It was too painful for each Black woman individually to have to teach the White feminists in her organization about the differences in their experiences. But through the written word, which can teach many at once, and through the controversies and understandings generated when people talk about what they have read, the movement as a discursive entity is now beginning to absorb, confront, and be transformed by these new insights. The feminist movement has never been simply one movement instead of many; but to stay in any sense one movement it must now encompass this important change.

As feminism becomes international, the movement will begin to look even more different, because the culture, concerns, and experiences of women in Asia, Africa, Latin America, and Eastern Europe will not be the same as those in the American and Western European tradition that has shaped the movement so far. Even in English-speaking Australia, the tradition of leftist class consciousness and trade union organization opens possibilities for the feminist movement that are inconceivable in the United States. American Catholics use discursive politics because they cannot use the state; Australians can use the state bureaucracy. Shelters for battered women in Texas use the permeable, non-unitary American state in ways different from those used by rape crisis centers in California (compare Reinelt, Chapter 6, and Matthews, Chapter 19). The organizational imperatives of the feminist movement and the ways it works with the state, with other progressive movements, and with men differ in every country and in every locale. Strategies differ by widely varying shades of class, ethnicity, sexual preference, religion, and past experience. The only thing we can expect to unite feminists across these differences is internal accountability to a discursively created, self-transforming, internally contested feminist movement. Co-optation by the state, by other movements, by individual men, and by male-dominated organizations will be held in check not by any set of rules but through the maintenance of feminist identity, created and reinforced when feminists talk and act together.

The feminist movement draws on, works closely with, and often is practically indistinguishable from other movements by women addressed to women's concerns. Women may organize locally to get a well in their village, for example, and become connected eventually to a larger movement of women in local development. What distinguishes feminist movements from movements simply by and for women is that feminist movements are directed to ending male domination. This line between feminist and women's movements is not completely clear. Movements by and for women, including antifeminist movements, may in the long run help end male domination by, among other things, promoting women's political consciousness. Movements by and for women are also vital for improving women's lives. Women's organizations, women's literature, women's politics, and even women's fashions, directed not toward ending male domination but toward producing whatever women now want, will inevitably intertwine with the feminist movement in collaboration and in combat.

If the movement is to maintain its discursive tension, and if its street theory and working ideals are to remain responsive to what is going on in women's lives, it will always involve internal combat. Uncomfortable and competing ideals will create personal anguish. The lack of formal accountability will generate rallies, phone calls, and statements to the media that will make many feminists miserable. Internal accountability will produce guilt. Even with the best "group process"—the greatest care to condemn the action and not the actor, or to say and think "I feel" rather than "you are"—a discourse that matters will often cause pain. The movement, if it is to live, will always be in turmoil.

This entity in turmoil, this process of ideals in creation, this generation by and through what people say to one another is the feminist movement. This is what gives feminists their inspiration, and it is this to which, in a form of representation not noted by political scientists, they hold themselves internally accountable. Without understanding that the feminist movement is discursive and that the accountability of feminists to the movement is internal, we cannot understand what we see in the Australian femocracy, in feminist organizations in Washington, in the Catholic Church, in rape crisis centers and battered women's shelters, among the workers at *Ms.*, and in any organization in which a feminist is trying to do feminist work.

Notes

Acknowledgments: I would like to acknowledge the support of the Russell Sage Foundation and the Center for Urban Affairs and Policy Research during the writing of this article. I thank Hester Eisenstein and the editors of this volume for their helpful comments.

1. Yankelovich Clancy Shulman, October 23–25, 1989; $N = 1,000$ women. (Data are from the Roper Center for Public Opinion Research, University of Connecticut.)

2. Princeton Survey Research Associates, December 18–21, 1989; $N = 1,284$. (I thank Diane Colasanto of Princeton Survey Research Associates for making these data available. For a more comprehensive survey of public opinion surveys asking for self-designation as a "feminist," see Mansbridge 1993.)

CHAPTER 3

Discursive Politics and Feminist Activism in the Catholic Church

■

MARY FAINSOD KATZENSTEIN

Most social movements give rise to a generation of routinized political practices (Freeman 1983; Costain 1982; Rupp and Taylor 1987). In the case of feminism, the movement has produced two important forms of present-day politics: interest group activism and discursive organizing.

It is not difficult to envision what feminists do when they engage in *interest group* politics. One can easily imagine feminist lobbyists walking the corridors on Capitol Hill, and we can fill in the words by rote. Feminist organizations, often Washington based, endeavor to influence political elites to support or oppose particular legislation, regulations, or policy decisions. In the United States, interest group activism is the way many feminists do politics. Not that this form of feminist politics necessarily elicits public acclaim: the selection of Geraldine Ferraro as the vice-presidential candidate provoked accusations that feminists had acted as an interest group, "biasing" the selection of Walter Mondale's running mate. Some feminists, too, are disquieted, albeit differently. When feminists do interest group politics, some suspect, they have bought into a world of political compromise. But on the whole, interest group politics is seen as politics-as-usual.

Discursive politics requires greater elucidation. Most succinctly, it is the politics of meaning-making.[1] It is discursive in that it seeks to reinterpret, reformulate, rethink, and rewrite the norms and practices of society and the state. It is about cognition. Its premise is that conceptual changes directly bear on material ones. Discursive politics relies heavily but not exclusively on language. Its vehicle is both speech and print—conversations, debate, conferences, essays, stories, newsletters, books.

These two kinds of politics are ideal types; in real political life, organizations combine something of both. Feminist interest groups are often very word conscious, usually out of calculated instrumentality as to what phraseologies will "work." Feminist interest groups are also well aware of the need to change *understandings* of gender stereotyping, but they strike the balance in favor of instrumental change. In discursive politics the careful thought given to word choices and language is sometimes instrumental but more often expressive. Its intent is to articulate clearly the differences in perspective and the revisioning of a feminist world view. Less attention is paid to measuring the progress or acceptance of these newly voiced perspectives.

I have considered terms other than discursive politics—cultural politics, identity politics, the politics of ideology, transformative politics—but find each one limited. "Cultural politics" has too much the connotation of operating on the plain of music, art, and literature; and it evokes the glacial process of changing deeply embedded norms. Discursive politics *is* intended to challenge deeply held beliefs, but it directly challenges the way people write and talk about these beliefs. That process is more immediate, more malleable. Discursive politics is also broader than "identity politics." Part of what feminists do when they think and write is to ask: Who am I, who are we as women, in what way are women different from men and from each other, in what ways do gender differences shape identities? But these questions are connected to a much larger discursive undertaking which requires a reexamination of society, the norms and rules by which society operates. As one form of discursive politics, identity politics (whether individual or collective) can be an unflattering misnomer for the larger discursive project of social analysis and assessment in which many feminists have engaged. "The politics of ideology" is simply too weighted by pejorative luggage. "Transformative politics" presumes an answer to the question that needs to be posed: what if anything does discursive politics transform?

In this essay I describe the discursive politics that feminists have pursued within the American Catholic Church and reflect briefly on its transformative potential. I conclude by asking why feminists in the Church have relied on discursive politics and in what ways this form of politics is important for the feminist movement more generally.

Feminism in the Catholic Church

For those unfamiliar with the politics of feminism in the contemporary Catholic Church, a capsule narrative may help, beginning with an anecdote: A friend's friend attended a dinner party given to bid farewell to the Vatican emissary to Washington, who was returning to Rome. The guest of honor was asked what he had most and least enjoyed about his many years in Washington. Rome needs to recognize, he said, only partly in jest, that feminism makes Washington a hardship post.

What he meant was feminism *in* the Church. The Catholic Church in the United States has never lacked for independent women, but it was not until the mid-1970s that feminism in the Church came out: Nuns, sisters, or women religious (terms I use interchangeably)[2] as well as laywomen came together at a national level specifically to address the issues of gender inequality within the institution and within society.

In the 1970s the combined force of Vatican II and the dawn of feminism's second wave galvanized women (both lay and religious) to reexamine their lives and the world around them as women. Particularly at the beginning, much of this process seemed to be about identity: In what ways can we believe in women's equality and be Catholic or Christian? In what ways is this patriarchal Church our church? To what spiritual and secular ends should we dedicate our lives? As women asked themselves these questions, however, the answers they formulated required a reanalysis of both Church and society. Initially, women came together to debate the issue of women's ordination. But as feminist groups proliferated, their concerns and agendas multiplied.[3]

In November 1975 the first Women's Ordination Conference was held in Detroit. It was called "Women in Future Priesthood Now: A Call to Action." Attendance exceeded 1,200, and another 500 people were turned away. The mood was one of excitement and promise as participants joined in liturgies and listened to talks on such topics as "Moral Imperatives for the Ordination of Women" and "Models for Future Priesthood." The willingness of the bishops and church authority to engage in dialogue on the ordination issue was questioned in bold, frank terms, but on the whole the speeches dealt with the hopefulness of a church that would prove more open to women's ministry. In a talk that anticipated the more radical themes of the 1980s, Rosemary Radford Ruether wondered about the wisdom of seeking ordination without "questioning fundamentally this concept of clericalism" (Weaver 1986, 113). But there was no disputing the sense of empowerment that came from women gathering together around a single issue—and the issue in 1975 was the priesthood.

In 1978 the second Women's Ordination Conference, in Baltimore, took on a more feminist and polemical tone. Shortly after the Detroit meeting the National Conference of Bishops had affirmed the proscription against women's ordination (Bernardin 1976, 42–44). In January 1977 the Vatican issued a declaration against women's ordination.[4] It was thus abundantly clear to the Baltimore participants that Church authority was uncompromisingly opposed to the claim around which the conference had gathered. Some participants continued to focus on the issue of ordination and change within the institutional Church, but a substantial group sought to connect the issue of ordination to a much broader call for systemic change. Sister Elizabeth Carroll, vice-president of the Religious Sisters of Mercy, Pittsburgh, told the conference: "Unless the women who are to be ordained are deeply conscious of the oppressions of the poor and racially different, unless they are deeply converted to the necessity of uprooting the mindset of dominance and dependence on which these oppressions rest, they will all too easily fall into the institutional framework of clericalism which now hampers the church" (quoted in Papa 1978, 1).[5] The discussion had clearly moved beyond ordination.

In 1979 John Paul II made his first papal visit to the United States. On October 7, when the pope was to visit Washington, Sister Theresa Kane was asked to offer a short welcome. As head of the Sisters of Mercy and then president of the Leadership Conference of Women Religious (LCWR), Kane was no radical. But with television cameras recording her words—and the fifty-three women religious wearing blue armbands to protest the pope's opposition to women's ordination—Kane urged him on behalf of women both lay and religious to open up all ministries of the Church to women and to "be mindful of the intense suffering and pain of many women in these United States . . . who are desirous of serving in and through the Church as fully participating members" (Milhaven 1987, 6). The pope, staying with his prepared text, did not choose to reply to Kane's entreaty.

By the early 1980s momentum had gathered for a national conference that would be framed around a set of issues broader than ordination. The Women's Ordination Conference had postponed the meetings scheduled for 1981 in favor of continued local conferences, thus creating space for a rethinking of the direction a new national conference effort might take. This change of direction made fissures among Catholic feminists more evident. The LCWR along with several other groups dropped out of the coalition. Although their reasons were not stated publicly, their withdrawal was assumed to have been motivated by the presence of Catholic lesbians and

Catholics for a Free Choice, the Washington-based pro-choice organization.[6]

In 1983 two conferences were held. A conference in Washington drew from mostly moderate, liberal quarters (Giveu 1986; Hansen 1987). The speakers addressed topics that focused largely on issues within the institutional Church. The talks were forthright and posed clear challenges, covering topics such as "Relationships between U.S. Women Religious and Hierarchical Authority" and "To Face or Not to Face Sexism: Consequences for the Institutional Church."[7] But the larger issues of social justice were for the most part not incorporated in the program. The other conference, held in Chicago, was markedly different from the Women's Ordination Conferences of the previous decade. Called "From Generation to Generation: Women Church Speaks," it marked the formalization of the movement that created what came to be called "Women-Church." It was organized as a bilingual program in English and Spanish; Hispanic women made up 10 percent of those attending and included migrant workers from Florida and women from the barrios of New York. The emphasis was no longer on ordination or on desired changes in the institutional Church that church authorities were sure to repudiate. Instead, conferees began to reflect on ways of creating a spirituality and a praxis for themselves. Rosemary Radford Ruether spoke of women being "Women-Church not in exile but in exodus." Mary Hunt, also a theologian and the coorganizer of a recently formed feminist ethics group, spoke of women claiming "a new baptism— a baptism into a Church which acknowledges that it is guilty of sexism, heterosexism, racism and classism" (Hays 1984; Ruether 1986, 67–68).

Immediately after the Chicago conference, the Women of the Church Coalition broadened to become Women-Church Convergence, a coalition of twenty-five groups whose names indicated the growing geographic and social dispersion of women's activism. In 1987 the Convergence sponsored a second Women-Church conference, held in Cincinnati, which drew on increasingly broadened constituencies. As before, it was organized as a bilingual conference and appeared to attract increasing numbers of laywomen. Along with feminist theologians and well-known activists in the Church, the conference was addressed by leaders of the secular women's movement (Gloria Steinem, Eleanor Smeal, Charlotte Bunch). Only a small number of sessions concerned the institutional Church; most covered a broad social agenda: the sanctuary movement, racism, abortion, sexual assault, lesbians keeping faith, community organizing South Bronx style, women and AIDS, economic literacy. On the Saturday evening of the conference a Feminist Eucharist ("Women-Church shares in the breaking of many breads and drinking from many cups") was scheduled for a ballroom-sized crowd. Attended by 3,000 participants, this second Women-Church conference was named, significantly, "Claiming Our Power."

Discursive Acts

It is not by chance that the sketch of Catholic feminism recounted above is most easily told as a narrative of conferences and workshops, an account of *ideas* rather than *policies*. This is certainly not to say that women (both lay and religious) in the Church do not "act" in the "real world" to effect social change. Many nuns as well as many committed Catholic laywomen are engaged in direct social justice activism (in prisons, shelters, hospices, and sanctuaries), working to redress problems of poverty and racism as they affect both women and men. Some others have sought positions in the Church (as educators, pastoral assistants, and chaplains) from which they hope to work toward a more just and faith-driven society. But much of the work women activists do when they come together is discursive: rewriting through language texts and symbolic acts their own understanding of themselves in relationship to both Church and society.

It may be helpful in specifying the character of feminist discursive politics to say a little more about what it is not: For the most part feminist groups in the Church do not lobby either the state or the Church. One organization called Network, with headquarters in Washington, does explicitly monitor congressional legislation, conduct letter-writing campaigns, and undertake the requisite visits to congressional offices, but it is the exception. Also, although individual women in the Church have brought their grievances to the courts, no feminist group in the Church is directly organized around legal action. Finally, few activist groups explicitly engage in parish politics. Mary's Pence (which describes itself as similar to the officially sponsored Peter's Pence collection in that both seek donations from church members to fund ministries to the poor) attempts to connect the interests of women in the pews to the efforts of grassroots organizers, but few groups explicitly aim at mobilizing women in the parishes. Instead, activist groups have spent much of their time in reflection and deliberation, in constructing new words, language, and meaning to describe their changing understanding of women and the Church.

WOMEN-CHURCH

One of the most dramatic expressions of feminist discursive politics is the linguistic construction "Women-Church." The concept grew out of the need shared by many feminists in the Church to find a home and identity within Catholicism. Unwilling to leave the Church yet to varying degrees alienated from its institutional practices, many women found connection and validation in the knowledge community that the phrase Women-Church evokes.

The term itself was adopted from the Second Vatican Council's affirmation of the laity's role, expressed in the phrase "We are the Church." In the 1980s, women who saw themselves as deeply spiritual with life roots in Catholicism and yet felt themselves to be a subordinated class within the institutional Church adopted the Vatican II language, declaring, "We are the Church and it is Women-Church."

Women-Church is less an organization than an idea. Organizationally, there *is* a coalition of the groups that came together under the auspices of the Women of the Church Coalition in 1983 and Women-Church Convergence in 1987. But there are other women, not active members of the twenty-five or so groups formally associated with the umbrella organization, who also find spiritual identity in Women-Church. Many women who are part of local liturgical communities reconceptualize their connections to the Church in terms of Women-Church. Two women writing for the newsletter of the National Association of Religious Women explain: "The ever present reality of patriarchy and clericalism forces us to consciously and deliberately marginalize ourselves from much that is 'Church.' Still we choose to remain, in identity and practice, Roman Catholic. . . . Functioning as a 'base community' or 'house church,' our WomenChurch group gathers regularly for inclusive liturgy, story sharing, and potluck meals. The leadership is 'roundtable'; we take turns planning, hosting and presiding at liturgy. Our affiliation with WomenChurch energizes and empowers us. It gives us the hope we need to continue as women in the church."[8]

The creative reconceptualization of women's identity within the Church in terms of a critical rethinking of women's relationships to the power of the institutional Church is captured so precisely by Rosemary Radford Ruether (1986, 62–63) that I quote her at length:

Women-Church means neither leaving the church as a sectarian group nor continuing to fit into it on its terms. It means establishing bases for a feminist critical culture and celebrational community that have some autonomy from the established institutions. It also means sharing this critical culture and sense of community with many women who are working within existing churches but who gather, on an occasional or regular basis, to experience the feminist vision that is ever being dimmed and limited by the parameters of the male-dominated institution. . . .

One must refuse the institutionally defined options either of continuing on its terms or of cutting off all connections with it and becoming sectarian and hostile to those who are working within established institutions.

In her book on the theology and practice of Women-Church, Ruether offers alternative liturgies for the use of Women-Church celebrants. Included are rites of healing from incest, wife battering, and rape and a coming-out rite for lesbians. Passages instruct women on the remembrance of foremothers, on the exorcism of patriarchal texts, on the blessing of symbolic foods (bread, wine, milk, honey, the apple). The text, Ruether emphasizes, is not a prayerbook "with words and forms to be repeated." Rather it "assumes that the creation of liturgy is properly a function of local communities who are engaged in a collective project woven from the fabric of many concrete stories that make up the lives of each member of that body" (1986, 7). The discursive politics of remaking the rituals, customs, visions, and norms of feminist worship as a collective endeavor is thus central to Ruether's project.

LCWR: REVISIONING WOMEN

Not all women engaged in equality issues in the Church identify with Women-Church. Nevertheless, even those who may not utilize the vocabulary of Women-Church have been deeply engaged in discursive politics. The Leadership Conference of Women Religious (LCWR), the official umbrella organization representing 90 percent of women religious in the United States, is generally on the more cautious, moderate side of feminist encounters with Vatican authority. It has nonetheless struggled over the last decades to foster deliberations, pass resolutions, and engage in discussions that subject issues about religion and society to major reexamination.

Constituted under Vatican direction in the 1950s, the LCWR has provided a forum in which the changing mission of American sisters has been debated and the delicate relationship between religious orders and the Vatican has been negotiated. Its early founding and official position give it a different cast from the politics of more recent (and in different ways more radical) groups such as Catholics for a Free Choice, the National Coalition of American Nuns, and the National Assembly of Religious Women. There is no question, however, that all these groups have been seen by the present-day Vatican as troublesome sources of feminist politics.

First established at the urging of the Vatican in 1956 as the Conference of Majors Superior of Women of the USA (CMSW), the LCWR changed its name in 1971 to move away from hierarchical nomenclature.[9] Via annual assemblies with the attendant workshops and discussions, copious correspondence with member congregations and the Vatican, and extensive surveys and documentation of its own membership, it has become the site for seemingly endless deliberations over the transformative processes engaging women religious in the last decades. The LCWR both mirrored and shaped this transformation. This was discourse politics at its most vivid—recording, reinterpreting, and reconstituting through talk and pen the relationship of women's lives to the world around them.

For the first decade of its existence, the organization looked inward, focusing on the religious life of the membership. With the Vatican II call for renewal and the societal changes in the 1960s that swept many American sisters into the civil rights movement, the women's movement, and third world political issues, the LCWR began its own self-examination. The 1971 bylaws redefined its mission as the "development of creative and responsive leadership" by conference members "within their communities but in the church and, through the church, in the world" (Quinonez and Turner 1992, 21). The changes precipitated opposition both inside and outside the LCWR. Inside, some sisters worried that the spiritual essence of the body's mission was being diluted. In Rome, when the new bylaws were submitted to the Vatican's Congregation for Religious, discussions led to the reinstitution of language acknowledging a "due regard for the authority of the Holy See and of the bishops" (Quinonez and Turner 1992, 27). Even the new name, particularly the designation of the word "leadership," met with objections from the Vatican. In one meeting both the conference president and the Vatican ambassador sat with dictionaries looking up the words "leader" and "leadership." According to a former LCWR president, church authorities could not tolerate the association of women with leadership (Quinonez and Turner 1992, 28).

Over the years numerous disputes arose between Vatican officials and the LCWR as well as within the LCWR. The sources of disagreement ranged widely: What should be the nature of religious life? What was the relationship between the sacred and the secular? In what way, if at all, did religious authority demand attention to experience, history, culture? In what way should religious life be seen as an unchanging essence? These questions translated into specific, often intense, disputes about sisters' apparel, about the rewriting of the constitutions of religious orders, about deference to Vatican authority, about the disciplining of sisters who were seen as disobedient. Debates grew intense over particular resolutions: supporting theologian Charles Curran, developing a deeper understanding of the right-to-life issue, supporting the legitimacy of conference alliance with communities in conflict with church officials (Quinonez and Turner 1992, 133).

Throughout, the LCWR reflected on epistemological issues, particularly the place of experience in shaping how sisters should be guided in their lives. The LCWR, like other organizations in the Church, came to insist on the authenticity of experience as a source of moral decision-making. The surveys and research into the views of individual sisters in member congregations were themselves an indication of the early attention that the conference felt should be paid to women's experience. The "Sister Survey" gave legitimacy to women's own experiential understandings and became an instrument of politicization (Quinonez and Turner 1992, 46). In national assemblies, LCWR women were encouraged to tell their stories. It became understood that members would be seated in circles of eight to ten persons and that in place of speeches, questions would be posed to generate discussion: "Tell about a time when you felt powerless." "What are the themes you want to include in a statement about the Vatican's censure of Charles Curran?" (Quinonez and Turner 1992, 110).

The LCWR leadership was very self-conscious about the role of language. As Quinonez and Turner (1992, 88) state: "Names signify. . . . The power to name a group can be the power to position it socially and politically. . . . To study the progress of American sisters in the past thirty years is to become aware of the exquisite attention lavished upon naming, more particularly renaming." At times the attention to language is instrumental. Quinonez and Turner (1992, 111) recount the huddles in the dimly lit basement down the street from St. Peter's Square where LCWR officers would rehearse for their meetings with Vatican officials: "They played roles, trying out language. They tagged words that under no circumstances should cross their lips because they evoked such hostility ('team,' 'empowerment,' 'dialogue'); others (like 'ministry') they would decide to risk . . .

because they thought meanings need to be expanded." But more often the attention to language was expressive rather than instrumental. Words were tried and chosen not with regard to how far an idea could be pushed, not calculating its reception, but because the word expressed an idea that required articulation. As Quinonez and Turner remark, the discussions at national conferences were considered indispensable for moral growth. But as ideas were explored, "to secure official approval of their views was not their primary object. Comprehending their own diverse views was" (Quinonez and Turner 1992, 129).

Other groups have taken their discursive politics more purposefully into the public arena. The signatories to the October 7, 1984, *New York Times* advertisement supporting a diversity in views about abortion were clearly targeting public opinion. So also was Catholics Speak Out when it commissioned a Gallup poll in spring 1992, the results of which were strategically released the day the U.S. Catholic bishops met to discuss the third draft of the pastoral on women. But for the most part, feminist organizations in the Church—in conferences, discussions, workshops, newsletters—have aimed primarily at self-reflection.

Discursive Politics as Transformative

Feminist discursive politics has been at once ineffectual and transformative. In numerous ways the Church seems unchanging and unchangeable: On women's reproductive rights, women's ordination within the Church, the place of homosexuality within Christianity the Vatican has been unbending. At the same time, feminist discursive politics has had a transforming effect summarizable under three headings: (1) the empowerment of women religious; (2) the change in popular attitudes toward gender issues in the Church; (3) the influence over the agenda of church authorities.

Discursive politics has created a "safe place" (Evans and Boyte 1986) where feminists in the Church can regroup and reflect on their daily encounters with hierarchy and oppression. Those engaged in the grueling work of social justice often see little coming out of their ongoing struggles to combat the oppression of poverty and racism. Those engaged in pastoral work (the woman who can minister to the dying but cannot perform last rites) are often in painful confrontation with the injustice of gender inequalities in the Church. To be able to come together to reflect in text and in talk on the immediate and far-reaching meanings of these experiences has been for many not just sustaining but life-transforming. Discursive politics has been the vehicle for the metamorphosis in the lives of women religious in the United States.

Moreover, feminist discursive politics has been at least party to, although by no means the sole cause of, the change in popular attitudes toward gender issues in the Church. The 1992 Gallup poll commissioned by activist groups revealed more than just the expected disagreements between laity and hierarchy on birth control and abortion (87 percent believe that the Church should permit couples to make their own decisions about birth control; 70 percent, that Catholics can in good conscience vote for political candidates who support legal abortion). It showed also that the number of those who think women should be allowed to be ordained as priests has now reached a high level: 64 percent of all those questioned, 74 percent of those under age thirty-five (Goldman 1992). It is hard to believe that the feminist-driven debates over the ordination question have not contributed to changing attitudes.

Finally, the speech and writings of activist women in the Church have reshaped the agenda of church leadership. The extraordinary story of the bishops' pastoral letter is testimonial. The 1988 letter, originally called "Partners in the Mystery of Redemption: A Pastoral Response to Women's Concerns for Church and Society," has now been through four full drafts with results unprecedented in the history of pastoral letters: it has failed to be supported by the necessary two-thirds vote of U.S. bishops.[10]

Conservatives saw the pastoral as "priest bashing" because of its references to attitudinal changes that clerics might reflect upon. Feminists (from moderate to radical) directed their criticism variously at the bishops' refusal to recommend women's inclusion in the priesthood, concede any of the feminist arguments over reproductive rights, or acknowledge the voluminous theological scholarship by feminists, and at their heavy focus on woman as nurturer, mother, and wife.[11] Widespread debate followed. Testimony on the first draft was received from hundreds of dioceses, sixty college campuses, forty-five military bases, and many groups representing different positions within the Church. As that draft circulated throughout the United States dioceses, more than 54,000 English and 6,500 Spanish copies were sold (Scott 1988).

The 1987 Synod of Bishops had also reflected the agenda pressures that feminist discursive politics were creating. Although the Synod considered few concrete proposals addressing gender equality, its discussions did dwell extensively on gender issues. The American delegation had voted to make gender issues one of two priorities, and Archbishop Rembert Weakland presented the delegation's reflections. Both bishops' and laypersons' voices addressed the synod with discussions about the admission of women to the diaconate, altar service, women's leadership on pastoral councils. Women were, by one account, very visible, addressing the assembly, reading the scriptures, leading prayers, talking in the coffee bars and in the "language circles" (Leckey 1988).

The impact of discursive politics on the bishops' discussions was most clearly revealed when the Gallup poll results were released to coincide with their meeting in June 1992. With the ordination question a central issue in the pastoral and with the Gallup poll revealing that a strong majority of the laity support women's ordination, the pastoral seemed destined to fail—as happened when a vote among the bishops in November 1992 did not provide the necessary support for its adoption (Steinfels 1992).

Capturing the ways in which feminist discursive politics has begun to shape the Church agenda, Annie Lally Milhaven (1987, xi) comments: "A final reason for (feminists) staying in this church is not spelled out, but I think it may be the most powerful reason of all: these women, on the whole, sense that they have clout precisely by remaining as dissidents within this particular church. This might surprise some of them, because, from an institutional, legal point of view, they would seem to be quite powerless. But institutional power does not lie only in possession of control over property and juridical authority. It lies, in the church particularly, in a cultural hegemony to define the meaning of the community and its mission."

Conclusion

In what way is discursive politics a form of power? Given the Vatican's intransigence on questions of gender equality, are there ways in which the discursive politics of feminists in the church can be seen to "count"?

In his study of Appalachia, *Power and Powerlessness*, John Gaventa (1980, 13–16) distinguishes three dimensions of power. Building on Steven Lukes's work, he identifies the power to make decisions, the power to set the agenda of policy and public debate, and the power—through the control of "social myths, language, and symbols"—to shape the way people define their concerns and options. In Gaventa's account of the mine owners' hegemonic control, all three dimensions of power converge to render the population quiescent. These three forms of power, however, need not operate in synchrony. The discursive politics of feminists in the Church illustrates the capacity of protest politics to mount a counteroffensive within the second and third arenas of power, even as the first realm of decision-making appears impervious to protesters' claims.

Although Vatican actions have proffered few concessions to feminist concerns, the discursive work of feminists in the Church has generated intense discussion both among women (lay and religious) and within the church hierarchy. Unlike the Appalachian miners, feminists in the Church have created a strong counterdiscourse in response to the words, rituals, and symbols that emanate from the Vatican. The voluminous writing by feminist theologians, by feminist leaders of religious orders, by feminist nuns committed to social justice work has meant that there is hardly a biblical passage, a moment in the Mass, an utterance in the bishops' pastoral letter on women, a clause in a Vatican pronouncement that has not been reflected on, debated, and queried.

To restate this in terms of Gaventa's three dimensions of power: At the first level, feminist discursive politics has had remarkably little effect on Vatican decision-making. At the second level, feminist discursive politics has impeded the "mobilization of bias" that would have allowed the hierarchy to keep women's issues off the agenda for public debate. Feminist speech and writing has engaged the Vatican, the American clerical hierarchy, and numerous parishes in public confrontation over women's roles in the Church, over exclusionary liturgical language, and over various ecclesiastical and secular forms that the "sin of sexism" (in the concessionary phrase of the bishops' pastoral letter) has assumed. At the third level, the discursive struggle to frame the issues, to provide the words, narrative accounts, and symbols that shape the language of debate, has helped feminists to reach their own diverse self-definitions.

In this three-dimensional struggle for power, there is no simple description of the influence of feminist discursive politics on the "hearts and minds" of American Catholics. One interpretation might be that the Vatican is increasingly isolated, since popular opinion among American Catholics on such issues as the ordaining of women, birth control, and support for pro-choice political candidates approximates the views of feminists far more closely than it does those of Rome. Mary T. Hanna, a scholar of religion and politics, speculates that if American bishops were free to set policy, the church might soon ordain women as priests. But, as she goes on to say, "It's not up to the Bishops. It's up to the Pope and to Rome and I don't believe we're going to see it happen in the lifetime of this Pope" (quoted in Goldman 1992, A16). Another interpretation suggests that conservative forces in the church hierarchy have isolated feminist and radical challenges to the status quo, as evidenced by the absence of any strong popular ground swell for change. Sociologist Andrew Greeley contends, for instance, that revolutionary change would be indicated only if the increasingly liberal views of Catholics nationwide on gender questions were so high on the popular agenda that "people started doing something about their convictions, like cutting off their contributions to the church" (quoted in Goldman 1992, A16). But even if popular momentum does not on its own bring a revolution, the transfigured popular attitudes that feminist discursive politics has helped to create may well support major institutional changes in the event of a future, more liberal Vatican leadership.

Why discursive politics? The relationship of the Church to the state is, in the end, what makes discursive politics the logical choice for feminists in the Church. Law provides little recourse to those who have claims against the Church.[12] Those whose speech has been silenced by clerical decree cannot turn to the courts for protection (Father Curran tried and failed; the "Vatican 24" who signed the 1984 *New York Times* ad never tried). Nor are the courts ready to intervene in support of those denied employment or promotion on account of their sex; if they were, would-be women priests now being trained in large numbers in theological seminaries would flood the courts. Outside the Church, feminists can pursue interest group politics because the law is sometimes on their side in their efforts to influence recalcitrant institutional personnel. Within the Church, it is no surprise that feminists turn to language in lieu of law.

Looking beyond the Church to the women's movement more generally, it is significant that the earliest expression of discursive politics occurred under similar conditions—when the pathways that led to the door of equal rights were still unmarked. Feminist discursive politics was, initially, the invention of small consciousness-raising and radical groups of the mid-1960s and early 1970s, a period that prefaced the establishment of any clear "standing" for feminist equal rights claims in the courts and the legislatures. It was this ten-year period that generated the new vocabulary of "sexism," "harassment," "battering," "reproductive rights," "sexual preference," and so on. In this period, women who were organizationally dispersed were connected in a discursive community through shared narratives and newly named experiences. It was in part these linguistic formulations identifying the systemic character of gender inequalities that gave many women the self-confidence and sense of connectedness that would later motivate their feminist organizational activity. It was also this discourse that would later become braided into the very language of the law itself.

As feminist reliance on discursive politics in the Church suggests, however, not all institutions in society march to the same cadence. The importance of discursive politics varies by institution and over time. When access to the judicial system and equal rights protection is unavailable, discursive politics remains an option. Unless the realm of discursive politics is taken seriously, it is too easy to miss the changes that precede and indeed precipitate the policy shifts by which advances in equal rights are so often gauged.

Notes

Acknowledgments: I am grateful to Myra Marx Ferree, Jane Mansbridge, Patricia Yancey Martin, Claire Reinelt, and Sidney Tarrow for their helpful readings of an earlier draft of this essay.

1. I owe this phrase to a discussion with Martha Minow. For definitions of discourse and counterdiscourse politics, respectively, see Fraser 1990; Young forthcoming.

2. Strictly speaking, "nuns are women religious who live in contemplative or cloistered orders; "sisters" belong to active or apostolic communities engaged in the active works of education, health care, social services (Ebaugh 1977, xiv; Quinonez and Turner 1992, 36).

3. For the sake of brevity, I omit from my account here the early stirrings of feminism that were visible in the Sister Formation Movement of the 1950s and in the rewriting of constitutions of religious orders that began in the 1960s with Vatican II. For an analysis of those early movements, see Bradley 1960; Chittister 1977; Ebaugh 1977; Ware 1985; Neal 1990. Two excellent accounts of women's activism in the Catholic Church, covering both the earlier and more recent periods, are Weaver 1986; Quinonez and Turner 1992.

4. "Declaration on the Question of the Admission of Women to the Ministerial Priesthood," sec. 27, Vatican City, October 15, 1976. This reads in part: "It is the unbroken tradition of the Catholic Church that women have never been admitted to Holy Orders, with which the Orthodox tradition also concurs. Jesus Christ did not call any woman to be part of the twelve, even his own mother. The apostolic Church faithfully carried out this exclusion of women from priesthood that was instituted by Christ. Moreover it should also be said that the maleness of the priest reflects the sacramental mystery of Christ and the Church. As representative of the

Head of the Church, the bridegroom, the priest must be male. There must be a 'natural resemblance' between the priest and Christ. For Christ himself was and remains a male" (quoted in Ruether 1986, 139).

5. Papa (1978) reports the reactions of several women attending the conference who were distressed at the fact that the meeting had taken on broad social justice aims (which could be pursued "elsewhere") rather than limiting itself to the issue of ordination (see also Weaver 1986, 112–16). The changed tone of the conference began to elicit criticism in the usually liberal Catholic newspapers (A. McCarthy 1978; Moan 1978, 433).

6. Weaver 1986, 245 n. 84. There is criticism of Women-Church from within the coalition as well, some of it quite specific to particular aspects of the conferences. Rosemary Radford Ruether, for instance, questioned the use of the phrase repeated aloud by the assembled women in the 1987 gathering: "I am holy, I am holy, I am holy"; she argued that it was too individualist and that some more collective expression should be used. Renee Golden, a leader in the sanctuary movement, has articulated what she sees as a more fundamental difference within Women-Church between a "liberal-faith response and the more radical-faith sector." Golden would argue that there is more than a strategic difference between these two sectors and that there are fundamentally two sorts of struggles, the more radical one being focused on an integration of women's issues with an analysis of imperialism, and a structural critique of race and class oppression in American society (author's interview with Renee Golden, October 1988). Marjorie Tuite (1986, 3) used to talk about the need to create "solidarity" rather than agreement and the importance of basing that solidarity in more than the shared opposition or critique of the institutional Church. I interviewed a number of women who consider themselves feminists but do not exactly identify with Women-Church; they talked about their need for tradition, for ritual, and the difficulty of substituting new religious forms for familiar ones.

7. See the list of topics in *National Catholic Register* 23 (July 17, 1987): 11 n. 35.

8. Moran and Schwarz 1987, 3.

9. It is ironic, given Rome's current antipathy to feminism, that the LCWR was founded at the initiation of the hierarchy. Pope Pius XII hoped that a cohesive association of Mothers (or Majors) Superior would provide effective leadership to help combat the ills of modern society; to do so, the Vatican urged, sisters must become well educated and "shed the accretions that had left them an anomaly in modern times" (Quinonez and Turner 1992, 18).

10. The second draft was titled "One in Christ Jesus: A Pastoral Response to the Concerns of Women for Church and Society" (1990).

11. The pastoral did offer a revisioning of Mary that attempted to portray her as a champion of the oppressed, and it talked about the "sin of sexism"—a linguistic frame that on the whole met with feminist approbation.

12. Women in Chicago have used the courts successfully in threatening to sue the archbishop's fund to make the diocese accountable for funds designated for sisters' use. Other attempts—such as Sister Rosa Martha Zarate's suit against the San Bernardino diocese, which in dismissing her, she charged, had discriminated against her as a woman—have been unsuccessful.

CHAPTER 4

"Like a Tarantula on a Banana Boat":
Ms. Magazine, 1972–1989

■

AMY FARRELL

In 1972 the first feminist, mass-media periodical, *Ms.* magazine, hit the American newsstands. Gloria Steinem, cofounder, described it as a "how to magazine for the liberated female human being—not how to make jelly but how to seize control of your life" ("For the Liberated Female" 1971). Within eight days all 300,000 copies had sold out nationwide, drawing 20,000 letters from readers—an amazing number, considering that magazines with four times that publication rate average only 4,000 letters per issue ("*Ms.* Makes It" 1972). Many readers signed their letters with a "click," referring to the "click of recognition" that Jane O'Reilly (1972) discussed in her article "The Housewife's Moment of Truth." The shift in consciousness that *Ms.* represented clearly resonated with the changing ideas and perspectives of women across the country.

When *Ms.* began, there were over 500 feminist periodicals—newsletters and magazines—being published in the United States, but none had the mass circulation that *Ms.* offered (Mather 1974, 82). As a crossover magazine that borrowed its content from the smaller feminist periodicals and its format from mass-circulation women's magazines, *Ms.* promised to reach those who had little formal connection to the women's movement. Despite some skepticism from mainstream journalists that such a "single-issue" magazine could last, and the Redstockings group's accusations that *Ms.* was part of a government conspiracy to displace the radical feminist movement, some sensed its revolutionary potential (Breasted 1972, 12; Redstockings 1975, 32). Onka Dekkers, a writer for *off our backs*, most clearly articulated this possibility: "*Ms.* is making feminist converts of middle class heathens from academia to condominium ville. A slick reputable looking magazine breaks down defenses and lets the word worm its way into the brain. *Ms.* is almost in violation of Truth in Packaging laws. There

is a female mind-set on those glossy pages slipping into American homes
concealed in bags of groceries like tarantulas on banana boats" (1972, 19).
Using the funding and the circulation that a mass-media magazine offered,
the *Ms.* founders intended to harness capitalism for the feminist movement.
The risk, however, was that capitalism—more specifically, advertisers—
would harness *Ms.* first.

Gloria Steinem had begun talking to activists and women's magazine
editors and writers about starting a feminist periodical in the early 1970s.
By 1972 she and Patricia Carbine, who resigned from her position as editor of *McCall's* to become publisher of the new magazine, had organized
this group into the first mass-media, feminist, magazine organization, one
that attempted to run itself in a more egalitarian fashion than traditional
magazines.

Under the leadership of Steinem and Carbine, *Ms.* survived for nearly
two decades, balancing precariously the demands of its feminist readership
and its commercial sponsors. The fact that *Ms.* discontinued publication
in 1989, to come out with an advertising-free magazine in 1990, suggests
that *Ms.* failed, unable to sustain itself as a commercial feminist magazine.
Its demise as a mass-media periodical was perhaps less significant, and
certainly less interesting, than the eighteen-year struggle over its symbolic
and literal ownership. This essay explores *Ms.* as a contested terrain, a
concept most clearly represented in the text of the magazine itself. In any
issue from the 1970s or 1980s one might find advertisements portraying
women's liberation as an American Express card or Benson and Hedges
smoke, colliding with poems by Adrienne Rich, an editorial proclaiming
the "sisterhood" of all women, an article bemoaning the housewife blues,
Alice Walker speaking on the limitations and racism of white feminism,
classifieds selling "matriarchal" jewelry, a "No Comment" section criticizing mainstream advertising, and letters from readers criticizing the magazine's own advertising policies. Not simply a postmodern bricolage, this
"mixing up" represents the results of the *Ms.* staff's attempts to construct
a feminist "tool" within the context and using the resources of corporate
capitalism.

In discussing the editors' strategies to negotiate between the advertisers,
who demanded that *Ms.* be a good "marketing opportunity," and the
readers, who expected *Ms.* to live up to its promise to be an "open forum"
for all women, I look first at the way advertisers colonized the magazine,
creating consumer feminism despite (and sometimes because of) the sales

staff's policies. Next, drawing upon an examination of the unpublished and published letters written to *Ms.* from 1972 to 1979 and the published letters from 1972 to 1989, I turn to the readers, who actively claimed the magazine as their own resource despite the power of the advertisers. Finally, I examine the latter years of the commercial *Ms.* to see how an extremely conservative political context, financial problems, and new editors destroyed the delicate balance between advertisers and readers.[1]

Financing Ms.

Initial funding for the magazine came from Clay Felker, the editor of *New York* magazine, who in 1971 agreed to publish a year-end special double issue including *Ms.* Part of Felker's motivation was a desire to attract the women's advertising *New York* magazine had been trying to gain. As Felker said in an interview with *Newsweek*, "We're going to make a lot of money out of it" ("Feminist Forum" 1971, 104). With the immediate sellout of the preview issues and the overwhelming response from subscribers, investors began to look seriously at *Ms.* In the spring of 1972 Warner Communications offered to invest $1 million in the magazine, making Warner the major investor. Steinem insisted that the magazine be woman-controlled, and Warner finally agreed to take only 25 percent of the stock. Far less than the amount generally considered necessary to start a new magazine, Warner's investment nevertheless separated *Ms.* from the regional and often more radical periodicals that were run on a shoestring budget.

Although the funding assured editors that they could run for a year even without strong responses from advertisers, the *Ms.* founders quickly had to forge strong ties with potential sponsors. They hoped not only to bring in enough business to support the magazine but also to transform the advertising industry itself, changing its practices of using sexist imagery and of hiring only male sales people. Carbine hired and trained the first female sales staff in the country (author's interview with Carbine, 1990). In a 1974 article the *Ms.* advertising staff explained their goals: to run more articles than ads; to choose advertising that "accurately reflects the way women spend our hard-won consumer dollars"; to accept only ads that treat "women as people"; and to train "advertising sales people who themselves would be agents of change" ("Personal Report" 1974, 58). Editors promised to reject ads that were either "downright insulting" or "harmful" (feminine hygiene deodorant, for example). They also sought more advertising for such "unfeminine" products as cars and stereos ("Personal Report" 1972, 7).

The *Ms.* ad staff had the daunting task of persuading advertisers that their goals were realistic. They had to convince advertisers that women actually bought cars and plane tickets, and that angry letters from *Ms.* readers proved that these were careful consumers who paid attention to advertisements, not anticonsumer radicals. As a result of the ad staff's insistence (the staff often returned to the office "battered down" from their meetings with doubtful advertisers), *Ms.* was the first women's magazine to publish ads for big-ticket, traditionally "male" products such as cars, insurance, and credit cards (author's interview with Levine, 1990). Besides promoting a less stereotypical image (women buy major appliances as well as groceries), these ads had the significant benefit of requiring no complementary editorial copy.

Ads in *Ms.*'s early years frequently urged women "into the mainstream," an aspect of a feminist philosophy that Ferree and Hess (1985) have identified as "career feminism." For instance, NOW's Legal Defense and Education Fund pictured a board room with nine white male executives; the caption read: "What's wrong with this picture? Somebody forgot to include the women" (January 1974). Large companies also began to speak to *Ms.* readers as potential executives and well-to-do consumers. American Express, one of the first national corporations to move into this new market, advertised a credit application "for women only" (January 1973). Throughout the 1970s other advertisers—for charge accounts, executive clothing, and business correspondence courses—picked up on this trend of portraying the women's movement in terms of economic advancement. In the 1970s *Ms.* instituted a regular ad section titled "Human Development," which featured corporations (ITT; Merrill Lynch) that wanted to hire more women on their executive staffs.

The advertisements also drew on some of the most compelling themes evoked by feminism—equality, freedom, personal transformation, and sisterhood—to justify a consumer ethic.[2] For instance, a common tactic was to acknowledge the women's movement, then to offer some specific consumer product as the solution to women's problems. In the preview issue an ad for the Redactron Company, which sold typewriters and word-processing systems, suggested that the "dead-end secretary was dead." The copy encouraged women to send for "Free the Secretary" buttons and then ask their bosses about the new machines.

During the late 1970s and into the 1980s, competition from new women's magazines, problems with advertisers, censorship in schools and on newsstands, and rising postal, paper, and ink costs forced *Ms.* to solicit ever more ads and limited the staff's ability to pick and choose. As early as 1974 the editors solicited ads for traditionally feminine products, legitimating their decision on the basis that the "full range" of women's lives would be represented (November 1974, 90). That change in policy did not immediately bring forth the desired response from advertisers. Not only did advertisers expect supporting complementary (also "complimentary") copy; they also doubted that feminists actually concerned themselves with personal appearance, children, or housekeeping. As a result, the most prevalent ads found in *Ms.* were for cigarettes and alcohol, two products that most companies would advertise without complementary copy and with slogans the editors perceived as relatively innocuous. The staff did reject certain ad campaigns they saw as most offensive, however (Dougherty 1975). One of the most lucrative was the Virginia Slims "You've Come a Long Way, Baby" campaign, which they refused after failing to convince the company to change the slogan to "You'll Go a Long Way" (author's interview with Carbine, 1990).

By 1978 a note of alarm had replaced the earlier enthusiastic tone, stressing the magazine's "unique connection with its readers" and asking them to help out with donations ("Personal Reports from *Ms.*" 1978). In 1979 the magazine attempted to avoid an economic crisis by switching to a nonprofit status. This would make *Ms.* tax-exempt (with the exception of advertising revenue) and would lower postal costs. In 1981, however, the Reagan administration slashed the postal breaks given to nonprofit and educational organizations, a policy that worked against media without strong commercial backing.

Despite *Ms.*'s move to a nonprofit status in 1979, the magazine continued to solicit advertising. Anticipating readers' questions, the editorial that introduced the new organizational structure explained: "As for advertising, *Ms.*, like other nonprofit magazines, will continue to carry it. Earnings from ad revenues are taxable as unrelated business income, and without them the economic burden on the reader and on tax-exempt contributions would be too great. Besides, one of the accomplishments of *Ms.* has been improving the image of women in advertising, and diversifying the kinds of products that are considered appropriate for women" ("Personal Report" 1979, 12–13). Muting the inherent tension between the commercial context in which *Ms.* was situated and the feminist resource that it aspired to be, editors focused on the successes they had in transforming the "image of women in advertising." Indeed, *Ms.* began publishing a section titled "One Step Forward," which printed examples of advertisements portraying women in a positive light.

The sales staff were under constant pressure to convince advertisers that *Ms.* provided a good marketing atmosphere. *Ms.* printed circulars and provided demographic statistics for potential advertisers and, by the 1980s, was even providing some complementary copy. Although it never published recipes or make-up "how-tos," one can see increased concessions to advertisers in the articles that focused on personal computers and related paraphernalia (July 1984, 36; October 1984, 68; December 1984, 111; January 1985, 89). These articles, listing brand names of specific products and prices, created more attractive space for computer companies to advertise; in 1984 and 1985, WordStar and IBM bought multipage spreads. *Ms.* provided services to other kinds of companies as well, such as publishing bound-in catalogues with editorial copy. The June 1984 "*Ms.* Sun Sampler" provided a coupon for ordering "this summer's hottest products." The regular May "Beauty of Health" issues promoted related products through two- to five-page advertising supplements (May 1984; May 1985; May 1986). *Ms.* frequently published other "theme" issues as well, such as "Women and Money." Theme issues were supposed to attract the "right" consumers and provide a supportive atmosphere for ad copy, but ads and articles frequently contradicted rather than supported each other. For instance, in the October 1983 issue featuring "Food: Secret Pleasures, Hidden Dangers," the cover story focused on an analysis of anorexia and other eating disorders primarily related to the societal imperative for women to be thin. Four ads in that issue, however, featured diet aids and foods, products that the article implicitly criticized. Another piece asked who profited from the new industry for treating premenstrual syndrome, while two ads—for Aqua-Ban and Pamprin—sought readers' money to treat this same problem. Incongruities like these, necessary for the dual purpose of maintaining a feminist perspective and attracting advertising, pleased neither the advertisers nor the readers.

In the 1980s the financial problems facing *Ms.* forced editors to repackage their magazine. An increasingly mass-media "look"—including more white space, shorter articles, sensational or "catchy" titles, and an increased reliance on images of "successful" women—coexisted with reviews of feminist films and books, feminist analyses of contemporary issues, and the continued outpourings from readers. This refocusing enabled *Ms.* to mask its oppositional perspectives so that it could continue to solicit advertisements from companies who were skittish about buying space in a "political" magazine. This is what made *Ms.* look more commercial—some would say dull—by the 1980s. Advertising demands not only influenced how *Ms.* looked but also helped to create a philosophy of consumer feminism (you are liberated if you buy certain products) and reduced the diversity of its intended audience. Paradoxically, *Ms.*'s decision to promote a less stereotypical image of women, by campaigning for ads of nonfeminine products, encouraged the development of a new stereotype. When liquor, car, airplane, credit card, and insurance companies overcame their reluctance to advertise in *Ms.*, the editors felt they had accomplished what the NOW statement of purpose encouraged: they had moved a women's magazine into the mainstream of the mass-marketed magazine industry. But *Ms.* now had to prove to these "mass" advertisers that it could attract and maintain an audience of readers who wanted and could pay for big-ticket items. This enforced a focus on a white, heterosexual, middle-class "career" audience. An ad for the magazine appearing in the *New York Times* in March 19, 1974, described the *Ms.* reader as being part of a high-income household, likely to hold a managerial or professional job, and young, between the ages of eighteen and thirty-four. Two promotional ads geared to potential advertisers in the late 1980s emphasized a portrait of a well-to-do, baby-boomer-age white woman as the *Ms.* reader. One, picturing a thin, well-dressed woman among champagne corks, passports, and credit cards, asked, "What do you call a woman who's made it to the top? Ms." Another pictured a four-photo spread of a white woman casting off her 1960s granny glasses and beaded headband, putting on lipstick, and emerging as an "up-to-date" woman of the late 1980s, complete with permed hair and gold earrings (Winegar 1988, 1E; Zuckerman 1988, 72). In short, *Ms.* portrayed the *Ms.* reader as the ideal consumer. Even as its editorials talked about "sisterhood," the promotional material circulated to advertisers presented a much narrower conception of the *Ms.* reader.

In the premier ad-free issue of the revived *Ms.*, Steinem (1990) wrote a lengthy article describing the pressures advertisers had placed on the magazine. In this article and in interviews both Steinem and Carbine spoke forcefully about the double standard that required complementary copy and supportive editorial atmosphere in women's magazines but not in more "general interest" magazines such as *Time* or *Newsweek*. The history of *Ms.* does demonstrate the power of this double standard, but it also points to the larger problem confronting any attempt to use commercial media for a political movement. Commercial media want to create a consumer ethic, not a culture of politics that ignores or perhaps even resists a culture based on the purchase of goods. Moreover, all commercial media must present their readers as good consumers; every magazine, from *Newsweek* to *Vanity Fair*, "sells" its readers to advertisers (Marc 1984; McCracken 1993). *Ms.* was no exception; indeed, because of advertisers' skepticism, the ad staff had to work doubly hard to convince potential sponsors that they would reach "desired" consumers. As we have seen, some of *Ms.*'s own policies, such as soliciting ads for big-ticket items, reinforced the need to prove that its readers were well-educated, monied, and consumption-oriented—far from the editorial descriptions of *Ms.* as a magazine for "all women, everywhere." Although its refusal to publish recipes or beauty hints had lost *Ms.* many potential advertisers, in her 1990 editorial Steinem apologized for the offensive ads that had been published: "Though we [did] refuse most of the ads that would look like a parody in our pages, we [got] so worn down that some slip[ped] through," she wrote (1990, 24). There is no question that sales staff and editors did get "worn down": the untenable position in which *Ms.* existed forced the sales staff to solicit actively whatever advertisers they could find, and necessitated a blind eye on the part of the editors. Readers, however, were not silent, and editors responded to their critiques.

Resistant Readers

By examining the text of *Ms.* we can see how advertisers, attempting to colonize the women's movement for their own purposes, led *Ms.* into representing feminism as a movement of and for "successful" women. Throughout its history, however, readers resisted the way these advertisements portrayed women and feminism. Moreover, readers questioned editors about the issue of ownership, criticizing what they saw as corporate control over "their" magazine. When it fell short of its promise to be a resource for the women's movement, they felt betrayed; angry and disappointed, they actively criticized and resisted what they found offensive. The language of the women's movement and the marketing promises of *Ms.* provided ample ammunition for making strong claims. One reader, for instance, concluded her angry letter with the skeptical and sarcastic question "yours in sisterhood????" (*Ms.* Letters Collection, box 2, folder 60). Readers wrote to *Ms.* with their personal stories of discrimination, their stories of triumph, their analyses of current events, and their strong and often contradictory opinions about feminism. Though they disagreed over what kind of feminism *Ms.* should advocate, nearly all readers were united in opposition to the advertising. From its first issue, when nearly 8,000 of the 20,000 letters received focused on ads, advertising provoked the majority of readers' critical letters.

Many ads in this first issue (the insert in *New York* magazine) were blatantly sexist. For instance, an ad for a beauty salon read, "Guys dig flabby girls. Guys blindly in love." *Ms.* published many of the angry letters and gave a lengthy editorial response as well. Explaining that *New York* magazine had chosen the ads for the preview issue, the editors wrote, "Now that we are responsible for our own advertising, we will do our best to emphasize ads that are a service to women, and reflect the real balance of our lives" (July 1972, 7). They promised to reject obviously offensive or harmful ads but asked the readers for help in less clear-cut cases. This exchange set the precedent for communication between readers and editors. Particularly when readers' critiques focused on advertising policy or selling techniques, *Ms.* responded publicly, a strategy that worked to encourage readers' identification with *Ms.* and allowed it to construct itself as a magazine for the movement.

Published exchanges between readers and editors raised the question of corporate control in a public forum and legitimated readers' criticisms. The *Ms.* text itself, specifically the "No Comment" section, also subverted the advertising. Nearly every month from 1972 to 1987, *Ms.* devoted space under this title to one or more sexist advertisements that readers sent in. Though readers submitted everything from offensive office memos to photos of billboards, much of the "No Comment" section was taken up by advertisements from the mass-media magazines, such as the 1984 ad from *Time* magazine for First Citizens Bank telling readers, "Show your wife you love her. Leave her out of your will," or the one from *Yachting* magazine picturing glamorous blondes on a yacht, with the caption, "Love Her on the Outside, Love Her on the Inside." As Linda Steiner argues (1988, 12), the "No Comment" department provided readers with "access and commitment to an alternative, oppositional definition of reality."

Significantly, readers used this feminist perspective on reality not only to critique other mass-media periodicals but also to question *Ms.*, frequently sending in ads from *Ms.* itself. These were not published, however, until the noncommercial *Ms.* presented a two-page spread of offensive *Ms.* ads in its premier 1990 issue. One might argue that the advertising-free *Ms.* needed to respond to these ads in order to regain legitimacy with disenchanted readers. In 1978 an ad *Ms.* published for the Lady Bic Shaver—picturing a tanned White woman from the buttocks down, the words "Bikini Legs" dominating the page—suggested that your legs had to be shaved smooth or you were condemned to a day under water. More than a hundred readers sent it in, often with only a slip of paper marked "No Comment." A few analyzed the Lady Bic ad in detail, referring to the skills in deconstruction that they had learned from *Ms.* itself. A woman from Michigan wrote: "Shame on you! . . . Your 'NO COMMENT' section backfired on you, and if many disappointed readers don't send this particular ad among 'NO COMMENT' mail, I'll be surprised." Another woman who sent it to the "No Comment" section also wrote to editors because, she said, "I do, after all, have a comment. . . . Do you think no one will notice and be offended by an ad that is, supposedly, condoned by *Ms.*? That we'll search magazines for offensive ads while ignoring the same in *Ms.*'s pages? (Be yourselves, girls, only shave those legs!) . . . You contradict yourself, *Ms.* I've spent my high-school years reading you and learning from you. So, please, DON'T CHEAPEN YOURSELF, *Ms.*, after teaching *me* not to" (*Ms.* Letters Collection, box 6, folder 204).

Visual misogyny was not the only source of discomfort for readers. Such ads provided tangible evidence that the magazine belonged not to the readers but to those who paid the most for it, the advertisers. Dissatisfaction with the power of advertisers can be seen most clearly in the letters concerning cigarette and alcohol ads. Throughout the magazine's history, readers were angry that *Ms.* advertised cigarettes and alcohol despite the editors' promise to refuse ads for dangerous products. These criticisms became particularly vocal after the 1987 issue on women and addiction, in which *Ms.* chose to include no cigarette or alcohol ads. In her editorial preface editor Suzanne Braun Levine wrote: "Like most national magazines, we depend on such revenue, but we have never let that affect our decision to publish important new research about women's health. In this case, because of the nature and the scope of this ground-breaking report, we have offered advertisers the courtesy of a choice not to appear in this particular environment. We will welcome them back in future issues and gratefully acknowledge their continuing support" (February 1987, 35). This statement failed to clarify why *Ms.* gave cigarette and alcohol advertisers the choice *not* to buy space in this issue: because it would be incongruent in an issue devoted to women and addiction, or because they might not advertise in *Ms.* again if they anticipated articles attacking their products. Clearly, *Ms.* was attempting to protect itself both from advertisers' boycotts and from readers' anger.

Many readers found the policy offensive, arguing that these were the products that *Ms.* had originally promised to ban because they were "hurtful" to women. In May 1987 the magazine published pages of letters responding to the addiction issue. One particular exchange highlights the tension among economic demands, readers' interests, and editors' negotiations. Rosemary Pitkin from Ithaca, N.Y., wrote: "I cannot help but wish *Ms.* would let go of *its dependency* on revenue from liquor and cigarette advertising that is so hurtful to the women *Ms.* claims to serve. Your statement that you will 'welcome them back in future issues and gratefully acknowledge their continuing support' smacks of incongruity. Continuing support of what? Women's dependency? It strikes me that one force that 'creates dependency in us' is our willingness to let the economics rather than our own values and integrity define the reality. *Ms.* is in a position to model something different. But then, change does have its price."

Immediately following this letter, editors responded that this was a dependency over which they had no power; it was not simply a matter of choice to retain cigarette and alcohol advertising but an economic necessity. They went on, defensively: "We're the only women's magazine to do a cover story on women and addiction, and to sacrifice advertising revenue to do so. We're proud of this fact and of the thousands of reader donations that made it possible" (May 1987, 8).

Readers identifying themselves as legitimate critics of *Ms.* raised pertinent and painful questions about the consequences of mass-media existence. As one woman from Massachusetts wrote, "While it can be argued that large scale advertising is the only way to support a mass circulation and thus reach more women, at what point do you sell your soul?" (*Ms.* Letters Collection, box 6, folder 204). It is important that *Ms.* legitimated readers' dissatisfaction by publishing their letters and responding to their criticisms in lengthy reports explaining the need for advertising and asking for suggestions. By promoting dialogue in this way—publishing three to five pages of readers' letters and two full pages of "No Comment" ads in every issue—*Ms.* was able quietly and gently to subvert the commercial matrix in which it existed. Ads that degraded women or that commodified feminism—making women's liberation appear to be synonymous with buying a car or using a credit card—could not be read in the same way within *Ms.* as they were in other magazines; women continually pointed out the different reading process they used with *Ms.* As a reader from Delaware asked, "Why can't I just read the articles and skip the ads like I do when I read *Newsweek?*" (*Ms.* Letters Collection, box 6, folder 186). Indeed, the published letters and the "No Comment" ads created a counter-discourse to the advertising and elitist narratives of feminism in the magazine. In writing *to* the magazine, then, readers literally worked to write the magazine itself.

As a mass-circulation periodical, *Ms.* reached thousands and thousands of women, many who were predisposed to the ideas of feminism but many as well who had little previous connection to the movement. Indeed, *Ms.* broke through much of the literal as well as figurative isolation of women living in nuclear families, in secluded communities and suburbs, and more generally in the alienating and disempowering culture of patriarchy. The lengthy letters section, publishing personal stories and critiques of the magazine, provided women with a "free space" (Evans and Boyte 1986) in which to articulate their changed perceptions of the world and their needs. The letters section transformed private talk into public discourse, allowing women to rehearse their arguments and critiques for an audience outside *Ms.* Once they connected to the magazine, readers did not easily abandon it, for it promised them oppositional politics and a democratic forum. Using the language of the women's movement, readers resisted the commodification and narrowing of feminism that they observed as the magazine moved into the 1980s.

Falling Off the Tightrope

Throughout its history *Ms.* balanced the demands of readers, advertisers, and editors rather tenuously; in the late 1980s, when it faced extensive financial difficulties and the *Ms.* Foundation sold the magazine to an Australian media firm, this balance tipped in favor of the advertisers (Fabrikant 1987; Wayne 1988; LaGanga 1990). Through the late 1970s and into the 1980s circulation remained relatively stable (about 350,000), but the new for-profit *Ms.*, owned first by Fairfax and then Matilda Inc., needed to reach more (and, from a demographic standpoint, "better") readers. To mollify advertisers who believed *Ms.* to be "too strident and too focused" (Fabrikant 1987, 39), *Ms.* worked to distance itself from its roots in the feminist movement. Sandra Yates, the new publisher, portrayed the decision to buy *Ms.* as completely "pragmatic," emphasizing the magazine's "potential for growth" in financial terms and ignoring its history as a feminist resource. Anne Summers, the new editor-in-chief, described it as "less angry, less militant, more focused and, we hope, more successful" (M. Hamilton 1988). For the first time in its history, *Ms.* explicitly refused the title of "feminist." It had increasingly shied away from feminism in its later issues in its effort to solicit advertisers more aggressively and stay in competition with the other women's magazines, but not until it changed owners did this attempt to avoid "feminism" become an explicit policy devised to reach the most (and the most "attractive") readers.

We can see how the balance tipped away from readers' favor in the policies instituted by the new editor and publisher in 1988. Summers and Yates shortened the letters section, published more edited letters, eliminated the classified section, and abbreviated "No Comment" to a quarter-page, anchoring it with their own caption rather than leaving it up to reader interpretation. They drastically reduced the possibilities for the reader interaction—and reader intervention—that had become institutions in the former *Ms.* Speaking about women's response, Summers referred to the "battle" she had with readers, who did not understand the demands of the commercial publishing industry (interview with Molli Hoben of the *Minnesota Women's Press*, 1989). Ironically, however, that sort of "battle" had been encouraged by the previous editors. If readers did not understand the commercial publishing industry, then Summers did not understand that readers had claimed *Ms.* as a feminist resource and used it in support of democratic, oppositional politics and a feminist community.

The final months of *Ms.*'s commercial history demonstrate the ultimate economic power of advertisers. Even if the demographics of the new *Ms.* were "right," the political connotations of the magazine proved too dangerous. When the new owners increased the circulation to over 550,000, the number considered significant enough to attract major advertising, advertisers still did not respond, finding the political content too controversial (Reilly 1989). They particularly shunned any discussion of abortion rights in the ultraconservative period of the late 1980s. Hence, when the July 1989 issue appeared with the words "IT'S WAR" emblazoned in bold red print across a jet black cover, referring to the anticipated anti-abortion-rights decision by the Supreme Court in the Webster case, advertisers reacted powerfully: they pulled out en masse. The December 1989 issue brought in only ten ads, too few to allow the magazine to publish (Allemang 1989), and the magazine folded—to reemerge in 1990 as a noncommercial publication.

Although advertisers rejected *Ms.* after July 1989, even previously disenchanted readers saw that issue as a possible direction *Ms.* might go in the future (Lathrop 1989, 12). I witnessed the power of the magazine's cover firsthand at a pro-choice rally I attended in Boston, where one of the major speakers for the day waved the "IT'S WAR" issue throughout her speech. For that speaker, the magazine was again an excellent resource to illustrate her anger and her determination. The issues following publication of the "IT'S WAR" cover contained pages of letters from readers sharing their frustration, their renewed energy, and their tactics for fighting the Webster decision. At the same time that the history of *Ms.* illustrates the power of corporate capitalism, then, it also suggests the power of a magazine to which readers felt connected and which they claimed as their own. The "IT'S WAR" cover evoked not only the shared memory of a powerful historical feminist movement and hope for future mobilization but also the collective memory of a magazine that had promised to give voice to and serve the movement.

Conclusion

The founders of *Ms.* imagined a magazine that would bridge the boundaries of the commercial and the political, creating a "popular" feminist periodical. By claiming a position on the commercial newsstand, *Ms.* could challenge the collective definition of a mainstream women's magazine, but that same commercial position also thwarted the magazine's potential to work as a resource within the women's movement. Ironically, though it was advertising that allowed *Ms.* to reach the mass population it did, to be sold so inexpensively (only $12 a year even in 1987), and to be available in supermarkets and bookstores where more radical journals were unavailable, this same advertising also portrayed women and feminism in a way offensive to most readers.

The *Ms.* organization dealt with these opposing demands by living a double life. Ad staff compiled demographic statistics and designed catchy circulars to convince advertisers that they would reach a desirable target audience. Editors encouraged advertisers by trying to make *Ms.* a supportive atmosphere with complementary copy and "upbeat" covers. At the same time, editors appeased readers by publishing their letters, writing responses, drafting longer explanations of advertising policies in their "Personal Reports from *Ms.*" By the late 1980s this had become a balancing act too difficult to maintain. An extremely conservative historical moment, advertisers' unwillingness to associate themselves with anything "feminist," and the sheer exhaustion of the staff forced *Ms.* to sell. The new editor and publisher, perhaps ignorant of the dangerous waters they would have to negotiate, found the readers' anger and the advertisers' threats surprising and disappointing. They did not know how to play the game of balancing the claims of these opposing groups.

The newest *Ms.*, advertising-free and completely subscriber-supported, doesn't have to play the game.[3] Publishing an even more extensive letters section than the old *Ms.* as well as lengthy articles expressing a wide range of views and voices, the new *Ms.* has become a useful forum for debate and communication among feminists (Goodman 1990). With no advertisers to please and no need to mask its politics, *Ms.* can now name feminism explicitly, actively construct an oppositional politics, and work unambiguously for the resurgence of the women's movement in the 1990s.

Inevitably, however, we must ask ourselves what has been lost. In sharp contrast to the "old" *Ms.*, the new magazine is expensive ($35 a year for a subscription, compared with the previous $12), has limited distribution, and seeks to reach those already considering themselves feminists. Most significantly, one can no longer find *Ms.* at the grocery store or on most commercial newsstands. Ironically, then, even as the new *Ms.* has the freedom to construct a more inclusive feminism, attentive to the voices of women of color, lesbians, and poor women, its noncommercial status is an obstacle to reaching any but those women who have the knowledge and the money to subscribe to it or to find it in alternative bookstores.

In many ways, the story of *Ms.* is paralleled in the stories of feminist organizations across the country, which must weigh the demands of their clientele with the demands of their funding agencies. For *Ms.*, readers were the clientele, businesses and corporations the funding agencies. The dependence on advertisers made the magazine look increasingly commercial and narrowed its representation of feminism. In the end, the advertisers forced *Ms.* to close its doors. For nearly two decades, however, the publication did balance readers' needs against the demands of the commercial publishing world so that this feminist magazine reached an estimated 3.5 million readers. Like a "tarantula on a banana boat," *Ms.* slipped feminist ideas into the mainstream. Though it may never have been the perfect feminist "tool," perhaps feminist movements could use a few more "tarantulas" as we move into the twenty-first century.

Notes

Acknowledgments: Funding for the larger project of which this essay is a part came from a Schlesinger Library Dissertation Grant in 1989, a University of Minnesota McMillan Travel Grant in 1990, a National Endowment for the Humanities Travel to Collections Grant in 1992, and a Dickinson College Faculty Research Grant in 1992. I thank Myra Marx Ferree and Patricia Yancey Martin for extensive comments on earlier drafts.

   1. All evidence in this essay is drawn from Farrell 1991, which explores in more depth the tensions among editors and readers as to what kinds of feminism *Ms.* should represent. All unpublished letters written to *Ms.* from the second issue on are collected at the Schlesinger Library at Radcliffe College. I studied all letters that were open for examination, those written from 1973 through 1979. Because letters are closed until ten years after their writing, I examined only published letters from 1980 to 1989 (Thom 1987 is a useful collection of published letters). In addition, I interviewed former editors of *Ms.* in 1990–93 and examined the *Ms.* editorial papers collected at the Sophia Smith Archives in Northampton, Massachusetts.

   2. The transformation of feminism into consumerism was not a new trend, as Nancy Cott demonstrates in her study of the first wave of feminism (1987, 171–75). In the 1920s, women's magazines frequently sold household products in the name of "freedom" for women.

   3. After the canceled issue of December 1989, Dale Lang Inc., owner of *Working Woman* and *Working Mother*, bought the magazine, and Robin Morgan, longtime activist and former contributing editor of *Ms.*, accepted the position of editor. The current editor is Marcia Gillespie.

CHAPTER 5

The Australian Femocratic Experiment:
A Feminist Case for Bureaucracy

■

HESTER EISENSTEIN

A "femocrat" is a feminist bureaucrat. The term is an Australian coinage, minted when members of the Australian women's movement first developed the strategy of entering federal and state bureaucracies as a way of bringing feminist concerns onto the public policy agenda. The femocratic experiment (my expression) began in the 1970s, and is ongoing.[1]

This essay looks at some aspects of this experiment, in order to illuminate the relation of feminism to bureaucracy and, more broadly, to look at the possibilities for implementing feminist ideals in the "real" world of political action. My research on this question is part of a broader scholarly and activist debate about the relationship of women, and of feminist concerns, to the state and the exercise of power. The feminist revival of the 1960s and 1970s produced many efforts to use state power on behalf of women. Women's agencies, ministries, and special advisers were established by governments in response to pressure from the organized women's movement in countries as diverse as India, Germany, Brazil, Jamaica, Greece and Australia.[2] Concomitantly, there has been a steady stream of feminist writing denouncing the state as inherently patriarchal and inimical to women's interests.[3]

My title refers to Kathy Ferguson's well-known book, *The Feminist Case against Bureaucracy* (1984), in which she argues that bureaucracy and feminism are natural enemies. I disagree with her, at least in part, as the result of my experience with the Australian femocratic experiment. Ferguson's argument relies on at least two assumptions: (1) she defines true feminism as the daughter of the New Left, accepting the division common in 1970s analysis between "radical" and "reformist" feminisms; (2) she defines bureaucracy as the characteristic social formation of modernity, based on the subordination and dehumanization of those subjected to it.

I do not have sufficient space here to go into her argument at length, but
it represents a widely held view within U.S. feminism, including academic
feminism, which basically rejects reformist or bourgeois feminism as a
form of co-optation, and defines administrative and bureaucratic structures
as intrinsically oppressive.

On the first point, in the 1990s it feels like a bit of a luxury to distinguish between feminisms that are radical versus reformist. Given the shift
of the political spectrum to the right, we are dealing with an "F" word
no matter what subdivision of feminism we individually embrace. When
I say this, I am talking about the short term. In the longer run I continue
to take very seriously the distinction between reformist (or "bourgeois")
and radical (in its 1970s sense: committed to fundamental social change)
feminism, but it is the stuff of at least another article or book to examine
these issues adequately.[4] On the second point, I am not defending bureaucracy as such but rather raising the question of how feminist ideals can be
translated into practice in a world that is organized, probably irreversibly,
into complex and hierarchical administrative structures. Vivien Hart has
suggested that an examination of the history of women's efforts within
bureaucracies, from the 1920s onward, may yield a more optimistic picture of the possibilities for feminist influence: "Women bureaucrats can be
active 'crusaders,' not passive 'servants of the state' " (1992, 7).[5]

The Australian experience is a striking example of this phenomenon,
most notably in its conscious decision to use bureaucratic structures as the
central instrument for effecting feminist reforms. In the period under discussion—from the early 1970s to the late 1980s—this mechanism was a
powerful vehicle for placing feminist issues on the political agenda and for
establishing a range of feminist institutions funded by governments. But
this set of developments is part of a unique political and social conjuncture
that needs explaining.

This essay gives a brief history of the femocratic experiment and provides some information on how femocrats saw their alliance with the state,
its costs and its benefits. The material is drawn from a series of interviews
I conducted in March–April 1990 with thirty-three present and former
femocrats in Sydney, Melbourne, Adelaide, and Canberra. The respondents
were selected by a "snowball" process, starting with feminist friends and
colleagues whom I knew from my experience working as an equal employment opportunity (EEO) officer in Sydney from 1980 to 1988, and then
expanding to people they recommended to me. I limited the interviews to
the capital cities where the femocracy had been the most developed under
Labor governments, but this was also a limit set by time.

My schedule of interview questions derived, in part, from my own experience as a femocrat. During the years I spent in Australia I became aware of a series of intense debates over the status of femocrats, their political commitments, their relations to state power and to the broader women's movement.[6] I was also interested in the issues of "gender experience" raised by the presence of women at senior levels of a white, male-dominated, and very traditional-minded civil service. In effect, my questions focused on the experiences of femocrats within the bureaucratic structures they inhabited. To whom did they see themselves as accountable? How did they select the issues on which they went to battle? How did they develop the structures that housed them in the bureaucracy, and how effective were these as centers for the development of policy on women's issues? After a brief excursion into recent Australian history, I focus on three areas: accountability to the women's movement; setting an agenda; and changes over time.

The Femocratic Experiment

The Australian national elections of 1972 brought to power a Labor government headed by Gough Whitlam. The change of government marked the end of an era. The right-wing Liberal-National coalition had governed Australia for the previous twenty-three years, in an unbroken regime that had come to seem "the natural government": conservative, colorless, and subservient to the foreign policy dictates of Britain and the United States. Whitlam's government came in on a wave of optimism and hopes for sweeping change. Domestically, the Labor government was committed to major reforms, including antidiscrimination legislation, urban renewal, and Aboriginal land rights.

The Women's Electoral Lobby (WEL), which was the major reformist feminist group, had lobbied heavily for attention to women's issues during the campaign.[8] The women's movement was seen as a factor in Labor's victory, and this was acknowledged in Whitlam's appointment of Elizabeth Reid as the first adviser on women's affairs. In concert with other feminists inside and outside government, Reid won a series of feminist policy initiatives: Commonwealth funding of child care, women's refuges, rape crisis centers, women's health centers, working women's centers, and policies for equal opportunities for women and girls in education, among other things. In the International Women's Year (1975, the first year of the United Nations Decade for Women), the government funded an astonishing variety of women's projects across Australia (Sawer 1990).

That was also, however, the fateful year in which Whitlam's government fell, in a complicated constitutional crisis. In the wake of this defeat, WEL activists concluded that tying their interests only to electoral victories was an unreliable strategy. The alternative was to seek the establishment of permanent women's advisers within the bureaucracies, nationally and at the state level.

The pattern of establishing a women's adviser to the prime minister was rapidly reproduced at the state level, so that between 1976 and 1990 women's advisers to the premier (equivalent to a state governor) were established in all of the six states and two territories (the Northern Territory and the Australian Capital Territory, or ACT), usually (but not exclusively) under Labor governments. Soon this strategy expanded, and women's advisers began pushing successfully for the establishment of specialist women's positions in other sections of the bureaucracy including health, education, social services, and industrial relations (labor). Along with the passage of antidiscrimination legislation in some states, these moves began to establish the substantial network of femocrats now in place. It was understood from the beginning that these women were feminists who owed their position to pressure from the organized women's movement, and it was broadly expected that they were in government to deliver policy changes that would advance the interest of women in general.

By the 1980s there was widespread acceptance of the femocratic phenomenon as part of ordinary political life. When Carmel Niland, head of the Anti-Discrimination Board, resigned after the defeat of the Labor government in New South Wales in 1988, the *Sydney Morning Herald* announced the news in a five-column-wide headline reading "Top 'femocrat' jobs up for grabs" (September 27, 1988, p. 2).

Accountability

The Australian strategy of creating femocrats has been to place women in the bureaucracy at key places to ensure that woman-friendly policies can be produced.[9] But what is to guarantee that once they rise to positions of influence and power, women will remain true to the interests of the mass of women? The name of Margaret Thatcher conjures up the worst-case scenario. Feminists have learned that it is entirely possible to empower women to oppress their sisters once they achieve high office.

In the Australian context, there has been a strong notion that the femocrats are in some sense accountable to the women's movement.[10] Placed in power by the strength of women's activism, they are widely seen to be the arm of the women's movement in government. But the situation is more complex than this.

In the first place, femocrats, like all bureaucrats, are accountable in a formal and legal way not to the women's movement but to government. The structure of Australian bureaucracy replicates that of the "mother" country, Great Britain. It is organized along the lines of the Westminster system of responsible government, in which the permanent bureaucracy is expected to carry out the policy of the government of the day. The elected government, in the form of the prime minister and cabinet, make policy decisions, which if necessary are embodied in legislation that goes through the Parliament. (Party discipline ensures that the government of the day, unlike the majority party in the United States, controls the outcome of parliamentary votes—unless there is a crisis of confidence, which will usually trigger new elections.) These decisions are conveyed by the responsible ministers to their heads of department, who in turn transmit the decisions to the bureaucrats under them, who do the work of turning policy into programs that are implemented on the ground. The lines of accountability thus run upward, in the bureaucracy, from the individual bureaucrat to the department head to the responsible minister and the cabinet. If the electorate dislikes the outcomes, in principle they have the option of "turning the rascals out" at the next election.

In practice, of course, this elegant scheme works in a more complicated and conflictual way. The bureaucracy has a powerful culture of its own, and senior members of the administration often seek to persuade cabinet members of their own views. Hence the line of accountability that runs from head of department to minister can be interrupted when these two are at odds. The expectation of loyalty within the bureaucracy tends to be to itself. The suspicion that someone is loyal to the minister, rather than to the head of the department, can count heavily against her.

In this field of forces, the accountability of femocrats to the women's movement has absolutely no formal legitimacy. Indeed, one ex-femocrat asserts that the notion that femocrats could "represent" women, widely held in the 1970s, was based on a misunderstanding of how the Westminster system operates. The notion of representation, she argues, needs to be broken into two halves. One half is the idea of representative bureaucracy. This is the notion that in order to develop policies that reflect the needs of the entire population, the bureaucracy must have within it members of all the groups within society. For women, their presence in the bureaucracy means that they can speak to the issues that confront women and get these placed on the agenda. They are representing women not in the electoral or parliamentary sense but in a bureaucratic sense: their life experience and the knowledge deriving from it provides them with the perception and the information that can be forged into woman-friendly policies.[11]

The other half is the idea that feminists in the bureaucracy can somehow report back to a constituency. This, she argues, was an illusion of the 1970s. Feminists in the bureaucracy are permanent public servants, whose loyalty must be to their colleagues and superiors. Given the requirements of a career service, where their promotions will in part depend upon their acceptability to their peers and especially to the hierarchy above them, they can in no way be seen to be loyal to the women whose interests they are thought to be serving. She believes that feminists were naive about the situation of femocrats and did not understand the constraints within which they had to work:

> I can still remember I think it was [name] years ago, . . . yelling at the Women's Refuge Movement . . . "Look, don't trust me, I'm a bureaucrat." And they said, "But we like you, [name]." She said, "Yes, but you still shouldn't trust me because structurally I'm a bureaucrat and if I've got to sell you out, I will." And . . . she talked to me about it afterwards, she said, "I just couldn't make them understand." (Respondent A interview) [12]

There is more to this issue than the rules of the Westminster system, however. There is also the issue of effectiveness. On this point Anne Summers, who served from 1983 to 1986 as the head of the Office of the Status of Women, with direct access to the prime minister, has argued that the femocrat is inevitably in a no-win situation; she is either a "mandarin" or a "missionary." A mandarin—a sardonic term in common parlance for Commonwealth public servants—operates strictly behind closed doors and gains the trust of colleagues by never leaking documents, regarding all transactions as strictly confidential. The result is that she is deeply distrusted by the women's movement, which has no evidence of her ever having stuck her neck out for a feminist decision and thus automatically concludes that she is a person who has sold out to the bureaucracy. Meanwhile, of course, her colleagues see her as a missionary, a "raver" (Australian term for a fanatic), whose commitment to the cause means she can never be taken seriously within the bureaucracy (Summers 1986).

One senior femocrat saw no alternative to becoming a mandarin. Helen

L'Orange, who served as head of the Women's Coordination Unit (women's adviser) in New South Wales from 1980 to 1988, and was head of the Office of the Status of Women in Canberra at the time of the interview, sees this as a choice that in the long run permits a kind of effectiveness that will bear fruit: "You're uniquely placed to influence mainstream policy. And the most important thing is to wield the influence that's available to you through your position. . . . Because unless you get the degree of acceptance from the other mandarins so that they can trust you, then I think you're dead in the water as a missionary. So I feel that the only chance you've got of being a really strong missionary is to be a mandarin first" (L'Orange interview).

The price of effectiveness is clearly winning the trust of the other senior officers, and this requires a commitment to confidentiality. What mechanism, then, can possibly keep the femocrats honest? According to many of my respondents, the only person each one really has to account to for her actions is herself. The bottom line becomes her own feminist conscience. One long-term femocrat, Jozefa Sobski, expressed it in these terms: "In the end . . . nobody can keep you honest because . . . out there they may not have an awareness of what you are dealing with inside anyway. So it is about your own . . . political commitments, to a lesser degree your personal loyalties, but . . . fundamentally the onus is on you. . . . Indeed, the bureaucracy is what can direct you. . . . Out there they have really no control over you. So it does depend entirely on your own political integrity" (Sobski interview).

Of course part of the complexity stems, in the case of this femocrat, from an increasing knowledge of the system and an increasing access to political power. As a very senior education officer in New South Wales, from being an outsider Sobski became over time an insider, with the capacity to initiate change. So while she felt that in principle people were entitled to information about government actions that were likely to affect them, the direct provision of information was not always, in her judgment, the most effective way to work: "It need not necessarily mean . . . every time something terrible happens inside, you run out the door, race down to the nearest feminist group, and tell them all about it so that they can take action. Because if you're operating effectively as a bureaucrat, you can probably solve a great many problems internally." She gives the example of establishing a child-care center at a Technical and Further Education College (roughly, a cross between a vocational high school and a community college in the United States):

Child care was a classic of this because we had a very fractious and difficult group out there which we could really not control in a way that would be most productive. We needed the pressure to be maintained by this group of women. . . . Now what we chose to do was actually not to conduct much debate with . . . the pressure group out there at all. . . . Three or four of us in key positions in the system worked to develop the policy that would be most politically palatable that we thought we could sell to the minister, and we reinforced each other. . . . Now that was a classic one where internal networks operated, reinforcing each other, supporting each other, providing the information on . . . what the timing should be. . . . And we didn't need to consult the group out there. (Sobski interview)

Setting an Agenda

The acceptance of femocrats went hand in hand with a general acceptance of feminism as a legitimate, if controversial, political stance. The legitimacy of the femocrats is linked to the success of Australian feminism more broadly in connecting itself to one of the mainstream themes of Australian political culture: namely, a commitment to egalitarianism and social justice. The agenda for change set by Australian feminists covered issues such as jobs and job training, access to higher education, child care, women's refuges (battered women's shelters), women's health centers, and increasing income support for women and children, along with antidiscrimination and affirmative action legislation. Obviously all these strands of activism are present in the U.S. movement as well, but I refer here to the mode of feminism that has become hegemonic.[13]

Partly, this emphasis was linked to the political climate. The feminist alliance with the Labor Party, in particular, had meant strong links to a mainstream progressive social democratic tradition with no direct counterpart in the United States. In addition, the issues of race and racism took a different form in Australia. The situation of Aborigines is comparable to that of Native Americans in the United States: an indigenous population subjected to the ravages of white settlement, including disease, alcoholism, murder, sexual exploitation, and theft of the land that was the basis of their civilization. Aborigines now make up less than 2 percent of the total Australian population. Although there is no direct analogy in Australian history to slavery in the United States and to its particular legacy of racism, this is not to minimize the history of Australian racism, which has also included severe discrimination against immigrants of non-English-speaking background, whose families now constitute 25 percent of the population.

In Australian society, the gap between rich and poor has been generally less marked than in the United States (although there are signs that this is beginning to change). The political traditions differ fundamentally, too, in that the United States is organized around a tradition of defending individual constitutional rights, whereas in Australian politics the defense of collective interests—as with the trade union movement—seems more firmly entrenched.

There was general agreement among my respondents that the issues taken up by Australian feminists, including femocrats, have been designed to address the needs of most women, rather than to advance the careers of an elite few. (The complicating issues of racial and ethnic discrimination mean that some of these needs—for migrant women of non-English-speaking backgrounds and for Aboriginal women—are only now being articulated.) One femocrat, at the time of interview a senior EEO officer in the federal civil service bureaucracy, translated this "non-elite" approach to mean that "we're keen at starting at the bottom of a pyramid and doing something about it rather than the top. When we moved into the bureaucracy . . . we moved in to do something about maternity leave, . . . part-time work, . . . things that were affecting the bulk of women. . . . One of the things which people constantly ask about is statistics for senior women. And it's only a very small number of women. I mean a lot of the other gains are more important to women as a whole" (Respondent B interview).

In thinking about what had shaped the agenda of Australian feminism, one of the crucial elements mentioned by my respondents was class background. Several argued that the issues taken up by femocrats reflected their own experience as members of the working class. In general, accounts of the femocracy have tended to assume that femocrats are privileged members of society, and this is certainly true in terms of their level in the bureaucracy.[14] But insufficient attention has been paid to their original class background.

Jenni Neary, a strong feminist activist who was the deputy head of the National Occupational Health and Safety Commission at the time of interview, reports that many femocrats are themselves of working class origin, and that their own memories of the economic struggles of their families help to shape their concept of what issues ought to be pursued as matters of policy: "I haven't done a class survey . . . of the feminists in the bureaucracy, but I'm sure that more than half of them come from working-class backgrounds because the public sector has always been a way for working-class kids to have a career" (Neary interview).

The experience of coming from the working class and in some cases from poverty and joblessness, of living close to the edge, means that femocrats have a keen sense of what most women might need in terms of economic assistance. One respondent, now the head of a major state government department, feels that most femocrats derive their sense of what is important from the experience of having to struggle for economic survival. The attention to grassroots issues, in her view, comes from the fact that "we all came from the working classes. . . . We would all have . . . mothers who did hands-on things. . . . My father still says to me, 'Don't you get too big for your boots.' . . . The kinds of things that were issues in our family were about money and paying the bills. And the person next door's lost his job . . . those kinds of things. And so . . . we know them in our core" (Respondent C interview).

But besides the class origins of some of the femocrats themselves, respondents pointed to several elements of Australian culture and history. One was the notion that Australian society has emphasized a sense of collective responsibility rather than individual rights. According to one of the most senior femocrats in the federal bureaucracy, then in her mid-fifties, "I think the kind of influences you're thinking about in Australian feminism come from people my age or younger who have a strong sense of a fair go for people who aren't as well off. . . . I think that's very important in understanding Australian social policy. . . . The feminist movement therefore fits within that broad ecology . . . of attitudes" (Respondent D interview).

Respondent A comments that this tradition influenced the Women's Electoral Lobby in the early years. Although WEL has always been what she terms "ineffably a middle-class organization," it was prepared to pick up the issues it saw as affecting the broad range of women, such as child care and education: "Certainly the philosophy of the seventies which fed into the eighties was very much that we were concerned about the least powerful women and saw ourselves as representing their interests in the system, not our own. . . . Or that we didn't see a huge barrier between our interests and theirs" (Respondent A interview).

The sense of a shared set of interests is deeply related to the Australian egalitarian ethos. Like most national myths, egalitarianism is clearly an ideological construction rather than a description of economic realities, but it remains a powerful idea in Australian life. Pat O'Shane, a magistrate who was Australia's first Aboriginal law graduate, sees the birth of white Australian society as still affecting its current attitudes: "Modern . . . Anglo-Australia was basically a penal colony. . . . We're just a graveyard for convicts. . . . That's given rise to what I consider to be quite a myth, although it's a workable myth: that Australia is an egalitarian society. . . . Naturally enough that kind of ideology . . . operates on the . . . Australian feminist consciousness as well" (Pat O'Shane interview).

Another element influencing the Australian feminist agenda is the tradition of strong trade union activism. One attempt to find ways for women to get out of poverty has been to encourage women to begin their own small businesses. A femocrat and activist from Victoria reports that in her state, discussions on this issue have always included questions about how to do so without exploiting other women:

> I was just appalled at the way in which industrial issues [that is, working conditions and union representation] were not discussed in America. . . . I heard women talking about setting up businesses using [piecework] at three and four dollars an hour. [This] would be dressed up as . . . the way of me becoming economically independent. And then I'd say, but . . . where are the union wages? . . . You couldn't have a discussion . . . in Victoria without taking in account the spinoffs . . . of what might be seen as an elite issue. Like women in business. You would still always get a discussion about the industrial issues related to the women that they may employ . . . I don't think that the . . . shoulder pads are quite as wide . . . as they are in New York or Washington. (Respondent E interview)

Changes over Time

The establishment of the femocratic network and the reforms achieved on behalf of women in Australia, from affirmative action to federal funding for child care and women's refuges, were due to the strong pressure from an organized women's movement. Obviously, there have been changes: the vociferous women's movement of the 1970s with its street demonstrations, sit-ins, lobbying, and other highly visible tactics has yielded to the women's movement of the 1990s. In the Western democracies this has meant the movement of women from the streets into some of the institutions that were the object of their campaigns from outside the system. In Australia, many of the activists of the 1970s have found their way into bureaucratic positions. Thus there is a much less visible and powerful women's movement than there was in the heady days when women's adviser positions were first being created under pressure from an organized movement.

The task of consultation has been complicated by the disappearance of this visible and vociferous pressure group. As a senior academic administrator, Denise Bradley, comments: "Where did the issues come from and are you taking the issues from the women's movement, however you define it? That's got more difficult I think in Australia as the organized women's movement has . . . stopped being so powerful. Once upon a time, fifteen years ago you could probably consult with WEL . . . and you can't do that any longer" (Bradley interview). Certainly there are lobbying groups that can "call up the troops if they want to and get a reasonable mass turnout on issues" (Bradley interview). But the proliferation of interest groups means that a variety of positions are represented, and a policymaker may not agree with the agenda of this or that group. The simple issues of the past have been replaced by more complex ones, and it is no longer possible simply to turn to the women's movement en masse for its wisdom.

In addition, the institutionalization of the femocracy has meant that there is a new generation of femocrats, some of them generated from the ranks of the bureaucracy, who lack a background in feminist activism. The process of keeping in touch with the women's movement, then, has become problematic. One femocrat argued that it is necessary to make a special effort to keep open the lines of communication with active feminists: "It's really important for various reasons for women in those units to go to the [women's movement] conferences. . . . There's so many things lately where there has not been anyone from [the women's units]. . . . I think it says partly that the people who work in those areas are from [the] mainstream and don't feel comfortable when they go because . . . they're not old friends. And I think that's a danger" (Respondent F interview). If these lines of communication are not kept open, there is the obvious fear that as a femocrat, one has been co-opted by the bureaucracy and is no longer serving the purposes for which she first went in. This respondent, who began her career in the bureaucracy as a "straight" economist and then developed into a femocrat as a result of being assigned to a women's unit, fears that she may be losing touch, in part because of the sheer weight of her duties as a bureaucrat:

The issue of being co-opted: I find that . . . really interesting because I can't make up my mind about it. It's very hard working here at times not to believe your own rhetoric. And to get really angry with people who criticize you. . . . But if you go the other way and blame the victim or the messenger, then you are beginning to be co-opted. . . . You . . . need some mechanism whereby you can keep clearly in your mind why you're there. . . . Too often you're so busy, you don't. (Respondent F interview)

For Jenni Neary, the women's units were a place where women educated themselves on women's issues and on the bureaucratic environment. From the women's movement point of view, the specialized women's units served as centers, where women's networks were created, and training grounds: "The networks that we created through the Women's Bureau [in Canberra] are still there and they still influence decisions in amazing places. These women carried their feminism wherever they go. Now, those women's units were a particular mechanism we used for a lot of women who were coming in out of the Women's Movement into influential positions in the bureaucracy" (Neary interview).

But the historical moment has passed, in some sense, in that bureaucracies are now staffing these units with women who are not feminists and who did not come out of the same political background. Hence the function of the units as training grounds, and as a source of feminist expertise, is being undermined. Other ways, then, may need to be found to accomplish the same ends.

Conclusion

The achievements of the femocracy have been controversial among Australian feminists since the 1970s. The high salaries and the civil service confidentiality requirements created an atmosphere of suspicion, as grassroots activists expressed both envy and distrust toward their high-flying sisters in the bureaucracy.[15] But in the current climate, with the femocracy under siege from neoliberal governments at state and federal levels, there is increasingly an acknowledgment that the alliance between grassroots activists and femocrats has produced tangible results for the women's movement.

Pace Kathy Ferguson, I would contend that the entry of feminists into bureaucratic positions in Australia has contributed to a significant shift in public attitudes and government priorities, and to a widespread legitimizing of feminist concerns in a traditionally macho country. On the other side of the ledger, one has to note that the achievements of the femocrats may be fragile and temporary. Although Labor under Paul Keating squeaked into an unprecedented fifth term in national office in 1993, with the help of women's votes, the international economic downturn is forcing severe spending cutbacks on Australian governments, of whatever political persuasion. With an unemployment rate of over 10 percent, Australian politicians with an eye on the interests of male "breadwinners" may have increasingly less sympathy for feminist concerns.

In addition, the large-scale entry of feminists into government has effectively siphoned off the energes of activists into a form of activity that is carefully shaped and limited by the possibilities of electoral politics: Labor reforms have ensured that state and federal bureaucracies are ever more responsive to government policy, and this includes policy designed by femocrats. Whatever its virtues, the femocratic experiment has proceeded via an acceptance of the bureaucratic form of politics, and therefore at some level has served in turn to legitimize, rather than to contest, state power.

Ironically, from the high degree of burnout reported by my respondents (and found in my own experience), one has to conclude that the interests of feminists and the permanent bureaucracy are probably fundamentally opposed. But I would still argue for the importance of the temporary alliance with bureaucracy forged by Australian femocrats. The long-run effects of the experiment, of course, will be measured only by future historians.

Notes

Acknowledgments: This essay is drawn from a book in progress on Australian femocrats. The research was funded by a Changing Gender Roles in Postindustrial Societies grant from the Rockefeller Foundation. My thanks go to *Australian Feminist Studies* for permission to reprint material from my article, "Speaking for Women: Voices from the Australian Femocrat Experiment" (H. Eisenstein 1991b).

1. The use of the term "femocrat" has spread to New Zealand, Canada, and the Nordic countries, where the related term "state feminism" originated; see Hernes 1988, 201–2.
2. See, among others, Ferree 1991–92; Alvarez 1990; and Stamiris 1988.
3. See MacKinnon 1989 (among her other writings). For useful summaries and discussion of feminist debates on gender and the state, see Deacon 1989, 1–11; and Alvarez 1990, 19–36.
4. On the original meaning of radical feminism, see Echols 1989. On the radical possibilities of liberal feminism, see Z. Eisenstein 1993.
5. See Martin 1987 and Hart 1992 for thoughtful discussions of Ferguson on bureaucracy.

6. There is a growing literature on Australian femocrats. The most comprehensive account is Sawer 1990. But see also Dowse 1983; Franzway, Court, and Connell 1989; Watson 1990; Yeatman 1990; and H. Eisenstein 1991b.

7. On this point see my essay "Gender as a Category of Analysis" (Eisenstein 1991a, 97–124).

8. Like the U.S. women's movement, Australian feminists were initially split into "women's liberation" and liberal or reformist feminist camps, although there is some evidence that in Canberra the women's movement was small enough that these divisions did not prevent unified political efforts. I am skipping over some of the details of a complex history. But the rise of femocrats was by no means uncontroversial, and some of the opposition came from women's liberationists who, like their U.S. counterparts, had deep suspicions about the role of the state.

9. The concept of a "woman-friendly polity" was introduced by Helga Hernes the Norwegian theorist and senior civil servant (see K. Jones 1990).

10. See H. Eisenstein 1991b for a longer discussion of the accountability issue.

11. For the concept of representative bureaucracy advanced by Australian public administration reformers in the 1970s, see Wilenski 1986 (esp. 57). Jane Mansbridge commented (at the Feminist Organizations conference, Washington, D.C., February 14–16, 1992) that this notion contradicts the mainstream political theory that bureaucracy represents the wishes of the majority as expressed through their elected representatives.

12. Quotations, edited for the sake of readability, are taken from transcripts of my taped interviews. Respondents who are identified only by a letter have not given permission for the use of attributed quotations.

13. Cf. Katzenstein (1987, 16), who notes that although the U.S. feminist movement has been powerful in advancing issues of sexual politics, "policies that would alleviate the situation of poor women in the United States lag well behind those of Western Europe."

14. See, e.g., Anna Yeatman's discussion (1990, 61–79) of femocrats as members of the "new class": that is, the managerial, professional third class between the proletariat and the bourgeoisie.

15. On this point, see Summers 1991, 45.

CHAPTER 6

Moving onto the Terrain of the State: The Battered Women's Movement and the Politics of Engagement

■

CLAIRE REINELT

> Undoubtedly the most pressing work before us is to build our own au-
> tonomous institutions. It is absolutely crucial that we make our visions
> real in a permanent form so that we can be even more effective and
> reach many more people.
>
> Barbara Smith, *Home Girls* (1983)

> Where we have not yet succeeded as a movement is in the structural
> arena. We have not brought this vast, decentralized revolution of con-
> sciousness and the small projects characteristic of the women's move-
> ment into sufficient engagement with the political structures to create
> lasting structural changes that would institutionalize some of the new
> possibilities for life that we seek.
>
> Charlotte Bunch, *Passionate Politics* (1987)

Is it possible to build and nurture autonomous feminist institutions and at
the same time engage with mainstream institutions? Or are these two strategies politically contradictory? Historically, feminist activists have tended
to emphasize one strategy over the other, depending upon their political
beliefs. Radical feminists, who were skeptical about transforming the existing system, favored creating alternative, autonomous institutions (Echols
1990). Liberal feminists, by contrast, sought legal reforms within that
system. These divergent political strategies characterized much feminist
activism throughout the 1960s and early 1970s.

By the late 1970s the boundary between liberal and radical feminism
had blurred (Taylor 1983). Feminist activists within alternative institutions
increasingly attempted to transform the politics and practices of mainstream institutions.[1] Women within mainstream institutions began orga-

nizing collectively to challenge institutional forms of gender inequality.[2] Self-defined feminists were moving into positions of power within bureaucratic structures (H. Eisenstein 1991a). And liberal feminist organizations, such as NOW, adopted proposals that required more than legal reform (Z. Eisenstein 1981; Taylor 1983). This blurring of movement and institutional boundaries transformed feminist political strategies.

In this essay I focus on the meaning of these changes for feminists within an alternative institution: I discuss how feminists in the Texas battered women's movement moved onto the terrain of the state by creating the Texas Council on Family Violence, hereafter referred to as the Council. Council activists brought a feminist movement agenda to local shelter activists, state agency employees, and legislators, among others. The Council is of particular interest because it has been instrumental in the funding, evaluation, and administration of state funds to battered women's shelters through a series of contracts with the state.

State-level shelter activists in Texas practice what I call *a politics of engagement*. A politics of engagement is based on a belief that long-term social change depends on mobilizing and educating women in their communities by creating autonomous institutions, and on establishing relationships and structures of communication with those who work in and set policy for mainstream institutions. This political approach starts with the insight of radical feminists that autonomous institutions are essential for women in a patriarchal society. At the same time, it views mainstream institutions as absolutely necessary terrains of political struggle.

Moving onto the terrain of the state is full of political contradictions for movement activists. On the one hand, there are new political opportunities for organizing and education; on the other hand, there are increased opportunities for divisions within the movement and for co-optation of the movement's agenda. The challenge for state-level feminist activists is to negotiate a path that provides support for services to battered women and at the same time promotes a feminist program for change. The case study of actual feminist practice presented here can help us understand how some feminists are defining and implementing a politics of engagement in the 1990s.[3]

Moving onto the Terrain of the State

During the 1960s and 1970s, radical feminists created alternative institutions such as battered women's shelters, rape crisis centers, and feminist health centers. One of the most vexing problems for these institutions was funding. At issue was whether an alternative institution could maintain its autonomy and political commitments if it received money from the very structures it was seeking to change, such as local and state governments. The debate over funding was particularly heated in the literature on the battered women's movement (Ahrens 1980; Johnson 1981; Morgan 1981; Sullivan 1982b; Tierney 1982).

In the 1980s there was a rapid increase in the number of battered women's shelters because large amounts of money from local governments and foundations were made available to fund local shelters. This influx of money was in many ways a mixed blessing. Shelters were more financially secure and could concentrate on building their programs to meet the needs of battered women, but funding also brought such changes as increased specialization, more hierarchy, and less autonomy for shelter residents (Schechter 1982). Resisting the depoliticizing effects of increased funding has been an ongoing political struggle.

Forming state coalitions of battered women's shelters (Schechter 1982) is one strategy feminists used to define and institutionalize a collective political vision. State organizations play a critical role in sustaining and building the battered women's movements nationwide. They are often organized by veteran shelter activists to engage in political and educational activities that local shelters find little time to pursue. Their vision and political perspective is likely to be explicitly feminist.

Most of the literature on the battered women's movement has focused on the creation, transformation, structures, and practices of local shelters (Ferraro 1981, 1983; Wharton 1987; Rodriguez 1988). Little attention has been paid to the state coalitions of shelter activists that operate now in almost every state.[4] State organizations act as a network for and provide assistance to local shelter activists by developing public education and outreach programs; producing manuals and newsletters; and holding conferences. Since state organizations are not involved in providing direct services to battered women, they do not face the same pressures to concentrate on service instead of politics; nonetheless, they confront many of the same issues that arise in local shelters. They make choices about organizational structure, political goals, values, and strategies for changing attitudes and structures that support violence against women.

During the time of my research in Texas, feminist activists mobilized to shape state legislative decisions and institutional practices that had an impact on battered women. They secured the passage of funding legislation in 1981 that created the Family Violence Program and thereby structurally solidified a set of relationships between local shelters, the Council, and the state. This process of politically engaging with the state opened up possibilities for political activism but at the same time created its own set of contradictions.

Historically, feminists have approached the state as either a neutral arbiter of competing interests or as a site of gender inequalities originating elsewhere.[5] Liberal feminists have tended to accept the structures and processes of the state as democratic and just, even though they recognized inequities. These they sought to redress primarily through existing political means, believing that their interests would prevail because they were politically consistent with democratic values. Radical and Marxist feminists have not considered the state a primary site for political struggle, believing its policies and practices to reflect inequalities structured either in the family or the workplace. Both these conceptions treat the state as a unified entity.

I suggest that the state itself is a contradictory and uneven set of structures and processes that are the product of particular struggles. The state is neither a neutral arbiter of gender nor simply a reproducer of existing gender inequalities. It is a site of active contestation over the construction of gender inequalities and power. Legislative decisions and institutional practices are made in historically specific social, political, and economic contexts that shape, by either perpetuating or altering, particular social formations of gender.[6] With this conception of the state, we can understand state policy outcomes for battered women as the result of social processes that include feminist mobilization.

Feminist Mobilization and Organizational Practice

During the 1970s and early 1980s, shelters for battered women formed all across the country. They had diverse organizational beginnings. Some were neighborhood-based (for example, Casa Myrna Vasquez in Boston). Others emerged from consciousness-raising groups (such as Women's Advocates in St. Paul, Minnesota). Still others were organized by formerly battered women (Boston's Transition House). In some locations women's centers became de facto shelters, as did the Women's Center South in Pittsburgh (Schechter 1982), or shelters were integrated into existing treatment programs (Johnson 1981). Many of the early organizational efforts were grassroots; many of them were also feminist, although this was not always a term that the women involved used to describe themselves.[7]

Many who did describe themselves as feminists embraced radical feminism.[8] Radical feminist ideology profoundly influenced the politics and practices of many early shelters.[9] It defined violence against women not as a personal or family issue but as a political issue; it argued that existing institutional practices were male-dominated and perpetuated violence against women. What women needed was a safe space of their own where they could escape the violence and begin to rebuild their lives. Shelters became those spaces.

Organizing local shelters was in many instances both exhilarating and frustrating. For many radical feminists, it offered opportunities to create nonbureaucratic, nonhierarchical organizations based on collective, collaborative work, consensus decision-making, and respect for the expertise that women have about their own lives. Even though actual shelter practices did not always measure up to such ideals, these ideals profoundly influenced the movement. Many shelter activists are committed to empowering battered women to take control of their own lives, rather than solving problems for them. There is a widespread belief that battered women are victims of male violence who primarily need practical and personal support, not therapy. Many shelters take seriously the need to be grassroots community organizations whose primary support comes from community members who volunteer time and money. Many shelters are committed to involving battered women in an ongoing way in shelter activities. Organizationally, many shelters create structures and practices that value collective consensus decision-making, ethical communication, and group empowerment. Institutionalizing radical differences in knowledge, status, and power is discouraged (Rodriguez 1988).

Despite their widespread influence on the politics and practices of shelters, radical feminist values have been difficult to sustain and implement. Some radical feminists have argued that this failure is political and ideological. Too many shelter activists, they say, are not commited to feminist ideology. They lose touch with communities through creating boards that are white and professional; they opt for hierarchical structures and job descriptions that make them more legitimate; and they engage in lesbian-baiting in order to secure their positions of power (Ahrens 1980).

Radical feminist values and practices have been difficult to sustain for economic and political reasons as well. Very few shelters can or choose to remain entirely autonomous and disengaged from existing institutions, whether those be funding agencies, state and local governments, law enforcement, welfare bureaucracies, or the courts. The considerable costs of running a shelter and working to end violence against women make fund raising a high priority. Many shelters rely on community support for both money and volunteer staff, but these are often not enough to cover expenses. Most shelters turn to foundations, corporations, or local and state governments to fund their programs. For some shelter activists this is done reluctantly, since it often can mean a loss of autonomy and control over the politics and organization of shelter practices; other activists believe that governments and foundations *should* be financially responsible for supporting work that aims to end battering and provide a better life for women and their children. Whatever the reason, most shelters devote considerable time and energy to fund raising, and as the literature makes clear, outside funding sources often have a depoliticizing effect (Johnson 1981; Morgan 1981; Ristock 1990).

Shelter activists engage with outside institutions for other reasons as well. A battered woman has numerous encounters with outside institutions, from the police officer she calls when her partner beats her to the courts that preside over her assault case or divorce proceeding. Hospitals, welfare offices, social workers, and housing authorities also have contact with battered women while they are at the shelter. These institutions operate with practices and values radically different from those of shelters; nonetheless, because they provide essential resources for women to rebuild their lives, shelter activists often find themselves challenging the institutional practices they see as unfair or discriminatory. Shelter activists have trained law enforcement officials, lobbied for legislation that will protect battered women, and provided technical assistance to programs that are working with abusive men. These are time-consuming and often frustrating activities, but few shelter activists refuse to engage in them.

In addition to the ideological, economic, and political forces that have made it difficult to implement radical feminist political practices fully, there are problematic aspects to radical feminist practice itself. Consensus decision-making, a hallmark of radical feminist practice, may empower group members and challenge hierarchical structures of decision-making, but as early as 1972 feminists also identified negative aspects. Resolving conflict is difficult (Mansbridge 1980); participation is very demanding and time-consuming (Wharton 1987; Rodriguez 1988), and homogeneity is fostered (Freeman 1972). Many shelter organizations have thus moved away from pure consensus-based decision-making.

Collectives, the defining organizational form of radical feminist practice, minimize the division of labor, specialized knowledge, and status differences between participants (Rothschild-Whitt 1979; Ahrens 1980; Schechter 1982), but pure collective forms have been difficult to sustain. Collectives often have no mechanism for ensuring worker accountability (Schechter 1982). Without a formal structure, informal power structures develop that are often more difficult to negotiate than formal ones (Freeman 1972). Intense face-to-face relationships among collective members personalize conflicts that make them emotionally painful (Rothschild-Whitt 1979; Mansbridge 1980). Thus, most shelter organizations today operate with some form of "modified collective" or "modified hierarchy" (Schechter 1982).

Radical feminist shelter organizations have worked toward eliminating professional hierarchies. Some shelters made commitments to hire primarily former residents (Rodriguez 1988); others tried to minimize differentials in status by paying everyone the same salary. Formal education and training were not considered relevant criteria in hiring decisions. By rejecting professional status, feminists were trying to create alternative systems of value and power that did not depend on institutional legitimation. For many working-class women who wanted the skills, money, and control over their work that professional status offered, this rejection was incomprehensible (Schechter 1982). By hiring only formerly battered women, shelters maximized group bonding but often created barriers between themselves and the rest of the women's movement (Rodriguez 1988). As shelters gained community legitimacy, more professionals (social workers, mental health workers, lawyers and other criminal justice workers) staffed battered women's shelters. For some feminists this signaled the depoliticization and co-optation of the battered women's movement (Ahrens 1980).

Practicing a Politics of Engagement

The question of whether the movement has become depoliticized and co-opted is a complex one. In part, the answer depends on the conceptual framework used to understand processes of social change and political transformation. During the 1960s and 1970s, blacks, students, and women pursued a politics of confrontation and protest. Underlying this political strategy was the belief that the state and mainstream institutions were the mechanisms through which the powerful maintained and managed the oppression of subordinate groups. Subordinate groups were outsiders whose only source of power was mobilization and protest against the establishment. The profound sense of being simultaneously outside political organizations and structures and oppressed by them shaped a political ideology and strategy of confrontation.

The battered women's movement in its early years drew its political strength and energy from defining itself in opposition to patriarchal and hierarchical institutions. By constructing itself as outside the political and institutional structures of mainstream society, the movement had the political space to experiment with and create new organizational forms. It was critical for the emergent movement to define what constituted radical, feminist, and transformative practices. In part this was achieved by reifying and dismissing what were considered masculinist, mainstream, and hegemonic practices. Creating an "us" versus "them" opposition was essential to this process.[10] The following sets of practices and values were grouped together and opposed in order to provide a basis for judging whether a shelter or movement organization was feminist or not.

feminist	patriarchal
collective	hierarchy
democratic participation	bureaucracy
empowerment	power
grassroots	professional
confrontation	co-optation
political	institutional
outside	inside
people	state

If a shelter or a movement organization was organized collectively to empower people at the grassroots level by engaging in political confrontation against patriarchal institutions, then it could be considered feminist. If it worked with mainstream institutions, developing hierarchical or bureaucratic organizational structures, then it was co-opted.[11]

Several assumptions underlying this conceptual framework are problematic for understanding a politics of engagement.[12] First, this framework assumes that an organization or a movement is either feminist or patriarchal, collective or hierarchical, and so on. There is no way of conceptualizing the politics of a movement that may include both collective and hierarchical processes, participatory and bureaucratic elements, outside and inside political strategies, grassroots mobilization and organizing within institutions. Second, this framework assumes that whatever is collective, participatory, and grassroots is open, democratic, and responsive to people's needs, while all hierarchies and bureaucracies are oppressive, static, and unresponsive. There is no room within this framework to explore the oppressive, unresponsive elements in collective practices or the democratic impulses in hierarchical practices. And third, this framework assumes that if the terms on the left come into contact with the terms on the right, the right will win; therefore, the left must maintain a rigid boundary between itself and all that is on the right. It is not possible within this framework to understand feminist mobilization within institutions, feminist engagement with existing institutions, and the formalization of feminism within alternative institutions.

As these forms of feminist politics grow in significance, we need a conceptual framework that allows us to understand how feminists are using institutional and state resources to build their movements and to open up terrains of political activism and education (Freeman 1975; Simon 1982; Matthews 1989). We need to explore new forms of feminist consciousness within institutions and look at how feminists are transforming institutional structures and practices (Katzenstein 1990). Toward that end I turn to the political strategies and practices of the Texas Council on Family Violence.

Building a Statewide Battered Women's Movement

In 1977, feminist activists from around the country met in Houston for the International Women's Year Conference. At this conference, shelter activists held several workshops. It was the first time so many women from that movement had gathered in one place. They shared information, traded stories, and felt empowered by being together. This conference was instrumental in the formation of the National Coalition Against Domestic Violence (NCADV).

It was also out of this conference experience that shelter activists in Texas decided to form the Texas Council on Family Violence. They moved quickly to define an agenda and a workable structure for the new organization. A working board of eight people was set up. Each board member was responsible for coordinating Council activities in one of several areas such as legislation, fund raising, membership, and research. Like many shelters, the Council decided on a modified collective structure. The board had a chair who was responsible for running board meetings, but decisions were made by consensus.

In 1979 the Council coordinated the passage of a bill to establish a pilot project that would provide state funds for six Texas shelters. This was the beginning of the Council's effort to involve the state in funding local shelters. Its decision to seek state funding was uncontroversial; in fact, the Council had formed in large part for this purpose. State funding was seen as a means to create a more stable funding source for local, community-based shelter programs.[13]

The legislation that Council activists drafted to increase state funding was carefully written to ensure that shelter programs continued to be autonomous, local, community-based programs with primary funding coming from community sources. State contracts were to be awarded only to those shelters that had been "in actual operation offering shelter services 24 hours a day with a capacity for not less than five persons for at least nine months before the date that the contract [was] awarded." This provision was designed to discourage those who might form a shelter solely for the purpose of getting state funds, reflecting the Council's belief that such shelters were less likely to be grassroots, community organizations. This commitment to community-based organizations, however, though consistent with feminist practice, does not acknowledge that some communities, particularly those that are poor, may find it extremely difficult to organize without state funds (Matthews 1989).

The law further provided a declining scale of state support over a six-year period so that after six years no more than 50 percent of a shelter's funding could come from the state. By limiting state support, the Council sought to encourage local shelters to continue raising funds in their communities in order to build acceptance and support for their work. Community support is one of the strongest guarantees that a shelter will continue to survive. Shelters that lack community support lose touch with the population and are not as responsive to community needs. Strong local shelters that have broad community support also strengthen the statewide movement. A legislator is more likely to back the Council's legislative and funding agenda if there is a community-supported shelter in his or her district. In addition, those shelters that are well established in their communities have more staff resources to contribute to political and educational work organized through the Council.

Council activists saw the state as a potential resource for their own activities as well. The enabling legislation they wrote required the Department of Human Services (DHS), which would administer the funds, to "contract for the provision of training, technical assistance, and evaluations related to shelter and service program development." This provision was meant to ensure that the Council would be actively involved in carrying out the mandate of the legislation. Its role was further reinforced by another section of the bill: "In implementing this chapter, the department shall consult with individuals and groups having knowledge of and experience in the problems of family violence."

The legislation was passed in 1981. Soon afterward the Council received a contract from DHS to visit every shelter in order to prepare them all for state funding. DHS contracted with the Council because they perceived it in their interest to do so. When DHS received the legislative mandate to administer the Family Violence Program, the staff had no knowledge of family violence or shelters. The legislation required that they contract for technical assistance, and the most knowledgeable source on family violence and shelters was the Council. In addition, the Council's community and legislative support made it highly unlikely that DHS would choose to contract with another organization.

This first contract marked the beginning of a contractual relationship with DHS that in 1991 generated $260,000 for movement-building activities, in addition to the money that local shelters received. DHS contracts funded a toll-free technical assistance hotline, a resource library, the Council's newsletter, training conferences, an information database, site visits, a statewide public education campaign, and Council members' active participation in shaping the DHS administration of the Family Violence Program (Texas Council on Family Violence 1990). The initial contract, along with a grant from the Levi-Strauss Foundation, made it possible for the Council board to hire a staff: two shelter activists from the Austin Center for Battered Women who had been instrumental in obtaining the grant and contract.[14] Under the new contract, they began visiting every shelter that qualified for state funding.

When an advocacy group contracts with the state for funding, it raises the possibility of conflict of interest. Whom does the Council represent: the state? shelters? itself? The potential for conflicts of interest was not very great under this first contract, since its purpose was purely informational. With this limited state agenda the staff was able to spend a lot of time talking with shelter directors about their programs and about the Council's agenda. The context for the visits was in fact very favorable, since it was the Council that had been instrumental in securing state funds for the shelters.

Evaluating Local Shelters

The potential for conflict of interest increased significantly with the next contract. In 1982 the Texas Council on Family Violence contracted with DHS to evaluate shelter services. It did this for several reasons. First, members were interested in developing a "competency-based evaluation system" that would be used as a basis for allocating funds to shelters. The idea behind this system was to encourage shelters to develop their programs in the direction of more public education and advocacy work. Second, knowing that DHS would want some form of evaluation to ensure that shelters complied with their contracts, the Council wanted to have input into how the state conceptualized these evaluations and, if possible, use the state's authority to implement its own ideas. Third, they saw the evaluation contract as a way to shape the state's perception of its relationship to local shelter programs. And fourth, they saw the evaluations as a means of learning about shelter programs, assisting shelter staff with problems, and encouraging them to take risks and innovate. This diverse agenda proved very hard to negotiate.

When the Council sought the evaluation contract, members were aware that some local shelters might misperceive their relationship with the state. Not all shelters were equally aware of the Council's history: when it first formed, there were only six shelters in existence; at the time of the evaluations there were twenty-nine.[15] Those shelter activists who had been involved in the formation of the Council had a very different relationship to it than did those whose shelters were established afterward. Having a part in creating a movement organization from scratch is a much different experience from coming into an already established organization. Some of the new shelters were formed through the active nurturance of Council members; others developed on their own. Most shelters were members of the Council, but some perceived it as a professional organization for shelter providers rather than a movement organization. Others did not feel that feminism spoke to their communities.

The evaluations took place during a day-long visit to each shelter.[16] The Council staff conducted the visits with the shelter staff in the presence of the DHS regional contract managers. The participation of the contract managers was required by the Council, which saw in such participation a political opportunity to educate state employees about battering and shelters, as well as a chance to define the state's relationship to local programs.[17] If during evaluation visits contract managers referred to the shelter program as a state program, the Council staff would correct them in no uncertain terms, pointing out that these were locally based community programs that the state was helping to fund. Often a conversation would ensue about the difference between the state's relationship to shelters and its relationship to other DHS-administered programs. The substance of the conversation was always that while DHS "owned" other welfare programs, it "funded" family violence programs. The consistency with which the Council staff corrected DHS misconceptions underscores the strategic importance they placed on maintaining the autonomy of local shelters. If DHS began to perceive shelters as "their" programs, then the shelter movement would lose a significant tactical edge. By maintaining the autonomy of local shelters, the movement strengthened its claim vis-à-vis the state to define how shelter would be provided.

The evaluation instrument that the Council designed had several purposes.[18] First, it met the needs of DHS by assessing whether shelters were complying with the law. Second, it provided a mechanism for the Council to gather information about how shelters handled batterers, children, staff-board relations, budget planning, personnel policies, and general organization. With this information, Council activists hoped to be better able to advise and consult with shelters. Finally, the evaluation instrument was designed to open up dialogue—on issues such as advocacy versus counseling, the use of volunteers, public education, developing community resources, and shelter accessibility—that would give the Council staff an opportunity to discuss shelter philosophy and politics with both shelter staff and DHS contract managers.

Most shelter directors actively engaged with the Council staff during the evaluation visits, using them as a resource and seeing them as allies. Engaging in practical, philosophical, and political discussions was a learning experience for both the Council staff and shelter directors. This was particularly evident in one South Texas shelter run by the Catholic Charities. The director, a middle-aged Hispanic woman, operated the shelter with a philosophy of "charity" that included viewing battered women as victims who primarily needed therapy. She was very reticent about doing public outreach. As she explained, this is "macho country," by which she meant that it was dangerous for women to challenge male power by discussing the rights of women—including the right not to be beaten.

The Council staff conducting the evaluation visit had never provided shelter in a hostile environment. Their experiences had been in a liberal, urban city where politicians and community leaders were generally receptive. The visit to South Texas caused the staff to reflect on how regional, racial, and cultural differences shape the way a community provides shelter. The Council staff worked hard to empower the Catholic Charities shelter staff to take the political risk of raising the issues of violence against women in their communities, pointing out that not only would a public presence build community support, but it would also increase their opportunities for diversifying their funding base. The two direct service staff (also Hispanic) responded positively to the Council staff's suggestions, but the shelter director was still afraid to "rock the boat."

The success of the battered women's movement in the 1990s will depend on how it handles issues of diversity and difference (Ristock 1990). At the time of these evaluations the Council's philosophy statement did not include any mention of how culture, race, and sexuality impact on battering relationships and on the movement's political agenda. They were afraid early on to raise issues of homophobia and racism because they believed such a focus would weaken their efforts to pass funding legislation for battered women's shelters, to transform the way police officers view battered women, and to encourage all shelters to become members of the Council. More recently the Council has taken on these issues through a series of training workshops aimed at new shelter staff. These include a work session on homophobia and lesbian battering, and one on racism and women of color.[19] The Council's willingness to confront these contentious and emotional issues signals its own greater feelings of political strength and recognition that understanding and working across differences are essential political work in the 1990s.[20]

Local Shelter Resistance

Some shelter directors were unhappy with the Council's approach to the evaluations. One shelter director said in a letter to the Council that she felt "the evaluators tended to impose themselves into the internal operations of a private agency, well beyond the scope of the [DHS] contract under evaluation." She considered any discussion of philosophy, politics, personnel policies to be inappropriate. Part of her resistance came from very real philosophical differences between herself and the Council staff. This director was neither a feminist nor a movement activist. At one point in the evaluation report, the Council staff objected to the shelter's policy of "limiting women's activities and problem-solving during the first three days of their stay." This, they argued, was "incongruous with accepted shelter practices." The shelter director objected by invoking her own "experts" and arguing that women in crisis experience "cognitive, behavioral and affective disequilibrium and need a three day waiting period to regain their sense of equilibrium" (personal correspondence). The Council staff, consistent with their approach, tried to engage the shelter director in a discussion about this policy, but without much success. The director was particularly angry that the Council's assessment of this policy was included in the evaluation report sent to DHS.

In writing up the evaluation reports, the Council staff included a full assessment of all the shelter's policies and practices. These reports were used simultaneously to give feedback to the shelter and to report to DHS. Such mixed goals were problematic. Feedback is an internal movement activity aimed at strengthening and supporting local shelters; to be useful, it should include frank assessments about the strengths of the program and the areas where improvement is needed. Reporting to DHS is an official act that can have consequences for the local shelter's share of state funding. By not distinguishing these two activities, the Council placed itself in an extremely contradictory position. Some local shelters protested that "their" organization was divulging negative information about them to their funders. Feedback from local shelters on the evaluation visits led the Council to reevaluate this strategy.

The Council wanted to maintain a mechanism for discussing philosophical issues and providing technical assistance to shelters but did not want to be in a position of providing DHS with knowledge about these discussions, thus adversely affecting their relationship to local shelters. As the Council's director said to me, "We have become much more circumspect about what we reveal to DHS." Consequently, the Council made a decision not to continue evaluating shelters for DHS. It does still engage in evaluative activities by investigating complaints or questionable practices engaged in by shelter staffs. But although DHS may ultimately be asked to intervene if a complaint or grievance is not resolved internally, the goal is to create internal processes for handling problems.

Re-visioning Feminist Politics in the 1980s and 1990s

I have discussed the politics of the evaluation contract at some length because it points to both the potential benefits and the contradictions of engaging with the state. Once the state is viewed as a terrain of political struggle, some form of political engagement is likely. Defining the parameters of this engagement in a way that maximizes autonomy for the movement and effectively challenges institutional practices is a major feminist challenge.

Successfully pursuing this dual agenda requires not only a more complex understanding of the state but also a revised understanding of the dynamics of power. Earlier movement activists understood power as the ability of the state, institutions, and those who held positions of authority to impose their will on others. Power was competitive, individualistic, and zero-sum. If some had it, then others did not. As feminist politics changed, power was redefined as the ability to act, the ability to transform oneself and the world. Power was no longer defined only as something that others possessed and wielded over you. Through working together collectively, creating organizations, and challenging patriarchal practices, feminists began to experience their own power, based on energy, strength, effectiveness, not domination and control (Hartsock 1979).

Andler and Sullivan, in an article that is quite skeptical about the possibilities of transforming and engaging with mainstream institutions, describe eloquently this sense of power within the battered women's movement.

> We can mobilize countless unpaid women whose commitment keeps numerous shelters operating and whose work is building a national movement to end women abuse. Bureaucracies are in awe of this because it is not within their experience. There is power in the knowledge that it is our groups that are providing the correct answers about issues of our work. Government agencies and funding sources recognize this, and that gives us clout. As recognition of our expertise increases, our political power will increase and we will be able to make demands and set directions within these same institutions. We should never lose the sight and ability to set directions for them. (Andler and Sullivan 1980, 14)

This sense of power is very different from control and domination. It is a collective power that is experienced by movement activists as they mobilize and gain recognition for their work.

Empowering movement activists to challenge bureaucratic and institutional practices has been one of the important political contributions of the Texas Council on Family Violence. During one regional meeting that I attended with local shelter activists, the Council staff spent a good deal of time demystifying the power of the state. Local shelter activists were angry that their contract manager was slated to be changed during a bureaucratic reshuffling. Feeling powerless to influence the DHS decision, much of their anger was directed toward the Council for not protecting their interests. The Council staff redirected the focus of local activist anger to the DHS decision and empowered those activists to work collectively to change it. This turned what began as a hostile encounter between the Council staff and local shelter staffs into a common struggle to find effective ways to challenge oppressive bureaucratic practices. Feelings of powerlessness that had caused anger and resignation were replaced by feelings of collective power.

Empowering others to act and take responsibility for their decisions is a political strategy that Council activists have also used with those in mainstream institutions. One of the most frustrating aspects of engaging with mainstream institutions is the bureaucratic and hierarchical processes that delay action and derail communication. From the beginning of its relationship with DHS, the Council sought to create structures and patterns of communication that held DHS personnel accountable for both decisions and indecisions. Through a joint Council-DHS advisory committee, extensive written correspondence, and regular phone calls, Council activists have been more effective than other advocacy organizations in demanding timely, honest, and open consideration of issues that affect the Family Violence Program.

In the beginning the Council's approach was particularly awkward for some DHS staff people because they were being asked to engage with the Council staff in ways that were highly unusual for agency personnel. In one case a DHS staff person responsible for the Council's contracts with the agency was initially quite antagonistic toward the Council and felt threatened by its power and its approach to dealing with the agency. Through extensive and persistent communication, Council activists gradually developed a relationship of trust and understanding with her, until she actually became an active advocate for the movement within DHS.

Is such a staff person a movement activist? What about the shelter director who has been active in the battered women's movement for years who takes a job with DHS working with the Family Violence Program? Has she been co-opted, or is she an advocate on the inside? In both cases the boundaries between the movement and mainstream institutions have been blurred. While this blurring has political risks, it also creates political opportunities for transforming institutional practices and furthering a feminist agenda using the resources and power of the state.

Conclusion

The blurring of boundaries between who is and is not a movement activist, between hierarchical and collective processes, and between movement and mainstream institutions leaves many feminists feeling shaky about the ideological ground they stand on. If firm determinations cannot be made about who is a movement activist and what constitutes feminist practice, then how can we know with any clarity whether our work is contributing to women's liberation or simply to more sophisticated forms of oppression? I believe that it is impossible to know for sure. Such uncertainty, however, should not be resolved by assuming that engagement is antifeminist.

Engaging with the state is a strategy that has risks. It is risky because state funding is contingent on economic and political forces that one does not control. It is risky because state engagement can threaten movement solidarity. But any strategy that has risks also has benefits. Funding for movement activities, access to policymakers, and opportunities for educating many people about the issues of violence against women are not trivial. Risks and benefits are present in any political choice. Organizations that acknowledge this are better able to cope with the uncertainty.

Feminism is a dynamic process. It is guided by values that include nurturance, democracy, cooperation, empowerment, inclusion, transformation, maximizing rewards to all, and ending oppression (Martin 1990a). These values provide a moral framework for action but do not entail specific organizational forms or political strategies. Because the process of social change is neither predetermined nor linear, all activism is historically contingent and shifting, replete with its own contradictions. Instead of denying this reality, many feminists in the 1990s accept this as the condition of their activism.

The battered women's movement has changed but this change cannot adequately be characterized as either a radical break from the past or a quiet slippage toward ever greater bureaucratization. Instead feminists continue to move into more and more arenas of political activism; they are developing innovative organizational and communicative structures and strategies; and they are continually challenging the structure and practices of mainstream institutions. While many of these changes may appear less radical than the early feminist organizing efforts of the 1970s, they may in the long run result in more profound and long-lasting transformation.

Notes

Acknowledgments: I thank Carmen Sirianni, Mary Katzenstein, Shulamit Rein-harz, Richard Alterman, Mindy Fried, Kamini Grahame, George Ross, and anonymous reviewers for giving me valuable feedback on this work. I also thank Myra Marx Ferree and Patricia Yancey Martin for their encouragement and support. A big thank-you also goes to Debby Tucker and Eve McArthur, who made this work possible.

1. For a discussion of how the battered women's movement has attempted to transform mainstream institutional policies and practices, see Schechter 1982.

2. See Katzenstein 1990 for a discussion of women organizing within the U.S. military and the Catholic Church.

3. Dobash and Dobash (1992) describe in some detail feminist efforts to define and implement an antiviolence agenda at the federal level in both Britain and the United States. Leidner (1991) provides an excellent analysis of feminist practice by looking at the internal organizational process of defining what it means for a feminist organization to be inclusive and representative.

4. Two exceptions are Andler and Sullivan 1980; and Schechter 1982.

5. For a thorough discussion of feminist approaches to the state, see Franzway, Court, and Connell 1989, chap. 2. For a summary of socialist feminist debates on the state see Barrett 1980. For earlier socialist feminist discussions of the state, see Wilson 1977; and McIntosh 1978. For a radical feminist theory of the state, see MacKinnon 1982. Liberal feminists have not articulated a distinct theory of the state, but for a discussion of liberal feminism and the state, see Z. Eisenstein 1981.

6. Australian feminists have been in the forefront of defining a feminist theory of the state that understands the state as a historically constituted set of social processes. "The state cannot be analyzed in abstraction from history. It does not exist as a reflex of the functional needs of a system, whether a class system or a gender system. It is the product of specific, historically located social processes. Quite specifically, the shape of the state is the outcome of particular social struggles. What kind of state we have depends on who was mobilized in social struggle, what strategies were deployed, and who won" (Franzway, Court, and Connell 1989). For further case studies and theoretical developments on feminism and the state, see Watson 1990.

7. For some women, defining themselves as feminists emerged through their work with battered women. One of the founders of Women's Advocates says, "Personally, I didn't call myself a feminist when we started, it sort of snuck up and embraced me as I lived it." Women of color often did not describe themselves as feminists because of the racism they encountered in the women's movement. Racism took the form of being excluded from leadership positions, being ignored when concerns that predominantly affected women of color were raised, and by an unwillingness to examine the interconnectedness of oppressions, in effect forcing

women of color to choose between gender and racial struggles. This racism has made it difficult for women of color to self-define as feminists even though many of them espouse feminist beliefs. See Moraga and Anzaldua 1981; and hooks 1984.

8. The definition of radical feminism has been and continues to be highly contested. For a history of radical feminism, see Echols (1989); see also Douglas's (1990) review of Echols' book and Echols's (1990) response.

9. I base this claim both on my personal knowledge and on my reading of Susan Schechter's account of the emergence of the battered women's movement. She states that "in many programs, locally and nationally, radical feminists organized first, setting the style and practice that continues to dominate in much of the battered women's movement" (Schechter 1982, 45). For a comparison of shelter organizing by radical feminists in both the United States and West Germany, see Ferree 1987.

10. Ristock (1990) notes in her discussion of feminist collectives that this political strategy allowed collectives to feel united and strong but it also assumed a false unity. Anyone who was different was considered a threat to that unity and had her feminism called into question.

11. This assessment has been particularly widespread in the literature on the battered women's movement (Martin 1990b).

12. Works that explore the need for a new conceptual framework for understanding feminist organizational practice include Simon 1982; Taylor 1983; Staggenborg 1988; Katzenstein 1990; Martin 1990b; and Sirianni 1993.

13. For more positive accounts of the impact of state funding on organizations and movements, see Simon 1982; and Matthews 1989. For more critical or pessimistic accounts, see Andler and Sullivan 1980; and Morgan 1981. For a more recent critical account, see Fraser 1989.

14. Both women are White, college-educated feminists with a long history of community activism, including anti-rape work and shelter organizing.

15. Most of the evaluation visits were held during 1983.

16. I accompanied the Council on eight shelter visits in the south and central Texas regions as a participant observer. The Council staff arranged my participation. I was introduced as a researcher interested in the evaluation process.

17. During the week I traveled with the Council staff in south Texas, one contract manager attended all five evaluations. At the beginning of the week he spoke continually about state requirements and seemed uneasy about the Council staff's approach to evaluations. By the end of the five days his bureaucratic concerns had been replaced by an interest in the programmatic issues shelters faced. He began to assume the role of an advocate, discussing strategy with shelter directors much as he had heard the Council staff do earlier in the week. In other words, he became an active participant in the evaluations on the terms that the Council had defined.

18. The instrument was developed and used in 1982–83.

19. There has been active resistance by some attendees at the sessions on homophobia and lesbian battering, primarily from women in the shelter community who

are fundamentalist Christians. For a discussion of feminism and fundamentalism, see Stacey 1990.

20. There is a growing literature that addresses battering in the African American community (White 1985), in the Latino community (Zambrano 1985), and among lesbians (Lobel 1986).

CHAPTER 7

Outsider Issues and Insider Tactics: Strategic Tensions in the Women's Policy Network during the 1980s

■

ROBERTA SPALTER-ROTH AND RONNEE SCHREIBER

The period from the election of Ronald Reagan in 1980 to the defeat of George Bush in 1992 was a time of open hostility to feminist public policy claims. Nonetheless, an active network of national women's policy organizations persisted and grew more sophisticated in their use of insider tactics such as lobbying, testifying, writing legislation, providing public education, mobilizing constituencies, and supporting women candidates (Schlozman 1991; Judis 1992). Compared with the heady days of feminist activism in Washington in the 1970s (Tinker 1983), their policy successes were limited. Yet despite the constraints placed on their language, style, and activities by their need to legitimate themselves to policymakers, funders, the public, and their own members, these organizations addressed feminist issues and maintained an institutionalized network for the staging of future feminist claims.

In this essay we examine the efforts of nineteen national women's organizations to represent women's claims in the policymaking process during the 1980s: the tactical choices they made to professionalize and to use insider techniques in addressing such issues as abortion rights, violence against women, economic inequality, racism, and heterosexism; the tensions of trying to place these feminist or outsider issues on the policy agenda as exemplified in their use of language, acquisition of resources, and attention to issues of diversity.

Some of the organizations studied—such as the American Association of University Women, founded in 1888—have been on the Washington scene since the first wave of the women's movement. Others, such as the National

"Organization for Women, the National Coalition Against Domestic Violence, the Center for Women Policy Studies, the Women's Legal Defense Fund, the Coalition of Labor Union Women, and the Institute for Women's Policy Research, were established in the 1960s, 1970s, and 1980s and grew directly out of the movement's second wave.

The compromises required by their quest for Washington-insider status, especially during the feminist backlash of the Reagan-Bush years, generated criticisms that these women's organizations represented the interests of a narrow elite, were too extremist, too concerned with Washington politics, and out of touch with the perspective of "ordinary" women (Faludi 1991; Judis 1992; Vobejda 1992). In short, they were accused of being simultaneously too insider and too radical. We contend that for these organizations the quest for insider status and the making of radical claims were not either/or choices. The lines between radical and mainstream organizations, which began to blur during the 1970s (Deckard 1979; Ferree and Hess 1985, 1994), continued to fade in the 1980s. The very use of insider tactics for outsider issues—feminist ideals of transforming structural inequalities—prevented these organizations from solidifying along a single radical to mainstream continuum. We categorize these organizations on the basis of their history and structure, analyze the tactical choices that they made during the 1980s and the tensions that resulted, and suggest how these tensions may be transformed under the Clinton administration.

The Authors and the Organizations

This study is drawn from organizational case studies produced by graduate students at the Women's Studies Program and Public Policy Center of the George Washington University between 1985 and 1990, under our direction. Spalter-Roth went on to become director for research at the Institute for Women's Policy Research (IWPR) in 1987, where she does policy research in conjunction with these same organizations. Schreiber worked in the Program and Policy Department of the American Association of University Women (AAUW), where she lobbied in coalition with several of the organizations discussed here. Both IWPR and AAUW are represented here by case studies (neither written by us, however). Though we have tried to enhance the case study data with our own insights and experiences, we do not feel we can share all our inside knowledge. Nevertheless, we think we accurately depict the tensions and practices of feminist organizations in the policy process. We should add that both of us are White, middle-class feminists, and this perspective is no doubt reflected in our analysis.

From all the case studies produced, we selected those describing organizations that fit two of Martin's (1990b) criteria for feminist organizations and two of our own. The organizations included attribute women's inferior status to processes of structural inequality, not individual actions or circumstances, and they work to "improve women's collective status, living conditions, opportunities, power, and self-esteem" (Martin 1990b, 184). Although many of the organizations deliberately eschew the "feminist" label, they recognize women as an oppressed group and are all "pro-women, political, and socially transformational" (Freeman, quoted in Martin 1990b, 184). We also required that groups be Washington, D.C.–based, private, nonprofit policy organizations that are not part of government agencies.

The organizations included in this study, their acronyms, and the date and purpose of their founding appear in Table 7-1. Not all major women's organizations are represented; the National Abortion Rights Action League, National Women's Political Caucus, the National Council of Negro Women, and the Women's Research and Education Institute are some notable omissions. On the other hand, some organizations are represented by several case studies that provide a window for examining organizational change over time.

All nineteen organizations discussed are national in scope. All participate in the Washington, D.C., policymaking process, but each has its own unique history, set of issues, resources, and organizational constraints. Despite their differences, they can be grouped into three general types: mass-membership organizations, coalitions of direct service providers or membership organizations, and staff-driven "expert" organizations.

Six were founded as national membership organizations: AAUW, the National Federation of Business and Professional Women's Clubs (BPW), the Coalition of Labor Union Women (CLUW), the National Council of Jewish Women (NCJW), the National Organization for Women (NOW), and the Women's International League for Peace and Freedom (WILPF). Along with the national offices, they have state and local affiliates operating under standards established by the parent bodies.

A primary goal of membership organizations is to recruit, educate, train, and mobilize members to participate in the policy process. To empower their membership, they attempt to encourage women to work directly for their own benefit. Members are organized to lobby, get media attention, and recruit and train other members. Organization staff act as power and information brokers. They gain access to decision-makers, educate the public, and mobilize their constituents. In turn, the membership provides

TABLE 7-1

ORGANIZATIONS AND ACRONYMS, FOUNDING DATES
AND PURPOSES

ORGANIZATION	ACRONYM	FOUNDING YEAR AND PURPOSE
American Association of University Women	AAUW	1888; to eliminate discrimination against women pursuing higher education
National Federation of Business and Professional Women's Clubs	BPW	1919; to be a national organization concerned with issues that affect working women
Coalition of Labor Union Women	CLUW	1972; organized at Chicago convention to represent the needs of labor union women
Center for Women Policy Studies	CWPS	1972; to be a research and advocacy organization focusing on the social, legal, and economic status of women
Displaced Homemakers Network	DHN	1979; to establish a national presence to advocate on behalf of displaced homemakers
The Fund for the Feminist Majority	FFM	1987; established by former NOW leaders to "feminize power" and remove the institutional barriers to women's attaining positions of power
Institute for Women's Policy Research	IWPR	1987; to establish a women-centered, policy-oriented research organization
National Association of Commissions for Women	NACW	1970; to bring a national presence and form a clearinghouse of information for the nation's women's commissions
National Coalition Against Domestic Violence	NCADV	1978; to establish a national office to represent battered women's shelters and programs
National Council of Jewish Women	NCJW	1893; to serve as a charity organization as well as to represent Jewish interests

TABLE 7-1, CONTINUED

ORGANIZATION	ACRONYM	FOUNDING YEAR AND PURPOSE
National Committee on Pay Equity	NCPE	1981; organized by labor and women's professional groups to support ongoing advocacy for pay equity
National Institute for Women of Color	NIWC	1981; to build a support network for and improve the self-esteem of women of color
National Organization for Women	NOW	1966; to be a national organization addressing existing discrimination against women
Overseas Education Fund/Women, Law and Development Project	OEF/WLD	1983; to define and confront legal constraints on women worldwide
Project on Equal Education Rights	PEER	1974; founded as a project of the NOW Legal Defense and Education Fund to monitor enforcement of Title IX
Women's Equity Action League	WEAL	1968; to offer a women's organization alternative to NOW
Women's International League for Peace and Freedom	WILPF	1915; to convince heads of states to stop World War I
Women's Legal Defense Fund	WLDF	1971; organized by feminist lawyers to advocate women's rights and to represent women in legal matters
Wider Opportunities for Women	WOW	1964; to establish a national organization to provide employment training and advocacy for women and girls

credibility, effectiveness, and financing to the staff. Membership surveys and national conventions select issues to pursue in Washington, and paid staff do the day-to-day work.

Four of the membership organizations discussed here, AAUW, BPW, NCJW, and WILPF, were formed during the first wave of the women's movement. AAUW and BPW have been equal rights organizations throughout their histories, involved with battles over woman suffrage and discrimination against women in education, business, and the professions. In contrast, NCJW and WILPF grew out of "social" rather than "equality" feminism (Black 1989), with social reform and peace as their primary focus. NOW and CLUW were formed during the second wave of the women's movement. NOW is currently the largest of the membership organizations; CLUW, the most recent, grew out of the labor movement and is especially concerned with workplace issues.

The second type of organization studied comprises coalitions of direct service providers such as the Displaced Homemakers Network (DHN)[1] and the National Coalition Against Domestic Violence (NCADV), and coalitions of local units such as state and county Commissions on the Status of Women (NACW). Unlike the membership organizations, these groups do not have founding parent bodies. Rather, the local units came together to establish Washington offices in order to represent themselves better in the national policymaking process. The networks are composed of representatives of funded organizations and their paid staffs. Rather than directly organizing "victims" and "survivors," the coalitions try to empower these women through programs and legislation primarily designed to increase their economic autonomy.

For example, the DHN, formed to lobby on behalf of displaced homemaker programs and issues of particular concern to displaced homemakers (such as increases in the minimum wage and access to training and apprenticeship programs) provides information about the needs of displaced homemakers to policymakers and technical assistance to direct service providers. They do not directly organize displaced homemakers. In the words of a former staff member:

> The network is a grass-roots organization in a different way from what I would call a classic grass-roots organization. It's not a membership organization. Our strength does not lie in the individual displaced homemaker. That group is largely unorganized except through employment and training service programs that provide their link to

some type of organizing. . . . Displaced homemakers as a group are not for the most part in a position to go out and take action and organize a movement because they are too busy needing services from our program in order to get their lives in order. It would probably not be very worthwhile or useful or effective to go out and say "OK, we're going to go out and organize displaced homemakers." (Patrick, quoted in Cilik 1988).

To overcome the hierarchical relationship between professional and client, and to give voice to the survivors of victimization, organizations such as NCADV and DHN often put "clients" on their national board. These coalitions also arrange for survivors to "tell their stories" to policymakers and to the media.

The third set of women's organizations, those that are staff-run and expert-based, include legal defense organizations such as the Women's Legal Defense Fund (WLDF); research organizations such as the Institute for Women's Policy Research (IWPR) and the Center for Women Policy Studies (CWPS); advocacy organizations such as the Fund for the Feminist Majority (FFM), the National Committee for Pay Equity (NCPE), Wider Opportunities for Women (WOW), the National Institute for Women of Color (NIWC), the Women's Equity Action League (WEAL); and single-issue projects of membership organizations such as the NOW Legal Defense and Education Fund's Project for Equal Education Rights (PEER) and Overseas Education Fund's Women Law and Development Project (OEF/WLD). These organizations often have "donor members" and organizational affiliates, who participate in organization activities. WOW, for example, has a network of state and local affiliates and a National Commission on Working Women; it is a kind of hybrid organization. In general, however, members or affiliates do not vote (although they often advise) in determining organizational priorities. Therefore, the staff has more flexibility (within the constraints of the need to obtain funding) to develop the organization's agenda and to define its issues and activities. The majority of these organizations were founded during the 1970s and 1980s.

Blurring Lines between Mainstream and Radical Organizations

Authors who wrote about the activities of the second wave of the women's movement during the 1960s and early 1970s distinguished between the organizational styles and issues of radical versus mainstream strands (Freeman 1975; Deckard 1979; Tinker 1983; Ferree and Hess 1985). Radical (or women's liberation) groups were described as relatively informal networks struggling for transformative feminist goals outside the conventional political arena. The mainstream (or women's rights) groups were described as more formally structured organizations established to pursue specific equity goals through legislation and the courts (Ferree and Hess 1985, 48).

This distinction was never fully descriptive of all the threads of the women's movement, especially the activities of women of color and working-class women (Bookman and Morgen 1988). By the mid-1970s, activities and issues of radical and mainstream organizations began to blur as more expert-based organizations were started and as more membership organizations and coalitions developed a presence inside the Beltway. The issues and techniques of these organizations began to overlap as younger, more radical feminists were motivated to bring their claims into the policy arena and assume leadership roles in Washington-based organizations. Simultaneously, more mainstream organizations began to work on issues initially staked out by more radical organizations (A. Fraser 1983; Gelb 1989; Schlozman 1991; Ferree and Hess 1994).

During the 1970s, both new and established organizations attempted to improve women's collective status through activities in the policy arena. They met with notable success in gaining passage of equity laws such as Title IX of the Educational Equity Act of 1972, the Equal Opportunity Credit Act of 1974, and the Pregnancy Discrimination Act of 1978 (Gelb and Palley 1982). But President Jimmy Carter's electoral defeat in 1980 led to the end of access to executive agencies and, eventually, of access to the federal courts. The Reagan administration looked benignly on a right-wing counterattack against the modest feminist legislative gains and organizational funding. As women's organizations faced conservative backlash in the 1980s, the distinction between "radical" and "mainstream" feminism continued to fade. Even the most mainstream feminist issues, such as educational equity, came under attack, and the Reagan administration began to dismantle welfare state programs that minimally protected women from total dependence on the capitalist marketplace or men (Boris 1991; Erie et al. 1983). During this period women's organizations, along with labor and civil rights groups, turned to the Democrat-controlled Congress for redress, but with only mixed success. Having brought women's issues to Washington and placed them on the public agenda, however, these organizations continued in the 1980s to gain sophistication in the use of insider techniques in order to influence and monitor the policy process, and "to protect what we've got" (Walker, quoted in Baxter 1987, 14).

Tactical Choices: Mastering the Arts of Insider Politics

The network of women's organizations operating in Washington, D.C., has been applauded, even by opponents, for its political sophistication and its polished use of insider techniques. As part of their insider style, organizations learned the techniques of packaging information in short and readable form ("put all reports on a 3 by 5 card" was the well-heeded advice of a congressional staffer). They provided information on a quick turn-around basis and developed effective contacts with congressional staff that allowed them access to policymakers. They located victims of discrimination from a legislator's home state. They developed media campaigns, focus groups, and other sophisticated forms of constituency analysis. They explained the bottom line of complex legislation to glassy-eyed legislators (it is no coincidence that some of the most sophisticated of the women's movement lobbyists were former schoolteachers). They attended innumerable coalition meetings. In short, these women's organizations learned to function as interest groups (Gelb and Palley 1982; Ferree and Hess 1985) in the hope that insider techniques would increase their power and influence, and raise the visibility of the issues they represented.

As Ferree and Hess note, "Playing politics increases the possibility of co-optation as organizations get absorbed into the policy making process, [and] goals can get displaced as organizations concentrate on maintaining themselves" (1985, 122). Yet the very issues raised by these organizations often challenged the legitimacy they gained from the use of insider tactics. Women's organizations support outsider issues that are hard to "hear." For example, WEAL's Women in the Military Project challenged the sexual harassment of both heterosexual and lesbian women in this male bastion, along with raising the more customary equal opportunity issue of women's exclusion from numerous military occupational specialties.

Although insider techniques have the potential to make the issues that organizations emphasize more conservative over time, this does not appear to have happened in many of these organizations. For example, as the Reagan and Bush administrations and an increasingly conservative judiciary began systematically to narrow women's access to abortion, mainstream women's organizations responded to the demands of their staff and their membership and joined the abortion rights lobby. AAUW, whose stated goal since its inception in 1888 has been "to achieve equity and education for women and girls," became one of the most active organizations in the pro-choice coalition. Likewise, abortion rights became a primary issue for WEAL, despite its years of avoiding the question.

In the 1980s, passing legislation was a herculean task because the support of two-thirds of Congress is required to override presidential vetoes. Goal-displacing compromises to pass controversial legislation became more likely. Yet rather than accept any and all compromises, groups often withdrew from particular legislative coalitions. For example, NOW and others refused to accept a compromise cap on damages in sex discrimination suits in the 1991 Civil Rights Bill and dropped out of the coalition organized by the Leadership Conference on Civil Rights to support the legislation. AAUW and other groups formed a separate child care coalition when the original coalition led by the Children's Defense Fund was ready to accept a provision allowing government to fund centers run by religious groups (Berry 1993). Once the tactical choice had been made to use a professional insider style, however, controversy arose when specific organizations tried to return to confrontational outsider techniques. The Washington pro-choice coalition of women's organizations was nearly torn apart when NOW announced its desire to use civil disobedience during the 1992 pro-choice demonstration. Ultimately, NOW yielded to the vehement objections of its coalition partners, who argued that such tactics would be counter-productive in an election year.

The proficient use of insider techniques by women's organizations succeeded in keeping feminist agendas alive in Washington, D.C., during the 1980s. Occasionally, these techniques were questioned even by the organizations themselves for being "too inside the Beltway" and "too professional." More confrontational techniques were suggested but seldom adopted at the national level. Although insider techniques did not appear to make organizational agendas more conservative over time, they did generate significant organizational tensions.

Tactical Choices and Resulting Tensions

These organizations continued to pressure Congress, mobilize constituencies, and educate the public despite political backlash and diminishing resources. All faced charges that they were irrelevant to most women, were outdated survivors of a more radical era, and had been co-opted and could no longer stir or mobilize the marching millions. Not all of the nineteen organizations survived this hostile environment. Those that failed to survive, at least in the same form, were WEAL, NCADV, OEF/WLD, PEER, and NIWC.[2] Others, such as the CWPS, were pronounced dead several times but nonetheless managed to attract new resources and are still functioning (Batchelder 1990).

Those organizations that survived constantly faced the tension between their insider techniques and their outsider issues. The daily choices they made combined elements of radical and mainstream feminism. Although such pragmatism and flexibility were needed to endure the long decade of the 1980s, the organizational tensions that were introduced also threatened their survival. The tactical choice made by many, but not all, of the organizations to develop their sophistication in the use of mainstream insider or interest group techniques resulted in three major tensions in their practices. First, there was tension between marketing feminist issues in the dominant language of individual liberalism, while simultaneously trying to raise collective consciousness, to mobilize, and to educate around structural issues. Second, there was the strain of relying on government resources for the treatment of women as clients or victims while simultaneously attempting to mobilize women to speak out in their own interests. Third, tension arose between claims to speak for all women and the limited success achieved in trying to recruit a more diverse membership, to participate in diverse coalitions, and to put issues of importance to women of color, lesbians, and working-class women on the policy agenda.

Not all these stresses were experienced by all the organizations. Our analysis of the case studies indicates that the first tension appeared most among membership organizations, and the second among coalitions of service providers; the third was found in all the organizations we studied.

TENSION 1: MARKETING FEMINIST ISSUES IN THE DOMINANT LANGUAGE OF INDIVIDUAL LIBERALISM, WHILE SIMULTANEOUSLY TRYING TO RAISE COLLECTIVE CONSCIOUSNESS TO MOBILIZE AND TO EDUCATE AROUND STRUCTURAL ISSUES

The spokeswomen for the organizations discussed here all recognized gender inequality as a structural rather than an individual problem, and all recognized the importance of working to empower women collectively. Yet especially during this antifeminist backlash, they believed that to gain legitimacy for their issues they needed to present them in moderate and universalistic terms. This meant speaking the dominant language of liberal

TABLE 7-2

ORGANIZATIONAL STATEMENTS OF GOALS AND PROBLEMS

ORGANIZATION	STATEMENT OF GOAL
AAUW	to achieve equity and education for women and girls
BPW	to address the lack of full participation, equity, and economic self-reliance for women especially in the workplace
CLUW	lack of organization of working women; labor union women need information and education about their rights in the labor force and labor movement
CWPS	to address the lack of equality and need for economic independence for women in U.S. society
DHN	displaced homemakers fall through the cracks of federal assistance programs; need programs and assistance to address specific needs of displaced homemakers both educationally and financially
FFM	feminization of power is the flagship; aim to move on five fronts—legal, business, campus, political, and media—to change the decision-makers
IWPR	to rectify the limited availability of policy relevant research that can contribute to the development of policies and programs that adequately consider women's needs
NACW	to eliminate discrimination on the basis of sex, race, age, religion, national origin, or marital status in all phases of American life
NCADV	to eliminate violence against women; violence against women is the result of patriarchy; sexism, racism, anti-Semitism, homophobia, classism, ageism, and ableism are forms of violence
NCJW	in the spirit of Judaism, to further human welfare in the Jewish and general communities; to educate the individual and the community toward their responsibility in advancing human welfare and the democratic way of life
NCPE	to rectify wage discrimination based on sex- and race-based discrimination and lack of worker participation in phases of employee evaluation projects
NIWC	necessary to promote economic and educational well-being and to affirm the dignity of women of color

TABLE 7-2, CONTINUED

ORGANIZATION	STATEMENT OF GOAL
NOW	to take action to bring women into full participation in the mainstream of American society, exercising all the privileges and responsibilities thereof in truly equal participation with men
OEF/WLD	need organization and reallocation of resources for third world women; to enable these women to develop their full productive capacities
PEER	unequal and inadequate access to equal education for girls; need for social changes and challenge of ideology that promotes traditional sex roles
WEAL	to address women's economic issues especially through public education projects, policy analysis, and support for litigation and advocacy
WILPF	to achieve by peaceful means those political, economic, social, and psychological conditions throughout the world which can assure peace, freedom, and justice; to forge a new vision of national security from a woman's perspective
WLDF	to secure equal rights for women through education, litigation, advocacy, and other lawful means, and to empower women through the delivery of legal services
WOW	need for economic independence and equality for women and girls through training and advocacy

individualism. In so doing, these organizations avoided the full brunt of the backlash but perhaps did so at the price of obscuring the structural nature of the issues they addressed. Although radical language that refers directly to gendered relations of domination and subordination might have alienated policymakers, the public, and some of their own membership, more liberal language fails to challenge the dominant discourse, which legitimizes structural inequalities.

Table 7-2 presents the public statements of the goals of all nineteen organizations. As the table shows, these organizations rely on the liberal feminist language of "opportunity and rights," "eliminating discrimination," and "encouraging full participation in the mainstream of American society." All but one avoid more radical or socialist feminist phrases such as "capitalist exploitation," "public patriarchy," and even "oppression" in promotional documents. They do not discuss eliminating existing systems or structures; they refer instead to "eliminating barriers" or "increasing women's participation" in systems that are dominated by white men.

In the FFM's "feminization of power" campaign the rhetoric of liberal individualism was deliberately chosen in order to increase the appeal of the campaign to a broader public. As Walls notes, "Despite the intrinsic radicalness of the feminization of power concept, the Feminist Majority have been able to package the idea as a liberal concern with equality. The effectiveness of this liberal packaging has been the true genius of the Feminist Majority. . . . The undertones of policy overhaul and radical change in the way society is structured are to be found in the Feminist Majority literature, but only if one is really looking for them. As a result the Feminist Majority have cleverly been able to combine an appeal to both liberal and radical sections within the populace" (1990, 6).

To address what they saw as structural problems, these organizations advocated policies designed to promote women's economic autonomy, eliminate sexual violence against women, guarantee employment rights, ensure reproductive freedom, and bring feminists to power. In defining solutions for the public, however, they chose terms that were seen as more mainstream and more palatable. Thus, "increased economic autonomy" became "pay equity"; "woman-battering" became "domestic violence"; "increasing job rights" became "family and medical leave"; and "guaranteeing abortion rights" became "pro-choice."

Organizations such as WLDF have promoted a women's agenda in the guise of "work and family" issues. The struggle for the Family and Medical Leave Act of 1993 was a primary example of an attempt to use palatable pro-family language to increase women's power in the workplace. "In our modern-day society when we talk about 'the family' we are talking about working women . . . which is why we are doing it. And because we think we can get some political capital from it" (Lenhoff, WLDF, quoted in Stoneback 1989).

In their quest to use palatable language to gain legitimacy, many of the nineteen organizations do not publicly label themselves as "feminist." This is intentional; some promote themselves as mainstream (AAUW, BPW) despite their feminist agendas. A WILPF staff member notes: "While WILPF is not by title a feminist organization, . . . if you want to describe them [WILPF members] as a bunch of women who have been of independent thought, action, conviction, commitment, creativity, leaving their husbands and going into women-identified organizations, taking leadership . . . recognizing that women's needs are first, but the world is organized by white men, of course they're feminist. They might not use the word, but of course they are" (Guy, quoted in Monaghan, 1990, 6). In a climate in which feminists are often portrayed as supporting the interests of a deviant elite, avoiding a feminist label was a survival tactic. The sole exception to this rule of using liberal language to convey feminist goals was NCADV, whose public goal statement is "to eliminate violence against women caused by patriarchy and the power of men over women." Its recent near-demise as a national coalition has been traced, in part, to the organization's refusal to soften its rhetoric (Gelb 1993).

Insofar as these organizations placed feminist issues on the public agenda, they did undermine male dominance and empower women, but by packaging these issues in less threatening terms, organizations also gained political capital and legitimacy. "Domestic violence," "family leave," and "pro-choice" became part of the public vocabulary and directed attention to women's issues (see Condit 1990 on abortion rhetoric). But despite the hopes of organizational leaders who wished to appeal to both liberals and radicals, the use of politically palatable language obscured relations of domination and subordination. Their efforts may have failed to raise the consciousness of the very women these organizations hoped to represent and empower.

TENSION 2: RELYING ON GOVERNMENT AND CORPORATE RESOURCES
WHILE SIMULTANEOUSLY ATTEMPTING TO EMPOWER CLIENTS

The stress that results from relying on government and corporate funds to empower victims and survivors of exploitation and abuse is most likely to be experienced by the coalitions of service providers. These coalitions are composed of networks of local and state-level organizations that started out in the 1960s and early 1970s as alternative service providers, with largely volunteer staffs, determined to overcome the paternalism of traditional service agencies. The frustration of working with the instability of volunteer staff and a constant shortage of resources led many of these organizations to fight for local, state, federal, and corporate funding. In their struggles for resources, radical and alternative organizations became more mainstream as funders insisted on more bureaucratic and hierarchical relations between clients and staff. In her article describing the change in one women's health clinic, Morgen (1986) notes that another result of state funding was the increased hiring of women of color, who could not afford to be volunteers, as paid staff members (see also Matthews 1989).

The coalitions of service providers faced financial concerns similar to those of their state and local member groups. Their primary sources of funds were government agencies and private corporations that "hired" them to provide direct client services or technical assistance to providers. Reliance on this type of funding opened them to accusations that they were no longer feminist organizations but rather "institutionalized social service agencies that have sold out to the state in exchange for financial resources" (Martin 1990b, 183). On the surface, the services they offered appeared to be typical of those of traditional service providers. For example, Johnson & Johnson (J & J), funded NCADV's national hotline for battered women (a grant that was later terminated by NCADV because of the company's relations with South Africa); and with funding from the MacArthur Foundation, WOW organized the Female Single Parent Literacy Project to improve the literacy of low-income single mothers. Yet according to staff members, these programs reflected a feminist analysis of the problem. For example, WOW's literacy project "has gathered information specifically concerning women and literacy, re-defined the issue in terms of women's economic self-sufficiency and presented the issue to constituencies, coalitions, policymakers, and the broader public from its own unique perspective: that is, in the context of women's employment and training issues" (Watson 1988, 13).

During the 1980s the organizations' relations with government funders, especially the U.S. Department of Justice (DOJ), became especially hostile. For example, an acrimonious battle began in 1985 when the DOJ announced it would award NCADV a $625,000 grant. Patrick McGuigan of the conservative Institute for Government and Politics stalled the grant when he announced, "I don't think pro-lesbian, hard-core feminists should be getting a grant from the Reagan Administration" (Ciolli 1985, 14). After months of debate and much media attention, the DOJ awarded $580,000 anyway, which NCADV accepted with great reservations. "Organizational Bottom Lines" to "guide them through the partnership" were established. The group pledged that "if a funding source refuses to support any part of our analysis, then other money must be secured" (NCADV *Voice*, Summer–Fall 1985). The coalition's analysis of domestic violence included racism, sexism, homophobia, anti-Semitism, classism, ageism, and ableism as forms of violence. The contract required that DOJ approve all text for the NCADV project, and DOJ refused to allow the words "lesbian" and "woman abuse" (arguing that men are also abused) in their publications. This led NCADV's board to reject the DOJ contract for its second year. Objections within the battered women's movement arose, and another organization quickly formed to accept the DOJ funding, creating a major rift within the movement.

A major goal of feminist organizations is to empower women to work collectively to overcome structural inequalities. Coalitions of service providers are less able than others to rely on their clients for resources and organizational support toward this end. During the 1980s they were more likely to rely on hostile government agencies or right-wing corporations for organizational survival. As a result, they were constrained to adopt mainstream models in dealing with their clients. Despite such constraints, the coalitions continued to lobby on behalf of radical causes and, in the case of NCADV, declined funding at great cost.

TENSION 3: CLAIMING TO SPEAK FOR ALL WOMEN WHILE FACING
LIMITED SUCCESS IN TRYING TO RECRUIT A MORE DIVERSE MEMBERSHIP,
TO PARTICIPATE IN DIVERSE COALITIONS, AND TO PUT ON THE POLICY
AGENDA ISSUES OF IMPORTANCE TO WOMEN OF COLOR, LESBIANS, AND
WORKING-CLASS WOMEN

To gain power and legitimacy in the policy process, women's organizations in Washington, D.C., need to be perceived as broad-based and able to activate and mobilize millions of women. Yet Washington's women's organizations have consistently been criticized by feminists inside and outside the Beltway for being too white, too middle-upper-income, and too heterosexual; for defining gender issues from that privileged perspective and falsely generalizing this perspective to all women. Critics argue that a narrow and elite leadership creates a self-serving movement that empowers only those women who already have the most relative power, thus failing to empower other women (Judis 1992; D. King 1988). From the perspective of these organizations, their desire to speak for a diverse but unitary coalition of women who vary by race, ethnicity, sexual preference, and class created tensions. Issues of race, sexual preference, and class were marginalized because these issues divided organizations and were sometimes perceived as a threat to their legitimacy with white, middle-class male policymakers. By the end of the 1980s most of these nineteen women's organizations were attempting to promote and recruit more diverse staffs, memberships, and constituencies. They admitted that issues of diversity were legitimate within the women's movement and thus part of their feminist agendas; they continued to participate in diverse coalitions and to support efforts to eliminate structural inequalities of race, heterosexism, and class privilege; but their success in dealing with these issues was mixed. Organizations tended to focus on one issue, such as race or class, in a particular program, and in doing so presented white, middle-class women as the norm. This construction no doubt added to the tension between white, middle-class women and all women of color, poor and low-income women, and lesbians. Each of these issues posed its own distinctive problems.

Race ■ Most of these organizations had specific programming designed to address racism by the end of the 1980s. For example, WLDF had an Employment Rights Project for Women of Color to encourage the participation of organizations representing women of color in the formulation of public policy. WILPF designed a Racial Justice Campaign to attack racism within both the organization and the "wider society." NCPE produced such publications as *Women of Color and Pay Equity*. NOW hired an antiracism coordinator, and antiracism work has become an increasingly important organizational activity. CWPS defined its issues "from a woman of color perspective." IWPR conducted research focused on race, ethnicity, and class as well as gender.

These programmatic attempts to address the needs of women of color were criticized as too little and too late; as expecting women of color to "join in" an already white-dominated group in the name of diversity; and as using women of color as spokewomen on issues of diversity and racism without allowing them the power to define organizational agendas (Higginbotham 1992). Char Mollison, a former director of WEAL, agreed with this analysis: "A number of women's organizations, including WEAL, in an attempt to build diversity, have endorsed 'outreach' programs and efforts. This 'outreach' has often involved asking women of color groups and individuals to join with established white women's organizations, go to their meetings, and fight for their issues. The attitude . . . is that many women of color groups and individuals will drop everything to be part of the established groups" (Mollison, quoted in Patty Martin 1989).

Predictably, such attempts at inclusion resulted in challenges to organizational goals, issues, and resources. For example, women of color edited a special issue of the NCADV newsletter, the *Voice*, in which they accused

NCADV of denying women of color equal access to resources, failing to elect women of color to positions of leadership, failing to reach out to communities of color, using language that degraded women of color, and assuming that gender is more important than race or ethnicity. In short, women of color claimed that NCADV marginalized both them and their issues. The raising of such concerns was divisive for the organization and may have contributed to its near-demise.

In attempting to participate in coalitions that put race as well as gender issues on the policy agenda, the decision as to which issue should have priority frequently became a source of tension. For example, in the effort to pass the Civil Rights Act of 1991, white women were both accused of failing to treat the issue as a priority and criticized for using a strategy that deliberately emphasized the act as a women's economic equity issue. In their turn, many predominantly white women's organizations criticized their civil rights coalition allies for failing to support them in the fight to keep abortion safe and legal.

Sexual Preference ■ Although tension and conflict often resulted, organizations appeared eager (at least in their organizational statements and programs) to promote efforts to include women of color. They appeared somewhat less desirous of advertising efforts to address lesbian issues and to educate their constituencies, policymakers, and the public about homophobia, despite the leadership roles lesbians often played in their organizations. Nonetheless, WLDF, NOW, NCADV, AAUW, and WILPF did add references to sexual orientation in their general mission statements or publications during the 1980s, and a few others offered specific programming to address these concerns. WEAL addressed the issue of harassment of lesbians in the military and worked with "mainstream" groups and congressional representatives to get their support. The WLDF ran a Lesbian and Gay Custody Project to "assist lesbian mothers, gay fathers, and their attorneys in obtaining custody and visitation determinations that are not based on prejudices, stereotypes or myths about homosexuality." NCADV published an anthology on Lesbian Battering and had a Lesbian Battering Task Force. And NOW hired a Lesbian Rights Project Coordinator.

By the end of the 1980s at least some of the nineteen organizations had included lesbian issues and homophobia in programming and policy agendas as part of their commitment to transforming relations of inequality. Some organizations lost credibility with policymakers, the general public, and even their own constituencies as a result of their support for "a lesbian agenda." NOW experienced considerable flak over President Patricia Ireland's "confession" of bisexuality.

Working-Class Women's Issues ■ Although most of these organizations gave at least token support to combatting racism or homophobia or both, few offered a class-based analysis of the U.S. economic system. Most did not explicitly address the economic disparities among women and the ways in which class differences affect the control women have over their lives. They were more likely to attempt to gain legitimacy by universalizing women's needs for economic equity relative to men. Some organizations were more likely to give awards for "best practices" than to criticize their corporate funders' drive for profits at the expense of working women.

During the 1980s "expert" organizations did address the needs of working-class women through research and advocacy. For example, IWPR conducted and disseminated research on low-wage jobs and workers and on strategies to decrease gender, race, and class inequalities. Its research has been used by other women's organizations and unions to do battle with, for example, the U.S. Chamber of Commerce and the National Association of Manufacturers. DHN was extremely active in lobbying for an increase in the minimum wage. WOW lobbied for and educated about the majority of women who were employed in low-wage, traditional women's jobs. NCPE challenged the ways in which corporations value women's labor. CLUW represented women in the ranks of organized labor, an institution especially under attack by the Reagan and Bush administrations. And since labor leaders are typically white men, CLUW battled these male-dominated unions to "inform and educate trade union women about their rights, opportunities and responsibilities within their unions," as well as advocating for a "more equitable sharing of the wealth of the nation" (Baxter 1987, 3).

The omission of a class analysis can be seen as an effort to avoid tensions and divisiveness, to continue to use inclusive language in order to increase women's economic participation, mollify corporate funders, avoid additional backlash, and keep the focus on women's losses in abortion rights. Yet the relative neglect of structural class issues during the 1980s—a period of increased economic inequalities between those at the bottom and those at the top—likely reinforced the notion that the women's movement represented an elite interested in only those women's issues that affected them.

Summary and Conclusions

During the conservative 1980s the distinction between radical and mainstream feminist organizations blurred as many national policy organizations gained sophistication in the use of insider techniques in order to place radical, structurally transformative issues on the policy agenda. Organizations found it necessary to use the language of liberal individualism to market policy issues that, if implemented, would result in the structural transformation of gender relations. In doing so, they ducked some backlash and prevented increased marginalization of their issues, but they also risked failing to stir or raise the consciousness of those not already committed to change. As a result of accepting funding from hostile executive-branch agencies and from corporations with exploitive practices, organizations ensured their survival but faced constraints in their ability to empower the women who needed it most. To gain legitimacy in speaking for all women, these organizations tried, with varying success and commitment, to recruit a more diverse membership, to participate in coalitions, and to introduce issues of racism, heterosexism, and classism into their program and policy agendas. As a result, some faced the loss of organizational unity and resources without successfully incorporating these issues. Others more successfully broadened their agendas and their membership.

As these organizations faced the tension between living up to feminist ideals and maintaining their legitimacy, they could have become more mainstream by dropping their commitment to transformative issues. Or they could have become more idealistic and dropped their efforts to place these issues on the mainstream national policy agenda. Most of the organizations that did survive the 1980s maintained their credibility while keeping feminist claims—for women's economic rights, overcoming violence and sexual assault against women, abortion rights, civil rights, and political empowerment—on the policy agenda, albeit not always in their purest form.

Insider/outsider tensions kept these organizations constantly deciding between the need for credibility, funds, and organizational unity, on the one hand, and accountability to feminist ideals, consciousness-raising, and empowerment of women, on the other. In facing the daily problems created by these tensions—deciding whether to accept a grant, remain in a coalition, rename an issue, support unpopular causes—they sometimes compromised and sometimes stuck with feminist principles. In general, these groups were not co-opted as a result of the trade-offs they made.

Radical issues such as sexual orientation, abortion rights, and racism were added to, not subtracted from, organizational agendas. The result was a continued blurring of the radical/mainstream distinction.

With the election of Bill Clinton, feminists in Washington celebrated the end of the long decade in the wilderness. After initial skirmishes in which the president-elect labeled them "bean counters" for their persistence in demanding that more women be appointed to the Cabinet, once inaugurated Clinton overturned the "gag rule" in Title X–funded abortion clinics, and signed the Family and Medical Leave Act into law. It is not yet clear how much a feminist agenda will benefit from this administration, even though women's groups now have more access, or what role will be played by these organizations now that they are no longer entirely on the defensive.

Although Clinton won the election on the issue of the economy, women's economic issues such as pay equity, job discrimination, a higher minimum wage, and training for non-traditional jobs are not emphasized in his economic agenda. Despite the endless faxes, briefing papers, and coalition reports sent by women's organizations, "economics as if women mattered" (Noble 1992, F25) has not yet materialized. The NOW Legal Defense and Education Fund organized a diverse coalition of women's groups (including the Welfare Rights Organization) to develop a women's economic survival agenda that is supportive of welfare recipients and low-income workers, but it has not received much of a hearing. Yet class, or at least economic issues, may become a more significant part of these organizations' agendas as a result of the impact of the economic recession on women, the continued restructuring of corporations, and the likelihood that the right to abortions will be more secure. The need for good jobs and control over the conditions of work, especially for those women without a college education, appears to be a structural issue that women's organizations are increasingly using their insider tactics to address.

As women's organizations struggle to get their concerns on the Clinton administration's agenda, more of their leaders are in contention for appointments in executive-branch agencies. Again, the potential results for feminist policy are not clear. In 1992–93 coalition meetings, some spoke in the voice of the administration, drumming up support for the Clinton agenda. The co-optation of these women into the administration (getting a "seat at the table") may result in less marginalization of women's organizations and issues but also in lessened ability to raise outsider issues. A decreased ability to raise outsider issues may lead to more use of confrontational tactics by those groups not on the inside. The result may be that a feminist agenda could again be pursued through both insider and outsider tactics. The organizations that survived the 1980s are now a critical resource in pursuing feminist goals in the 1990s.

Notes

Acknowledgments: We are grateful to the graduate students in the Women's Studies Program at the George Washington University who did their internships in policy organizations and who participated each spring from 1985 through 1991 in the practicum seminars "Training Women to Make Public Policy in Women's Interests." Without their questions, their insights, their analyses, and their case studies, this essay would not exist. We also thank the staff members of the women's organizations in Washington, D.C., who served as field supervisors, organizational guides, information providers, and critical commentators on the case studies. Lisa Tomlinson collected additional information; Felicia Lynch (now of the Hitachi Foundation), who was the project officer at the Fund for the Improvement of Postsecondary Education during the initial years of the project, provided advice and support. Finally, we thank Patricia Yancey Martin and Myra Marx Ferree for putting together the conference that spurred us to write what seemed like endless drafts of this essay, and Jill Braunstein, Melinda Chateauvert, Joyce Gelb, Hank Leland, Jane Mansbridge, and especially Myra Marx Ferree, who read them all.

The case studies not elsewhere cited in this chapter that form the basis for our analysis include Arnold (1989, 1991), Barnett (1987), Bowleg (1990), Crim (1987), Foley (1987), Gire (1990), Hordosch (1987), Jenkins (1990), Mulligan (1987), Nadel (1991), Quinn (1986), Reiner (1988), Satake (1990), Schreiber (1986), Sonosky (1988), Sottile (1985), Travis (1989), and Wolf (1990).

1. "Displaced homemakers" are defined as women who have lost the economic support of a spouse on which they had long depended; many are neither old enough for Social Security nor mothers of children eligible for AFDC and are thus not able to depend on the state for support of their work as homemakers. The Displaced Homemakers Network renamed itself Women Work! in 1993.

2. The NCADV has not failed but has significantly reconfigured itself and limited its scope. Joyce Gelb is currently doing research on why all the organizations listed have either ceased to exist or changed dramatically.

CHAPTER 8

Feminist Organization Success and the Politics of Engagement

■

JOYCE GELB

The essays in this section have dealt with various aspects of organizational transformation and change in second-wave feminist groups. As social movement theorists have noted, the "staying power" of these groups is unusually good. Recently, for example, Mayer Zald (1988, 10, 29) wrote: "Of the social movements on the current scene, . . . because of its specialized organizations and constituencies . . . the feminist movement appears to have the best chance for continued high levels of mobilization and activity." Nonetheless, the persistence of feminist organizations brings its own problems. Processes of "aging" occur in all social movement organizations, creating pressures to alter their structures, missions, and strategies, or to put goal maintenance ahead of goal attainment (Zald and Ash 1965; Minkoff 1992). Changes in the political opportunity structure—the external environment of the movement—such as economic crises and retrenchment, a more hostile political climate, organizational proliferation, and competition for scarce resources force groups to make choices, some of which are less than ideal. In any environment, movement organizations must balance their desire to create change against the need to accommodate the demands from funding sources and political decision-makers to moderate their tactics. They walk a political tightrope as they seek to respond to claims by their allies in government, the media, foundations, and other movement groups while also remaining faithful to their mobilizing principles and supporters.

Defining the meaning of success for a movement organization is important (see also Staggenborg, Chapter 22). Some groups have gone out of existence or modified their structure and goals so much that they have become unrecognizable as movement organizations. Even those that "self-destruct" may be effective, however, if they leave behind a substantive policy impact, cadres of experienced activists, and belief systems and models of collective action that can be utilized by succeeding generations of movement partici-pants (cf. Mueller 1987; Chapters 10, 12, 13, and 22 by Strobel, Whittier, Barnett, and Staggenborg). Resources for further mobilization appear to be a clear legacy of even those feminist groups that cease to exist. Institution-alization may itself be the most durable resource produced by movement mobilization because it protects gains, sustains commitment to enforce-ment of new laws, and facilitates efforts for further change over the long term (Ferree and Hess 1985, 175; Martin 1993).

The essays in this section tell us much about the issues of organizational change and success. They emphasize the relationship between organiza-tional dynamics and the external environment. They draw attention to the organizational issues raised by homophobia, racism, and class divisions, and they suggest directions that future research on these problems might explore. For example, one might ask how organizations change as aware-ness of the problems of achieving inclusiveness grows. The chapters show us how movement groups deal with pressures for organizational modera-tion arising from disparate organizational constituents, such as staff mem-bers, financial supporters, and political allies. Few organizations fail to alter some positions, yet the picture overall is not one of renouncing radi-calism. Whether in Washington policy groups, a Texas battered women's agency, or *Ms.* magazine, strongly feminist perspectives remain or even grow in institutionalized settings. Pressures to remain faithful to founding ideology and principles often successfully confront demands for funding support, skills and expertise, and political pragmatism. But the external environment that provides sponsorship and patronage also produces alter-ations in policy priorities, rhetoric, and agendas. An unresponsive politi-cal climate and negative economic conditions can adversely affect social movement groups. Feminist groups may be especially vulnerable to such changes, given their frequent reliance on nonmember support (Reming-ton 1991).

Chapters in this section also draw attention to the significance of dif-ferent organizational forms: decentralized versus centralized groups, par-ticipatory versus hierarchical groups, multi- versus single-issue groups, service versus advocacy groups, coalitions versus individual groups, and so on. They suggest the need for research on several issues. For example, are groups that attempt to combine the goals of personal transformation and policy impact as likely to gain access and win concessions as those that focus on political transformation alone? What is the role of coalitions among feminist organizations of diverse types and orientations? In the absence of strong political parties, left politics, and a centralized, co-ordinated state (which are typical in most European nations), do coalitions of feminist groups provide a basis for agenda development and effective intervention in the policymaking process? Or do they lead to dilution of principles and excessive emphasis on pragmatism and compromise?

Additionally, what is the relationship between radical and moderate groups in the feminist movement? Some scholars argue that both are neces-sary for movements to influence policy change successfully. Many contend that the structure of contemporary American feminism, with professional-ized interest groups at the national level and more radical feminist social movement groups at the local level, has provided maximum flexibility and the rare opportunity to pursue varied goals and shifting priorities (see Gelb and Palley 1987; Buechler 1990b, 79, 84). Eisenstein, Reinelt (Chapters 5 and 6), and others point out that although co-optation is a possible outcome for feminist organizations that engage with the state, it is not an inevitable one. Taking issue with the findings of writers such as Ferguson in *The Femi-nist Case against Bureaucracy* (1984), these authors suggest that grassroots feminist groups often adopt modified bureaucratic norms, goals and be-havior, and pragmatic political practices to good effect (see Burt, Gornick, and Pittman 1984). New styles of management, often less hierarchical and directive, and new priorities on issues are moved onto "the terrain of the state," as Reinelt says (Chapter 6; see also Dodson 1991). Feminist groups have sought new organizational forms, including "modified collectives" and other structural hybrids, in order to sustain their original commit-ments but also to operate more effectively and efficiently (Gottfried and Weiss 1992).

Constant experimentation to ensure accountability and democratic par-ticipation and consensus has been ongoing since the beginning of second-wave feminism in such groups as the National Organization for Women, Women's Equity Action League, and the National Coalition against Do-mestic Violence, as well as in countless grassroots feminist community groups; see the chapters by Spalter-Roth and Schreiber (7), Farrell (4), Eisenstein (5), and Morgen (15). One can make the case that continually confronting and reinterpreting the issues of power, centralization, profes-sionalization, voluntarism, and financial support, though often a painful and conflictual process for individuals and organizations, has contributed to dynamism and maturity in the movement as a whole.

Anne Costain (1992, 141) argues that the "peak period" for feminist organization has passed, political opportunities have narrowed, consciousness has diminished, and organizations are preoccupied with "just maintaining themselves." The struggles to do more than merely survive make this death warrant for feminist vitality and continuity seem premature. The groups, processes, and activities analyzed in this section provide little evidence for claims that the U.S. feminist movement has become complacent, is beset by organizational inertia, or is in a state of decline or retreat. Neither deradicalization and conservatism nor increased professionalization and bureaucratization appear to have taken their toll of feminist groups, despite the predictions of numerous social theorists. Rather, as Buechler (1990b, 69, 217) suggests, the continuation of grassroots activism, ongoing commitment to the progressive goal of transformation, and the existence of a large constituency that has maintained its independence from "official circles" have contributed to sustaining the movement's vitality and strength. In its more than a quarter-century of existence, American second-wave feminism has been able to enter the decision-making process, shape a distinctive policy agenda, and alter the way in which people define their concerns and options, in both the public and other sectors (see the discussion of Gaventa 1980, in Chapter 3).

Feminism as a social movement was resurgent in virtually every Western nation in the 1960s and 1970s. In each nation, however, differences in the institutions, values, and ideologies that together constitute the political opportunity structure of the country influenced the movement's organizational development and impact. The movements in the United States, Sweden, and the United Kingdom, for example, share many joint objectives but differ sharply in their styles of political activism and their organizational values. These, in turn, interact with specific political opportunities to shape feminist movement success (Gelb 1990, 138). At this nation-state level, the extent of corporatism vis-à-vis pluralism and the degree to which the state is centralized or fragmented affect movement emergence and activism. Comparatively, Sweden is the most corporatist and centralized; the United States, the most pluralistic and fragmented. The extent to which such systemic factors have contributed to creating an American feminist movement that differs from its sister movements and that is, in many respects, highly successful is an important question for feminist organization scholars.

How might different political structures shape the effectiveness of feminist mobilizations? In Sweden, for example, progressive social policy has benefited working women in many ways, but the country's social demo-

cratic and corporatist agenda for all workers has accounted for these benefits more than has autonomous mobilization by women's and feminist
groups. Labor-oriented policy gains for women have been impressive, but
they have not been accompanied by movement activism on a major scale.
Rather, the state has preempted or co-opted movement ideas and structures almost totally. In *Feminism and Politics* (Gelb 1989), I argue that the
absence of a distinct women's voice in the policy process has left women
politically and economically subordinate, with limited ability to advance a
dialogue about feminist objectives in the policy arena. In Britain a strong,
locally based women's liberation movement has emphasized transformation of personal consciousness and lifestyles—rather than national policies
and institutional change—from a decentralized base. From the late 1970s
to 1986 the U.K. women's movement interacted with local (district) governments, facilitating a rare convergence of local socialists, Labour Party
activists, and feminist groups. This process came to a virtual halt in the last
years of the conservative Thatcher ascendancy. Movement resources and
coalitions proved difficult to maintain apart from local government. Ideological conflicts limited efforts to resolve differences between radical and
socialist feminists and to create linkages to the masses of British women, a
limitation leading to marginalization of the movement's political impact.
American feminism may be unique in its blending of disparate wings with
different orientations, styles, and organizational styles. This hybrid style
is not without its tensions and costs, but it also offers the potential for
significant influence on policy.

U.S. feminists have made considerable policy gains, including the winning of new, substantive rights and the adoption of progressive policies
in once "private" areas such as rape and violence against women. Policy
transformations have occurred at the national level and, thanks to the presence of grassroots activists, in the fifty states as well. In Britain too, laws
that regulate the sexual abuse of women have been passed, but implementing and enforcing them have been difficult in the absence of an effectively
mobilized national women's movement. Grassroots groups facilitate discussion and theorizing but have little direct effect on policy. In Sweden,
feminism plays a minor role. Feminist goals and aspirations have been secondary to a Social Democratic agenda that emphasizes family and equality,
and little discussion of issues that are not on this agenda has occurred. The
lack of legitimacy for an autonomous women's movement has made it difficult for feminist groups to mobilize support for dialogues with the state

on issues of sexual abuse, power relations, and other issues not addressed by Social Democratic policy.

Surveys of "collective consciousness" in the United States show widespread support for many feminist goals and the feminist movement itself. In the United Kingdom, by contrast, conventional values continue to prevail; and in Sweden, questions regarding feminism—a suspect term in this consensus-oriented society—are not even asked in survey research. The United States appears to be somewhat unusual in winning both policy change *and* widespread acceptance of the feminist movement and many of its principles. Nonetheless, in all three nations, movement activists continue to interact with political parties, state institutions, and local politics in an ongoing process in which further change is likely.

Katzenstein (1990) points to another unusual feature of U.S. feminism: the *unobtrusive mobilization* of feminist constituencies in professional organizations and other mainstream institutions, including the church and military. The fragmented and decentralized nature of American politcal culture may have contributed to this development. By comparison, as Eisenstein (Chapter 5) shows, feminists in Australia have mobilized, with Labor Party support, within their state governments. Each strategy may be particularly adapted to the specifics of the national system, but perhaps some cross-national lessons can also be drawn. Mobilization at the local level in the United States—including women's shelters, rape crisis centers, women's health and abortion clinics, women's studies programs, and self-help initiatives—has persisted and, in many cases, expanded in pursuit of feminist values and goals. Although many of these activities have counterparts in Sweden and the United Kingdom (indeed, the movement against domestic violence began in England), their cumulative impact appears to be greatest in the United States, where the national and local levels are most strongly linked. At a minimum, such U.S. organizations provide an ongoing means of recruiting new activists and mobilizing new resources.

Change in the feminist movement is inevitable in the United States, as elsewhere, but decline and demise are not the assured outcomes. Conservative forces that gained preeminence in the 1980s constrained opportunities for feminist mobilization in the United States and in most European nations, including Sweden and the United Kingdom. The defensive posture of U.S. feminist groups during twelve years of antifeminist, right-wing domination had an inhibiting impact on feminism, which calls for scholarly exploration and analysis; see the chapters by Spalter-Roth and Schreiber

(7), Hyde (20), and Marshall (21). New and qualitatively different challenges to the movement and to feminist organizations will emerge from the present, more receptive Democratic administration. Feminist groups will still have to address issues related to goal attainment, group identity, issue specialization, funding and support, and the dynamics of internal and external relations, but in different forms. Adapting to a more receptive political opportunity structure and environment may result in new possibilities, but new problems are likely to arise as well in the ever changing dynamic of the political process. Organizational change need not necessarily lead to any one outcome, but it surely should not be understood as the death knell of feminism.

PART III

Inside Feminist Organizations:
Struggle, Learning, Change

CHAPTER 9

Feminist Goals and Organizing Processes

■

JOAN ACKER

Feminists, and others who are committed to egalitarian organizing to change society, have faced many dilemmas. The essays in Part III raise two questions. First, is it possible to organize in a collective, nonhierarchical, participatory way and still achieve other organizing goals? Second, is it possible to create organizing efforts that include people from diverse racial, ethnic, class, and gender locations? These dilemmas have been discussed extensively in both the feminist movement and the research literature (e.g., Freeman 1973; Rothschild-Whitt 1979; Ferree and Hess 1985; Echols 1989; Collins 1990; H. Eisenstein 1991a), but they are by no means resolved.

The organizations represented in these essays range from the overtly feminist organizing of collectives (Whittier, Chapter 12), women's liberation unions (Strobel, Chapter 10), and a women's bank and associated training program (Tom, Chapter 11) to the grassroots organizing of women around civil rights (Barnett, Chapter 13). Although the historical contexts, societal locations, and goals of these organizing efforts are different, each provides material for reflecting on these persisting issues.

I begin with an explanation of my use of the term "organizing" rather than "organization" to name the process involved, a distinction made by Helen Brown at the conference on feminist organizations that was the basis for this book. In using "organizing," I intend to emphasize that organizations are continually constituted through practices and processes that occur through the actions of organizational participants. Many of these practices are grounded in fundamental social arrangements and understandings, are supported by powerful interests, and persist over time and the coming and going of particular people. But they become nonexistent when no one carries them out, when people stop organizing.

With this usage I want to underscore the point that agency resides in people, not in abstractions such as an "organization." Certain organizations do have the legal status of individuals and are understood as actors.

It is convenient, as well as consistent with this reality, to think of them as having agency, and as existing outside the actions of people. This is a legal and theoretical fiction, however, achieved historically by corporate actors in pursuit of goals such as minimizing individual owner or manager responsibility and maximizing power (Friedland and Robertson 1990; Perrow 1986; Powell 1991). Conceptualizing organizations in abstract, gender-neutral terms is consistent with the processes through which power is organized. But this reification mythologizes and entrenches the power of large organizations and those who hold privileged positions within them.

My emphasis on organizing and agency does not imply a theory based upon an individual actor making lonely—however well-informed—decisions, for I take organizing to be a profoundly social activity that arises from and often aims to change the prevailing social relations. Of course, this is what women's and feminist organizations try to do.

Participation and Democracy versus Getting Something Done

Is it possible to remain true to the feminist ideals of collectivity, respect, and democracy and at the same time create or take enough power to make the changes in the society that are needed to meet feminist goals (Freeman 1973; H. Eisenstein 1991a)? Many of the people in these stories of organizing were aware of this dilemma, faced it in a number of concrete circumstances, and dealt with it in different ways.

The overtly feminist organizing efforts recounted by Whittier and Strobel (Chapters 12 and 10) were, with some exceptions, products of radical feminist organizing of the late 1960s and early 1970s. They started with emphases on collectivity and consensus of various degrees, but over time they moved to more hierarchy, whether planned or unplanned, or to representative rather than participatory democracy. In the Ohio women's movement described by Whittier, success in the form of outside funding contributed to hierarchy as core members of various organizations in the coalition became paid staff and were perceived by newer members as an elite with illegitimate power. For their part, older core members were frustrated with newer members, whom they saw as inexperienced and requiring induction into the organization at the cost of scarce time and energy. Differences in age, organizing experience, and knowledge led to difficulties in maintaining collective practices. Members of the Chicago Women's Liberation Union, many with previous experience in the New Left, recognized these problems and created mechanisms for organizational learning by new members (as Strobel recounts). The CWLU faced increasing needs for leadership, however, as the organizing involved more and more women. Although they hoped to retain democratic participation through adopting explicit structures of learning to organize and lead and to assure accountability for leaders and members, problems of participation were not completely solved, because participation demands intense involvement and large amounts of time. Women with family or other obligations often found such participation impossible, effectively barring them from membership.

These two examples illustrate the pressures toward conforming to what I have called a gendered logic of organization (Acker 1990). This logic of organization is an implicit blueprint for how things are to be arranged to produce an efficiently functioning whole; as such, it may include elements of bureaucracy. Fundamental to efficient functioning is an abstract, ostensibly gender-neutral worker whose central commitment is to the organization and who has no competing time or emotional obligations, such as those to children or spouses. This worker is, in reality, a man. Organizational logic is anchored in and helps to reproduce the fundamental structuring of industrial societies, in which the production of things and services for which money is exchanged is clearly separated in time, place, form of organization, and conceptualization from the reproduction of human beings and daily life. This division and the organizing practices that support it are deeply gendered, and include sets of taken-for-granted organizational practices that assume a male participant.

Although feminist and other alternative organizations have often tried to disrupt and replace this logic, pressures toward its re-creation are severe. Pressures are implicit in the reality of organizing within the structures of contemporary society, which operate according to this logic. Feminist organizing occurs in opposition to the existing ways of doing things. To oppose them, feminist organizing must contest in arenas in which hierarchy, divisions of labor, timing, and procedures are already defined. Potential members already have lives structured by previous organizational demands on their time and energy. Other organizations on which action for change must often be focused have *their* established and hierarchical ways of doing things. To survive, a feminist bank must provide services in accord with outside regulations to customers who have substantial resources and other organizational demands on their time, as Tom notes (Chapter 11). In doing so, the bank also accepts an implicit organizational logic that undermines its commitment to training low-income women for permanent jobs.

Pressures toward hierarchy and away from collective practices may be direct and overt, presented as conditions for receiving outside assistance or support (see, e.g., Ferguson 1984). The Chicago and Ohio cases, as well as the feminist bank, illustrate this point. As state funding becomes available, state agencies begin to define the conditions under which feminist organizations can be funded (see Martin 1992; Ferguson 1984, 221). Some of these conditions, as Matthews's study of rape crisis centers (Chapter 19) shows, directly undermine the collective practices of these centers and, over time, influence them to shift their focus from confronting oppressive gender relations to servicing victims of those relations. State support may be essential to the survival of feminist organizations, but it often undermines their intended goal.

This pervasive dilemma for feminist organizing is a consequence of relative powerlessness. Organizations of many kinds survive and prosper through a supportive and legitimating environment composed of other organizations (Perrow 1986; Granovetter 1990). Leaders of powerful organizations have complex linkages with leaders of other powerful organizations: for example, defense industry corporations have ties with the leaders of the military establishment. Most feminist organizations, in contrast, have few links with powerful sectors of the state, and they come with few resources for reciprocation to the funding agencies that exist. Consequently, the implicit rule for them may be "conform or die." These pressures may be ameliorated when feminists have been able to help create funding agencies and see to it that they are staffed by feminists (see H. Eisenstein 1991a, and Chapter 5). The existence of "femocrats" (H. Eisenstein 1991a) within state bureaucracies does not eliminate the contradiction but does begin to develop the sort of supportive and ideologically affirming organizational environment that promotes organizational survival, though probably often at the expense of participation by ordinary members.

It seems to me, on the basis of these studies and other evidence, that the ideals of completely egalitarian, collective decision-making and action are impossible to achieve over any substantial period of time, given the existing organizational structure of our society and the embeddedness of organizing efforts in that structure. This, I think, is due not to an iron law of hierarchy but to the historically contingent way that organizing has developed. Collective decision-making is impossible when there are large differences of knowledge and experience between participants, accompanied by time pressures for effective action. Excessive focus on internal processes to achieve consensus interferes with actions to achieve change in a world that does not wait (see Starr 1979). Some division of labor and allocation of authority and responsibility are necessary—given the social relations within which we are all embedded—to reach organizing goals. But, this does not mean that feminist organizers must abandon efforts to keep hierarchy to a minimum and create favorable conditions for democratic participation.

Certain conditions improve the possibilities for greater degrees of egalitarian participation in organizing. These include small group size, common goals (including the goal of equal participation), relatively equal knowledge and experience, individual members who are flexible and noncompetitive, and a benign organizational environment that supports participatory practices (Rothschild-Whitt and Whitt 1986). As Ferguson (1984) points out, there are examples, although they are rare, of flourishing cooperatives and collectives. In Sweden, where there has been a great deal of experimentation with work democracy, numerous flat, almost leaderless groups survive and work quite well (Acker 1994); however, although the members make small decisions about their daily work, they do not decide the big questions of product, technology, or larger organizational goals. In addition, working collectively requires tremendous energy and time, and members who lack these resources are disadvantaged relative to others. Though voluntary women's movement organizing is not the same as organizing paid work in the state or private corporations, some of the same pressures exist. I believe that it will take radical transformations of the entire society, which we cannot yet imagine, to create conditions that will support alternative and humane forms of organizing. In the meantime, the feminist image of nonoppressive organization can serve as an ideal against which to judge our actions.

Gender, Class, and Race in Women's/Feminist Organizing

Is it possible to create feminist organizing efforts that include as participants people from widely differing locations in the intersections of gender, race, ethnicity, and class? Differences in political issues and ideology, as well as differences in the sociopolitical climate of time and place, may create variations in the likelihood that people with disparate life situations will

come together. In the women's/feminist organizing described here, homogeneity along lines of class, race, political position, and sexual orientation
is pervasive. One reason is that all the organizations were local; organizing
was done through preexisting networks of friends, family, neighbors, co-
workers, or colleagues in other religious, political or social groups. Local
communities tend to be homogeneous in societies that are race and class
structured; friendship networks rarely stray across lines of class and race.

Moreover, the issues around which organizing occurred were often local
issues, increasing the saliency of organizing through local networks. Thus,
in Montgomery, Alabama, women organized through their personal grassroots networks and, along with other organizations, supported the bus
boycott. Barnett (Chapter 13) describes two class-homogeneous women's
organizations, both within the Black community: the Women's Political
Council was predominately middle class; the Club from Nowhere was
working class. In spite of class homogeneity, however, class barriers were
not rigid, and some women belonged to both organizations.

Pardo (Chapter 23) describes Latina activists who organized across
racial and ethnic lines, in one case because the community was multiethnic
and a local issue affected all residents. But such multiracial action is unique
among the organizing experiences reported in this volume. In Tom's study
of a feminist bank we see the dilemmas of class separation, and the life
circumstance and orientation differences that these entail, for the middle-
class women who ran the bank and the working-class women who were
supposed to receive training, skills, and support for a new way of life from
the program. The rape crisis centers discussed by Matthews were organized
along racial/ethnic lines.

The feminist coalition organizations in Chicago and Columbus, Ohio,
had predominantly young, white, and educationally advantaged members.
Efforts to involve women from other age, class, and racial locations were
unsuccessful. These two organizations differed in some important ways
in their feminist analysis, in their organizing strategies, and in the central
issues they tried to address, but they were similar in their white privilege.
Class, race, and age probably contributed to the resources of time and
energy that were necessary in these organizations. The Columbus coalition
moved more and more toward lesbian separatism, which may have been
possible partly because of race and class privileges. Although the essays
describing these organizations do not specifically comment on this issue, it
is probable that class and racial privileges, sometimes expressed in racist

ways, doomed any attempts to expand beyond their boundaries of race, class, and age homogeneity.

The Chicago Women's Liberation Union had some limited success in making coalitions with groups organized around other class and racial locations. Since the CWLU died in 1977, we do not know whether this strategy would have succeeded further. One surviving group, the Mothers of East Los Angeles, entered coalitions that crossed class and racial lines, as Pardo reports. Perhaps organizing coalitions is the best way to work together across lines of difference to reach shared goals (though Arnold, Chapter 18, notes their limitations as well). At present, the common bases of community and personal networks rarely exist, except in isolated places, for organizing people from disparate social locations (Zavella 1991). Of course, this issue has been widely discussed in the feminist movement and feminist scholarship (e.g., Collins 1990; Ferree and Hess 1985) and promises to remain problematic for activists.

Segregation along lines of sexual orientation is also evident in these stories of women's and feminist organizing. Except for the Chicago Women's Liberation Union, these organizations appear to have appealed primarily either to heterosexuals or to lesbians, but not to both. As sexual orientation became a political issue in the late 1970s and early 1980s, it, too, may have increased the difficulties of organizing in inclusive ways. At least, this seems to have been the case in Columbus, Ohio, and the Latinas in Los Angeles were apparently all heterosexual: the basis of their organizing was their identities as mothers and wives. (Of course, separation between lesbians and heterosexuals may have occurred in many other times and places, but invisibly, when lesbians could not acknowledge openly this aspect of their existence.)

In concluding these reflections, I want to look at organizational success and decline in these particular examples. All these organizations were successful for a time. Some faded away because they had met their limited goals. Other declined when their supportive organizational or state environments changed and state funding dried up. Still others were destroyed by political opponents. In Montgomery, Alabama, women leaders and activists in both organizations were subject to various forms of retaliation, including being fired from their jobs. The Women's Political Council stopped functioning when its leaders were investigated by a state committee; its members lost their college teaching jobs and had to leave the area to find employment. The reasons for the demise of the socialist-feminist

Chicago Women's Liberation Union are somewhat less clear (Strobel notes the differing interpretations, as does Echols 1989). Obviously a complex of ideological as well as organizing problems undermined the organization's functioning. Some participants and observers argue that a primary reason for its decline was debilitating argument over the correct political line fomented by various left sectarians who infiltrated the group, possibly at the behest of the FBI (see Echols 1989, 8, 136, 302, 330).

According to Echols (1989, 302 n. 26) the FBI stopped its surveillance of the women's movement in 1973, four years before the Chicago group folded. Because I am skeptical of this claim, however, I end on a cautionary note. Feminists who seek fundamental change should not underestimate the role of the FBI and other antiradical organizations in undermining civil rights, feminist, and socialist movements. New evidence is appearing even today about the extensive and successful efforts of the FBI against feminist organizing in the 1970s. What looked like organizing failures may have been, partially, the result of successful attacks. Many feminist organizations that survived enjoy relatively secure niches, with relatively safe activities, usually carried out through rather traditional organizational processes. But what happens when feminist organizing truly challenges the way things ordinarily are? FBI oppression may seem long ago and unlikely, now that the Cold War is over, but studies in this volume by Simonds, Hyde, and Marshall (Chapters 16, 20, 21) show that feminist organizations are still the objects of study, surveillance, and attack when they openly promote values and practices that antifeminist groups abhor.

CHAPTER 10

Organizational Learning in the Chicago Women's Liberation Union

■

MARGARET STROBEL

The Chicago Women's Liberation Union (CWLU) was a major force in the women's movement in Chicago in the first half of the 1970s.[1] Moreover, it influenced developments in other women's unions nationwide. Its eight-year existence, from its founding in 1969 to its dissolution in 1977, was longer than that of most of the dozen or so other women's unions sharing similar politics: a radical vision that came to be identified as socialist feminism (K. Hansen 1986; Strobel 1990).[2]

I utilize the example of the CWLU to examine how individuals learn about organizational process and structure, how they use that learning in organizations, and what structures organizations put in place to promote members' learning. When I refer to organizational learning—that is, learning about organization—I am referring to one of these three questions. The CWLU experience transformed the lives of women members; in addition to learning about organization, they learned significantly about themselves and the world. Here, however, I narrow my focus to learning that is related to issues of organization. From studies of the origins of second-wave feminism, we know that many of the women's liberationists of the late 1960s came from the civil rights movement, the New Left, Students for a Democratic Society (SDS) and other parts of the student movement, and the antiwar movement. These studies emphasize how women's liberationists took away ("learned") from these experiences the understanding that the male domination within society at large was also found in oppressive hierarchical organizations dedicated to achieving justice, equality, and freedom from oppression. I argue that those who formed the CWLU learned other, more positive, lessons about organization as well (K. Evans 1980).

My interest in working on the CWLU developed when I moved to Chicago in 1979 to become director of the Women's Studies Program at the

University of Illinois, Chicago Circle (as it was then named), and discovered over time that many of the women I worked with and liked had been
members of the CWLU. During the period of its existence I was a member
of the New American Movement in Los Angeles, a socialist feminist group
that shared the CWLU's politics in many ways. Hence I am both an insider
(in terms of shared beliefs, friendships, and the historical moment) and an
outsider (not a participant in CWLU events). The CWLU began placing its
documents in the Chicago Historical Society as early as 1973, which shows
an unusual self-consciousness of their role as agents of history compared
with other women's and radical organizations. I have used and added to
this archive. In addition, I have interviewed forty-six members and leaders
of the CWLU, many of them several times, as well as thirty-two members
of other women's unions, and two other individuals.[3] The forty-six CWLU
women are broadly representative of the organization's membership, num-
bering perhaps one-quarter to one-third of its most active members over
its lifetime.[4] They were involved in all the major and most of the minor
work groups, projects, and chapters. They represent all the major political persuasions. They were both leaders and followers, central and more
peripheral actors. They include heterosexuals, lesbians, and bisexuals. All
are European American except for one Asian American.

An Organizational Overview

The CWLU was founded in 1969 as an umbrella organization that brought
together individuals and groups of women who had been active in a variety
of activities: for example, consciousness raising, community organizing,
or underground abortions. The founders saw themselves as supporters of
women's liberation, as radical women who argued for tying women's issues
to other issues (such as the war in Indochina, Black liberation) and for
establishing a broad base among Black and White working-class women.
The CWLU's "Principles of Unity" stated a feminist, anticapitalist, anti-
racist position; a "gay principle" was added in 1972.

From its founding, the CWLU was structured to demand a great deal
of participation on the part of its members. Not uncommonly, a woman
who was involved in a CWLU project (called "work groups") was also
in another affinity grouping (called "chapters") for purposes of discussing CWLU business and personal development. The organization early on
rejected the impulse to form consciousness-raising groups, instead choosing to establish action projects. This preference for action, a New Left

legacy, characterized the Chicago union throughout its existence and differentiated it from others more theoretically oriented, such as the Berkeley-Oakland Women's Union (interviews: Lawhon, Ehrensaft). Indeed, the widely circulated paper for which the CWLU is best known, *Socialist Feminism: A Strategy for the Women's Movement*, was written as a strategy for and evaluation of direct action (Booth et al. 1972; CHS/1/7).

Members could select from a wide variety of work groups, which were classified as involving education, service, or direct action (these categories are further discussed below). Educational initiatives included public speaking engagements handled through the Speakers Bureau, courses offered through the Liberation School, and various newspapers. Organized earlier than most women's studies programs, the Liberation School offered a series of courses that enrolled about two hundred students per session. The Union produced several newspapers designed to interest women in women's liberation and in the CWLU itself. *Womankind* introduced women to various aspects of women's liberation, often linked to CWLU projects in health, employment, and so on. *Secret Storm*, named after the soap opera, had two incarnations, the first with a group organizing in a factory, and the second for those women who organized teams and challenged Chicago Park District discrimination against women. Later, *Blazing Star* was produced by and for the lesbian community.

Music, art, and film formed an early focus within the Union, crossing the categories of education and service. The Chicago Women's Liberation Rock Band, which made a record, played for fund-raising and other events. They "saw their role as both outreach [to diverse constituencies] . . . and internal unification and stabilization, scheduling dance concerts when they perceived conflict and low morale in the Union" (personal communication: Weisstein, August 26, 1993). Band members wrote a "Culture Paper" in which they assessed the sexism and insurgent potential of rock music and posited the role of such groups as theirs in advancing a visionary, socialist feminist movement (*CWLU Newsletter*, January 5, 1973, CHS/19/6; "Developing a Revolutionary Women's Culture" 1972). In addition, the Graphics Collective produced a wide range of posters and other materials, and CWLU members helped produce *The Chicago Maternity Center*, a film about the medical establishment's closing of a home-delivery center (interviews: Cooper, Davenport, Rohrer).

The CWLU provided various services for women, including pregnancy testing (in the days before kits were available at the local pharmacy), the Legal Clinic, and the Prison Project. The Legal Clinic offered legal advice,

primarily about simple divorces, plus some work on landlord-tenant problems (interviews: Pascal, Geraghty). Prison Project members did support
and advocacy work for female prisoners at Dwight Correctional Institution
and taught classes there.

Perhaps the most dramatic of the service projects under the Union's
umbrella was the Abortion Counseling Service, an underground abortion
collective some of whose members had helped found the CWLU. "The
Service," as they called themselves, later came to be popularly known as
"Jane." From 1969 to 1973, members performed an estimated 10,000 abortions and achieved a safety record better than or comparable to that of
licensed medical facilities in New York or California (Bart 1987; Schlesinger and Bart 1983; interview: Arcana).[5]

Jane was concerned with more than merely providing an immediate service, and the umbrella structure of the CWLU facilitated linking different
types of projects and forging connections across issues. For example, service members also taught courses on women's bodies and women's health
in the Liberation School (interview: Arcana). Then, after abortion was
legalized, the Abortion Counseling Service disbanded, and the Abortion
Task Force worked to ensure that Chicago area hospitals actually provided
safe abortions.[6]

Other CWLU direct action groups engaged in struggle to bring concrete
changes, not only service, as a strategy. Direct Action for Rights of Employment (DARE) had various incarnations. DARE women supported strikes
and organized in local factories. They lent support to African American
"janitresses" at City Hall and successfully joined with NOW to sue the
city for sex discrimination. Also as part of a direct action strategy, CWLU
members organized ACDC, the Action Coalition for Decent Childcare,
a multiracial coalition that succeeded in bringing about changes in city
codes regarding licensing of day care centers and gaining $1 million in state
funding for child care (interview: Booth).[7]

CWLU members often worked on one or more of these projects. If a
member was also in a chapter (the affinity-based group) or in a leadership
position or volunteering in the office, she could easily attend four or five
meetings a week. Although such a high level of participation made the
experience very intense for those who could maintain it, many women—
those with children and/or full-time jobs—found it hard to embrace so
heavy a commitment.

Thus, for all its theoretical understanding of the importance of reaching
working-class women and women of color, the CWLU was in fact rela-

tively homogeneous (see Rothschild-Whitt and Whitt 1986) in terms of age, race, and socioeconomic status (for comparison with Bread and Roses, see Popkin 1978). Over its lifetime, its membership hovered between 200 and 250 dues-paying individuals, of whom the members I interviewed are broadly representative. All forty-six were born between the years 1915 and 1954, with the median year being 1945. Except for one Asian American, all were European American, including a substantial Jewish contingent (43 percent). Although they tended to be single and childless, a large minority (35 percent) were married or were parents. A substantial portion were lesbian (39 percent) or bisexual (26 percent). Most grew up in suburban areas (54 percent, compared with 50 percent urban, 28 percent small town or rural), although a substantial minority reported their family as below middle class (17 percent working class, 28 percent lower middle class, 48 percent middle class, 24 percent upper middle class). The vast majority were getting or had received college degrees while in the CWLU (15 percent had only a high school diploma; 39 percent had a B.A. or B.S., 24 percent an M.A. or M.S., 15 percent a Ph.D. or equivalent). Their parents were relatively liberal but not radical (52 percent Democratic, 20 percent liberal; 24 percent Republican, 7 percent conservative; 7 percent socialist; 7 percent communist).[8] Despite periodic efforts to recruit beyond a homogeneous base, CWLU members remained concentrated in the Lake View and Hyde Park neighborhoods that were home to many progressives. This overall homogeneity hindered recruitment among women who did not fit the profile. For example, one older woman whose daughter had recommended that she "belong to the women's lib" did attend one meeting, she wrote to the CWLU, but decided that she wanted a group of women her own age.[9]

Although the Union had few women of color as members, it successfully worked in coalitions with Black and Latino organizations. The Abortion Task Force early on linked legal abortion with the need to stop sterilization abuse, a link that led the CWLU, the Puerto Rican Socialist Party, and Mujeres Latinas en Acción to form, in Chicago, the Coalition to End Sterilization Abuse. This coalition work resulted in other cooperation: in 1975 the Puerto Rican Socialist Party asked the CWLU to provide a speaker for its May Day celebration.[10] And in 1974 the CWLU organized a large and diverse coalition to celebrate International Women's Day, attracting nearly 4,000 people.[11]

The CWLU had little interest in employing mainstream structures or playing mainstream politics. Apart from the janitresses' case, which it undertook with the Chicago chapter of the National Organization for Women, the Union preferred to agitate rather than sue. The late Mayor Richard J. Daley's grip on the Chicago machine made work with reform politicians seem futile, even had the CWLU been ideologically predisposed to electoral politics, which it was not.[12]

What held all these disparate projects and affinity-based chapters together? Where did the vision come from for creating the CWLU as an umbrella with a unifying center? How did the CWLU develop new structures, approaches, and strategies? The answers to these questions lie in an exploration of organizational learning.

Structure, Change, and Organizational Learning

Organizational learning was evidenced in the CWLU in two ways. First, individuals used legacies from previous movement experience to shape the Union. Key founders brought from their prior SDS experience ideas about organization, structure, and accountable leadership. Second, the CWLU structured organizational learning into its processes through formal courses and elaborate evaluations of individual performance, actions, and programs. I examine several critical moments in the CWLU's development that illuminate both the lessons its members drew and the process by which the group approached making decisions, and I analyze the various mechanisms the CWLU used to foster organizational learning. In the latter analysis I look at mechanisms for skills transfer in, for example, the Speakers Bureau, the extensive practice of evaluation and criticism/self-criticism, and, finally, the CWLU's reflexive examination of its activity using a grid of education, service, and direct action.

NEW LEFT LEGACIES

The founders of the CWLU came out of the New Left and brought what they had learned from that experience. According to Wini Breines, "participatory democracy, small group consciousness raising, and the slogan 'the personal is political'" constitute the New Left legacy to the women's movement in general (1982, xiv). Specifically, several key founders of the CWLU came from SDS, a central New Left organization with national headquarters in Chicago after 1965 (Miller 1987, 235). Jo Freeman claims that "Chicago, more than any other city, had a movement almost entirely rooted in the New Left" (interview: Freeman).[13] The SDS and former SDS women who founded the CWLU came from the "Old Guard" period of

SDS, rather than its disintegrating, Weather Underground period; their experience in community organizing and other organizing gave them an appreciation of the need for organization, strategy, and program.

SDS moved into community organizing in summer 1964 with Economic and Research Action Projects (ERAP) in northern cities. ERAP sought to address urban poverty and powerlessness under the rubric of organizing "an interracial movement of the poor" (Gitlin 1987, 165–66; Miller 1987, 184–217).[14] SDS women had more organizing success than did the men. They had the one-on-one communication skills, and the women they talked to were rooted in the communities. In contrast, the men's constituency was largely guys on street corners—unemployed men, teenaged gang members or potential gang members—and the men's skills, such as speechmaking, were less significant in community organizing (S. Evans 1979, 145–55; Gitlin 1987, 366; Miller 1987, 203, 257).

Several women central to the CWLU's founding had been active in SDS and community organizing. Vivian Rothstein had worked earlier in JOIN—"Jobs or Income Now," Chicago's ERAP project.[15] Heather Tobis (now Heather Booth) worked in the Coordinating Council of Community Organizations and Student Nonviolent Coordinating Committee (SNCC) in Chicago.[16] Amy Kesselman worked as an organizer with Citizens for Independent Political Action, one of whose activities was to organize a community-based women's group. All were part of the Westside group, an informal gathering that met in Jo Freeman's apartment from approximately September 1967 to April 1968 (interview: Freeman).

The Westside group's legacy to the CWLU lay in the organizational structure that embodied principles of the women's liberation movement and New Left. Schooled in community organizing and other kinds of organizing, and in contrast to most other women's liberation organizers,[17] the CWLU founders sought to establish leadership positions that were accountable to the membership and also to develop democratically the capacity of many women to become leaders. CWLU members adopted a clear (if awkward and not completely effective) umbrella structure intended to assure democratic participation at a time when many women's liberation groups, chary of authoritarian structures, fell victim to the "tyranny of structurelessness" (Freeman 1973). And, in a critical early period, CWLU leaders, mindful of the collapse of SDS and seeking to preserve the integrity of their organization, affirmed its right to remain a multi-issue autonomous women's group and successfully avoided takeover by the Socialist Workers Party/Young Socialist Alliance.

The CWLU's unique and most valuable contribution to women's liberation was its notion of accountable leadership and structured democratic participation (see Sirianni 1993). Its leadership initially created a decentralized structure and modified the structure as their experiences warranted.

Those who attended the CWLU's founding conference established a structure involving a Steering Committee of representatives from each work project group and chapter, plus periodic citywide membership meetings at which policy decisions would be made. Thus, Steering Committee members represented only a minimal level of leadership; individuals voted directly on policy. But this structure proved unwieldy, because the Steering Committee was the only authorized group that could respond quickly to requests for endorsement of activities. Since it was not clear where the ultimate political authority lay, the Steering Committee devoted part of its July 1970 retreat to that issue. The chapters and work projects, committee members argued, were the "basic functioning units." The Steering Committee was largely an administrative and supervisory body whose task was to "guide the general policy and politics of CWLU activity." The citywide meeting was "a membership, action, and policy forum."[18] Whereas the Steering Committee was representative of the chapters, the citywide meetings provided at-large members who were not in chapters with a forum. In reality, both these types of members were part of the CWLU, but the tension between them continued throughout the life of the Union.

In addition to citywide meetings, at periodic conferences CWLU members evaluated the effectiveness of these structures and modified them over time, empowering leaders to speak and act for the benefit and in the name of the CWLU. Moreover, they strengthened representative, rather than direct, democracy by authorizing the Steering Committee—not only the general membership—to make policy decisions. By 1973 the organization had decided to elect co-chairs to provide accountable leadership beyond that of the Steering Committee. A year later a Planning Committee was established to do long-range planning for financial security and outreach, which often got lost amid everyday activity. At each of these levels of political responsibility, leaders were elected, given concrete tasks, and asked to report back to those who had elected them.

The question of defining membership emerged in the first year, and the debates surrounding this issue illustrate several points. First, the founding leaders with SDS and community organizing experience brought that experience to bear. Second, their definition of membership showed CWLU leaders' profound commitment to organizational learning, to the evaluation of past activity and redirection of effort based upon that evaluation.

At issue was who might attend the first annual membership conference in a decision-making capacity.

The 1971 conference was the first major conference since the CWLU's founding. The founders had negative past experiences with the Socialist Workers Party/Young Socialist Alliance, a Trotskyist organization: "The [SWP/YSA] would recruit people off the street to vote their way" (interview: anonymous). Hence the founders took decisive action to protect CWLU from what they saw as infiltration and takeover by the SWP/YSA.[19] As one member recalls, "A fundamental difference [between us and the SWP/YSA] involved our sense of sisterhood and sectarianism, so a small grouping decided to, in effect, go to war on this question. Not to move for exclusion on the basis they were SWP[/YSA] and fall into red-baiting,[20] but to try and figure out . . . a self-definition of what we stood for."

Laying out the philosophy that decisions and change should develop out of an organization's evaluation of its past activity, Vivian Rothstein argued that those attending should "be in similar places politically in order for discussions to get anywhere." People should come who had worked together and could therefore evaluate that work. Having done some work with the Union should be seen as a requirement for membership, and only those people should attend the spring 1971 conference.[21] Essentially labeling this notion as elitist, SWP/YSA supporters argued for very open criteria, based simply on agreement with the CWLU's political principles. Their statement appealed to notions of sisterhood and democracy: "Each woman's experience because she is a woman is valid and valuable for our movement. It is on the basis of our common experience *as women* that we must come together and not on the basis of some esoteric knowledge of the inner workings of a select group of active women" ("Position Paper #2," *CWLU Newsletter*, November 11, 1970, CHS/19/3). Ultimately, the membership voted in support of Rothstein's notion of a conference of members who shared and could evaluate activity instead of the broader SWP/YSA proposal (written communication: Wessel).

If the membership debate was a critical moment in which CWLU members learned about establishing organizational boundaries and debated issues of structure and democracy, it also contributed significantly to their understanding of how to organize. Because of their notions of sisterhood and commitment to inclusiveness, it was difficult to persuade union members to exclude other women, even on principled grounds. "People felt it was a terrible thing to ask them to do," explained one member. "As the vote came close, we felt an enormous pressure to move for that victory and didn't build enough of a core that in fact felt participatory enough and owning enough of the core decision. . . . We alienated people who were close to us, though we won the vote overwhelmingly. . . . I still feel, for the survival of the Women's Union, it was the right outcome." Reflecting on the episode, Heather Booth noted that "the questions of when [one is] organizing, creating a core of support, ensuring that friendship patterns reinforce political objectives, and keeping the human relationships primary—that lesson will stay with me for the rest of my life. It reinforced my antagonism to 'pure line' sectarianism."

In addition to establishing organizational boundaries by defining membership in terms of participation, the 1971 conference affirmed representative democracy (decision-making by the Steering Committee) over direct democracy (citywide votes on organizational matters). And, reflecting women's experiences in such large groups as SDS, they decided that "important decisions will be talked over in the small groups with women we work with and know, rather than made in large meetings in which many of us do not speak, or understand the procedure." [22]

Thus, CWLU members consciously learned from the experiences of those with prior organizational and movement experience, in terms of maintaining organizational integrity (preventing takeover by the SWP/YSA) and promoting internal democracy (ensuring representative democracy and small group structures).

In addition to voting changes in structure in 1971, CWLU members changed their attitude toward paid staff. From the beginning, the Union had a (barely) paid staff of one to three women, who coordinated activities of the various work groups and, with volunteer labor, produced a fairly regular monthly newsletter. "Initially," wrote Day Creamer (now Piercy) and Carole Whiteside, "we argued that since capitalism is so concerned with money, we should not be." Most workers were volunteers, since "paying someone to do it would be a new form of oppression." [23] Over time, however, members came to believe that paying staff made it possible for low-income women or single mothers to take these jobs and experience the benefits in terms of personal growth. They accepted a division of labor between paid staff and members, while clearly articulating expectations that chapters (but not work project groups) held some responsibility vis-à-vis routine maintenance of the organization. The Union staff echoed sentiments similar to those of Old Guard members of SDS regarding the importance of effective organization (Breines 1982, 76). In the words of staffer Betsy V., "If we don't deliver better than the institutions we are attempting to supplant, how are we going to make a revolution?" ("Please Note," *CWLU Newsletter*, May 1972, CHS/19/5).

The particular influence of the Chicago SDS/JOIN experience on the CWLU can be seen in differences between the Union and Bread and Roses, the more anarchistic Boston area group of similar politics, which was formed three months earlier in 1969 and collapsed much sooner (Popkin 1978, 1979). The two groups drew members from the same segment of the population in terms of age and ideology. But Bread and Roses members were suspicious of formal structure. Their structure, based upon primary affiliation with a small group, work groups, and mass meetings, did not include a formal center that held the organization together; formal leaders were not selected. In comparison with the CWLU's vast array of minutes of meetings (in some cases summarizing the statements of each person on each issue), Bread and Roses kept no minutes of meetings and had no organizational newsletter. Two part-time staffers were chosen by lottery from among members. Meredith Tax, who later joined the CWLU, summarized her Bread and Roses experience this way: "Inevitably, most of the real decision-making got done informally, . . . leading to a feeling of exclusion and resentment on the part of the majority and a feeling of overwhelming responsibility on the part of the informal leadership. I learned all about anarchism in practice in Bread and Roses; the experience turned me into a Leninist for a while. Fearing an SDS model of leadership, we fled from representatives and elections and ended up with de facto leadership of people who had the most experience and confidence: rule by friendship clique, a popular form of oligarchy in the feminist movement."[24]

The early membership of the CWLU drew upon the same kinds of women as Bread and Roses and other women's liberation groups around the country; indeed, two JOIN organizers became leaders in Bread and Roses. Yet Bread and Roses members did not draw the same conclusions as did the CWLU membership: to create accountable leadership, representative democratic committees, and membership based on shared political work.[25]

INTERNAL LEARNING PROCESSES

Organizational learning in the CWLU did not consist merely of heeding the political advice of more seasoned activists. As the organization evolved, its leaders and members adopted a number of procedures that institutionalized organizational learning. They established a Liberation School course on the political history of the CWLU in order to transmit to new members the lessons learned from their past CWLU work and struggle, as well as the policies of the Union. Both individuals and work projects as a whole were evaluated periodically in an effort to learn from experience and correct emerging problems. They drew upon Chairman Mao Tse-tung's notion of criticism/self-criticism, incorporating into each meeting an evaluation of self and of the group. As member Sarah Bornstein reported, "I've been through formal and informal constant appraisals of what I did, through criticism and self-criticism. I felt [that I was] held very accountable for my work in the Women's Union, more so than I've been on paid jobs" (interview: Bornstein; communication: Davenport; see also Rothschild 1986, 84–91). In addition, each work project published an elaborate evaluation in the newsletter for public discussion at the annual conference.

In its first year the CWLU developed an important schema for evaluating and analyzing its activity. In this analysis, the overall work of the Union was to be balanced in terms of education, service, and direct action. (As another example of organizational learning, this schema was adopted by other women's unions.) These three aspects were intended to be mutually supportive and to define success in relation to the CWLU's call for fundamental changes in U.S. society. Without taking direct action to challenge power, education and service activity could not bring about real change.[26] Without education, discrete actions could be viewed in isolation rather than seen as part of a broad strategy; in addition, education was necessary to change and deepen women's understanding of themselves and their world. The service component of the Union's work was intended to meet the real needs of women, but merely building counter-institutions nurtured the illusion that "problems can be solved in the spaces between existing institutions"; moreover, service-providing activities could not "alter the power relations if they [made] no demands on those in power" and hence needed to be combined with direct action (Booth et al. 1972, 14). Although the Union continued to experience the centrifugal force wherein women's intense identification with a particular project competed with their identification with the organization as a whole, the leadership attempted systematically to unify the organization by having members utilize the education/service/direct action schema to discuss the relationship of projects and chapters to one another and to the CWLU's overall program.

Members and leaders also built on their experiences to develop strategies for democratic participation. Initially, Steering Committee representatives rotated frequently, reflecting an implicit assumption that the role of the

Steering Committee was to be a conduit for information rather than a leadership and decision-making body; for the former purpose it was useful to rotate representatives, thus encouraging participation and familiarity with the larger group. In mid-1971, as the role of the Steering Committee became more important, the membership conference voted for staggered three-month terms (extended to six to nine months at the November 1972 annual conference), and the Steering Committee discussed the political implications of regular representation. Some women believed that requiring regular attendance by representatives was "anti-working class, because many women can't leave home regularly on every second Thursday." Yet irregular attendance made it hard for a woman to follow and contribute; therefore, others responded that her chapter or work group should bear the responsibility to "make it possible for her to come, doing child care, etc."[27] Ultimately, the CWLU was not able to address the kinds of problems that made it hard for some women to participate or to serve in leadership roles, but the Union did structure opportunities for members to learn concrete skills related to effective organizational work.

One such skill was public speaking. The CWLU established the Speakers Bureau in response to the barrage of requests for information about women's liberation. Within its first six months the bureau scheduled fifty speaking engagements and averaged twenty-three per month for some time after that.[28] Although the CWLU did not share the women's movement's suspicion of structure, it did reject the notion of media stars, and this attitude is reflected in its Speakers Bureau policy: everyone in the Union was expected to give speeches. Speaking engagements were rotated among chapters or work projects. The Speakers Bureau actively taught the public speaking skills necessary for spreading a message and building a movement (Strobel 1995). Women were sent in pairs to speaking engagements, and training sessions helped them learn and improve. They shared sample presentations for particular audiences and critiqued one another's efforts.

While training individuals, Union members learned from their experience and modified the speakers' policy over time. Replacing voluntarism with an expectation that everyone would learn to speak publicly helped members develop skills and self-confidence and ensured a basic level of political knowledge. Supporters saw this Speakers Bureau policy as "structur[ing] out elitism" and as evidence that not all structure was bad. Critics, however, labeled it as coercive and claimed that the rigid policy was blind to differences in people's abilities and placed "the need of developing our members before the need of making an impact on the audience" (Rothstein and Weisstein 1972).[29] By 1973 the policy was modified to make the elected co-chairs responsible for important media contacts and speaking engagements; and work project groups were responsible for speaking on their particular subject area.[30]

Training occurred in both the Liberation School and the various work projects. Liberation School courses included such practical skills as auto mechanics, which contributed significantly to women's sense of accomplishment even if they had little relation to building an organization. Classes in silk screening encouraged neophytes to learn how to produce inexpensive political art. Those who worked on the various newspapers learned writing and layout skills, typically by being paired with more experienced women and by rotating responsibilities. Other training included such technical skills as running pregnancy tests. In all these ways, CWLU members learned the skills needed to organize effectively around whatever goals the group established (written comments: Wessel, July 1992; interview: Davenport).

In both the definition of membership and the empowering of a representative Steering Committee over the general membership meeting, CWLU members rejected the notion of a barely involved but dues-paying membership and a leadership whose influence derived in part from the marginal involvement of the membership. In various decisions that empowered elected leaders (for example, creating co-chairs and a Planning Committee), union members sought to ensure accountable leaders. In their structures of evaluation, criticism, and mentoring, they sought both accountability and growth from themselves (Strobel 1995).

Lessons Learned and Not Learned

Staggenborg (Chapter 22) identifies various ways in which the CWLU was successful in terms of "mobilization outcomes and broader cultural outcomes," even if it "exerted little direct influence on public policy and accomplished none of its radical goals." Indeed, part of its success lies in the lessons about organization learned by members who went on to utilize the skills and ideas developed in the CWLU in other organizations, from women's studies programs to women's health groups.

There is not space to analyze in detail the lessons *not* learned by CWLU members, although these remain critical to the development of effective feminist organizations. Tensions existed between more feminist and more left-oriented members—for example over the Equal Rights Amendment (written communication: Weisstein, August 26, 1993). Like that of many other women's unions, the CWLU's demise was linked to an inability to deal with ideological heterogeneity within a left-feminist framework.[31]

Its other shortcomings are manifested in many other organizations. It tried to be, in Paul Starr's categories (1979), both an exemplary organization, "exemplify[ing] in its own structure and conduct an alternative set of ideals," and an adversary organization, "primarily concerned with altering the prevailing social order." This contradiction led the CWLU to try simultaneously to be an organization of organizers (of cadre) and an organization of the masses. For all its discussion of structure, it did not find a structure that was democratic and inclusive and also served the needs of people with minimal available time. The problem of how to integrate at-large members, who for lack of time or commitment never joined a particular work group, was never solved.

For all its energy, the CWLU never succeeded in broadening its base beyond a fairly narrow range of the population in terms of ethnicity, class, education level, and lifestyle. The enormous outlay of time that was expected of members built intense friendships but effectively limited the possibility of membership for many people. The intensity of relationships built solidarity but also created the sense of an in-group (Popkin 1978). Although the structures for evaluation contributed to members' learning from their own and other members' experiences, the requirement of active participation limited the extent to which CWLU members could learn from experiences of people outside the Union.

Further, largely because of the youth and countercultural orientation of its membership, the CWLU had unworkable notions about work and money. After a few months on the job, staffers, who claimed to have learned enormous amounts, would decide that it was time to move on to another position. People moved in and out of communities, barely there long enough to meet neighbors, much less develop roots upon which to build an organization based in neighborhoods. The idea of paying people to do political work was abhorrent initially and the Union included several voluntarily downwardly mobile individuals. The homogeneity of the group, which reinforced this countercultural ethos, contributed to its ineffectiveness in developing a movement in Chicago that could include working-class women who identified with neighborhoods and aspired to raise their standard of living.

Like other socialist organizations, the CWLU did not successfully communicate to the anticommunist/antisocialist society around it a compelling vision of democratic and feminist socialism.[32] The problem of developing a strategy that linked concrete reforms and victories to a larger goal of socialist transformation was not solved by the Union; neither was it solved by those who criticized the Union in its dying days for its lack of such a strategy for revolutionary change.

For all these shortcomings, the CWLU did bring some changes to the Chicago area. It helped keep a left-wing presence alive in the 1970s in the years following the end of the Vietnam War. It brought a socialist feminist perspective to the gay and lesbian rights movement. It strengthened reproductive rights activity in Chicago (see Staggenborg, Chapter 22). It helped win the janitresses' suit against the city.

Many women learned organizing skills they brought to later political work in Third World liberation, antiracism, disability rights, labor, community, peace, reproductive rights, lesbian, or other feminist activities. Thus the CWLU contributed leadership to various other progressive organizations. Many people I have interviewed comment upon the skills they learned in the Union, and, although I do not have a random sample, a remarkable number report that their present jobs embody the politics they held while in the CWLU (McAdam 1989). Membership in the CWLU affected some women's eventual career decisions. Some Jane workers went on to work in health care fields, for example (Schlesinger and Bart 1983). One woman found relevant to her later degree in marketing the collective decision-making that she had learned in the CWLU (interview: Kloiber). Others have gone into community organizing, labor organizing jobs, youth work, or nontraditional careers (interviews: Blacksin, Norris, Schmid, Hurst).

The impact on personal lives too is striking. One Jewish woman attributes her marriage to a Mexican American to the exposure she got in the CWLU to a broader range of people and cultures (interview: Morales). The radical questioning of heterosexuality generated by the women's liberation movement in the early 1970s occurred in the CWLU as well.[33] One woman who came out as a lesbian during her years in the Union says, "It gave me . . . the ability to be able to look a little deeper into myself and explore my own sexuality, which took a long time, a lot of years. But I felt that there was always a lot of support from the people in that group to figure out who you were" (interview: Maloney). Another lesbian agreed that as a married housewife with children, living in the suburbs at the time, she would not have come out as a lesbian without the CWLU. Although it was sometimes criticized by the lesbian separatist community as basically heterosexual (a claim the CWLU rejected), the Union provided her with space and acceptance that she did not find in the separatist community (*Secret Storm* group interview). The CWLU provided a deep sense of sisterhood. As one woman put it: "I grew very fond of all the women in the group. . . . They gave me a feeling of self-worth in being a woman. . . . I had never had [the camaraderie] from a group of women before, in high school, whatever. Women were just somebody you knew. This was the first time I could ever be close to women and not be afraid to tell them how I feel."

In retrospect, many view the Union as having been an appropriate vehicle for its time and its ending as closure on an intensely meaningful period, organizationally and personally.[34] In the words of former co-chair Jennifer Rohrer, "It had been for most of us, certainly for me, the most important organization for developing leadership, for transition from the left into the mainstream. . . . I have never felt more confident than I did then. Politics has never been more fun, and my social life has never been better than it was in the Women's Union." For most, the perspective on society learned in the CWLU—the importance of linking women's issues to those of people of color and the working class or poor people—remains, in Suzanne Davenport's words, "burned into your consciousness." That consciousness, along with the individual and organizational lessons learned, may turn out to be the CWLU's most important contribution to today's feminist movement.

Notes

Acknowledgments: Interviews and written communications are from Judith Arcana, Sarah Bornstein, Heather Booth, Victoria Cooper [Musselman], Suzanne Davenport, Diane Ehrensaft, Jo Freeman, Miriam Geraghty, Cady Hurst, Judith Kloiber, Jane Lawhon, Jean Maloney, Esther Moscow Morales, Coral Norris, Erica Pascal, Jennifer Rohrer, Margaret Schmid, Meredith Tax, Naomi Weisstein, and Elaine Wessel.

Many former CWLU members have commented on drafts of my research. I thank them and, for their comments on this article in particular, Judith Arcana, Bill Barclay, Heather Booth, Victoria Cooper, Suzanne Davenport, Myra Marx Ferree, Jo Freeman, Patricia Yancey Martin, Vivian Rothstein, and Elaine Wessel. The interpretation and any errors are my own. Carol Mueller suggested the phrase "organizational learning." Research was conducted with the assistance of University of Illinois at Chicago Campus Research Board grants and a National Endowment for the Humanities fellowship.

1. Because being identified as a socialist in the United States can be hazardous to one's livelihood, if not health, I have taken precautions in identifying individuals.

Those who, when I interviewed them, gave me permission to use their names are cited by name. Others whose names appear in CWLU documents are referred to by first name and last initial only. As a historian, I am uncomfortable with social scientists' notion of not naming individuals at all. The women I interviewed are not merely representatives of points of view; they are particular individuals who have gone on to do other things in their lives. I wish to preserve their identities both so that the reader can follow the thread of a particular person's contribution and ideas within the article and so that this part of their lives is not lost to the historical record. Unless otherwise noted, archival references are to files in the Chicago Historical Society (CHS), identified by box and folder number. These materials were indexed *after* I read them. With the assistance of Vickie Kukulski, I have tried to cite the present location of all the documents I use.

2. Briefly, socialist feminists shared with Marxists a critique of capitalism and the vision of a society in which resources would be broadly shared; however, they agreed with feminist critiques of the male bias in Marxist theory and socialist practice.

3. Quotations not cited from documents come from these interviews, conducted between 1986 and 1993. Transcripts are in the CWLU archive at the CHS.

4. In preparation for a reunion in 1984, former members compiled a list of 436 names, which represented everyone in the extant records and in the memory of people who had been in the Union; many were names of transitory members, however. One-third to one-quarter is my estimate.

5. As was the case with various CWLU projects, members often developed a more intense commitment to the project than to CWLU itself. Thus, the Service had a tenuous connection with the CWLU: often it did not send a representative to the Steering Committee; rather, the Steering Committee sent a representative to Jane's meetings (interview: Arcana). The CWLU staff took calls for Jane, which constituted, according to one log for a six-month period, one-third of calls to the CWLU office (CHS/6/8).

6. Reports for May 1973 program meeting, CHS/19/6; *CWLU Newsletter*, May 10, 1973. CWLU's health work evolved over time into the Health Evaluation and Referral Service (HERS), which continued into the late 1980s. Some members formed the Emma Goldman Women's Health Center.

7. CHS/22/1. Heather Booth indicated that it was the most multiracial group in which she has ever worked: about half the members were White, the other half were Black and Latina.

8. The percentages do not add up to 100 because not all respondents answered all questions, and often they reported occupying more than one category in the course of their membership in the CWLU.

9. Correspondence, S.B.M., October 21, 1970, CHS/5/7. One chapter consisted of older, white, working-class women, but it was atypical demographically (interview: Starr).

10. "CWLU Planning Committee Report—1975," CHS/4/7.

11. Report and evaluation, my files; interviews: Tax, Cooper.

12. Several CWLU members, however, were involved in Citizens for Independent Political Action (CIPA), which engaged in electoral campaigns as an organizing tool rather than with the expectation of winning power (personal communication: Kesselman and Weisstein, December 30, 1989).

13. Indeed, some contemporaries joked, "If you ever wondered what a female SDS would look like, check out the CWLU" ("Evaluation/History of the CWLU," p. 82, CHS/2/5–6).

14. Jennifer Frost, a graduate student in history at the University of Wisconsin, Madison, is researching these projects (Frost and Strobel forthcoming).

15. Interview: Rothstein. Vivian Rothstein was married to Richard Rothstein, whom Breines (1982, 60) credits with "one of the most extensive and damning accounts of participatory democracy in SDS." He argued that the dismantling of formal structures in an attempt to eliminate hierarchy led to, in Breines's paraphrase, "an elite not answerable to the membership."

16. Interview: Booth. Both Rothstein and Heather Booth were married to national SDS leaders who argued for more effective national structure and against excesses of participatory democracy (Miller 1987, 246–59, on Paul Booth).

17. Feminist organizations such as NOW adopted more traditional hierarchical structures. In contrast, women's liberation groups, organized by the younger branch of second-wave feminism, eschewed hierarchy and, often, formal structure itself (see Carden 1974; Freeman 1975).

18. "On the Issue of Structure," by Carole Whiteside, notes of July 10–11, 1970, Steering Committee retreat, mailed August 21, 1970, as a *CWLU Newsletter* (CHS/4/10).

19. SDS collapsed in the late 1960s, in part because of a takeover by the Progressive Labor Party; the Old Guard had already lost influence by then, and the CWLU founders were no longer close to SDS (interview: Booth; Breines 1982; Miller 1987). After the demise of the CWLU, a group of independent Marxist-Leninists who met and evaluated the CWLU, identified the SWP struggle as decisive in a different way, setting the tone for what they viewed as a pattern of anti-communism.

20. "Red-baiting" is the tactic of discrediting a person or group by linking them or their ideas with socialism or communism.

21. Vivian Rothstein position paper, endorsed by the Steering Committee for citywide discussion, *CWLU Newsletter*, November 11, 1970, CHS/19/3.

22. Karen W., "Report from the CWLU Conference"; and "Structural Decision Made at CWLU Conference April, 1971," *CWLU Newsletter*, April 1971, CHS/19/4.

23. "An Evolutionary Perspective," n.d. [1973], CHS/1/2.

24. Personal communication: Meredith Tax; a portion of this material appears in Tax 1988, 457–62.

25. Rothstein communication, July 17, 1993. According to Jennifer Frost (personal communication), ERAP women organizers left the other communities where

ERAP projects were begun; hence there is no way of studying, with a control group, whether SDS women with community organizing experience established groups similar to the CWLU in their notions of structure and organization. I have dropped my initial hypothesis, that community organizing experience was the definitive cause of the difference between Bread and Roses and the CWLU; the precise explanation for the difference is more complex and requires examination beyond the scope of this essay. Naomi Weisstein argues that Vivian Rothstein deserves much of the credit for the CWLU's structure of democratic, accountable leadership (personal communication, August 26, 1993).

26. These ideas were developed in *Socialist Feminism* (1972). One of its authors, Heather Booth, built upon the ideas of author and political strategist Andre Gorz (1967) (interview: Booth). Breines (1982, 102, 104–5) discusses the influence of Gorz's thinking on SDS.

27. "CWLU Steering Committee notes April 8/71," personal copy.

28. "State of the Union" [1970], CHS/4/4; 140 engagements from September 1970 to February 1971, conference packet April 1971, CHS/7/7.

29. Critics: "Reconsidering the Speakers [*sic*] Policy," Ellen A., Pat McG., Jody P., CHS/18/3.

30. Steering Committee minutes, March 15, 1973, CHS/5/1; *CWLU Newsletter*, March 19, 1973 CHS/19/6.

31. This issue, and the particular manifestation of it in the CWLU, is very complicated. Some former members believe the organization was infiltrated and broken up by *agents provocateur* of the federal government, who deliberately provoked ideological battles. Others, including independent Marxist-Leninists and one of the alleged agents, believe the CWLU foundered because it did not—for lack of more systematic study of Marxism, Leninism, and Maoism—have the appropriate strategy for bringing about the revolution. Still others felt that although the CWLU had met a need at a particular historical moment, they wished to participate in more mainstream organizations. See K. Hansen 1986 for the demise of the women's unions; for discussion of the difficulty of maintaining an ideologically diverse and democratically structured feminist organization, see Leidner 1991, 1993.

32. Suzanne Staggenborg (1989) minimizes, I believe mistakenly, the effect of being a socialist organization in the midst of a capitalist society and instead identifies organizational features in discussing the differences between the CWLU and Chicago NOW. She is correct, however, in pointing to NOW's ability to set priorities, in contrast to the CWLU's more voluntarist, experimental approach.

33. The CWLU managed to avoid the gay/straight split that fractured much of the movement. In the early 1970s, however, tensions arose over claims inside and outside the Union that lesbianism was the authentic expression of feminism (written communication: Weisstein, August 26, 1993).

34. Others see its demise as a result of political errors that could have been corrected (interview: Davenport).

Children of Our Culture?
Class, Power, and Learning in a Feminist Bank

■

ALLISON TOM

Feminists are increasingly trying to grapple with the ways that dominant feminist thought privileges the experiences of white, middle-class women, taking the meanings of their lives as if they were the meanings of women's lives in general (Spelman 1988; hooks 1990). Feminists trying to help other women have also had to confront the need for a deliberate theoretical perspective on their feminism and on the impact of their helping on others. As more and more feminist theorists have pointed out, treating "women" as if they were a homogeneous group covertly sets an agenda based on the experiences and orientations of the most powerful women in the category (Jaggar and Rothenberg 1984). Even the recognition of "difference" is problematic because it retains the implicit norm against which such differences are to be measured (Spelman 1988). Many feminist organizations that were founded by White, middle-class women with the resources and commitment to work for change take as a significant portion of their mission meeting the needs of low-income women and women of color (Spalter-Roth and Schreiber, Chapter 7). But how are such "needs" to be defined and, more significantly, by whom? Needs interpretation, rather than being a straightforward process, often involves a political struggle among competing interests that are based on gender, race, and class (N. Fraser 1989).

In this essay I present conflicts between groups of women in a feminist job training program and argue that the lack of a strong feminist theoretical position—specifically, a lack of a position on "difference," and a lack of clarity about what I call the "deliberate" requirement of helping relationships—drove conflict underground and undermined the well-intentioned efforts of job trainers.

In this feminist bank and the training program it established specifically to address the needs of low-income women, invoking a presumptively common womanhood was a way of privileging the perspective of the trainers over that of the trainees. The hidden assumptions were that the trainers could "speak for" the trainees and that the goal of the trainees was to emulate the trainers. Other organizations that wish to work "as women" and "for women," such as women's studies programs or rape crisis centers, have to struggle with problems similar to those facing this bank, particularly when power differences in their particular settings (between teachers and students or providers and clients) are reinforced by structured inequalities of race and class in the wider society. By exploring the perspectives of both the trainers and the trainees, I attempt to suggest the nature of the differences that the myth of a common female experience disguises.

The bank was not a collective and did not aspire to be one, but it did operate with the "flattened hierarchy" that is typical of many feminist organizations (Martin 1990a). Although it was therefore less self-conscious than some other feminist organizations about the power dynamics that characterized it, its founders were actively attempting to bring a form of feminist practice into banking, an area that is notoriously male dominated and insensitive to the needs of women and low-income people generally. The training program within the bank also faced structural constraints that were hardly unique. Educational programs are intrinsically limited as agencies of social change: they can offer personal gains for individuals but cannot change the occupational structure in which students seek work (Tom 1987).

Although trainers and trainees tended to blame each other for their difficulties, both were caught in a confusing tangle of good intentions, limited opportunities, and a system of structured inequalities. William Ryan (1976) describes as "victim-blaming" the attitudes that often develop in programs intended to change individuals. In an important sense, however, these trainers were not typical "victim blamers"; they had a sharp sense of the injustices of the economic system and of the inequalities between men and women. But they did not have a theory of how gender and class interacted in shaping women's experiences, and thus they took the category "women" as uniform rather than varied. The trainers' and trainees' different life situations and occupational expectations were not simply factors in an economic equation; both groups found meaning in these differences, attributed characteristics to each other on the basis of these meanings, and interacted in terms shaped by these attributions (see Tom 1986). What the bank's trainers lacked was a theory that allowed them to articulate these differences as more than individual preferences, shortcomings, or virtues. The trainers' analysis, though sophisticated enough to articulate a sense of women's general oppression, nonetheless lacked the depth that would have allowed them to face challenges to their program in a flexible way.

This research is based on ethnographic fieldwork carried out in the bank from February 1984 to February 1985. As a daily participant observer in the bank's activities, I worked closely with and interviewed all the trainers and trainees involved with the bank during this period. Between thirteen and twenty-one women worked there at any one time; four of these were trainers. Trainees' program entrance was staggered; one trainee graduated and a new one entered approximately every six weeks. I came to know fourteen trainees well during the fieldwork period; with others I was able to develop a less complete relationship. My data were the opinions and experiences of these fourteen trainees and the four trainers, supplemented by shorter interviews with and observations of other paid staff and trainees whose terms at the bank overlapped with mine for a short period. I also draw here on conversations with individuals associated with the bank's founding.

In what follows, I recount the history of the bank and its training program, and the paths that brought the trainers and trainees into the bank. I then turn to a more detailed examination of the way the trainers thought about the trainees and the training program, and the way the trainees thought about the trainers. Finally, I attempt to draw out some general issues of inclusiveness and power, in particular the importance of a theoretically strong feminist practice, in relation to teaching and learning in feminist organizations.

The Bank and the Training Program

There were two histories of the women's bank, one that I call the "official" history and one that I call the "dissenting" history.[1] The official history held that the bank had been founded by a group of women of roughly the same background and attitude as its current directors and staff; this was the view held, with some inconsistencies, by the staff I met. The dissenting historians argued that the organization and goals of the bank at the time of the study were directly antithetical to those of its founders and that the current manager had carried out a coup that had changed the focus.

The bank was founded in 1978. The official view held that the founders were a group of women employed in various "helping" occupations who were working with single mothers and others living in public housing. The dissenting view agreed that the idea for the bank was born in public housing, but it identified residents of the housing project, not the professionals assigned to help them, as the original founders. In this view, professional helpers came into the picture later, after residents themselves had conceived and nurtured the original plan.

This difference was not a simple one of determining who was responsible for the original idea of the bank; clearly the idea evolved over time. Rather, it was a fundamental difference over the purposes the bank was founded to fulfill. In the official history the goal of serving poor women—providing financial services and job training to low-income women—was merged with the goal of creating a financial institution that would serve as an advocate for all women in the financial world. In the dissenting history, issues such as providing small loans for household purchases and emergencies to women on fixed incomes dominated, and the needs of women with higher incomes were clearly secondary, if considered at all. Both histories maintained that the idea of a training program evolved, without conflict, out of the idea of a women's bank as the founders heard of other women's financial institutions that had received government funds and as they began to consider the other needs of the low-income population they were serving. In the opinion of both groups, these needs included financial services as well as job training.

The official and the dissenting histories differed in their view of how the training was to be accomplished. As it stood at the time of the study, the training was conceived of as services delivered to one group of women by another relatively distinct group. The dissenters argued that the original idea was to form a coalition of poor women who could help each other; control of the bank and the training program were to have remained in their hands. The dissenting historians did not play a role in the running of the bank at the time of the study. The official story of the gradual replacement of the original staff with new staff was that the original staff were "well-intentioned people who didn't know the first thing about banking." At the time of the study, three of the four staff came from banking backgrounds and none from the ranks of the women who were served by the training program.

Bank staff maintained their allegiance to the ideal of serving poor women through the bank's training program and special banking services, but they also expressed exasperation with the poor women's advocacy groups who criticized them for directing attention to professional women and "neglecting" the women the bank was created to serve. At the time of the study, the bank was structured as a nonprofit, board-directed organization, and the language of its goals directed equal attention to the needs of professional and higher-income women and to those of low-income women. The bank manager articulated a philosophy that the bank's purpose was to serve the needs of all women rather than the needs of a particular group of women; she did not distinguish ways in which these women's needs might be in conflict: "I always feel very good when women who do have options bank here because of the kind of objectives that the organization has; the stronger it is and becomes, the more capacity it has to do both the training and providing banking services to a number of different kinds of women for different reasons."

The training program was supported by federal government funds to prepare ten to fourteen women at a time for jobs as tellers, receptionists, secretaries, and loan clerks. The training was specifically aimed at "long-term unemployed" and "disadvantaged" women in the labor force. As a matter of policy, only unmarried (divorced or never married) mothers were accepted as trainees. The four permanent staff were also the trainers; the bulk of the daily work of the bank was done by the trainees. Both the training program and the bank were heavily dependent on government funding; in 1985, over 55 percent of the operating budget of the bank came from a single job-training grant.

The Trainers

Of the four trainers at the bank, only one, the manager, can be said to have come deliberately into the bank because of its feminist goals. Although the others also used the word "feminist" to describe themselves at the time of the study, they came because the bank offered them job opportunities they could not find elsewhere. These three women embraced the ideal of serving other women through their work at the bank, but they did not hold a clearly articulated view of feminism.

The manager was involved with the bank from its inception in 1978 (with a brief hiatus) through the fall of 1986, when she left to open an exclusive women's club offering health and beauty services to professional women in combination with a public restaurant. Her feminism must be deduced from her behavior as her discussion of feminism—like that of all of the staff—was limited to the occasional use of the word itself. She was generally credited with "saving" the bank. She had taken over as manager at a time of financial crisis and had aggressively promoted the bank and sought the government grants that allowed it to continue operating. Her management style could not be characterized as inclusive; she tended to make decisions by herself and to inform staff of them. For example, when she agreed to my research, she interviewed me, talked with me several times, and finally gave me a date to appear at the bank without discussing the decision with anyone else. Staff were not encouraged to solve problems with her in a team setting; they were expected either to leave problems for her to solve or to present her with suggested solutions for her approval or disapproval.

Within this frame, the three other staff expressed a tentative and unclear commitment to "feminist" goals. One staff member's comment illuminates the general lack of a clear perspective on what feminism might mean for the bank's practice: "When I first started, I kept thinking I'm working with a bunch of feminists, I gotta be careful, you know. I was even wondering which finger to wear a ring on, you know, and this kind of stuff, but then you realize that they're just women like me, they're not ardent women's libbers . . . you can get married and you can change your name."

These trainers frankly admitted that their reasons for joining the bank had little to do with feminist ideals. One commented that she took her job at the bank "because it was a job. I had no idea what the women's bank was. I had never heard of [the government project providing funding]. I didn't know anything about the training program. I moved to the city when I had considerable banking experience and no banks were hiring. . . . But I jumped on it, it was a full-time job and when I came to the city there was not jobs available . . . so I jumped on it as a job, knowing that I was overqualified and underpaid." Although at other times this woman demonstrated a strong commitment to the trainees and the training program, neither she nor her two colleagues had come to the bank with either a clearly articulated sense of themselves as feminists or of the intricacies of the power dynamics of the helping relationship. They set to work with great good will and energy but considerably less theoretical perspective on their task.

In general, the trainers had no general theory of how their actions fit into the larger picture of the society they were trying to change. They spoke vaguely of equal opportunity for women, building women's financial "presence" and sophistication, and offering a "chance" to trainees. But this vague sense of purpose offered them little defense when faced with some of the fundamental decisions of the organization—such as explaining the bank's refusal to grant joint checking accounts to women and their male partners, even though some women left the bank in order to have joint accounts with men. They were similarly limited in their perspective on what helping women different from themselves might entail. In general, they subscribed to personal or exceptionalist rather than global social explanations of the problems facing the trainees (W. Ryan 1976). This lack of a general theoretical perspective was aggravated by the trainers' busy schedules and the constant crises facing the bank.

The Trainees

The trainees were selected to participate in the bank's one-year program on the basis of their status as sole-support mothers, their need for job training, and their potential to benefit from the training. They had only vague conceptions of what being a teller meant but had high hopes for dramatic changes in their work opportunities; they also knew that the city generally offered no other training program. Under the arrangement of staggered entrance into the program, the bank was always able to draw upon the skills of more experienced trainees in carrying out its public tasks. New trainees quickly learned from more senior trainees how their terms of training would progress and what their range of options would be.

The fourteen trainees I observed most closely were all single mothers with children whose ages ranged from eighteen months to sixteen years. Most had one or two children, the majority of whom were between six and twelve years old. Half the trainees had become mothers before they were nineteen. Twelve had been married; for these women, divorce had been a major turningpoint in their lives. After a period of depression, they came to believe that divorce had been a positive experience for them, and they were committed to meeting their own needs and making their own decisions. Although all but one of the trainees had had previous labor market experience, divorce and motherhood had propelled them into seeing themselves as permanently in the labor force, as supporting their families—in short, as breadwinners. They expressed regret for what they had lost by becoming mothers so young but were also determined to take charge of their lives and genuinely enthusiastic about being self-supporting.

The trainees came into the program with perspectives on feminism that were even less clearly articulated than those of the three trainers just discussed. The difference between the trainees and the trainers came from the differences in their assessment of their life experiences and, most significantly, of their life chances. Although the trainers could evade the ways in which their practice might not adequately meet trainees' needs and might fail to take advantage of the differences in the trainees' experiences, trainees had less investment in such a perspective. Trainees needed to face the reality of the structural odds against them. They struggled with trainers to get them to acknowledge the reality of their situations and to shape the training program accordingly. This conflict was never played out openly in public discussions but was confined to individual struggles over issues such as rights to specific training opportunities or "problems" with trainees who "stepped out of place." Discussion of such issues were held in hushed tones between serving bank customers or at coffee and lunch breaks, rather than openly or in a group setting. Such talk carried the stigma of "gossip."

The Trainers' View of Trainees

The four trainers were different from each other in experience and perspective, but they shared certain views of the trainees. Two important commonalities were their understanding of the trainees as "women like themselves" at a lower level of development, which I call the *developmental assumption*; and their belief in their ability to understand and meet the trainees' needs, which they equated with their own understanding of what the organization needed to survive, which I call the *managerial imperative*.

The developmental assumption manifested itself in several ways. When the trainers were asked to reflect on the differences between themselves and the trainees, their analyses shifted quickly from identifying class as important to making attributions of individual deficiency. For example, the head trainer suggested that "the core staff had an initial aspiration to have a career, and I don't think the trainees did; I think the trainees expected to be taken care of. And I think that's evidenced by the fact that they all got married very young, had babies very young." This lack of what she also called "a more educated outlook" was further interpreted as evidence that the trainees had not come as far as trainers *down the same road*: they were on the same developmental trajectory; they simply were behind the trainers. The trainers felt that the trainees lacked "a desire to move forward," and that the trainers needed to foster their ambitions. As the assistant manager said, "They're going to have to learn to be more independent and do more things for themselves." Either the trainers were unable to see or the trainees were unable to convey the trainees' ambitions and goals for an independent future.

The training was expected to impart "work attitudes" such as proper dress for the office, office demeanor, norms of timeliness, and the like. As feminists the trainers felt ambivalent about insisting upon feminine styles of dress and demeanor, but as managers they believed they had a "realistic" notion of how to conform to the system. Their notion of what it meant to be a working mother presented itself in the framework of their own experiences of having a job and children, rather than that of the trainees' needs. For example, as one trainer commented, many trainees entering employment for the first time had to learn that "they don't have time to fix fresh vegetables for dinner every night. You might have to use frozen vegetables some of the time." This observation came from her own experience of what it meant for a mother to adjust to full-time employment, rather than from any trainee's expressed need or experience.

The managerial imperative meant that the interests of the bank as an organization were the first priority of the trainers. Because the bank's survival as an organization that "served women" was seen as necessary to all other goals, the trainees' immediate interests could be sacrificed for this end. For example, the bank's efforts to attract professional and self-employed women as clients meant that the trainer-managers felt compelled to maintain a competitively "professional" atmosphere and rapid service (short teller lines). The most efficient trainees were therefore often kept working as tellers rather than being moved on to other training positions, even though their future employability was thereby compromised. The program experienced difficulty placing its graduates in general. The rise of automatic teller machines was displacing those women already working in this low-wage, gender-stereotyped field, yet the training program was preparing women to enter this shrinking job market. The focus on meeting the need for bank staff through a rotating pool of trainees made it impossible for the bank managers to question seriously how the trainees were used and the benefits of the training to their future.

Ironically, as the bank's financial statements made clear, the government funds supporting the training program subsidized the bank. Since it could not have existed without the training program, the bank was in effect using training funds that targeted low-income women to sustain an organization increasingly dedicated to serving higher-income women. Any new services were developed to fit the trainers' image of what the bank needed to do to "serve women." The managers believed that providing (welfare) check cashing and loans of small amounts was all that the bank could do for low-income women, and no other avenues of service were explored. The trainees were not consulted about ideas for future bank services or their awareness of unmet needs.

Lack of awareness of the trainees' different life experiences as a potential resource for the bank was also evident in the trainers' reactions when one graduate of the program ran for membership on the bank's board of directors (all account holders were eligible to vote). The trainers were exasperated with her and angry when she was elected. They complained that although they had no objection to "some" trainees becoming board members, the graduate who was elected was "unreasonable" and "wanted to make trouble." Their belief that they were in a position to evaluate who would be a "good" member of the board reflected their conviction that they knew what was best for the bank.

The confluence of the managerial imperative with the developmental assumption led trainers to talk about trainees as if they were children of their own culture.[2] In the trainers' eyes, the goal of the program was to remedy whatever it was that kept the trainees from being like the trainers, rather than to help them to develop an agenda of their own. All decisions about the training program—times for meetings, work schedules, development of training opportunities, assignment to training posts—were made by the trainers alone; there was no real consultation with or participation by trainees. When the trainers were contemplating changing the hours of the training program, for example, the bank director articulated this scheme for including the trainees in the decision: "Use child psychology. Give them two choices, one of which they'd clearly prefer, and then let them think they've made their own decision. . . . They'll choose to come in early, and they won't kick so much because they'll have felt that they had some input."

Despite their control of the training program, the trainers felt overextended and inadequate. They recognized that the training they provided was often disorganized and haphazard, but they felt that they could not do more themselves. They had no time to reflect on the intricacies of the helping relationship and their responsibility to carry the power of their role carefully. They likewise never considered what the trainees could do for one another. The head trainer offered advice on dealing with credit agencies and other such matters, but when trainees offered each other similar advice, it was denigrated as "gossip" that interfered with their work. At the same time, one trainer felt that the advice-giving role she had unilaterally assumed was a distraction from her real purpose of teaching the women their jobs. It was a form of "mothering" that she would not have needed to do if they had not been "lacking."[3]

Thus the trainers saw the trainees as less advantaged but unproblematically different versions of themselves, as children are often seen, and were willing to impute to the trainees the same commitment to the survival of the bank as an institution that they themselves held. Rather than acknowledging differences as something that could be a challenge and a resource, they defined differences as deficiencies and as the source of demands on them that they were valiantly struggling to meet. They were too often exhausted, impatient, and manipulative, as parents often are. The lack of a feminist theory to support analysis of what differences meant in this context produced frustrations for the trainers that they blamed on the trainees.

The Trainees' View of Trainers

The reverse was also true: trainees blamed their frustrations on the trainers. In the trainees' eyes, the training program was an opportunity to learn work that would offer them more personal as well as more financial rewards than either their earlier work or their marriages had. They felt that they had been strengthened by the trials they had been through and had learned valuable lessons that they could share with other trainees. They were surprised to discover from more senior trainees that their opportunities were limited and that the program was not structured to allow them to share support freely among themselves.

Although the trainees' initial hopes for well-paying and satisfying jobs were high, by the time they finished the program, they had more concrete and less ambitious goals. As tellers, they found that the glamour of handling large sums of money quickly wore thin and that the responsibility of their position was more apparent than real. As the trainees progressed through the program, their ability to differentiate between jobs that had looked the same to them, such as bank telling and word processing, also grew. They were angry when the trainers failed to make the same distinctions or devalued the small chances they held dear. Thus, when a change of trainers caused one trainee to miss out on her coveted word processing assignment, she saw the director's effort to reassure her that she "really wouldn't like word processing anyway" as arrogant. The trainee continued to work as a teller but with ill grace, and her disappointment and anger at the trainers were labeled her "attitude problem."

She and her fellow trainees, however, wanted the training program to be a first step on the road to a new life, and many valued the program because "it showed me I had potential." The trainees stressed both the differences and the similarities between themselves and the staff. As one reviewed her experience, she noted that when she entered the program she had thought that "these women making $40,000 a year, you know, they don't give a hoot about us. But I don't, no more, I understand what they go through. . . . I understand that sometimes they have to, to look at us this way, to get what they want to, to get better things for us or to better things, to better the situation." She also understood the bank's need to refer to its trainees as "disadvantaged" in order to ensure the continued flow of training funds.

Nevertheless the trainers' disparaging attitudes to them were resented, as was the trainers' interference with the trainees' own support systems. Trainees mentioned over and over their sense that they had the resources and the understanding to help one another with their problems, and they saw the trainers as actively blocking such efforts. In one instance, a trainee "got into trouble" in some unspecified way for doing other trainees' income tax returns for them (on her own time), and she was prevented from doing so the following year.

Trainees saw their coming together in the program as an opportunity to learn from one another on a wide range of issues, not simply to focus narrowly on the skills needed to become bank tellers. They taught each other how to apply for subsidized housing, how to deal with issues that arose in their children's schools, and how to deal with ex-husbands and the legal system to get their child support payments. None of this was seen by the trainers as legitimate within the workplace, and they continually denigrated such activities as either fruitless "gossip" or troublemaking. Trainees wanted to share inside knowledge on how to live with the welfare stigma; in their eyes trainers were ignorant of the fact that such knowledge was even necessary, since, unlike all the trainees, none of the trainers had ever been on welfare.

In the view of the trainees, the program was missing an opportunity by not allowing trainees to construct support networks that could be useful to them in practical ways. When such mutual assistance was defined as a waste of time or an interference with "real" learning, the trainees felt that their skills were being overlooked and their needs ignored. One trainee commented on the trainers' perspective: "I think sometimes the program thinks that, okay, we've put a bunch of women in the same situation together, that should help them, but that's not enough. . . . You know, we can talk amongst ourselves, but our problems, there's no solution to it, because we don't have the time or we don't have the resources among us to do that. . . . So you have to do it on your lunchtime or [when there's a minute], and because you don't have much time to talk, well, it takes a long time before you start talking to somebody about this, because you don't know, really know anybody." Since the trainers were not seen as capable of "helping" them, what the trainees wanted from the trainers was acknowledgment that their mutual assistance was a necessary and valuable part of "training for self-sufficiency." But that would have demanded that the trainers admit the limits of what they could do for the trainees.

Unlike the trainers, the trainees had an acute sense of themselves as being different. The trainers spoke of the trainees as women who might have been like them if they had not made some unfortunate early choices, but the trainees saw the trainers as coming from a different world with wholly different priorities and experiences as women. Generally, they expressed the differences in terms of class, seeing the trainers as women "who make $40,000 a year and don't care."

The process of the training program tended to bring the trainees closer to the perspective that there was a common womanhood and some shared interests between themselves and women whom they had initially perceived as alien and indifferent or even threatening; some tentatively used the label "feminist" for themselves. But the trainees' perception of some common gender interests did not erase their continued belief in fundamental differences and their abiding skepticism as to whether the trainers could understand or care about them. They often said they did not understand the trainers, yet their understanding of the contradictions facing the trainers may have been greater than the trainers' comprehension of the situation.

Conclusion

In this case of a training program for low-income women, the trainees were more willing and able than the feminist trainers to critique the program's limitations. The trainers focused their energy on defending their good intentions and demonstrating how hard they worked, rather than on creating mechanisms that would encourage more input from the trainees. One consequence was unnecessary distance between the two groups and a waste of scarce resources. Because the trainers believed that all learning in the setting had to be structured by them, they were resistant to hearing trainees' suggestions for diverse learning opportunities. If the trainers could have believed as much as the trainees did in what the trainees had to offer one another, they might have been more willing to allow trainees to help and teach each other.

The trainers lacked a clear philosophy of themselves as feminists and their practice as feminist "helpers." Their identification of themselves as feminist was not grounded in a theory of women's oppression through which they could work out conflicts that arose in the training program. The trainers' feminism was a fragile veneer, which they were afraid to expose to the difficult and necessary strains of challenges from the trainees and from advocates in the larger women's community. Their fragile theoretical position left them in a defensive position from which they were unable to find places to grapple with the difficult issues that arose in their practice. In the context of the unquestioned managerial imperative, conflict threatened rather than enriched their practice and was consequently driven underground. Trainers expressed their sense of conflict and frustration as frustration with the trainees as individuals; trainees likewise often turned their frustration on the trainers. Trainers and trainees shared a vague sense that the program had somehow failed to deliver the promised changes in trainees' lives. Lacking a clear vision of how they were challenging society, the women in this program were unable to articulate their conflicts in a way that would have allowed them to challenge broader social inequalities.

The critique that is increasingly leveled at white women's feminist organizations by women of color can be shown to be relevant in this setting as well. The "ownership" of an organization and the managerial imperative that goes with it block real communication and genuine inclusiveness. Differences based in class and culture, like differences based on race, provide obstacles that feminist organizations are learning only slowly and with difficulty to navigate. My research suggests that this learning process could be facilitated if the perspectives of women in subordinated groups were heard with less defensiveness and more commitment to genuinely mutual efforts.

Notes

Acknowledgments: I am grateful to Myra Marx Ferree for her assistance on this chapter and to Patricia Martin and Judith Lorber for comments on earlier drafts.

1. I learned the official history from current bank staff. I was alerted to the dissenting history in talks with former board members. Thus informed, I was able to discern ways in which current staff also acknowledged the divergent stories of the bank's inception.

2. This is not to suggest that I believe the way they approached the trainees is an acceptable way to treat children.

3. At one point when I was negotiating my contribution to the bank with the manager, she suggested that I could do some teaching. I proposed meeting regularly with the trainees to discuss issues they were concerned with and to work on strategies to learn more about how they could approach these issues. The manager requested that I instead "deliver" a prepackaged "life skills" course that she thought was more suited to their needs. In the end I did not teach, not wanting to reinforce their "top-down" approach.

CHAPTER 12

Turning It Over:
Personnel Change in the Columbus, Ohio,
Women's Movement, 1969–1984

■

NANCY WHITTIER

Women's movement organizations often endure for many years or even decades, but their personnel changes as new members continually enter and old members leave. How does turnover in membership affect women's movement organizations? This case study of a cluster of such organizations in Columbus, Ohio, between 1969 and 1984 examines the effects of the entry and exit of successive cohorts of activists. The organizations changed gradually as they emerged in the late 1960s, peaked in the mid-1970s, and declined in the early 1980s. As successive waves of activists gained influence, new organizations began, existing organizations changed or disbanded, and conflicts developed among feminists who entered the women's movement at different times. Although turnover in membership was not the only factor that shaped the course of women's movement organizations in Columbus during this period, it helps explain change and conflict in women's movement organizations.

My analysis draws on political generations theory, the major theoretical perspective that addresses the impact of changing personnel on social institutions. Theorists working in the tradition of Mannheim (1952) define a "political generation" as a group that experiences shared formative social conditions at approximately the same point in their lives and that holds a common interpretive framework shaped by historical circumstances (Braungart and Braungart 1984). A generation is not simply people of the same age, then, but rather a group bound together by a shared perspective on the world which arises from their common social location (Schneider 1988). The major difference between political generations is their outlook on the world, which social movements theory has conceptualized as their collective identity. Collective identity refers to a group's understanding of itself and its conditions, and it is constructed through interaction within movement contexts (Cohen 1985; Melucci 1989; Taylor and Whittier 1993). Applied to social movements, political generations theory suggests that activists who entered the women's movement at different times experienced distinct politicizing experiences that shaped their collective identities and thus their perspectives on movement organizations and social change. As each cohort gained influence in women's movement organizations, it reshaped the organizations' culture, ideology, strategies, and tactics.

Building on political generations theory, I have coined the term "micro-cohort" to describe small-scale variations among participants in the women's movement at different times between 1969 and 1984. Micro-cohorts are groups of participants with distinct formative experiences and collective identities that emerge at and shape distinct phases of the women's movement. Each micro-cohort entered the women's movement at a specific point in its history, engaged in different social movement activities, had a characteristic political culture, and modified feminist collective identity. Micro-cohorts differed from one another because they were politicized at different times. The women's movement in Columbus experienced rapid turnover in its leadership and core membership throughout the 1970s, and new micro-cohorts emerged every two to three years. Many feminist collectives, in order to prevent the formation of an elite within the movement, specified that key leadership positions could not be held by one individual for more than one or two years. Even in organizations that did not formally require the rotation of positions, leaders regularly "burned out" or were attacked and forced from their positions, thus creating a similar effect. In addition, a movement that is centered on a university, as in Columbus, has an almost automatic turnover in membership as participants graduate or move on.

My analysis employs two types of data. First, documentary and archival sources include the papers of the Women's Action Collective (an umbrella organization founded in 1971 that brought together many of the key women's movement groups and individuals in Columbus), personal files and correspondence provided by some respondents, and reports of women's movement activity in the Ohio State University newspaper, the *Lantern*. Second, I conducted thirty-four in-depth interviews with participants in the Columbus women's movement of the 1970s. The respondents were core activists in various groups, including the Women's Action Collective, Women Against Rape, OSU Women's Liberation, Lesbian Peer Support, Central Ohio Lesbians, the National Organization for Women, and OSU Women's Studies. The interviews were open-ended and semi-structured, lasting from forty-five minutes to four hours, most approximately an hour and a half; they were tape-recorded and transcribed in full. Thirty-three of the women interviewed were White and one was Latina. Their ages ranged from thirty-three to eighty-four years, with an average age of forty-five. Ten women identified themselves as heterosexual, twenty-one as lesbian, two as bisexual; one did not disclose her sexual orientation. The year in which they first participated in the women's movement ranged from the 1940s to 1976, with all but two of the respondents becoming involved between 1969 and 1976.

The Columbus Context

Studies of the women's movement in the Midwest are rare. Most previous researchers have focused on New York, Washington, D.C., San Francisco, and Chicago (Carden 1974; Freeman 1975; Cassell 1977; Echols 1989). Yet much nationally significant activism began at the grassroots, pointing to the need for local studies (Isserman 1989). The women's movement in Columbus was large and active; it proved important to the larger national movement, providing influential personnel as well as ideological and tactical innovations that were widely adopted and remain significant.

During the late 1960s and the 1970s the policy wing of the women's movement was relatively small in Columbus, because conservative Republican state and city administrations kept most policy goals out of reach for feminist activists. For example, when activists sought to establish an Ohio Commission on the Status of Women, Governor James Rhodes refused to authorize its creation, making Ohio the only state without an official commission. As a result of such opposition, the most vital feminist organizing occurred outside the realm of state government, both in autonomous feminist organizations and at Ohio State University. There was a small group of feminists working on policy questions, notably the Equal Rights Amendment, but they remained less influential than other segments of the women's movement in the state until the 1980s.

Because the policy arena was inaccessible, radical feminist collectives remained vital into the late 1970s and early 1980s. These organizations, rather than those working in the policy arena, are my focus here. This analysis addresses organizations that worked for feminist goals, saw themselves as part of the women's movement, and defined themselves as "radical feminist," regardless of their goals or tactics (Martin 1990b). They often worked in coalition with other organizations to achieve the reform of dominant institutions, however, particularly the establishment of Women's Studies at Ohio State University. In fact, many of the people who protested in support of the women's studies program, lobbied for feminist delegates to the 1977 International Women's Year conference in Houston, and worked for the ratification of the ERA also worked in what they considered radical feminist projects, such as consciousness-raising (CR) groups, lesbian counseling, demonstrations against sexist advertising, and rape crisis centers. Although I focus on women's movement organizations that described themselves as "radical feminist," there was often no sharp distinction between the liberal and radical wings of the women's movement.

The case study of the Columbus, Ohio, women's movement suggests four micro-cohorts. *Initiators* entered the women's movement as new organizations were emerging in 1969 and 1970 and shaped their course through 1971. *Founders* entered in late 1970 and 1971 and established lasting organizations in 1972 and 1973. *Joiners* entered the movement during the highly mobilized years between 1974 and 1976 and, together with founders, were influential through 1978. *Sustainers* entered women's movement organizations between 1977 and 1979, as mobilization was decreasing, and maintained organizations from 1979 through 1984. The following sections describe the organizational changes that occurred during the period when each micro-cohort came to prominence and document the impact of personnel turnover on those changes.

Emergence

The years between 1967 and 1971 saw the beginning of the women's liberation movement in Columbus. The first organization, Columbus-OSU Women's Liberation, was founded during that period, and two ad hoc organizations associated with Ohio State University—the Women's Studies Ad Hoc Committee and the Columbus Women's Media Co-operative—were established. Using demonstrations, guerrilla theater, and direct action tactics, as well as negotiation with university officials, these organizations pressed for an end to sex discrimination at the university, abortion rights, birth control, child care, the establishment of a women's studies program, and positive media representations of women. None established formal structures during these years and, despite the large numbers of women involved, none possessed notable financial resources.

Numerous works on the resurgence of feminist activism in the late 1960s indicate that radical feminism grew from the civil rights and New Left movements beginning around 1967 (Carden 1974; Freeman 1975; Cassell 1977; S. Evans 1979; Echols 1989). Women's liberation in Columbus emerged from the New Left later than it did nationally, yet the patterns of recruitment and mobilization were quite similar. In the spring of 1970 a group of women began holding consciousness-raising (CR) meetings and formed Columbus-OSU Women's Liberation (WL). As in other locations, the first wave of activists had been part of the civil rights, antiwar, and student movements and began to work for women's liberation because of dissatisfaction with male dominance and the lack of attention to women's issues in other movements. This first cohort of women's movement activists, whom I have termed "initiators," served primarily to raise issues, develop and make visible a critique of the status quo, form initial organizations and networks, and articulate the issues that initially mobilized feminists into action.

The emerging women's liberation movement in Columbus retained close organizational and cultural ties to the mixed-sex New Left. Shortly after WL began to meet, it joined a coalition of New Left groups that called a student strike at Ohio State University in the wake of the Kent State shootings; after the strike, women's and mixed-sex organizations continued to cooperate on issues such as the establishment of a campus child care center (Wilkey n.d.). The culture of WL emphasized militant tactics and the willingness "to put your body on the line." An awareness of FBI infiltration and surveillance pervaded the consciousness of early feminists, most of whom brought up the question of informants in WL during their interviews. Later entrants did not generally share this culture; one woman who entered the movement in late 1970 described the earliest activists as "too wild for me." Early feminist activist Carol Anne Douglas (1990) suggests that this distinction existed nationally: "Those of us who were politicized in those years feel a depth of alienation, a sense of ourselves as revolutionaries, that seems a little different from the feelings of many radical feminists who were politicized at a later period. We were aware that state violence could be turned against us." The unrelated murders of two Columbus feminist activists (apparently by their male companions) added to the sense of being under attack.

Because initiators were first politicized in the New Left and civil rights movements, their collective identity reflected the links between the women's movement and the mixed-sex left. Most activists described themselves as "women's liberationists," drawing on the terminology of the Black liberation movement (S. Evans 1979). They viewed themselves as part of a broad struggle against oppression in all its forms and talked about themselves as "sisters" to all women, writing, for example, about the need to cooperate with "our sisters in the North Side Welfare Rights Organization."[1] The major conflicts in this period were over *how* closely WL should be linked to other struggles. In August 1970, a few months after WL was founded, some activists split off to form a more "politically oriented group." They criticized WL for focusing excessively on "making life more comfortable for white middle-class women," instead of liberating women of all classes. This "politico-feminist" split mirrored conflicts in the women's movement nationally (Echols 1989).

The organizations begun in 1969 and 1970 were informally structured and did not last beyond the first few years of the movement. But consciousness-raising groups organized by WL (often called "rap" groups) brought in a new cohort of activists. Whereas initiators were closely tied to the student movement, and thus their demands focused on conditions for women at the university, incoming activists were less willing to work primarily within OSU or under the constraints the university imposed on student organizations; they were more interested in forming autonomous women's organizations. Echols (1989) found in her study of the radical feminist movement nationwide that the earliest activists left the organizations they established in the early 1970s and were replaced by others with a different collective identity. In Columbus, many members of the initiator micro-cohort moved out of town as they graduated from school or took other jobs, thus opening a space for newer feminists to organize. Other initiators remained active but took a back seat to newer activists as women's movement organizations proliferated and became institutionalized in the early 1970s.

Growth

In 1972 and 1973 members of a WL-organized consciousness-raising group founded formally structured organizations that later became the mass organizations of the mid-1970s. Most of the new organizations were part of the Women's Action Collective (WAC), an umbrella group founded in late 1971 and early 1972 that included a variety of autonomous member groups. WAC was founded with the stated goals of developing radical feminist theory, providing feminist services to women, and establishing feminist businesses; it saw these tasks as steps toward societal transformation. Member groups sought to develop alternative feminist institutions that could provide women with new skills, services, and autonomy. Toward this end their tactics included demonstrations, educational forums, discussion and study groups, and direct services. In 1972 and 1973 members included the Women's Co-op Garage, which taught women automechanics and provided tools and garage space; the Legal Action Group; the Women's Community Development Fund, which provided start-up money for new organizations; Women Against Rape, which focused on establishing a rape crisis hotline; the Women's Publishing Group, which compiled a bibliography of non-sexist children's literature; and Women's Health Action, which referred women to health practitioners. From its inception, WAC and member organizations made decisions by consensus and were rigorously collective in structure, rotating key tasks and leadership positions (Rothschild-Whitt 1979). During its first two years WAC possessed no financial resources beyond small donations from individuals, and relied on its members' volunteer time.

Virtually all writing on the women's movement of the late 1960s and early 1970s posits a division into two wings: a liberal wing that grew from the President's Commission on the Status of Women and was composed of older women, and a radical wing that emerged from the New Left movements and was staffed by younger, college women (Freeman 1975). In Columbus, however, the two wings of the movement overlapped far more than other studies suggest. WAC and its members were central to the burgeoning campaign to establish a women's studies program at OSU; in their demand for women's studies courses, student and community radicals joined women faculty and administrators. Although members of WAC and WL used disruptive tactics such as demonstrations, while faculty and administrators took a more moderate stance with university officials, they coordinated their tactics with each other in what one participant described as a "good cop, bad cop" strategy. "Liberal" and "radical" feminists worked cooperatively toward the same goal.

The founders of feminist organizations ranging from the Women's Action Collective to the Women's Studies Ad Hoc Committee saw themselves as a distinct group within the larger movement, as one explained: "It seemed like there was just one group of people who were starting everything. Maybe I'm misguided, but I don't think there was that much going on then other than the things that we were doing. There was the Music Union, there was the Action Collective, and Women Against Rape, and

Women's Studies. . . . It was all sort of a cohort of people that were doing it all at once."

I have termed "founders" this micro-cohort of activists who entered the movement after initial activism had begun but before lasting institutions had developed. They translated the ideas, dissatisfaction, and ad hoc organizations begun by initiators into lasting feminist institutions. This was possible because of the organizational foundation and social changes brought about by initiators. One member of the WL-sponsored Rap Group Number One explained how this CR group led to the establishment of other organizations: "Our CR group had a lot of people who had lots of leadership skills, and we tended to branch out and start projects. We met for about three and a half years once a week, and then we were activists the rest of the week doing other projects. . . . It's from that group that a lot of projects began." Many of WL's initial demands, such as the availability of birth control to unmarried women at the student health center, the establishment of a campus day care center, and legalization of abortion had been met by 1972 or 1973. Feminists were then freed to focus on a wide variety of other issues, including the establishment of alternative institutions.

While the women's movement remained politically aligned with the New Left on many issues, it diverged culturally. Women-only events and activities increased. Although membership remained decidedly mixed in sexual orientation, lesbians became increasingly visible. Growing numbers of activists in women's movement organizations came out as lesbian, some before joining feminist groups and others as an outgrowth of their feminist activism. An explicitly lesbian organization, Gay Women's Peer Counseling (later Lesbian Peer Support) emerged in 1973, which helped politicize lesbians and encourage feminists to be open about their sexual orientation.

It was during these years that the term "radical feminist" began to be used to describe individuals and organizations. This signified an important shift in collective identity from "women's liberationist," with its link to the New Left, to an emphasis on building an autonomous feminist movement and women's institutions. The use of alternative institution-building as a strategy, the increasing cultural distance between the women's movement and the New Left, and the growing lesbian presence in women's movement organizations all linked radical feminist collective identity more closely with separatism. As a result, WAC was poised for its subsequent growth into an extensive "women's world."

The Feminist Heyday, 1974–1978

In the mid-1970s the women's movement underwent rapid expansion. Organizations expanded, membership grew, and substantial funds poured in from outside sources (Carden 1974; Ferree and Hess 1985; Mansbridge 1986; Buechler 1990b; Staggenborg 1991). In the national political arena the fight to ratify the Equal Rights Amendment drew together feminists of all varieties (Ryan 1992). In Columbus, however, the policy arena remained a hostile one. The Ohio legislature ratified the ERA in 1974 at the end of Democratic Governor John Gilligan's one term, but during the remainder of the 1970s the state and local administrations were controlled by conservative Republicans, and gains were few. Nevertheless, outside the policy arena feminist service and cultural organizations flourished. New organizations founded in Columbus between 1974 and 1978 included Central Ohio Lesbians, a concert production company called the Women's Music Union, and four member groups of WAC: Single Mothers' Support Group, Women's Broadcasting Group, *Womansong* newspaper, and Fan the Flames Feminist Bookstore.

More striking than the emergence of new organizations, however, was the expansion of existing ones. The Women's Action Collective incorporated as a nonprofit corporation in July 1974; it established a formal structure with officers and trustees from each member organization and adopted a statement of philosophy.[2] Member organizations, able to receive tax-exempt status under the collective's umbrella incorporation, contributed a percentage of their earnings to the Women's Community Development Fund, which provided seed money for new organizations. Women Against Rape (WAR), a member group of WAC, moved its hotline from a member's house to an office and began rape prevention programs; the Women's Co-op Garage, another member of WAC, rented a garage and purchased a wide selection of tools; the newspaper *Womansong* published regularly; and support and advocacy groups for single mothers and for lesbians thrived within WAC. The former Gay Women's Peer Counseling changed its name to Lesbian Peer Support and joined WAC. Outside WAC, Central Ohio Lesbians (COL) and the Women's Music Union both sponsored frequent events and drew in large numbers of new feminists.

An influx of resources permitted much of this expansion. In 1976, WAR received a grant from the National Institutes of Mental Health (NIMH) for research on community rape prevention (called Community Action Strategies to Stop Rape, or CASSR). The grant amounted to $425,000 over four years and included funding for indirect costs, which went to WAC as the sponsoring organization. This money enabled WAC to hire staff and rent a house that served as a geographical center for the feminist community and gave member organizations meeting space, access to office facilities, and a measure of legitimacy. For example, Fan the Flames Feminist Bookstore, after finding a permanent location in the WAC house, greatly expanded its stock and business.

Large numbers of new activists entered the women's movement between 1974 and 1976. I have called this micro-cohort "joiners," since they primarily expanded existing organizations. Most of the joiners I interviewed were first politicized in the women's movement, unlike members of earlier micro-cohorts, who had often had experience in other social movements. Although most founders continued to play central roles in the organizations they had begun, participants drew a distinction between the "Old Guard" or "founding mothers" and newer members.

The hallmark of the women's movement during the mid-1970s was its success: it established organizations, acquired outside funding, won legalized abortion, pushed the ERA through Congress and many states, and achieved at least some decrease in the public acceptability of blatant sexism (Ferree and Hess 1985; Staggenborg 1991; Ryan 1992). In Columbus, Ohio State University funded a Center for Women's Studies, a gain that activists had pressed for since 1970. Joiners were highly optimistic about the possibility of achieving social-structural change on a large scale. Many core members held paid positions in WAR, WAC, or OSU Women's Studies; membership grew rapidly, and WAR received its almost half-million-dollar grant from the federal government. It is not surprising that joiners expected, as one put it, to be able to "make feminist revolution." Their goals were broad, and the scope of the organizations they joined and expanded was similarly far-reaching.

Echols (1989) has suggested that the mid-1970s were critical years when radical feminism declined and what she terms "cultural feminism" took hold. WAC, in fact, increasingly viewed its mission as the provision of services for women and the development of an alternative culture. Its "Statement of Philosophy," adopted in 1974, reflected this view, defining WAC as "women working together who are proud and happy to be women. . . . Using a self-help approach to the development of women's services we are building a radical feminist alternative culture."[3] Yet WAC continued to engage in direct confrontation of the social system. That members viewed building a feminist culture as a strategy for changing the external environment is illustrated by another excerpt from the 1974 statement:

> We are committed to change in our lives NOW. We believe the personal is the political and we must live what we believe. We must withdraw our support from existing sexist institutions and create new ones expressive of our philosophy. While we recognize the value of other forms of struggle, we are committed to building an alternative feminist culture NOW, even on a small scale, rather than expending our energy on large scale reformism.[4]

Service-providing organizations such as Women Against Rape's crisis line and the Women's Co-op Garage sought to change women's status as well as provide specific services. For example, a 1976 flyer for the Women's Co-op Garage argued that teaching women to repair their own cars encouraged women to enter into other traditionally male arenas: "The Women's Co-op Garage brings women together to learn from each other and expand their abilities into a traditionally masculine field. . . . As women increase their skills they become more confident, not only in auto mechanics but also in their ability to tackle situations once considered non-feminine."[5]

Revisions of WAC's bylaws in 1977 indicated the collective's view of cultural change as integral to feminist societal transformation; organizational goals included: "to build a cooperative community of women with free space where we can learn to depend upon one another, work together, and live an alternative free of sexism; to create services for women that are responsive to women's expressed needs; to encourage innovation in any form that will move us closer to non-sexist relationships and institutions."[6] In short, despite the flourishing of cultural and service organizations, members remained committed to changing the external world and saw changing the way women lived as a means of doing so.

Although the label "radical feminist" remained the one that participants applied to themselves and their organizations, its meaning changed. Most strikingly, feminism was increasingly tied to lesbianism. Not all WAC members were lesbians, but the vast majority were, and a new lesbian organization also grew outside of WAC. Central Ohio Lesbians, a campus-based group that lobbied for gay and lesbian legal rights, organized the first local gay pride march and provided a lesbian speakers' bureau. In 1974, in keeping with theoretical developments in the larger women's movement (see Johnston 1973; Radicalesbians 1973; Atkinson 1974; Myron and

Bunch 1975), members of WAC and COL saw lesbianism as a challenge to male domination and an important component of women's liberation: "We recognize a woman's right to free discovery and expression of her sexuality. Lesbianism is a positive expression of women loving women which resolves splits that are present in our relationships if we cannot express ourselves physically and sexually with each other."[7] Three years later, the link between lesbianism and feminism was much more explicit. A statement adopted by WAC in 1977 framed lesbianism as an explicitly political rejection of male dominance: "Lesbianism . . . affirms the process of challenging traditional institutions forced upon women and constitutes a primary commitment to women. The WAC recognizes Lesbianism as a positive means for eliminating one facet of the power relationship of men over women. As such, Lesbianism is an integral part of the Women's Movement."[8]

At the same time, radical feminist collective identity increasingly entailed separation from men. Whereas in 1972 and 1973 forming alternative institutions for women outside of the dominant culture was seen primarily as a strategy for achieving social change, after 1974 separatism became a more central ideological principle and, at times, an end in itself: "The work of the women's movement must be done by women. . . . No man can experience women's oppression; therefore, no man can be a spokesperson for the women's movement."[9] Members argued that women needed "women-only space" to develop a strong opposition and to contradict the cultural devaluation of women, and the WAC house was accordingly specified as "women's space."[10] In 1977, when WAC began holding orientation sessions for new members,[11] facilitators defined radical feminism as focusing on the connections between the personal and the political, including the "woman identified woman."[12] In short, theory about the connections between women's personal experiences and political causes cast both lesbianism and separatism as politically beneficial as well as personally preferable.

Because of the large influx of personnel into preexisting organizations, the period between 1974 and 1978 was characterized by conflict between more and less experienced members. Those who had been around for longer sought to teach new members the skills necessary to participate fully. As one founding member of WAC explained: "We were operating in a completely collective environment where supposedly everybody had equal access to decision making, but some of us were just damned skilled by that time. . . . We ran endless workshops to try to train women so they could make competent decisions. But some of us still became known as sort of the kitchen cabinet of the Action Collective." Such attempts at skill sharing, regardless of their success or failure in transmitting skills to incoming members, underscored the gap between experienced and new members. One founder remarked that those who were perceived as elitist were often the founders of the organization: "The folks who were on salary [with the CASSR project] I think were perceived to be some kind of an elite. And certainly they were the people with the longest history with the organization, and the people that had been around since the early '70s or maybe late '60s. So by virtue of their history with the organization, they had a fair amount of power. And I think eventually that some of the newer people chafed under that sort of thing."

In fact, founders of the two new organizations established during this period, Central Ohio Lesbians and the Women's Music Union, explicitly stated that they started the new groups because they felt closed out of WAC. As one founding member of COL explained: "Some of the older and more established groups had very much their idea of how they wanted to run things, and it was our perception that no one was really to tread on that. And there was this vague invitation to provide input, but you never really got the impression that that input was going to be taken seriously or acted upon in any way." On the other hand, more experienced women felt frustrated with what they perceived as the lack of political sophistication of incoming women. One woman who joined WAR during the mid-1970s explained that her greater familiarity with feminism made her impatient: "I think the longer you were there the less patience you had with brand-new women coming in. . . . There was always a continuum of women who had been there forever and ever and had read everything, and grappled with all these issues for so long, and [then there were] the women who just joined. . . . And we were eons apart."

Orientation sessions served as an institutionalized means for experienced feminists to transmit ideology and movement history to incoming members. WAC's orientation sessions, beginning in 1977, were instrumental in the political socialization of new members. One participant reported that the bulk of time was spent defining radical feminism so that, as she perceived it, "we could see what we were supposed to be if we were going to be radical feminists." The women who entered WAC in 1977, 1978, and 1979 through these orientation sessions became the next micro-cohort. These usually younger women entering a well-established organization in which the founders were still present complained about treatment by earlier members: "We were all referred to as the baby feminists for a time, and I really hated that. I really wanted to be accepted simply as a feminist, WAC member, and for people not to just see me as this young person. . . . But there was a little bit of, I guess you'd call it maternalism." Despite such resentment, orientation sessions provided a setting where new members read and discussed feminist tenets developed by earlier members, and thus existing orientations shaped new members' collective identity.

The joiner micro-cohort, in part because of its size and the boom it brought to the women's movement, led the growth of an alternative feminist culture. Its members took for granted that they would work outside the mainstream of society but that they could co-opt the resources of the state for feminist ends. This was a powerful combination while resources remained available, but the decline of the nonprofit sector hit women's movement organizations hard. As the 1970s gave way to the 1980s, the micro-cohort politicized in WAC's late-1970s orientation sessions took over leadership of the organization.

The Ebbing of Protest, 1979–1984

The radical women's movement in Columbus was active and well-funded and had many participants through 1978. But organizations started disbanding in 1977, and by 1980 membership had dropped drastically, funding was vanishing, and many organizations were defunct. Many of the core groups in WAC disbanded in the late 1970s, including the Women's Co-op Garage, the Single Mothers' Support Group, the Women's Health Collective, and *Womansong* newspaper. WAC as a whole and its member organizations had trouble keeping members active. They were continually urged to take on more "collective responsibility," but such exhortations met little success. By the end of 1979, members were wondering in print about decreasing involvement in WAC activities, as in this comment in a November newsletter: "Is this apparent 'malaise' at WAC just *our* problem, or symptomatic of a general 'slow down' in activity in the women's movement at large? Are there actions we can take to turn things around or is it time to think about closing our doors? The question now is not, 'How to raise more money,' but 'WHAT ARE WE FUNDRAISING FOR?' "[13]

WAC went from plentiful funding in the late 1970s to shortages and financial insecurity by 1980 as the economic climate worsened and the Reagan administration reduced funding for social services. As early as 1979 WAC was in its first major financial crisis, needing to raise $7,000 in six months in order to keep its house. The end of the rape prevention grant from NIMH meant that WAR cut back on many services and activities.

WAC moved from its house to a smaller space in 1983; it was dismantled in 1984 (Haller 1984). Only two of its member organizations, Women Against Rape and Fan the Flames Feminist Bookstore, survived.

Several short-lived study and support groups formed between 1978 and 1981, none of which lasted a full year. These included groups focusing on women and economics, international women, lesbianism, religion, radical feminism, the book *Fat Is a Feminist Issue*, heterosexual feminists, feminists in the workplace, pornography, lesbians who want children, substance abuse, and Jewish lesbians. A few longer-lasting organizations also formed between 1979 and 1981: Feminists in Self Defense Training (FIST); the Child Assault Prevention Project (CAP), which began as a task force of WAR and later became an independent organization; and Women's Outreach to Women, a twelve-step program for recovery from substance abuse. WAC, the Women's Music Union, and other organizations continued to sponsor cultural and social functions, including dances, concerts, film festivals, and an annual event dubbed "Famous Feminist Day." By 1981 cultural events were arguably the most vital segment of the radical women's movement.

The micro-cohort that entered WAC between 1977 and 1979 was politicized by the gains of the earlier women's movement. The success in establishing a Center for Women's Studies at OSU meant that students were politicized in women's studies classes, and the institutionalization of WAC's orientation sessions opened another route for politicization. This micro-cohort became influential in 1979 and 1980 as earlier cohorts took less active roles. I have termed them "sustainers" because it was they who passed the ideas of the peak of the women's movement to activists entering the movement in the 1980s. They modified the collective identity of the previous years by emphasizing a feminist spirituality, lesbianism, and issues of race, ethnicity, and class. The period was marked by conflict over these issues and the painful exits of long-term members.

All the women I interviewed who joined WAC between 1977 and 1979 were lesbians, both because the flourishing lesbian feminist culture helped bring in new recruits and because many heterosexual women felt outnumbered and unwelcome. Yet even as the organization became more nearly homogeneously lesbian, members debated the centrality of lesbianism to feminist collective identity. Some argued at a 1981 WAC meeting that the statement of philosophy should declare: "WAC believes that lesbianism is the lifestyle most consistent with radical feminist theory." Others argued that "we are feminists first and lesbians less obviously" and that heterosexual women should not be excluded from the women's movement.[14] The centrality of lesbianism to the definition of "feminist," in other words, was contested. There was substantial debate over whether WAC should attempt to appeal to heterosexual women, even though the organization was almost exclusively composed of lesbians by this point.

A second issue of increasing debate was race and class homogeneity within the women's movement. Earlier feminist theorists had analyzed sexism as if all women were an undifferentiated "sex class." In the late 1970s, however, women of color and Jewish women had begun to raise the question of differences among women, and by the early 1980s the issues were being widely discussed within the women's movement and in several books (Beck 1980; Moraga and Anzaldua 1981; Hull, Scott, and Smith 1982; B. Smith 1983). Homogeneity was hotly debated within WAC at a series of meetings in 1981 and 1982 at which members concluded that WAC had been a White-dominated and racist organization and that White members should examine their own racism and classism in order to encourage minority women to join.[15] In response, "racism and minority women's issues" were added to WAC orientation sessions,[16] and WAC newsletters more frequently discussed issues of race and class. Yet as in the matter of recruiting heterosexual women, there was little effect on the organization's composition.

A third area of conflict, feminist spirituality, also centered on collective identity, or the definition of what constituted a feminist issue. In September 1982 the WAC newsletter sported a new logo showing a crescent moon with the female symbol, and the new title "Womoon Rising." An accompanying letter from the newsletter committee explained the change in format: "As radical feminists we have all made the commitment to ending the patriarchy and re-establishing Matriarchy. One of the ways we do this is by claiming as our own the strong ties between ourselves and the Mother Spirit. In Prehistorical societies . . . the moon represented this Mother Spirit. We take the name WOMOON RISING because we are Womoon. And, although we may not yet be full, we are definitely rising." [17]

The change of name sparked controversy within WAC, as many members objected both to the name itself and to how the decision was made to change it. A letter from eight active members—some sustainers, others founders and joiners—protested: "What is a Womoon? No one knows, but it certainly doesn't sound like a political activist. . . . Equally disturbing is your reference to a "Mother Spirit". . . . The whole concept, down to the name being capitalized is traditional in many ways." [18] A subsequent letter,

however, countered that WAC ought to focus *more* attention on the issue
of spirituality: "I have seen this spelling [womoon] in popular womyn's
literature for the past year, at least. Womyn's spirituality is a 'hot' topic
in the many, many womyn's journals nationwide and in many womyn's
lives. The Women's (sic) [*sic*] Action Collective has been in the forefront
of womyn's theorizing and the movement itself. WAC now seems, by our
lack of forward progress, to be isolating ourself. . . . This is an issue WAC
will need to deal with soon, as, unfortunately, WAC is becoming very
mainstream feminist." [19]

The conflict was essentially a debate over whether to redefine the collective identity "feminist." Advocates of "womoonhood," who were predominantly sustainers, defined feminism to include matriarchal spirituality and
to emphasize personal transformation as an important means of creating
broad social change. In their view, an orientation toward external confrontation was "mainstream" and therefore undesirable. Their opponents, on
the other hand, sought to maintain a definition of feminism that linked it
to external political change and did not include what they saw as "flaky"
spiritual concerns.

In addition to substantive controversy over lesbianism, race, class, and
spirituality, conflicts raged between members of different micro-cohorts.
Some sustainers criticized many long-time members of WAC for making
decisions without consulting the collective, for "power-tripping" and elitism. Many members of both founder and joiner micro-cohorts moved out
of town, either for personal reasons or because they were criticized and
attacked. Those who remained in Columbus adopted an advice-giving role
rather than remaining active participants. One founder of Women Against
Rape, describing her relationship to the organization around 1980, commented wryly: "I was tired, basically, and I felt like I kind of sat around
as the wise old lady who dispensed advice. Because I no longer had the
energy to do anything. But I didn't mind talking to people about what they
could do and how they should do it. [I said] 'Oh, yeah, we tried that, in
19-da-da-da.'"

The loss of large numbers of experienced members as a result of internal
conflict, combined with shrinking resources and the increasingly hostile
climate, left women's movement organizations foundering. By the 1980s
feminists were increasingly pursuing their goals within mainstream institutions such as social service and governmental agencies, the judicial system,
colleges and universities, and the Democratic Party (Ferree and Hess 1985;

Staggenborg 1991; B. Ryan 1992; Whittier 1995) and within other social movements (Meyer and Whittier 1994).

Conclusion

Because social movements are made up not just of organizations but of people, membership turnover is an issue. Different people staff social movement organizations over time, even when the organizations as a whole endure, and this may produce conflict and change in the organizations. I have argued that women's movement organizations experienced conflict and changed as successive micro-cohorts entered and redefined the feminist collective identity.

This approach adds to our understanding of the recent women's movement in several ways. First, it views the discord that ripped through feminist organizations as stemming in part from the divergent politicizing experiences of different micro-cohorts rather than solely from ideological disagreements. Second, it suggests that change in women's movement organizations, like conflict, resulted in part from the continual entry and exit of micro-cohorts with varying collective identities. Third, it gives us a more accurate picture of the development of the women's movement after its origins in the late 1960s. The focus by many pivotal studies on the origins of the women's movement led to the description of radical feminists as having been initially politicized in the civil rights and New Left movements, and then building on those experiences in the feminist movement (Carden 1974; Freeman 1975; Cassell 1977; Echols 1989). Yet as joiners and sustainers entered radical feminist organizations, without first having been part of the mixed-sex left, their perspectives grew within the women's movement and changed the course of the movement as a whole.

Finally, as a new wave of feminist activism grows in the 1990s, a generational analysis can be instructive for both feminist scholars and activists. Contention between micro-cohorts in the 1970s meant that the lessons learned by earlier activists were not completely passed on to incoming members. Extensive controversy diminished chances for organizational learning. A better understanding of the origins and dynamics of generations in the women's movement over the past quarter-century may help us to comprehend and address those that are emerging now.

Notes

1. *Columbus-OSU Women's Liberation Newsletter*, November 5, 1970. This is contained in box 3—filed under Historical, Quinn, Karen—of the Women's Action Collective Papers, housed at the Ohio Historical Society in Columbus. Subsequent citations are in the form *OHS*, box number, file name, subfile name (if any), document title (if any).

2. "Women's Action Collective Condensed Organizational History" (Mary Haller collection).

3. Women's Action Collective (WAC) "Statement of Philosophy," adopted by consensus May 21, 1974 (Teri Wehausen collection).

4. Ibid.

5. *OHS*, box 3, Automechanics.

6. *OHS*, box 5, Annual Meeting 1981, Bylaws, Purpose and Policy sect., Art. II (revised July 1977).

7. WAC "Statement of Philosophy," 1974.

8. WAC newsletter, August 1977 (Debbie Chalfie collection).

9. WAC "Statement of Philosophy," 1974.

10. WAC newsletter, November–December 1976 (Debbie Chalfie collection).

11. WAC newsletter, April–May 1977 and June 1977 (Debbie Chalfie collection).

12. "Outline for Sessions" (Teri Wehausen collection).

13. WAC newsletter, November 1979 (Debbie Chalfie collection).

14. *OHS*, box 7, Minutes of Struggle Session no. 1, Lesbian separatism (September 12, 1981).

15. Ibid., Struggle Session no. 2, Mass vs. elite movement (October 24, 1981), and no. 3, Racism–minority Women (November 22, 1981); Process Narrative of Struggle Session no. 4, Mass vs. elite, pt. 2 (Teri Wehausen collection).

16. *OHS*, box 7, Minutes of Struggle Session no. 3.

17. WAC newsletter, September–October 1982 (Teri Wehausen collection).

18. WAC newsletter, November–December 1982, p. 9 (Teri Wehausen collection).

19. Ibid.

CHAPTER 13

Black Women's Collectivist Movement Organizations: Their Struggles during the "Doldrums"

■

BERNICE McNAIR BARNETT

My arrest [in 1946] convinced me that my defiance alone would do little or nothing to remedy such situations. Only *organized* effort could do that. But where to start? . . . *I was a feminist before I really knew what the word meant* [emphasis added], and so I dismissed the hardfaced men . . . but I felt that I could appeal to some of the women. I played bridge with them, but more important, I knew that they [middle-class Black women] must suffer from the racial abuses and the indignity accorded to all Blacks, even though they were somewhat insulated from it. Their outward indifference was a mask to protect both their psyche and their sanity.

Mary Fair Burks, "Trailblazers" (1990)

In the 1970s, Freeman (1973, 1975, 1979) argued that the modern women's movement had a distinctively "feminist" mode consisting of two "branches" that differed in age, organizational structure, and style. The one branch comprised women who were older, had a certain amount of money and other resources, had some specialized time, developed organizational structures that were centralized, and had hierarchical leadership styles (for example, formal position leaders). The other branch comprised younger women who had little or no money, had much unspecialized time, developed organizational structures that were highly decentralized, and had nonhierarchical leadership styles (for example, grassroots leaders). Ferree and Hess (1985, 49) described these different feminist branches as a "bureaucratic strand" and a "collectivist strand" in the new women's movement and suggested that both "emerged in the mid-1960s" and "inter-

199

twined" in the 1970s and 1980s but remained "two different organizational modes . . . reflecting the history and needs of their members."

This scholarship on the organizational modes of the new women's movement raises some crucial issues regarding modern Black women's collectivist movement organizations and the origins of these "new" feminist modes.[1] First, the period that Ferree and Hess (1985) have characterized as an unorganized phase in the women's movement and Rupp and Taylor (1987) have referred to as "the doldrums" saw the emergence of several Black women's collectivist organizations, two of which I examine in detail here. Second, in spite of the triple constraints of gender, race, and class, various groups of Black women (not just elite, educated Black women) were far from passive or apolitical in the 1950s. In their homes, communities, churches, and collectivist organizations, African American women actively engaged in protest against the oppression they encountered on a day-to-day basis (Gilkes 1980, 1982, 1988; Giddings 1984; Sachs 1988; Barnett 1989, 1990, 1993; Collins 1990; S. Evans 1992). Third, African American women were never simply a homogeneous group. Black women political activists developed different organizational modes that reflected their unique history and structural location within interlocking systems of gender, race, and class stratification.

This research compares two Black women's collectivist movement organizations located in Montgomery, Alabama: the Women's Political Council (WPC), founded in 1946, almost ten years before the momentous 1955 Montgomery bus boycott; and the Club from Nowhere (CFN), founded in 1956 during the bus boycott. The Montgomery boycott set in motion one of the most significant protests in modern American history. It was the first successful mass protest by African Americans in modern times. And Black women, working in their communities and their voluntary associations, served as initiators and organizers of this protest. Yet their stories as "leaders" (Barnett 1989, 1990, 1993) and key activists are just beginning to be told (Giddings 1984; Robinson 1987; Burks 1990; Crawford, Rouse, and Woods 1990; Mueller 1990). Though not narrowly "feminist" in primary aim or manifest intent (that is, in privileging gender oppression as the only or main target of political action), these groups illuminate women's particular organizational preferences and styles. I thus attempt to analyze their organizational modes (a) from the standpoint of a *Black women's* movement organization (for example, to view their organizational forms as gendered politics, separate from the dominant Black, male-headed civil rights movement organizations such as the NAACP and the Urban League) and (b) from the standpoint of a modern *feminist* organization (for example, to view these organizational modes in terms of their feminist values, goals and practices, and transformational outcomes for women).

My research utilizes data from a larger study of leadership in the civil rights movement and the ongoing collection of data on Black women's leadership roles in social protest. This essay is based on analysis of (1) archives, organizational records, published works, and personal papers of civil rights activists and (2) sixteen in-depth personal interviews with civil rights activists.[2] A major portion of the archival data was collected between 1986 and 1987. Personal interviews were conducted immediately thereafter and intermittently since 1988. Interviews with the women were conducted primarily in person in a variety of settings, including my hotel room and their homes and places of work (day care and community centers, universities, city council meeting places). Follow-up interviews were conducted over the telephone and during special civil rights movement commemorative events.

It is important to note several things about the sixteen Black women activists I interviewed.[3] First, these women came from diverse educational and socioeconomic class backgrounds. Some were public school teachers and college professors; some were lawyers and are now judges; some were office secretaries and insurance salespersons; some were the wives of elite Black professionals and did not work outside the home for pay; and some were, and remained, domestic workers and cooks, basically poor and working-class women. This last category is too often incorrectly assumed to be apolitical and thus inconsequential to social movement mobilization, maintenance, and success. But poor and working-class Black women as well as elite and middle-class Black women contributed to the success of the Montgomery bus boycott and many other protests (King 1958; Giddings 1984; Morris 1984; Barnett 1989, 1990). Second, though several of the women are nationally known, many are known only inside the movement and in their local communities. This may be true of most Black women activists. Third, all sixteen women were participants in multiple organizations. These community leaders were also active members of their churches, and most of them—especially the professional women—were members of the NAACP, the Urban League, the PTA, and several other voluntary associations as well. A few belonged to both the WPC and the CFN.

Finally, it is important to keep in mind that these Black women, even the most educated "elites," had to organize within the 1950s southern social structure (Bates 1962; Clark 1962, 1986; Giddings 1984; Robinson 1987;

Barnett 1989, 1990; Burks 1990). The triple constraints imposed by inter-locking systems of gender, race, and class stratification in this racist setting made a mockery of organizing on the basis of a common gender. As Black feminist scholars have pointed out, however, it is extremely important to understand that for Black women these multiple statuses cannot be sepa-rated or prioritized (hooks 1981; Hull, Scott, and Smith 1982; Gilkes 1988; D. King 1988; Collins 1990). Giddings's pioneering work (1984) illustrates that Black women's struggles for equality have been ignored by both Black men and White feminists. Anna Julia Cooper's 1892 declaration, "When and where I enter . . . then and there the whole race enters with me" (quoted in Giddings 1984, 13), puts Black women at the center of analysis and cri-tiques the exclusionary tendencies of both Black men civil rights activists and White women feminists.

Women's Activism and Models of Movement Organizations

Social movement scholars have argued that social movement organizations (SMOs) are significant and even necessary vehicles for noninstitutional-ized social change (Freeman 1979; McAdam 1982; Morris 1984). Schol-ars of the new women's movement have argued that the organizational modes developed by the movement of the 1960s and 1970s are very differ-ent from those employed by the movement in the late nineteenth and early twentieth centuries. These new organizational modes have been seen as uniquely "feminist" in their structure, values, and practices. As ideal types, they are nonbureaucratic, nonhierarchical, participatory, and democratic (Rothschild-Whitt 1979; Ferree and Hess 1985).

Recently, feminist scholars (see Martin 1990b) have argued for reducing the emphasis on ideal-type organizational modes and broadening the focus to include organizations that perhaps do not claim to be feminist but do in fact employ feminist values, practices, and outcomes. I argue that Black women's movement organizations exhibited such "feminist" organi-zational patterns. Just as organizational modes in the women's movement emerged from unique structural and historical circumstances, each of these Black women's movement organizations emerged from unique historical circumstances and reflected the needs of its members. Moreover, Black women civil rights activists and leaders such as Ella Baker were important role models for the White women who later became activists and leaders in the new women's movement. The emphases on participatory democracy, community, collectivism, caring, mutual respect, and self-transformation that have been viewed as distinctive characteristics of White women's organizing in the late 1960s and 1970s can be found in Black women's political activism and organizing several decades earlier (S. Evans 1979, 1992; Morris 1984; McAdam 1988; Barnett 1989; Breines 1989; Mueller 1990; Sirianni 1993).

The origins of participatory democracy in Black women's organizing in the 1940s, 1950s, and 1960s have seldom been acknowledged (S. Evans 1992). Exclusion of Black women's political history from feminist accounts is not new. Terborg-Penn (1978, 27) writes of the lack of acknowledgment of Black feminists' contributions in the earlier waves of feminist mobilization as well.[4] Black feminist scholars view this neglect as a basic failure in the feminist movement to come explicitly to grips with its unwillingness to acknowledge the diversity and multiplicity of women's experiences and women's consciousness (Terborg-Penn 1978; hooks 1981; Terrelonge 1984; D. King 1988; Collins 1990):

> Sexism and racism have so informed the perspective of American historiographers that they have tended to overlook and exclude the effort of black women in discussions of the American women's rights movement. White female scholars who support feminist ideology have also ignored the contributions of black women. . . . An example of the trend can be found in June Sochen's work *Herstory*, where she discusses white women's organizations in a chapter titled "The Women's Movement" but discusses black women's organizations in a chapter titled "Old Problems: Black Americans." (hooks 1981, 160–61)

Certainly, Black women's experiences are unique, especially in the way that racism and sexism intersect in their lives, but their experiences *as women* are often overlooked (hooks 1981; Hull, Scott, and Smith 1982; Barnett 1989, 1993). Emphasis on their uniqueness should not result in a failure to recognize commonalities among women and their organizations. I believe that it would be a mistake to marginalize or exclude the movement activism and organizing strategies of modern Black women in the scholarship on "feminist" organization simply because their environment demanded a focus on racial oppression.

Black women's roles as "organizers" in the churches, in work- and school-based associations, in sororities such as Delta Sigma Theta and Alpha Kappa Alpha, in male-dominated SMOs such as the Urban League, and in various clubs and associations such as the National Association of

Colored Women and the National Council of Negro Women have long
been recognized. Their tremendous organizing skills and effective practices served as the foundation of the civil rights movement and were later
adopted by youth, peace activists, and White women (S. Evans 1979, 1992;
Morris 1984; McAdam 1988; Barnett 1989; Mueller 1990; Payne 1990).
Nonetheless, their roles as "leaders" in modern social movements have
seldom been recognized. Elsewhere I argue for a rethinking of the traditional conception of leadership as formal, public "spokesman" because it
is gender-biased and one-dimensional, and it limits both women's actual
opportunities and their recognition as "leaders" (Barnett 1989, 1993).[5] My
research on modern Black women civil rights leaders is an attempt to put
leadership back onto the theoretical agenda of movement scholarship, to
challenge the dominant male-centered assumptions, and to conceptualize
the roles of women in grassroots community groups in terms of leadership. In my multidimensional view of leadership, organizing is a significant
dimension. Black women of different socioeconomic classes were organizers of distinctively communal and participatory movement organizations,
which in turn empowered them.

The Women's Political Council
and the "Club from Nowhere"

In comparing the styles of two Black women's movement organizations,
I focus on three main areas: (1) historical and political context (including founding date, purpose, scope of goals, membership, and strategies
and tactics); (2) structural dimensions (including authority and leadership,
social relations, and differentiation); and (3) feminist characteristics (including feminist values, goals and practices, and outcomes). As Table 13.1
shows, though there were many important commonalities in these two
organizations, there were also some significant differences.

THE WOMEN'S POLITICAL COUNCIL AND ITS MIDDLE-CLASS BASE

The Women's Political Council (WPC) was founded in 1946 in Montgomery, Alabama, by Mary Frances Fair Burks, head of the English Department at a historically Black school, Alabama State College in Montgomery. This organization was headed by formally educated, middle-class,
"elite" Black women who were college professors or the wives of elite
professionals (dentists, professors, doctors, lawyers, ministers). The socio-

TABLE 13-1

STYLES OF TWO BLACK WOMEN'S MOVEMENT ORGANIZATIONS

	WPC (professional/middle-class base)	CFN (poor/working-class base)
Historical/Political Context		
Founding date	1946 (before boycott)	1956 (during boycott)
Founding purpose	long-term political; response to Black women's treatment and exclusion from League of Women Voters	short-term economic; response to financial needs of the boycott
Scope of goals	multiple; broad; structural	single; specific; immediate
Membership	highly educated professionals: college professors, teachers, "elite" and affluent housewives; 100–300 members, all women	informally educated service workers: maids, cooks, beauticians, housewives, secretaries; 10–15 members, all women
Strategies and tactics	direct political confrontations, voter registration drives, letter writing, leafleting, lobbying, boycotting, citizenship education and training, organizing	fund raising: door to door, bake sales; organizing, boycotting (walking to work)
Resources	specialized and unspecialized	unspecialized
Structural Dimensions		
Authority/ leadership	somewhat hierarchical, positional leaders: "president" and other formal officers	nonhierarchical, grassroots leaders: "head" but no formal officers
Rules	formal and sometimes situational	ad hoc and situational
Social control	low member supervision	low member supervision
Social relations	internally associational and communal; externally autonomous from male organizations; little status in polity	internally communal; externally dependent on male organizations; no status in polity
Recruitment and advancement	professionalism and expertise; some personality and volunteerism	personality and volunteerism

TABLE 13-1, CONTINUED

	WPC (professional/middle-class base)	CFN (poor/working-class base)
Structural Dimensions		
Incentives	political empowerment, solidarity, community improvement, justice	solidarity, community improvement, justice
Social stratification	basically egalitarian	egalitarian
Differentiation	low to moderate division of labor	low division of labor
"Feminist" Characteristics		
Feminist ideology	justice, equality, Black women's political and economic consciousness	social justice and equality
Feminist values and practices	participation, cooperation, mutual caring, fairness	participation, cooperation, mutual caring, fairness
Feminist goals	political awareness, women's action agenda as part of racial and social justice	racial and social justice
Feminist outcomes	empowerment (e.g., politics, skills, self-esteem)	empowerment (e.g., skills, self-esteem)

economically secure and "well-connected" women of Montgomery made up the membership core.

The WPC had a formal, somewhat hierarchical authority structure with a president, secretary, treasurer, and heads of assorted committees, or "groups." During the life of the organization there were only two presidents, both college professors and both formally elected by the membership. Leaders were formally chosen for the four main groups—also referred to as "chapters"—on the basis not of issues but of geographical coverage. A WPC officer recounts: "Issues really were not the main reason someone was chosen a group leader. . . . Normally the president chose a reliable and dedicated person to make sure everything got done on her side of town. Of course, the person was usually a professional woman. . . . We thought this was the best thing because we wanted to make sure that the north, south, east, and west sides of Montgomery were always covered and had a leader."

The circumstances surrounding the WPC's founding are ironic. It was established in response to White racism in Montgomery's League of Women Voters (LWV), which denied membership to women who were Black. Burks and most of the forty Black women who later formed the WPC had all experienced some mortifying incident, such as an unwarranted brutal arrest by White police, and initially tried to use the LWV as a means to empower themselves to improve their treatment, but were rebuffed. One WPC member described the particular circumstances surrounding its emergence:

> If the League of Women Voters had not denied our participation and membership in its organization, we wouldn't have had reason to establish the Women's Political Council. . . . When they refused to allow Black women to participate simply because of our race, we had no other alternative but to form our own if we wanted to be part of an organization that allowed us *as women* to participate in political life and to address our political concerns. . . . It seems so irrational as I look at it—they refused to allow Black women to be members of a *women's* organization. I guess they thought we were something *less than women*." (Emphasis added)

It was White women, rather than Black women, who placed their primary emphasis on race over gender by insisting on segregation. Hence, Black women organized the WPC to fight racial segregation practiced by White women as well as the oppressive White male power structure in Montgomery. The name of the group—which Burks successfully persuaded the members to adopt in a close vote over the alternative "Women's Human Relations Committee"—made its direct *political action* concentration manifest (Burks 1990). Between its founding in 1946 and its crucial role in the bus boycott in 1955, the WPC worked to improve conditions for all Blacks but especially for Black youth and Black women. Expressing Black women's orientation towards community and family, one WPC member recalled:

> Black children didn't have playgrounds and recreation areas in their neighborhoods. Our Black youth especially didn't have any places to go [for] recreation. Young people need these things. And then whenever they were together, we were always afraid for them because they were harassed by the law. The teenagers, very fine teenagers, couldn't participate in much because of the way they were treated by police

officers, who didn't care that they were fine boys and girls who were active in the schools and the churches.

Black women often took the brunt of racially oppressive segregation laws and sexually oppressive behaviors in the South. Many, regardless of their socioeconomic class, experienced daily insults in their work settings and in public, especially on public transportation. When she traveled on the interstate bus home to Macon, Georgia, college professor JoAnn Robinson experienced the same kind of abuse as seamstress Rosa Parks when she traveled on the city bus in Montgomery. Constance Baker Motley and other Black women civil rights lawyers who were litigating in the southern courts faced public insult and physical abuse by the very people sworn to uphold the law and to provide equal protection under the law (Barnett 1991).

In 1950 JoAnn Robinson took over "Group One," the most politically active committee of the WPC, and led the WPC in lobbying and letter-writing campaigns, including threats of a refusal to pay for segregated parks and of a bus boycott (Robinson 1987, 22–24). In 1955, after news circulated that Rosa Parks had been arrested for refusing to give up her bus seat, Robinson put into action the boycott that the WPC had been planning as a response to the long list of insults directed against Black women in Montgomery. She called Burks, other faculty, and students to start the distribution of leaflets, which, together with word-of-mouth dissemination and newspaper headlines, resulted in almost 100 percent Black participation. The bus boycott began on Monday, December 5, 1955 (Morris 1984); in less than four days the arrest of Rosa Parks had precipitated a WPC-planned event that ushered in the most significant phase of Black protest ever to occur in the United States.

Such a leadership role was risky and demanding. One respondent recalled: "JoAnn could have been fired from her job at the college [Alabama State]. . . . Most of us [professors] had families to support and had to be careful about being openly involved. . . . JoAnn was something else . . . so determined . . . didn't even seem to be afraid if they [Black as well as white administrators] found out. . . . Hah! She used the mimeograph machines in the college to run off leaflets about the boycott!"

Like Ella Baker and many other Black women activists, Robinson was a behind-the-scenes leader (Barnett 1989, 1993). In her memoir (Robinson 1987, 10) she expresses a collectivist orientation and lack of self-promotion that are persistent themes in Black women's activism from slavery to modern times:

I was one of the first persons arrested in the course of the boycott; that was my first direct experience of what takes place when people are incarcerated. In general, however, I kept a low profile and stayed as much as possible in the background. That I did so was not from fear for my own well-being, but rather out of deep respect for Dr. Trenholm, for Alabama State College, and for its faculty and student body—all of whom would have been unavoidably implicated in case of trouble.

When Robinson was forced to resign from Alabama State in 1960, after being investigated by a special state committee, she took a position in the English department of Grambling State University in Grambling, Louisiana (Robinson 1987, 168–69). One WPC member expressed admiration for Robinson and other activists employed in places of such high vulnerability:

> Many women had to be undercover for fear of losing their jobs. This was a real threat. Some of us who worked for Black businesses . . . didn't have to worry about this type of retaliation. I worked for [a Black business], . . . which encouraged me, supported my activities, even donated money to the movement. Women such as Mrs. Robinson and Mrs. Burks and Mrs. Glass had to be careful or else they could lose their jobs. Being brave is one thing. Being sensible is another, especially when you have a family obligation. This is why I admire those women who did what they did.

Lamenting the loss of so many "good women" who risked their jobs and were forced to discontinue their activism, another activist and WPC officer explained: "The two or three remaining presidents of various auxiliaries were finally frightened out of operating. . . . It really just boiled down to about five of us who were left at the university. . . . We continued in the churches."

Such opposition reduced the historical visibility of the organization. Almost all the records of the WPC and the Montgomery Improvement Association (MIA), the organization headed by male ministers to coordinate boycott activities, were destroyed during this time: when White supremacists used the tactic of subpoenaing records for trial, leaders in the WPC countered by destroying the organization's records. When I asked to see the names of officers and committees in the WPC, one of the officers told me:

> We don't really have any records anymore. We had to destroy them during the boycott because we knew that this same thing had been used

to try to run the NAACP out of town many years ago. The Whites subpoenaed the NAACP's records and publicized the membership lists.
When we were subpoenaed to testify at the boycott trials, we knew
that they were trying to use the same thing to get back at us. . . .
So, we decided we had to destroy the minutes and our membership
roster. . . . That's why I really can't tell you everything you want to
know, especially who all were members. I have very few papers left.

Burks, Robinson, and others, such as Faustine Dunn, Thelma Glass,
Geraldine Nesbitt, Irene West, Johnnie Carr, and Sadie Brooks, developed
very ingenious ways of organizing. One respondent illustrates the creative
and effective fund raising of these Black women: "In all my speeches I used
to tell the people: if you are afraid, and I know you are, and you can't stand
up, [then] George Washington, Abraham Lincoln, and Alexander Hamilton—all those boys are dead and they are not going to tell *nobody* . . .
so just give us some of those boys' pictures and let us do the work. . . .
The women in our organization will just get out there and do the work"
(original emphasis).

The WPCers used a variety of tactics to obtain information and resources
as well. For example, even though the White women in the LWV had
denied the Black women membership, the WPC leadership nevertheless
invited LWV leaders to WPC meetings and after-church gatherings to provide information on White candidates whenever there was an elected office
to fill. Years before the 1955 boycott the WPC was seeking political empowerment through electoral politics, self-consciously using "subversive"
tactics. One such tactic was to establish a Negro Youth Day, similar to the
day set aside for the White high schools to elect students who replaced
government officials for a day (Burks 1990). Like the adult citizenship education and training pioneered by Septima Poinsette Clark (1962, 1986) in
the 1950s, this program was aimed at fostering in Black youth the desire
for and belief in the efficacy of change through electoral politics. Many of
the youth trained by WPC members and public school teachers later became SNCC activists and leaders who fearlessly initiated voter registration
campaigns in Mississippi and other parts of the Deep South (Barnett 1989;
Breines 1989; Burks 1990).

Finally, Robinson's use of the mimeograph machines in the public college, operated by the very power the WPC was fighting, is an excellent
illustration of how the professional, college-based leadership had access
to what Freeman (1979) labels "specialized resources." The WPC not only
had status and access to decision-makers within the movement but also a

little status and access to the mayor and other decision-makers in the larger White political structure. The leafleting that the WPC used so effectively required access to professional expertise, money from the city's affluent Blacks, and professor-teacher-student-government service networks. These resources had already been mobilized by the WPC to engage in direct political confrontations via letter-writing campaigns, taxation protests, and "hearings" before the mayor in the decade preceding the boycott. Both their willingness to take risks and their access to resources made the WPC women *leaders* in the civil rights movement in Montgomery, even though the gender dynamics of the movement tended to obscure their significant contributions.

THE CLUB FROM NOWHERE AND ITS WORKING-CLASS BASE

In addition to the WPC, other movement organizations helped to sustain the boycott in Montgomery. The key organizers and leaders of some of the collectivist organizations were not professional women or wives of professionals, but rather poor and working-class Black women (Barnett 1990). One little-known activist organization that can serve as an example of the type was the "Club from Nowhere" (CFN), founded in 1956 by Georgia Gilmore, a domestic worker and restaurant cook, to support the boycott just then getting under way in Montgomery.[6] One leader of the Montgomery boycott tells of the innovative tactics used by Gilmore and other members:

> The Club from Nowhere was truly something Mrs. Georgia Gilmore should be proud of. She headed this club and even lost her job working in a cafe when she started it. The club went door to door asking for donations and selling dinner plates and baked goods. . . . [They] made weekly reports on all the money collected from all kinds of people—Blacks and Whites. Some of these people didn't want it known that they had given money to the movement, so they wouldn't give Mrs. Gilmore and the other ladies checks that could be traced, only cash. And Mrs. Gilmore made sure they didn't tell anybody who had made the donations. That's why it was called the Club from Nowhere, so that none of the people giving the money could be in the least bit accused of supporting the movement.

Unfortunately, Gilmore, like most southern Black women domestic workers, was especially vulnerable to economic retaliation. Her employer learned of her activism, fired her from her job as a cook, and blacklisted her from other jobs. Undaunted, however, she continued cooking and baking in her home, selling the items door to door, and turning over all the money to the boycott's organizing unit, the MIA.

While these poor and working-class women didn't have access to the specialized resources available to the WPC's professional women, the CFN did have access to other valuable resources. As Freeman (1979, 195) points out: "Movements that seem to be poor, that draw from seriously deprived constituencies, may in fact be rich in some less obvious, but still tangible resources," such as time and commitment. The maids, cooks, and service workers of the CFN also had access to information in the homes of their White employers. As they went invisibly about their domestic work, the CFNers were alert to news about the strategies and tactics of the White opposition. They had resources in their particular churches and neighborhoods as well. Although they had no status in the polity at large or even in the male-dominated organizations in the movement, the church conferred status on poor Black women who gave their time and personal commitment. These church networks were important for organizing boycott activities (Morris 1984).

The fluidity of status and the permeability of class boundaries among women in the Black community, especially before integration, is indicated by their common involvement in the Black churches and the occasional overlapping memberships of the activists. For example, Gilmore's and Robinson's mutual friend Johnnie Carr, a former cook and later a successful insurance salesperson, participated in both the WPC and the CFN. Carr was the youngest of seven children born to a farm family near Montgomery and for much of her early life was forced to earn her living by working as a cook and maid to White families—the typical low-level domestic service jobs available to most poor and working-class Black women in the South—though she had entered the insurance industry by the time of the boycott. Carr and the other women in the various "clubs" and "councils" in Montgomery were extremely active in the church, the community, and the NAACP. Carr and her close friend Rosa Parks served alternately as secretary of the local NAACP, headed by Pullman porter E. D. Nixon, and helped to organize for the bus boycott. Several years after the boycott, Carr became the only woman ever to serve as president of the MIA, which remains a viable organization in Montgomery and which Carr still heads today. The mobilization of the CFN in particular was a significant experience of empowerment for its participants.

Empowerment was in part a result of the deliberately nonhierarchical structure of the group. Unlike the somewhat formal, hierarchical structure of the Women's Political Council and the male-led Montgomery Improvement Association, the Club from Nowhere was a loosely structured network of neighborhood women who had no formal rules or regulations. Although Gilmore was referred to as the "head," authority and decision-making were vested in the group as a whole. Professionalism and expertise were not the basis of leadership. The CFN operated in an ad hoc manner, using "generally agreed upon ethics" (Rothschild-Whitt 1979; Martin 1990b). On the east side of town (like the WPC, poor and working-class women divided the city into organizing sectors), Gilmore's counterpart Inez Ricks operated "the Friendly Club" in the same manner. There were no fixed rules, no supervision of member activities, no formal recruitment, no special incentives for membership, and no functional or hierarchical division of labor.

Such groups were not entirely independent, however. Whereas the WPC was a completely autonomous Black women's organization, separate from the male-headed MIA, NAACP, and Urban League, the CFN was a single-purpose Black women's organization that lacked power relative to the male-dominated civil rights organizations. Although the WPC often conferred with the male-dominated organizations, it did not see itself as an appendage of them; they in turn recognized the autonomy and influence of the WPC in the community. In contrast, the CFN "looked up to the MIA" for guidance and directives. Unlike the women of the WPC, the women of the CFN saw themselves only as an "arm" of the male-dominated movement organizations.

The short life span of the CFN reflected the organization's short-term, one-dimensional purpose, as described by one respondent: "The Club from Nowhere was really not an organization like the Women's Political Council. The Club from Nowhere was formed for the sole purpose of raising money to finance the Montgomery boycott. It went out when the movement died down." In contrast, the WPC's fourteen-year history reflected goals that were multiple, broad, and geared to structural change. The WPC as an organization, however, ultimately succumbed to the repressive effect of job retaliation by the opposition.

The Politics of Empowerment

The WPC and the CFN had tremendous impact on the lives of their members. Like the women described by Gilkes (1980, 1988), Giddings (1984),

Jones (1985), and Collins (1990), the Black women in these two organizations were individuals of courage and inner strength, who were further empowered through their activism. Gilmore, for example, responded to being unemployed and blacklisted by going into business for herself with movement support. Recognizing the political vulnerability of being a renter, she used the organizing skills and contacts she developed during the movement to finance the purchase of her own home.[7] Her involvement in the boycott transformed not only her material conditions but her political consciousness (Barnett 1990). She continued to organize poor and working-class Black women around issues of day care and voting rights and inspired at least one of her children to pursue a formal career in politics.

The middle-class and affluent women of the WPC learned to be directly proactive for political change. In fact, one of the very first tasks of membership in the WPC was to succeed in registering to vote by passing the citizenship tests that the White opposition was using to keep Blacks from voting in the South (Robinson 1987; Burks 1990). The poor and working-class women aided and assisted the recognized movement leaders and engaged in self-help strategies and activities of their own as well. The women in the WPC and CFN considered it a duty to help one another and sacrifice for the cause. The middle-class women of the WPC and the working-class women of the CFN also shared a sense of community; they were willing to stand up for each other. One activist said: "I was always in a kind of position where I could stand up anywhere anytime. I was not afraid to ask people to volunteer their time or their money, but if they were afraid, I understood and did not push. I told them I'd do it for them. And I could get out there and do it because I was secure in my job [with a Black-owned business] and could afford to do it."

In summary, the Black women in these two organizations did much planning and organizing in the civil rights movement. The WPC and the CFN were founded at different times, had different purposes, and used different tactics. Their members' self-conscious quest for social justice, however, transformed not only their lives but also the structure of society. Yet these women and their organizations have received relatively little recognition, especially compared with the male activists and male-dominated movement organizations. One WPC member and longtime NAACP worker compared this exclusion and subordinate status of Black women in Montgomery during the time of the boycott to the historical exclusion of women throughout society's institutions:

Throughout history, you'll see women being left out in almost every area. . . . If you read the Bible, of course you'll find mention of significant women, such as Esther and Ruth; however, you'll never find these women mentioned in the same glowing manner as Peter and Paul and Moses. . . . Women throughout the Bible and history had done outstanding things that they were not considered capable of doing, but when they did them, they simply were not recognized as much as the men.

Another activist suggested a relationship between racism and private patriarchy in Black man-woman relations in the South.[8] She pointed to Black women's cognizance of the "fragile" position of Black males:

In the South, women still look to men as leaders when women are actually doing the work. . . . A lot of this comes from the tradition of the church and the male minister as the leader, the person whom you're suppose to obey. The movement was no different. . . . Women obeyed and supported their husbands, looked up to them as leaders, and didn't take any credit even if it was offered. . . . Black women especially had to work hard, but never ever threaten the fragile position of their Black men.

One veteran civil rights leader interviewed suggested an explanation beyond traditional gender role differences and expectations among Blacks and pointed to the larger problem of public patriarchy in American society: "When Europeans came to America, women had to take a back seat to males. . . . Men didn't do the work that women did, and yet they got all the praises. This European patriarchal influence is evident not just among Blacks but also among Whites. . . . Women don't get credit and praise for the work they do because that's how the White European tradition sets things up."

In her memoir, WPC president and Montgomery boycott organizer JoAnn Robinson (1987, 172) summarized Black women's courage and resolve in organizing for change:

Those who stayed behind in Montgomery carried on what we had begun, as they should have. Since 1957, the WPC members, now retired and scattered around the country in various walks of life, still feel that a woman's duties do not end in the home, church, or classroom. Members have sought to determine the ills of dissatisfied Black people and, through intelligent approaches to proper sources, to find solutions to the nagging problems that turn good men into beasts and kill the hopes, dreams, and faith of those who would strive toward something better.

Conclusion

There are both similarities and differences among Black women's social movement organizations. On the basis of conventional criteria, the middle-class women's organization, the WPC, is more recognizably "feminist" than the working-class organization, the CFN. Because African American women are not a homogeneous category, one does not fully challenge the definitions of what is feminist politics by simply adding studies of those African American women's organizations that look most like White feminist organizations. Both the WPC and the CFN were organizations that encouraged participation by all women. Such participation is a "feminist" goal, practice, and outcome. Though often unsung, the Black women who belonged to the WPC and the CFN fought for "their" rights as well as those of their children, husbands, fathers, mothers, sisters, and brothers. Certainly, those Black women, just like their White sisters in the "new women's movement," were empowered by their activism.

The class differences among African American women also mattered, however. From the beginning, the middle-class women of the WPC were prepared to take political action. For them, the boycott was an *opportunity*. It had been their idea and their initiative, and in that sense they were leaders from the start, however unacknowledged. But the CFN women needed more than an opportunity. They needed to learn that they could be effective political leaders, and the nonhierarchical structure of their organization both reflected this need and made it possible to overcome it. As an organization the CFN was never more than an auxiliary, but as members of the CFN poor and working-class women empowered themselves to become leaders. Their leadership was then evident in later years in Montgomery. Such grassroots empowerment of women was a common outcome of civil rights organizing in the poorest sectors of the Black community.

My research illustrates that when the standard categories of feminist organizations are applied to Black women's historical experiences, they are simply inadequate. Indeed, these standard questions point to the need to rewrite the history of women's organizing in a way that gives voice and visibility to the experiences of Black women, who were not "in the doldrums" in the 1940s and 1950s or newly mobilized in the 1960s. Instead, despite vigorous opposition, they provided leadership throughout this period.

In these Black women's movement organizations, founded during the period considered "pre-feminist," feminist organizing patterns and orientations emerge. Yet Black women's movement organizations have a different history from White women's movement organizations. The dimensions of gender and race and of self and family/community are not separable in their experience. These Black women's organizations were also different from the male-dominated civil rights organizations of the time—the MIA, SCLC, NAACP, CORE, and Urban League—which were all very hierarchical and bureaucratic. Collectivist in orientation, these women's groups offered innovative plans, took risks, and supported each other, as well as Black men, in the quest for justice and equality. The strategizing, organizing, fund raising, communicating, and leadership roles of the women of the WPC and the CFN were critical. Finally, Black women's SMOs differed from each other. They reflected diverse needs and ways of organizing within their community and differential access to specialized and unspecialized resources.

Black feminists have pointed out that "feminist" scholarship contradicts itself when Black women's activism is marginalized, seen only in terms of race, or excluded from feminist theorizing (hooks 1981; Hull, Scott, and Smith 1982; Collins 1990). Indeed, there is much to be learned from the organizing strategies of all women, particularly those who have been marginalized (Sachs 1988; Barnett 1989, 1990, 1993). As Giddings (1984, 5–6) has argued: "Despite the range and significance of our [Black women's] history, we have been perceived as token women in Black texts and as token Blacks in feminist ones. . . . Black women had a history of their own, one which reflects their distinct concerns, values and the role they have played as *both Afro-Americans and women. And their unique status has had an impact on both racial and feminist values*" (emphasis added). This research should be seen as a step not only toward reclaiming that history for its own sake but toward understanding the feminist implications of organizing on gender and race and class dimensions simultaneously.

Notes

Acknowledgments: I want to express my sincere gratitude to the Black women civil rights activists who generously granted interviews and shared their organizing experiences with me. I am also grateful to many people who provided helpful comments on earlier versions of this essay, particularly Cheryl Townsend Gilkes, Hester Eisenstein, and Jo Freeman. Finally, I owe a very special debt to Myra Marx Ferree and Patricia Yancey Martin for their priceless encouragement, feedback, and editorial advice.

1. There has been considerable scholarship on White women's movement organizations such as NOW, on various women's liberation "first groups" (cf. Freeman 1975, 1979; Rothschild-Whitt 1979; Ferree and Hess 1985), and on both White male-dominated and Black male-dominated movement organizations such as SDS, the NAACP, SCLC, CORE, the Urban League, and SNCC (Zinn 1965; Morris 1984; Breines 1989; Stoper 1989). Explicit analysis of modern Black women's movement organizations, however, has been noticeably absent in the literature.

2. Time has taken its toll on veteran civil rights activists; the recent deaths of several of those I interviewed precluded follow-up on significant questions that their participation raised and insights that they provided for our initial interview. That some of those who are still living cannot readily recall the names and activities of all of the women involved makes the destruction of organizational records and membership rosters (to avoid their being subpoenaed; see below) all the more unfortunate.

3. The names of the women respondents are not used here because they were promised anonymity. I acknowledge my sincere appreciation to them for sharing with me their organizing experiences and their insights.

4. For example, Lottie Rollins and other Black feminists founded the racially integrated South Carolina Women's Rights Association (SCWRA) and attended the American Suffrage Association Convention of 1872. When the *History of Women's Suffrage* was written in 1900, however, the starting date of the movement was given as 1890, and no reference was made to the SCWRA, founded twenty years earlier (see discussion in Terborg-Penn 1978).

5. Though there is a rich historical and sociological literature on leadership, much contemporary social movement scholarship views "leaders" as one of many "resources" needed for and mobilized by a social movement organization. For additional discussion of this point, see Barnett 1993.

6. One might argue that this collectivity called a "club" is not an organization. In addressing this issue, however, Martin (1990b, 185) defines an organization as any "relatively enduring" group of people (one that exists for more than a few meetings) structured to pursue goals that are collectively identified. By this criterion, the CFN was a movement organization; it was intentional and had an emergent plan of action and organized strategy.

7. The political as well as material transformation that ensued for her was similar to the effects that involvement in voter registration had on sharecroppers Fannie Lou Hamer and Unita Blackwell.

8. Research by Martin, Wilson, and Dillman (1991) makes the point that social,

cultural, and structural conditions shape gender relations in the South. They argue that the intersecting of patriarchy and slavery in the antebellum South "fundamentally confounded gender and race relations" in the region and that slavery and White men's sexual "exploitation of Black women hindered the development of common bonds or identity among White and Black women" (1991, 105–6).

PART IV

Emotions:
A Hidden Dimension of
Organizational Life

CHAPTER 14

Watching for Vibes:
Bringing Emotions into the Study
of Feminist Organizations

■

VERTA TAYLOR

Anyone who has ever participated in a feminist organization would have to admit that emotions sometimes have a way of taking center stage in the women's movement. Acknowledging the impact of emotions on the functioning of feminist organizations, the planning committee for the first National Lesbian Conference (held in Atlanta in 1991) actually appointed several women as "vibes watchers." Vibes watchers were responsible for "staying alert to the collective emotional climate and advising us when to stop for a deep breath, a moment of silence, or a group scream" ("Choosing a National Lesbian Conference Steering Committee" 1989). Whether feminism is practiced in a community of activists, a women's health center, a women's studies program, a lesbian support group, or a large national organization, there is always an emotional subtext. For that matter, emotions are essential to antifeminist movements as well. A recent example is the Reverend Pat Robertson's attempt to capitalize on fear of feminism in his 1992 fund-raising letter for the Iowa Committee to Stop E.R.A., in which he accused the women's movement of encouraging "women to leave their husbands, kill their children, practice witchcraft, destroy capitalism, and become lesbians."

Two different concerns have called my attention to the importance of emotions for the study of feminist organizations. The first is my experience as a feminist trying to live in a nonfeminist world; bell hooks (1992, 82) evokes this daily struggle when she reminds us that "there is no one among us who has not felt the pain of sexist oppression, the anguish male domination can create." The second is theoretical. Over the past fifteen years, I have been studying submerged networks of women who continued to fight gender inequality in periods when mass feminism receded and there was widespread opposition to women's rights. This work led me quite naturally to the role of emotions in the feminist movement. I have found that women who carried the torch during the darker periods of feminism's history have often been motivated not only by a deep sense of anger at gender injustice but by the joy of participation, the love and friendship of other women, and pride at having maintained their feminist convictions in the face of strong opposition (Rupp and Taylor 1987; Taylor 1989; Taylor and Whittier 1992).

In this essay I argue that bridging the gap between feminist practice and theory requires recognizing the centrality of the feelings as well as the ideas and strategic actions that frame women's resistance to male domination. Recently the study of emotions has emerged as an important topic in the field of sociology. With only a few exceptions (see Lofland 1982, 1985; Morgen 1983; Morris 1984; Taylor and Whittier 1995), this work has yet to find its way into research and theorizing on social movements. Examining theoretical developments in collective behavior and social movements over the past several decades, one is forced to conclude that social movement scholars have been exceedingly ambivalent about the role of feelings in collective action. Prior to the surge of activism of the 1960s and 1970s, the dominant paradigm of collective behavior theory treated social movements largely as the nonrational or irrational responses of alienated and anomic individuals to social breakdown or strain (LeBon 1960; Smelser 1962; Blumer 1969). In effect, protest was distinguished from routine social behavior on the basis of its emotionality, and the emotionally driven beliefs and ideas of protesters were discredited by some scholars as akin to "magical" thinking (Smelser 1962, 8).

Research on the movements of the 1960s and 1970s undertaken by scholars more sympathetic to the views and actions of challenging groups questioned the notion that participants were irrational and marginal, reinvigorated the field, and led to a major shift in theorizing about contemporary social movements (McAdam 1982; Jenkins 1983; Morris 1984). Social movement theory subsequently took three directions. First, in the United States some collective behavior theorists continued to hold that the fields of collective behavior and social movements are empirically and theoretically linked. They advocated the emergent norm perspective, which recognizes the rational as well as the affective dimensions of protest and the cultural as well as structural influences on collective action (Turner and Killian 1987; Aguirre, Quarantelli, and Mendoza 1988).

A second major perspective, resource mobilization theory, developed among a group of scholars who viewed collective behavior and social movements as distinct subject matters. Questioning what they saw as the "irrationalist" assumptions of classical collective behavior theory, resource mobilization theorists emphasized the rationality of social movement actors and looked to variations in political opportunities and changes in group organization and resources for understanding the rise of collective action (McCarthy and Zald 1977; C. Tilly 1978; McAdam 1982; Jenkins 1983; Morris 1984; Gamson 1990). Influenced by neoclassical economic assumptions, resource mobilization approaches view social movement actors as driven by the same forces of self-interest that propel social actors in any setting. In effect, social movement participation and tactical choices are predetermined by the innate human drive to maximize rewards and minimize costs, rather than by any higher set of values, moral purposes, or affective commitments.

Resource mobilization theorists, therefore, hold organization to be essential for sustained protest, not only because formal organizations are capable of garnering and providing the material incentives necessary to offset the costs to individuals of participating in protest, but also because they are capable of providing secondary incentives—namely, bonds of friendship—that enhance participation (Olson 1965; Oberschall 1973). Feelings come into play in classical resource mobilization formulations only as affective ties that bind participants to challenging groups, and they are secondary to questions of strategic success in motivating activists. During the 1980s resource mobilization theory came to dominate the field of social movements and had substantial influence on scholarship on the American women's movement (Freeman 1975; Ferree and Hess 1985; Chafetz and Dworkin 1986; Gelb and Palley 1987; Katzenstein and Mueller 1987; Rupp and Taylor 1987; Buechler 1990b; Staggenborg 1991; B. Ryan 1992). Given its emphasis on instrumental rationality, organization, and strategic planning, early proponents of resource mobilization theory relegated the study of emotions, oppositional values, and affective bonds to the fringes of the field. It is not surprising that several analysts have recently sought to incorporate grievances and discontent into resource mobilization approaches (McAdam 1982; Klandermans 1984; Snow et al. 1986; Buechler 1990b; Friedman and McAdam 1992; Gamson 1992; Morris and Mueller 1992; B. Ryan 1992).

A third approach, often dubbed "new social movement theory" because it addresses the 1960s movements and the feminist, peace, environmental, gay and lesbian local community movements, and other struggles that were their heirs, originated among European scholars (Klandermans and Tarrow 1988). New social movement theorists question the rationalist assumptions underlying resource mobilization theory. What such scholars find distinctive about recent social movements is their emphasis on consciousness, self-actualization, and the expression of subjective feelings, desires, and experiences—or new collective identities—as a strategy of political change (Inglehart 1977; Pizzorno 1978; Touraine 1981, 1985; Habermas 1984, 1987; Cohen 1985; K. Eder 1985; Melucci 1985, 1989; Offe 1985). In this model the notion of freestanding individuals engaged in self-interested actions is replaced by the concept of persons as members of social movement communities. These communities, constrained of course by resources and their relative power, nevertheless supply the values, bonds, and affect that shape individuals' actions (Etzioni 1988).

European approaches to social movements pave the way laid by collective behavior scholars for considering the link between emotions and social protest. But it is feminist scholarship, with its critique of Western rationality for devaluing contextual modes of thought and the emotional components of reason, that provides the best signposts. My intent is to draw from feminist theory, research on a variety of feminist organizations, and the literature on the sociology of emotions to outline links between emotions and the women's movement. First, I discuss the significance of emotions to understanding women's motivations for participating in feminist activism. Second, I address the ways in which feminist organizations develop a distinctive emotion culture that challenges and redefines dominant emotion norms. I conclude by urging that we generalize from the study of women's movements to elaborate a model of social movements that breaks down the artificial barrier between the concepts of organization, rationality, and choice, on the one hand, and affective bonds, emotions, and impulse, on the other.

Emotions and Feminist Mobilization

Both popular and scholarly writings brim with accounts of the intense feelings that underlie participation in the women's movement. Women mobilized into the antiviolence movement, for example, direct anger not only at the men who perpetrate violence against women but at the institutions and cultural ideas that perpetuate sexist oppression. The upper-middle-class members of the National Woman's Party, to take a very different example, were passionately committed to the cause of the ERA in the 1940s and 1950s, leading one woman to exclaim about the joy of commitment: "It is as thrilling as a love affair, and lasts longer!!!!" (Rupp and Taylor 1987, 97). The extent to which radical feminists of the second wave saw emotions as central to protest is suggested by the comments of a Redstockings member: "Our politics begin with our feelings. Feelings are a direct response to the events and relationships that we experience; that's how we know what's really going on. For centuries women's information has been categorized as magic, instinct, intuition, witchcraft, and more recently, projections, distortion, personal hangups, and other variations on a theme designed to render our knowledge meaningless and empty" (quoted in Wasielewski 1991).

Feminist scholars have been among the most vocal critics of the "rationalist" or cognitive bias in Western thinking that privileges rational, independent, self-interested action over action that is driven by emotion, undertaken collectively, and motivated by altruism or the desire to affirm the group (Mansbridge 1990; Ferree 1992b). Women have generally been deemed—even if largely as a result of gender stratification—more emotional, subjective, and relational than men. Feminist theorists contend that the separation of passion and reason serves not only to dichotomize thought and feeling but to elevate what has come to be called "abstract masculinity" over women's standpoint (Jaggar 1983; Harding 1986; D. Smith 1987). This dichotomy so informs our understanding of nature and social relations that it has been applied fairly uniformly to differentiate most disempowered groups: people of color; the working class; ethnic, religious, and sexual minorities. The ideals of Western rationality have often served to legitimate the interests of powerful groups who aspire to dominate the uncontrollable by rising above it through logic or reason. The dualistic opposition of the rational and the emotional, as Ferree (1992b) observes, runs through both the collective behavior and the resource mobilization literature: whereas in the classical collective behavior tradition, social movement participants are denigrated for being too emotional, resource mobilization theorists legitimate protesters by insisting that they are *not* emotional (McAdam 1982; Klandermans 1984). In either case, reason and passion are segregated, and passion is considered a lesser motivation for protest.

In the recent literature on the sociology of emotions we find clear guidelines for understanding how emotion figures into feminist resistance. This work treats emotions as a site for articulating the links between cultural ideas, structural inequality, and individual action (Hochschild 1983, 1990;

Kemper 1990). Power and status inequalities may provoke predictable emotional responses—anger, fear and anxiety, guilt, shame, hate, depression, love, pride, satisfaction, happiness—but the expression and management of these emotions is ultimately governed by social processes (Kemper 1978, 1981; Scheff 1990). Depression, for example, is widely understood to be linked to women's low status (Mirowsky and Ross 1989; Jack 1991). Depression depends not only on status deprivation but on the perception that the forces responsible for one's situation are irremediable. Depression is common in women engaged in full-time mothering, poor women, lesbians, women of color, and women who survive rape, incest, battering, sexual harassment, and other forms of male violence (McGrath et al. 1990). Its link to women's mobilization can be found in the booming self-help and recovery movements that have swept up so many women in recent years (Kaminer 1992; Simonds 1992; hooks 1993).

Anger is another common response to sexist oppression. Kemper's interactional theory of emotions holds that when individuals view a status loss or deprivation as arbitrary and remediable, they are more likely to get angry than depressed. Man-hating, which J. Levine (1992) defines as the "volatile admixture of pity, contempt, disgust, envy, alienation, fear and rage at men" that women feel, is a powerful motivation for feminist protest. For example, the failure of Anita Hill's testimony about the sexual harassment she experienced at the hands of Clarence Thomas to block his appointment to the Supreme Court provoked widespread anger among women. These feelings galvanized a large constituency, as evidenced by the massive increases in membership and funding reported by national feminist organizations in the months following the hearings (Abramson 1992).

To suggest that emotions play a part in mobilizing women to participate in feminist organizations does not negate the body of scholarship on the women's movement that emphasizes the instrumental and strategic nature of feminist activism (Freeman 1975; Ferree and Hess 1985; Buechler 1990b). Rather, my point is that a full understanding of the factors that motivate women to take up feminist protest requires that we attend not only to the ideas and strategic actions of those victimized by gender subordination but to the feelings, generated by male domination, that drive women's resistance.

The Emotion Culture of Feminist Organizations

Scholars of the women's movement have pointed to both the love and caring, on the one hand, and the anger, pain, and hostility, on the other, that characterize feminists' interactions (Freeman 1972; Rupp 1980; B. Ryan 1992; Taylor and Rupp 1993). An analysis of the way feminist organizations channel the emotions that arise from inequality is basic to understanding the culture of contemporary women's movements. Although researchers have explored the distinctive structures of feminist organizations that accentuate pluralism and diversity (Leidner 1991; Sirianni 1993), they have overlooked the fact that communities of women devise what Hochschild (1990) has termed distinctive "emotion cultures" as well. To varying degrees, feminist groups tend to cultivate a unique set of feeling rules and expression rules that both draw upon and challenge the dominant ideal of women as nurturers. These emotion cultures grow out of a conscious awareness of the significance of emotional control for upholding gender differences, but they also struggle to resist this imperative by (1) channeling the emotions tied to women's subordination into emotions conducive to protest; (2) redefining feeling and expression rules that apply to women to reflect more desirable identities or self-conceptions; and (3) advancing an "ethic of care" that promotes organizational structures and strategies consistent with female bonding.

To take up the first point, being a woman in a male-dominated and misogynist society evokes a wide range of feelings. Through consciousness raising and other tactics, feminist organizations aim to channel women's fear, shame, and depression into feelings conducive to protest and activism rather than resignation and withdrawal. Ritual is an important mechanism in this process. At demonstrations, marches, and cultural activities such as concerts, films, poetry readings, exhibitions, plays, conferences, and music festivals, ritual evokes and channels women's emotions, dramatizes inequality and injustice, and emphasizes the connection between women's individual experiences and their disadvantaged status as a group (Eder et al. unpublished). For example, songs and poems use vivid and moving terms to describe homeless women, or lesbians incarcerated in mental institutions, or victims of battering and incest, or women activists from third world countries who have been persecuted for their resistance. Slogans such as "No woman is free until all women are free" express anger and remind listeners of their continuing subordination as women. Speakouts by women who have had illegal abortions or been raped or suffered forced sterilization, poetry readings by incest survivors, testimonies from recovering alcoholics all reframe feelings of shame over past events into pride over having survived such ordeals. Support groups linked to feminist self-help campaigns for sufferers of breast cancer and postpartum depression use consciousness raising to transform women's emotional distress into feelings that are empowering.

The anti-rape movement relies heavily on rituals that channel the fear, guilt, and depression women experience following victimization into emotions that reflect more desirable self-concepts (Matthews 1994). Confronting pornographers, picketing the businesses of sexual harassers, and posting lists of unconvicted rapists in public places are demonstrations that arouse anger and mobilize grassroots activism among women. Participants in "Take Back the Night" marches, held in major urban areas around the country, chant slogans such as "Out of the house and into the streets, we won't be raped, we won't be beat!" This sort of discourse, as well as the use of the term "survivor" to refer to victims of rape, incest, or battering, explicitly encourages participants to recognize women's collective strength and legitimates the expression of anger. The use of militant and dramatic tactics is another means of signifying anger. For instance, in the early 1980s, feminists against pornography attacked adult book stores by vomiting on the books and magazines they found objectionable. In Columbus, Ohio, after an unpopular judge dropped charges of rape against a local man on the grounds that his four-year-old victim was a "promiscuous young lady," members of a feminist group expressed their anger by sending pig testicles to the judge.

The second characteristic of feminist emotion cultures is the redefinition of feeling and expression rules that apply to women. The hallmark of contemporary feminism is the belief that "the personal is political." Among feminists, therefore, emotion is both a basis for defining oneself and a tool for change. To resist patriarchy means to challenge norms for the expression of emotion inside feminist communities as well as in everyday interactions in the outside world. The expression of anger, for example, is less acceptable for women than for men. One woman active in the movement to combat postpartum depression was told by a male interviewer not to express anger at the medical establishment in a videotape being made for the public because people tend to be "uncomfortable with women when they say that they are angry." Yet, as we have seen, feminist organizations encourage women to trade fear and shame for anger. Within predominantly White, middle-class feminist organizations, women of color and working-class women meld anger and pride to affirm and re-define their differences. Feminists involved in organizations that confront male violence admit hating and fearing men, thus rejecting the heterosexual imperative that controls women (Rich 1980). Lesbian feminists, defying the taboo on same-sex bonding, use tactics that depend on the open expression of affection and commitment. Two women who announced their lesbian union on the wedding page of the *Austin American-Statesman*, for example, viewed their action "as an outright frontal attack on the most holy institution—the institution of marriage" ("Bells Are Ringing" 1992). It is perhaps because feminism promotes the display of deviant emotions, both positive and negative, that participation in feminist organizations can be such an intense experience. The open expression of fear, hostility, anger, and pain that erupted between White women and women of color at the 1990 National Women's Studies Association conference, for instance, precipitated major structural changes in the organization and a substantial loss of members (Ruby and Douglas 1992).

Finally, feminist organizations make explicit claims to an "ethic of care" that promotes female bonding, even if in reality it may not always be practiced. The emphasis placed on the primacy of women's relationships not only molds everyday interactions among women; it also dictates democratic organizational structures and separatist tactics that challenge the hierarchical structures and self-interested behavior that are seen as undermining collective commitment and strong emotional ties between women.

Even if we abandon the conventional assumption that women are, by nature, more "emotional" than men, it would be difficult to deny that the traditional patterns of social organization dictating women's caring roles prescribe different feeling rules and expression norms for women (Hochschild 1983; Thoits 1990). In defining an Afrocentric feminist epistemology, Collins (1990, 216) states that "a central component of the ethic of caring concerns the appropriateness of emotions in dialogues." The feminist emphasis on caring is conveyed through women's references to each other as sisters and open expressions of love and affection between women who have participated in a common struggle. In lesbian feminist communities, the feminist emphasis on caring is reflected in the fact that relationships between women are thought of not only as personal but also as political, a view captured in what has become a classic slogan: "Feminism is the theory and lesbianism is the practice." In feminist self-help groups, caring and nurturant personal relationships provide a point of connection and identification with others that is not only therapeutic but empowering, permitting women to cultivate new understandings of their problems which counter orthodox medical views.

The expression rules of feminist organizations and communities dictate open displays of emotion and empathy and legitimate extensive attention to participants' emotions and personal histories (Morgen 1983; Chapter 15). Given the pain that women bring into the movement, it is not surprising that what Stevens (1992) has called "oppression sickness" sometimes leads feminists to turn on one another. Undoubtedly this contributes to the kind of interpersonal conflict—often dubbed "trashing"—described by so many feminists and scholars of the women's movement (Freeman 1972; B. Ryan 1992). Nevertheless, the way emotions are dealt with in the women's movement is meant to serve as an example of the new feeling rules and expression norms advocated by feminism; in other words, the women's movement practices emotional prefigurative politics (Breines 1989).

Conclusion

Sara Ruddick begins her book *Maternal Thinking* (1989, 3) with the statement: "My life has been shaped by a love affair with Reason." She goes on to describe the myriad ways that rationality has, until now, helped her find order in chaos, confusion, alienation, and despair. Reason seems to have served social movement theorists in the same way. To be fair, the neglect of emotion by at least some social movement scholars has been motivated by a desire to avoid depicting social movement actors as irrational and impulsive. That I have used research on the women's movement to challenge the excessive emphasis on rationality in contemporary theorizing on social movements is in no way meant to imply that emotion is uniquely associated with feminist movements. The civil rights movement, for instance, was particularly skilled at using music and religious symbolism that evoked strong emotions to mobilize participants (Morris 1984). As this example illustrates, emotional expression often serves rational and strategic purposes. Furthermore, strong emotional ties often underlie even the most formal of organizations. Recent military objections to allowing women into combat positions, for example, were justified by the argument that women's presence would threaten the traditional patterns of male bonding deemed critical to the success of military organizations. Finally, formal organizations condone the expression of a wide range of feelings. To illustrate, the articulation of woman-hating is routine in certain types of work organizations where sexual harassment serves to limit women's advancement (Fonow 1993).

Juxtaposing feminist theory and work by scholars interested in the emotional climate of feminist organizations to theorizing on social movements raises serious questions, then, about the polarization of emotionality and rationality as well as about the connection between rationality and organization posited by resource mobilization theorists. I conclude by suggesting that the study of emotions may be a site for articulating the links between individual protest and larger cultural and structural processes, for it is emotions that provide the "heat," so to speak, that distinguishes social movements from dominant institutions. Attention to the emotions of protest should be added to the contemporary agenda of those who are working to expand resource mobilization theory to incorporate the grievances, new self-understandings, and oppositional ideas that drive protest groups (see, e.g., Gamson 1992; Morris and Mueller 1992).

In a recent article, bell hooks (1992) admitted that she came to feminist theory because she was hurting. To recognize the role of emotions in mobilization and activism is not to deny that we are thinking as well as feeling actors. Just as "watching for vibes" may help to close the gap between theory and feminist practice, attending to the role of emotions in social movements suggests new directions for resource mobilization theory and from a feminist standpoint has the potential to alter what Audrey Lorde (1984) so eloquently described as "the master's tools."

Note

Acknowledgments: I would like to acknowledge the support of the Ohio Department of Mental Health during the writing of this essay. I am grateful to Leila Rupp, Myra Marx Ferree, Jo Freeman, Nancy Whittier, Carol Mueller, and Bert Klandermans for helpful comments and advice.

CHAPTER 15

"It Was the Best of Times, It Was the Worst of Times": Emotional Discourse in the Work Cultures of Feminist Health Clinics

■

SANDRA MORGEN

"It was the best of times, it was the worst of times." With these words, Charles Dickens opens *A Tale of Two Cities*, introducing his readers to a paradox of revolutionary times—the headiness, the dreams and hopes; the disillusion, the failures and pain. Affective intensity and conflicting emotions are part of political activism in the contemporary feminist movement as well. I use Dickens's words to stand as an evocation of the stories I have been told and the experiences I have been part of during my research on the women's health movement.

Feminist health organizations have both accommodated and resisted the powerful pressures they encounter from organized medicine, the state, and the New Right (Morgen 1986, 1988, 1990). Here I look at how this embattlement and feminist ideology and practice shape work culture in feminist health clinics. My approach is guided by a focus on the actual *experience* of participation in social movement organizations. Experience is examined as it is a part of and grounded in social relations of power.

A crucial dimension of the experience of involvement in social movements that is often neglected by researchers is what I have elsewhere defined as "the politics of feelings" (Morgen 1983). In calling attention to feelings as a dimension of social movement experience, I contend that political actors are feeling persons whose involvement in social movements encompasses intense passion and affect.

The neglect of emotion has deep roots in theories of social life, academic vocabularies, and the social relations of power characteristic of modern Western societies (Lutz and White 1986; Lutz 1988). Jaggar (1989, 145) argues that in Western thought "not only has reason been contrasted with emotion, but it has also been associated with the mental, the cultural, the universal, the public and the male, whereas emotion has been associated with the irrational, the physical, the natural, the particular, the private, and of course, the female." Stearns (1988, 3) suggests that the assumption of a dichotomous division between the realms of the public and the private has relegated the study of emotions to their perceived "appropriate" place, within the family. This has resulted in approaches to research on politics, work, and organizations that presume "the abstract, bodiless worker, who occupies the abstract gender-neutral job [and] has no sexuality, no emotions, and does not procreate" (Acker 1990, 151).

In recent years, there has been a growing social scientific interest in emotions as a dimension of social life (Lutz and White 1986). Social scientific studies of emotion have contributed an expanded appreciation of the social construction of emotion, and the related understanding that "ideas are infused with value, affect, and direction, just as feelings are used to understand and communicate about social events" (Lutz and White 1986, 430). Recent work on the anthropology of emotions has begun to politicize and historicize these insights concerning the social construction of emotions. For example, Abu-Lughod and Lutz (1990) move beyond seeing emotions as socially constructed to situate emotional discourse within power relations in concrete historical instances. Feminist scholarship has been one particularly important source of new theoretical insight about how profoundly emotion is conditioned by, and is a dimension of, the dynamics and reproduction of hegemonic power relations (Hochschild 1979, 1983; Lutz 1988; Abu-Lughod and Lutz 1990).

This essay represents a preliminary effort to develop a framework that integrates political economy, political passions, and ideology in examining the experience of involvement in the women's health movement in the United States since the 1970s. Specifically, I demonstrate how powerful political and economic forces external to feminist health clinics, as well as internal struggles spawned by the difficulties of implementing feminist ideology in organizational practice, were experienced, made meaningful, and transformed in the everyday lives of the health activists in these organizations. My approach is decidedly sociological: I explore the specific social practices in which emotional discourses are created, interpreted, and contested in the work cultures of feminist clinics.

The analysis of women's work cultures has been primarily a project of feminist anthropologists, sociologists, and historians who examine the ways women create networks, values, relationships, and social spaces that contest the wholesale control of work by management within mainstream workplaces (Bookman 1977; Benson 1978; Melosh 1982; Lamphere 1987; Zavella 1987; Sachs 1988a). This research conceives of work culture as a relatively autonomous sphere of action on the job, a realm of informal, customary values and rules that mediate the formal authority structure of the workplace and distance workers from its impact.

Since most research on women's work cultures examines conventional workplaces that are organized and tightly controlled by management (such as factories, hospitals, or department stores), this essay breaks new ground by exploring women's work culture in staff- and woman-controlled work environments. In general, the work cultures constructed in women's health clinics embody an active contestation of bureaucracy, hierarchy, and the valorization of rationality in public life. In the wake of feminist critiques of bureaucracy and hierarchy, grassroots activists developed organizational structures and processes to challenge inegalitarian social relations, to foster a sensitivity to individual needs and feelings, and to take "process" seriously: that is, to recognize that how things get done is as important as what is done.

After a brief discussion of the women's health movement as a social movement, I examine the difficult political-economic conditions that shape feminist work cultures and the specific strategies feminists have developed to legitimize and handle the affective dimensions of working for social change.

The Women's Health Movement in the United States

The women's health movement emerged in the United States in the early 1970s as women organized for abortion rights, reproductive freedom, and dignified and affordable health care. The movement articulated a radical critique of the U.S. health care system, including a condemnation of medicine as an institution of social control, of racism and sexism in health care institutions and policies, and of the failure of the system to meet the most basic health needs of many, most particularly the poor (Boston Women's Health Book Collective 1984).

According to movement sources, by 1973 more than 1,000 women's health projects existed in the United States (Ruzek 1978). These organizations formed the infrastructure for a movement that focuses on health education, on organizing to change medical practices and social policy affecting women's health, and on the development of alternative woman-controlled health services. Among them some one to two hundred woman-controlled, feminist health clinics.

Although these clinics varied from location to location and changed during their years of operation, they shared certain general features that set them apart from mainstream medical facilities and defined their connection to a movement committed to empowering women in health care decision-making, practice, and policy. Feminist clinics stressed self-help; lay involvement in all phases of patient care; and accessible, affordable, and woman-centered services. Most of them were run not by medical professionals but through some combination of worker and community control. Their organizational structures emphasized participatory democracy, and, especially in the early years, collectivity and decision-making by consensus (Ruzek 1978; Boston Women's Health Book Collective 1984; Simmons, Kay, and Reagan 1984; Morgen and Julier 1991).

My research on the women's health movement spans almost fifteen years. It combines fieldwork (1977–80) done in one feminist clinic with data from a questionnaire and interviews collected a decade later from the larger movement. Between 1990 and 1992 I interviewed thirty-six health activists whose combined experiences includes twenty-one different feminist health organizations. In addition, I collected data from fifty women's health organizations through a mail questionnaire that compares each organization at its founding, in 1979 (if it existed then), and in 1989. The questionnaire was designed to ascertain patterns of change in these movement organizations over two decades (Morgen and Julier 1991).

Here I examine data from four of these feminist health clinics. Two are on the east coast, two on the west coast. Two perform abortions as part of their health care; the other two do abortion counseling and referral, but not abortions, as part of their "well woman" gynecology and family planning services. Each organization was founded during the early years of the women's health movement; all but one are still operating. I do not claim that these four clinics are typical of the fifty organizations I have studied, but they are representative of some of the broad patterns and dynamics I encountered in my ongoing work.

The Experience of Work in Feminist Health Clinics

The interviews with women's health activists revealed a wide range of work experiences, but almost all the women emphasized the *intensity* of them. To hark back to the Dickens quotation that titles this chapter, women commonly described their experiences as both intensely good and intensely bad: a time of exhilaration, hope, and personal empowerment but also of pain, stress, and—often—demoralization. For example, one woman who worked for three and a half years at Feminist Women's Health (a pseudonym, hereafter FWH) spoke warmly of her years at the clinic: "I got so much out of working there. . . . I mean talk about . . . personal empowerment—I learned everything I know about working from working at the health center." Sentiments like this were articulated frequently in the interviews. But another longtime staff member at the same clinic shared a more negative assessment of her experiences, especially those in the last months before the clinic closed in the early 1980s: "I'd already seen a fair amount of personal tragedy . . . and a lot of growth and a lot of empowerment. . . . [But] it was just too hard to stay there . . . people were so tired, and people left, and your best friend from the last year was telling you she couldn't take it anymore, and it would be the most incredible desertion, and you were pissed off because she was leaving."

Located in a large city in the Northeast, FWH spent almost half its organizational life battling local and state officials—building inspectors, zoning ordinance personnel, and public health staff—during a long struggle to secure a clinic license. Shortly after the clinic's founding the powerful anti-abortion movement in the state had been victorious in passing legislation forcing abortion clinics to secure state department of health licensure before they were eligible to receive third-party reimbursement for abortion services. This mandate was a strategy to constrain and ultimately close down grassroots health facilities, as the process of licensure was at best long and costly, subjecting the organization to extensive external scrutiny.

Across the country in the Pacific Northwest, Feminist Health Care (a pseudonym, hereafter FHC) suffered a different but no less powerful assault from the anti-abortion movement. In the mid-1980s the clinic became the target of weekly picketing, extensive vandalism, and several blockades. In 1986, FHC filed what was to become a precedent-setting lawsuit which, after a long legal battle, resulted in findings against a number of the protesters and limited damage awards. The clinic's director used the words "terrifying" and "depressing" to describe the long years of harassment by anti-abortion foes: "It was terrible, just awful. . . . Sometimes there were as many as 150 picketers, and they would be, you know, just right up against our front door. . . . When they got in people's faces, screaming and yelling, it was really bad." The costs of vandalism and concern for personal safety forced the clinic to board up its windows for months until they were replaced by steel grates. The director was emphatic about the emotional toll on her staff: "I cannot believe we psychologically survived all this. . . . People were so depressed. . . . A lot of good people left. . . . You felt like you were just barely hanging on and there was hardly anything you could do anymore."

Experiences such as these are echoed in the literature on the violence that has been directed at abortion facilities, including feminist clinics. Lynne Randall, the director of a feminist clinic in Atlanta, admits fearing for her safety and is graphic in her description of the impact of the long-term and routine harassment of her clinic staff from anti-abortionists: "It's been pretty devastating. We've done a remarkable job of holding ourselves together, but it has certainly caused a lot of stress on our employees and their families . . . [and] it has caused a number of people to quit" (Hairston 1990, 15).

As of 1990, according to the conservative estimates of law enforcement officials, U.S. abortion clinics had been the victims of eight bombings, twenty-eight documented acts of arson, twenty-eight additional attempted bombings or arson, and 170 acts of vandalism (Hairston 1990, 15). In addition, groups such as Operation Rescue routinely use picketing, blockades, stalking, verbal assault on workers and their families, and threatening phone calls in their arsenal of harassment. In 1993 there were two attempts by anti-abortionists to murder doctors who perform abortions—one of which was successful.

Although the other two clinics avoided the direct wrath of the anti-abortion movement, both experienced profound economic insecurity. Since they did not perform abortions, they lacked the stable and generous fees associated with providing those services. Consequently, these clinics had to depend on state or foundation monies to supplement the sliding-scale fees paid by their clients for gynecological and family planning services. Feminist clinics (along with many other grassroots health facilities) faced continuing economic crises during the 1980s when Reaganomics on the federal level and taxpayer revolt plus revenue shortfalls on the state and local levels meant shrinking public funds for health care.

Increasingly scarce funds led to clinic closures, and in other cases, either the anticipation or reality of budget cuts fostered painful changes in clinic activities, structures, or goals (Morgen and Julier 1991). To generate external funds, clinics faced wrenching periods of self-reflection, restructuring, and often dramatic organizational changes. As a rule, these changes meant more hierarchy and bureaucracy in internal structures, decreased political autonomy, and an attenuation of the political goals of the organization (see Newman 1980; Simmons, Kay, and Reagan 1984; Morgen 1986).

Economic pressures and organizational changes often catalyzed internal division and protracted conflict in feminist clinics. A former director of one of the first feminist clinics in the country, Community Women's Health (a pseudonym, hereafter CWH), resigned by letter during one such crisis. After months of heated internal conflict about changes in organizational structure, decision-making processes, and clinic activities in response to state policy changes in the wake of budget cuts, she decided to leave because working at the clinic had become too emotionally costly:

> Because I'm afraid I'll be scapegoated at the meeting, my presence would serve only the purpose of creating further tension and stress. . . . I don't believe given what's coming down the road because of [the governor's] budget cuts that [CWH] will survive without serious change. . . . I wish you all the luck in resolving the issues [CWH] must come to terms with. . . . Any plan will fail if the group continues to assume the worst of and expects to be screwed by and refuses to work with each other. I've put my heart and soul in here. I love the place . . . and shed a lot of tears over having to leave this way . . . but . . . I can no longer work in a group that lacks a sense of process, compassion, and cooperation.

In addition to conflicts generated by external political and economic forces, feminist clinics often become embroiled in internal division and controversy arising either from ideological "splits" in the women's movement or from differences and distrust that emerged as women from different race and class backgrounds articulated divergent visions, priorities, or interpersonal expectations (Morgen 1988; Albrecht and Brewer 1990; Ristock 1990). For example, in 1977 the clinic in which I did fieldwork, Women's Health Center (a pseudonym, hereafter WHC), received a grant from CETA (Comprehensive Employment and Training Act) to hire fifteen low-income women as staff for a year and a half. This funding enabled the clinic to fulfill a long-envisioned goal of creating more race and class diversity within the staff. But with the diversity came years of painful conflict over race and class issues. Confronting the ugly realities of racism, homophobia, and class prejudice *within* their organizations meant new scars for women of color, lesbians, and women from working-class families. It also meant pain, shame, anger, and defensiveness in the relatively privileged women forced to recognize their complicity with dominant social relations of power.

The conflicts over racism, class issues, and homophobia were not unique to the clinic I studied but endemic in the women's health movement. Feminists were learning that the transformation of dominant social relations of power was not easy and did not follow automatically from a conscious political position about "sisterhood" or the empowerment of women. During the 1980s women of color formed several important national and local women's health organizations to articulate their particular perspectives on changing health care for women (A. Davis 1981; White 1990), even as they continued to challenge oppressive social relations within white-dominated feminist groups.

A number of factors contribute to the emotional intensity of the work cultures of feminist health clinics. The nature of the work means that staff are constantly engaged with clients who are in crisis, and feminist clinics often face crises stemming from both external pressures and internal divisions. Research on staff "burnout" suggests that this combination of factors is not unique to feminist organizations (Freudenberger 1975; Cherniss 1980; Joffe 1986). All human service work is stressful precisely because so often the organizations have pathetically limited financial resources for dealing with overwhelming human need. Alternative grassroots services, however, face even stiffer assaults and thinner resource bases than most mainstream service organizations.

Additionally, alternative organizations in the women's movement have articulated political goals that transcend progressive service delivery. Most of these groups reject hierarchical, bureaucratic organizational structures and decision-making processes, opting for participatory democratic processes that are time consuming, emotionally charged, and difficult to sustain even in the best of circumstances (Morgen 1990b; Rothschild-Whitt 1982; Mansbridge 1982). These organizations are ideologically committed to taking seriously the subjectivities of their members. Thus, concern for "process" and a desire to form organizations that reflect, and not just work toward, the empowerment of all women underlie basic aspects of work culture in feminist clinics.

Given these factors, it is no surprise that feminist clinics are intense, rewarding, draining, conflict-ridden places to work. Although a number of scholars have begun to examine the emotional intensity and conflict which have been endemic in feminist workplaces (Mansbridge 1982; Rothschild-Whitt 1982; Schechter 1982; Ristock 1990), the affective dimension of political activism and work in social movement organizations is still infrequently addressed and is even more rarely implicated in analyses of organizational change. Most commonly, when scholars do analyze the emotional intensity and conflict so often a dimension of feminist work cultures, they turn to psychological or psychoanalytic explanations that rarely consider how power relations and structural factors shape the feelings that are part of the experience of work in feminist organizations. For example, Eichenbaum and Orbach (1987, 136, 138) analyze conflict in a new women's studies program in starkly psychoanalytic terms: "In a sense it was as though this [particular] dispute and others similar to it, carried the weight of all the unexpressed difficulties that do exist between women. . . . Psychologically, the group turned from being experienced as a good and nurturing mother, who is enabling and helps one grow through the merged attachment, into a disabling, venomous, withholding, mean traitor that must be destroyed." Similarly, Joanna Russ (1985, 44) focuses on how women's terror of female strength, fear of success, and acceptance of victimization operate in women's organizations.

I see value in exploring the intersections of political economy, ideology, and emotions in the work cultures of political organizations. Rather than accounting for the nature of women's relationships with one another and for the emotional intensity of feminist workplaces solely with psychological explanations, I argue that emotional experience and discourse are shaped by and constitute an important dimension of hegemonic power relations.

Gloria Anzaldua aims toward this kind of analysis in discussing what she calls "entregueras, a kind of civil war among intimates, an in-class, in-race, in-house fighting" (1990, 144). She brings together history, political economy, and experience to comprehend how colonial and imperial processes have "indoctrinated [women in] . . . the old imperialist ways of conquering and dominating, adopting a way of confrontation based on differences while standing on the ground of ethnic superiority" (1990, 142). Anzaldua exemplifies an approach that historicizes and politicizes styles of conflict and interpersonal relations. Feminist theory needs to elaborate this kind of analysis if it is ever to be able to capture what power relations feel like and how processes of domination and resistance "work" in everyday life. In this vein the following section examines the specific social practices through which discourses about feelings and emotional expressions are formulated, then shows how the analysis of emotional discourse can help us understand the dynamics of change in feminist workplaces.

Emotional Discourse in Feminist Work Cultures

Among the social movements that arose during the past quarter-century, the women's movement was unique in the extent to which it authorized the concepts of *experience* and *feeling*. One of the earliest and best-known feminist organizational forms was the consciousness-raising (CR) group. CR groups were organized as forums where women could share their personal experiences and feelings in a supportive social context designed to foster their understanding of how they were oppressed as a social group (MacKinnon 1982). As other feminist organizational forms emerged over the next decade, feminist theory and organizational practice gave women's experiences and feelings a special place in feminist epistemology (Smith 1979; Jaggar 1989; Collins 1990; Harding 1991), organizational ideologies, and interactional codes.

Feminist clinics developed a variety of strategies to put into practice three interrelated organizational goals: restructuring power relations among workers, organizing labor so that workers could develop their individual potential and skills, and challenging the "dualism of private-expressive and public-instrumental selves" (Glennon 1979, 18). It is this last that I focus on here in examining emotional discourse as a crucial dimension of work culture in feminist organizations. As I suggested earlier, despite the importance of feelings in feminist theory and organizational practice, few studies of feminist organizations explicitly examine emotions as part of organizational cultures.

Feminist clinics have developed work cultures that variously absorb, mediate, foster, and transform emotional discourse as part of their strategies of organizational development and survival. Some feminist organizations, including many women's clinics spawned by women's activism in the 1970s, incorporated consciousness-raising into their organizational activities (K. Evans 1980; MacKinnon 1982). Consciousness raising has often been used in training programs for new staff and, in some clinics, as part of the weekly or biweekly staff meeting. Structuring CR into initial training fosters an organizational emphasis on self-disclosure and the public discussion of feelings, socializing staff to express feelings as part of their everyday work life.

Staff meetings in feminist health clinics are routinely punctuated by the expression of strong feelings, ranging from the taking of passionate positions in the process of decision-making to the more everyday expression of both "good" and "bad" feelings about interpersonal relations. These work-places tolerate and in some cases encourage personal sharing between staff and clients and among staff. For example, it was not unusual at the clinic in which I did fieldwork for agendas to be interrupted and occasionally replaced by attention to the feelings of a staff member about something going on in the workplace.

When decisions are made by consensus, meetings can become reposi-tories of strong feelings in a divided staff. "Consensus" often meant that an individual or group that disagreed with a decision went along with it as long as she or they had ample opportunity for the passionate expres-sion of dissent. Mansbridge (1982) and Rothschild-Whitt (1982) argue that the face-to-face relationships in collectivist organizations entail both emo-tional rewards and costs. The primary reward is that of "community," but community often comes at the cost of heightened interpersonal tensions and intensely emotional decision-making processes.

Emotional discourse in feminist clinics is not restricted to these expres-sions of conflict and tension. Much of the day-to-day interaction among staff and many decision-making processes are carried out in an affect-laden vocabulary (Morgen 1983, 212–13). Decrying the "maleness" and abstrac-tion of much political debate (for example in the antiwar, student, and civil rights movements, where many feminists cut their political teeth), some feminists opt for forms of political expression and discussion that give as much authority to statements of feeling as to those of belief or ideology.

Other forms of emotional display contribute to an atmosphere of open emotional expression. Staff often greet each other with hugs or kisses, or comfort each other with a hug or caring touch after a troubling counseling session or a difficult staff meeting. Other features of the work cultures of these clinics foster intimacy among staff. Close friendships are common, as friendship networks become both a source for recruitment of co-workers and a product of working together for shared political goals. In some cases co-workers become lovers, and because many feminist organizations sup-port lesbianism, lovers feel they can be more open in these workplaces than in many other public settings. Furthermore, since so much time is spent in meetings (not uncommonly a full afternoon or day each week), a sense of knowing one another well creates bonds and a range of expectations and emotional obligations (Morgen 1990b). As one woman said, "We spent I would say twelve to twenty hours a week in meetings. We really got down to it. We really knew each other very very very very well."

In addition to emotional intensity, social relationships in these workplaces are frequently emotionally dense. Staff know and feel accountable to one another on multiple levels, as co-workers, political allies, friends, and, sometimes, lovers. This multiplicity of roles contributes to the intensity of the relationships, and sometimes creates conflicts among roles.

Clinics sometimes provide space for emotional discourse by creating regular or occasional meetings for the purpose of airing tensions and expressing feelings. During my fieldwork at WHC, I participated in two retreats and four "crisis meetings," each of which lasted five to ten hours. These meetings were planned because of a perceived crisis within the staff, and each one unearthed considerable anger, pain, distrust, and frustration. The emotional fallout was rarely contained by the boundaries of the special meetings.

Some clinics institutionalized this process. For example, FWH held "feelings meetings" because the staff perceived a need to process the feelings they experienced about both issues and interpersonal relations: "I can't remember where 'feelings meetings' ended and 'issues meetings' began, I think we were alternating the two. At 'issues meetings' we would discuss racism, or classism. . . . 'Feelings meetings' were more like, I'm getting hurt by your personal style. Let's air everything, get to know each other better."

More than most work settings then, feminist workplaces tolerate, encourage, and create institutional forms for the public expression of feelings. These practices have been developed both because there is an ideological commitment to creating humane workplaces and because the confluence of passions and difficult political-economic conditions that shape them bear down hard on the women who work there. The political and economic conditions that challenge and undermine feminist clinics create both organizational *effects* (for example, structural change or co-optation) and organizational *affect*, women feeling deeply about what is happening to their organizations.

My focus on emotional discourse in feminist workplaces is more than an attempt to round out our understandings of what it is like to work in such organizations. Beyond describing the emotional texture of feminist work cultures, it is important to explore how particular emotional discourses germinate in the interstices of alternative workplaces and how emotion is implicated in the dynamics of change in organizations. The following example illustrates how the analysis of emotional discourse can help illuminate both the direction and meaning of particular organizational changes.

During 1977–78 the health center where I was a fieldworker grew substantially, receiving unprecedented new monies from outside agencies which enabled the clinic to expand services and staff. Just before and during this period of expansion, important changes were taking place in organizational structure and processes, including an increasing hierarchy and specialization in the division of labor, and a gradual erosion of collectivity and of the political and advocacy goals of the clinic (Morgen 1986).

The staff had just secured the large CETA grant that allowed them to hire fifteen low-income women, including a substantial number of women of color. Despite the excitement and hope this success generated, a difficult period in the organization's history ensued. Staff morale fell; marked interpersonal tensions emerged between the old staff and the newly hired CETA staff; and a series of crises associated with the inauguration and development of the CETA project erupted.

During this period a longtime member of the staff was fired for her "inability to function collectively" (Morgen 1990b). The firing took place at a long "crisis" meeting in late January, but three previous meetings had laid the groundwork for the evolving consensus that she should go. This was not the first time a staff member had left the collective (because she felt pushed out or unwelcome), but it was the first time the collective had *fired* a staff member.

Elsewhere, I have analyzed these events as a complex instance of scapegoating (Morgen 1990b). I argued that this staff member was fired because her attitudes and actions represented (in an exaggerated form) problems the staff was experiencing in trying to function as a collective under the constraints of outside political and economic conditions and in the context of their newly diversified staff. My original analysis of these events was filled with descriptions of the emotional intensity of the meetings and the specific feelings of pain, fear, sadness, confusion, guilt, anger, and relief. Those descriptions of emotion, however, served primarily as a vivid backdrop to an analysis that foregrounded how political pressures emanating from the New Right and economic retrenchment in federal and state support programs for community health created the conditions that led to the firing. I now see this explanation as incomplete because it does not adequately address *why* the staff chose to expel one of their most hardworking and committed members (albeit one who was sometimes abrasive and insensitive to others), or why they labeled their action a *firing*, despite her agreement that it was best for her to leave. When I turned to an analysis of emotional discourse, it was possible to understand these events more fully.

During this period, the staff frequently expressed the feeling that they were *losing control* of the organization, a feeling accompanied by confusion about why things seemed suddenly so hard and conflict-ridden. Under these conditions the staff singled out one woman whose actions represented some of the contradictions that were emerging, but had not yet been explicitly recognized, between their ideals (collectivity, feminist practice) and their everyday practices. Put simply, features of their organizational structure and decision-making processes increasingly resembled the kinds of hierarchy and bureaucratization they ideologically opposed.

I suggest that for a staff that felt it was losing control of the center, *firing* one of their staff *felt* like an assertion of control. The flow of sentiments within the group and the need to feel in control created the emotional climate in which the staff privileged the ideological principles of autonomy and woman-control (set into action by being self-determining and firing someone who violated feminist principles) over those of equality and consensus decision-making. Given that the fired staff member explicitly agreed to leave, this decision could easily have been framed as a consensus decision, a plausible alternative representation that would have reinforced feminist ideals of equality and collectivity. Instead, the group's ideological choice was influenced by their *felt* powerlessness, which was generated by complex political-economic realities over which they had little control.

This incident demonstrates the difference between describing feelings as part of the backdrop of an analysis and constructing an argument in which political economy, ideology, and emotions together shape social events and meanings. Emotional discourses are created, interpreted, modified, and contested in specific social practices, and feelings are a vital component of organizational and work life.

The point is not simply that emotions, like thought and action, are also socially structured or also influence individual and collective action. Like other dimensions of experience, feelings are profoundly affected by historical and political-economic processes. Moreover, strong feelings catalyze actions, including involvement and particular modes of action in social movements and social organizations. Feelings, ideas, and actions together are experience. They are interwoven dimensions of subjectivity that must all be recognized and addressed if we are to understand human agency in social analysis.

CHAPTER 16

Feminism on the Job:
Confronting Opposition in Abortion Work

■

WENDY SIMONDS

This essay explores ways in which feminism is conceived of and acted upon in the work lives of women. With the goal of illustrating how feminist identity and practice are constructed on the job, I show how abortion workers in a private nonprofit abortion clinic in the southeastern United States build feminist methods of thought and action through their encounters with antifeminist, anti-abortion opposition. Workers deal intermittently with anti-abortion protesters and continually worry about restrictive legislation, potential dismantling of procreative rights for women, and the attitudes that foster these threats. Staff members must negotiate the ambivalence and emotional stress involved in providing abortion in a hostile environment, and confront a moral minefield of anti-abortion rhetoric to arrive at feminist "truths" that support abortion. In this context, workers' activities appear both as *feminist* work and as *defensive* practice. My investigation fits into feminist sociological attempts to uncover how personal views about abortion and feminism are shaped by social forces (e.g., Freeman 1975; S. Evans 1979; Luker 1984; Echols 1989; Ginsburg 1989; Martin 1989), as well as into a tradition of ethnographies of controversial, service-providing, "dirty" workplaces (e.g., Ball 1967; Hughes 1971; Walsh 1974; Lipsky 1980; Detlefs 1984; Joffe 1986; Simonds 1991).

In 1976, a small group of women in a moderate-sized city in the Southeast organized around their interest in the women's health care movement and formed a self-help group, which shortly became The Womancare Center (TWC, a pseudonym). TWC began as a nonprofit collective but gradually expanded into a clearly delineated hierarchy, though it remains a nonprofit organization. TWC has moved in and out of debt over the years and by 1992 had an annual budget of over $2 million. Approximately 90 percent of its income comes from abortions. In 1991, TWC performed an average of seventy abortions each week while serving an average total of 189 clients weekly. Since the mid-1980s TWC has been targeted by anti-abortion protesters and, beginning in 1988, by members of Operation Rescue (OR).

At this writing, TWC staff numbers forty-five workers: three upper-level managers (two of the original founders hold the positions of executive director and clinic coordinator, and the director of administrative services joined the center two years after its founding), one director of development, seven administrative workers (two work part time), one health educator, one lab technician, six nurses (five work part time), three doctors (two work part time), four supervisors, and nineteen health workers (four work part time). The staff ranges in age from the early twenties to the early fifties; most health workers and supervisors are under thirty. The top three administrators are White and heterosexual; eleven of the staff are African American (two administrative workers, six health workers, the lab technician, one supervisor, and one of the per diem physicians), and one is Latina (a health worker). Approximately one-fourth of TWC staff members are lesbian.

Between April 1992 and December 1993, I spent one-half to one day each week as a participant-observer at TWC. In addition, I conducted interviews with twenty-nine TWC workers between fall 1990 and fall 1992. Each interview took place in private and lasted one to three hours; all but one were tape-recorded. I asked each respondent to describe her history at the center and as a feminist, the ups and downs of her work, her views about the workings of the organization, and her feelings about the current and future politics surrounding abortion in the United States.

The interviews defy neat categorization and, often, even comparison with one another, because the macro- and micro-level circumstances under which they occurred were not the same. Interview transcripts seem to impose an artificial sense of closure on each woman's views, yet public events continually transform the conditions of each participant's work and thus her experience and evaluation of it. Over the course of the interview project, anti-abortion protests diminished locally, so workers' direct experience with anti-abortion attitudes at TWC lessened. At the same time, ironically, legislative restrictions on abortion increased both locally and nationally. A parental notification bill has gone into effect in TWC's state. The Supreme Court's Webster decision of July 1989, making legislative decisions about abortion a state matter, was backed by the Casey decision of June 1992, which upheld most proposed state restrictions on abortion as constitutional. As the potential for a democratic presidential victory grew, however, TWC workers spoke more optimistically about the future of abortion rights. At this writing, workers are guardedly optimistic that the Clinton administration's commitment to abortion rights may translate into legislative changes that reverse the conservative trend of the Reagan-Bush years.

Arriving at Feminist Truths

TWC workers develop a conception of what it means to be feminist through their experiences as workers in the organization. The clinic encourages each woman to adopt a conceptualization of abortion that explicitly counters the fetishizing and sanctification of the fetus promoted by anti-abortionists (called "antis" by clinic staff), and to challenge the medical profession's common portrayal of women and fetuses as antagonistic entities (Rothman 1986, 1989; Petchesky 1987).

From what TWC workers told me, the events that are most capable of both challenging *and* affirming their commitment to procreative freedom are second trimester abortions. Several workers related that they were disturbed by their initial exposure to late abortions. One supervisor describes using a sonogram to assist a physician during a late abortion: "The first time I did a sono throughout a whole D & E, and the doctor did this thing: he wanted to wait until the fetus was dead, so he ripped . . . through the placenta and got the cord and waited—we all waited—on the sono until the heart stopped beating. It was *gross*. That upset me, you know." Though she found the procedure unpleasant, she asserted that she saw the clinic's decision to extend abortion services to women who are up to twenty-six weeks pregnant as a "*good* thing." The availability of D & E (dilation and evacuation) abortions at TWC means that clients can avoid referral to another area clinic for induction abortions, which are much more painful procedures (because labor is actually induced). The supervisor also affirmed her support for women's having late abortions, despite her "gut" response of disgust, saying, "You have your reality check if . . . you talk to these women, and you find out why they're having [abortions] . . . and you go, 'you know, I know why I'm doing it.'"

Several TWC workers called working in the sterile room (where fetal tissue is weighed, evaluated, and packed for disposal) during late abortions their least favorite part of their jobs. Many of the health workers acknowledge that they experience second trimester sterile room work as more difficult than first trimester sterile room work for several reasons: the fetuses are larger and "look like babies," especially if they come out whole, which is more likely in later abortions; the fetal tissue is very warm and "feels creepy"; and there is much more blood.

For a few health workers, working in the sterile room remains a problematic part of their jobs, but most strive to resolve their negative feelings with the feminist ideology of the self-help movement: they deliberately focus on the women they know they are helping and speak about their empathy with these women's experiences. Even in empathy, however, there often remains a sense of distance. In the words of one TWC health worker, "My experience with women who are having D & E's is they're—I hate to generalize, but . . . most of them have lives that are so out of control and tornado-ish, and in a whirlwind. And they experience themselves as victims." She sees her role as enabling women to take control over one crucial event in their lives. Another says: "I remind myself that it's not me" having a late abortion.

In an effort to protect themselves from emotional overload, TWC women shield themselves from the pain they see in their clients' lives and in their abortion experiences. A third woman discusses her ambivalence about late abortions by imagining what would happen if a hypothetical second trimester client did not abort: "I think of the big picture, that this woman knows what she has to do. She knows that she can't take care of this baby. . . . Sterile room and late D & E's, though, sometimes make me feel sad, because . . . [the fetuses] look like little babies. But I always just have to put it in the proper perspective, that . . . it could have been here [born], and still you would feel sad when you saw the news report about that baby on TV." The bottom line, for this woman and her co-workers, is that no one should have an unwanted child. Though they may wish to distance themselves from their clients' distress or "whirlwind" lives, they repeatedly express their understanding of every woman's struggle to have children only when she feels the time and circumstances are right.

When I first began interviewing TWC workers, my sense was that several women *confessed* their unease over sterile room work in a way that indicated they would not openly talk about such responses on the job. When I began doing ethnographic work, however, I found that this was no secret. Health workers speak openly about their feelings about handling fetal tissue, and everyone knows who likes or dislikes sterile room work. The reticence I encountered early on was, I think, an uneasiness about discussing the issue with an outsider. Uncomfortable responses to aborted fetuses are, after all, what anti-abortion activists hope for and seek to encourage.

Workers discussed ways in which they had attempted to share with other people, both on and off the job, their views about how important procreative rights are, but they tended to avoid talking about their work in superficial social situations. Many participants told stories about how discussing their work off the job could mean instant arguments, unpleasantness, broken or strained relationships. According to one worker, "Even the clients look at you and go . . . 'thank you so much—I don't know how you can *do* this.' "

TWC's director, focusing on the aborting woman rather than the abortion worker, elaborated on the theme of abortion as stigmatized: "I think that the anti-abortion people have been very successful in making the public view women who receive abortions in a bad light, and also make the women themselves feel really guilty. I think that's been something that's remarkably different here in our clients over the past thirteen years. . . . Women are still getting abortions, but they feel a lot worse about it." In the 1970s, she explained, because the right to abortion was newly won, "everybody who came for an abortion knew somebody who had had an illegal abortion, or they themselves had had an illegal abortion; [women] were just really *happy* to be able to have an abortion with more dignity." Now, she said, young women do not confront the dangers of illegal abortion, but they do experience the wrath and determination of anti-abortionists. Women "are bombarded everywhere they go with this message: '*abortion's murder.*' They hear it in school; they see it on TV; they get it in church. Their own lives are less significant than the lives [*sic*] of the fetus in the way that abortion's being debated now." Because of the prevalence of anti-abortion rhetoric, she believes clients do not see having an abortion as exercising a crucial right but, rather, experience it as a deviant act to undo a personal failure.

One TWC worker articulated the belief that maintaining a veil of secrecy around abortion helps to perpetuate stigmatization: "We do everything that we can to retain confidentiality. We treat the woman like no one in her life knows that she's having an abortion. . . . And if they knew, we assume they would, like, totally ostracize her or kill her, you know. We . . . really go about taking confidentiality so seriously. And I think on the one hand, that's really good that we respect that. But on the other hand, we're just perpetuating this myth. And we're perpetuating this shame about abortion." In her view, the pro-choice movement's focus on the right to privacy, along with the inequitable gender relations concealed in such a focus (cf. MacKinnon 1983), contributes to a silencing of women's voices.

TWC workers talked at length about how anti-abortionists' activities, rhetoric, and visual props had worked to stifle any *honest* public discussion of abortion, a discussion they see as essential to continued procreative freedom. One worker said, "I think that legal changes [prohibiting or restricting abortion] will be a lot easier if people are afraid to talk, or don't know that they *can* talk" about abortion.

Another woman described the closeting of abortion as a failure of the pro-choice movement, resulting from feminists' reluctance to address the emotional issues that abortion evokes for many people:

> The reason why . . . we've been falling back in terms of abortion rights is because we haven't been talking about abortion. . . . We've been so afraid to dialogue honestly about it, that when we talk abortion . . . it's like this constitutional right. We talk about it as, you know, "what can we do to help?" You know, you go and you write your congressman a letter. . . . We have our armor on, like we're ready for this battle. . . . We've just been on the defensive so long that we haven't changed the language about abortion. . . . We still say "products of conception." Well, why don't we say it looks like—you know, a twenty-week fetus looks like a baby. Why can't we say that in public? Because that's what the *antis* say, you know. But you know, it's pretty much true, and you'd better say it. . . . The antis have this one extremist language, and then the pro-choice movement has this other extremist language, and there are all these people in the middle and they don't believe either one.

Most participants attribute the infusion of anti-abortion sentiment into public consciousness to the persistence and aggressiveness of the antis, whose views are bolstered by conservative, misogynist politics, rather than to feminists' reticence about abortion. Many workers feel resentment that pro-choice activism does not seem to be "taking" the way it once did, and they do not understand how society can remain apathetic. They believe the American public does not understand the centrality of abortion's importance to women's freedom. As one TWC employee eloquently stated: "Part of what abortion is about is a woman's *wholeness* . . . And *that's* what's at stake. It's not just having a cannula put in your uterus. It's whether the world has enough room for you."

Confronting the Opposition in Person

I asked participants to tell me about their interaction with anti-abortion protesters and its effects on their work. Confrontations with antis make evident to workers the fact that abortion rights are threatened. Participants frequently said they felt deeply frightened about the future.

Their fears are informed by TWC's history. Anti-abortion demonstrators picketed the clinic sporadically during the mid-1980s. During the summer of 1988, Operation Rescue (OR) staged "rescues" at most abortion clinics in the city, and because of its avowed feminist stance, TWC was a favorite target. Despite a city injunction barring many of the group's more assaultive tactics, OR protesters continue to demonstrate at city clinics (though no longer on a regular basis or in great numbers at TWC) and routinely disobey the injunction.

When hundreds of antis arrived from out of state in 1988, their mission was to shut the city's clinics down. Fortunately, workers say, OR communicated its mission to the police. Until this point, the city police had been uninterested in the upcoming protests and refused to promise clinics that they would become actively involved. Once it became clear that OR was coming, TWC's executive director recounted,

> I met with other providers and the police to try to start up preparation. . . . The police's response was: "Well, just shut down to avoid confrontation." And we were adamant that there was no way that we were going to shut down, and that was never going to be an acceptable solution for us . . . [and] we demanded that they protect . . . us. At first, I'd say the police were pretty reluctant to agree that it was really any danger. And then Operation Rescue met with the police and were very arrogant—as they always are—and just told the police: "We don't care about your protest area. We don't care what you say. We're coming to town to break the law." So the police all of a sudden thought, "Well, maybe these clinics have something to say here."

OR's bragging about its plans seemed to awaken the sensibilities of the police. They vowed to prevent OR from breaking the law, and since that time, police have been allies of TWC. Clinic workers recognize that this relationship is a fragile one; they often talk about how strange it has been to come to see police as allies and about what it would be like to be working against the police to provide abortion.

Employees who were present during the 1988 protests remember those months as a long and seemingly never-ending nightmare. Many say that at the time they thought their work was like what war must be like for soldiers. A few TWC women described the OR blockades as also exciting or wonderful because of the unexpected consequences of enduring the intense ordeal: they say it brought the staff together as a group and gave them a sense of daily accomplishment when the antis were unable to shut the clinic down. In the words of one participant: "Nothing in the history of the health center had drawn all of the staff together like being under the assault of anti-abortionists. You know, it was the one thing that we could all bond on, 'cause you know there are a lot of divisions at the health center. . . . And it was really like we drew together and we fought them off, you know? Everyone was just so committed to winning that battle."

For women who have remained at TWC since 1988, working through the experience of OR blockades strengthened their commitment to providing abortion. But in the six months after the summer when TWC was heavily targeted by OR, eleven clinic workers quit. Though none said the experience was their reason for leaving, the clinic director said she was sure that OR's attack was the impetus.

In *The Managed Heart* (1983), Arlie Hochschild contrasts the occupations of flight attendant and bill collector to demonstrate the types of emotional labor expected of workers. In this case, TWC employees performed emotional work across the spectrum, being called upon to demonstrate empathy and nurturance to their clients and with each other, yet at the same time to appear controlled, united, and assertive in the face of the enemy. Sandra Morgen (1983) writes about a case study she conducted in a feminist health center where emotions acted as "filter" for ideology in the day-to-day running of the clinic. The reverse is true as well: ideology also filters emotion. TWC women spoke repeatedly of not wanting to let the antis see how they felt, telling how they often resisted displaying their anger and fear because they worried that, unleashed, these emotions could become uncontrollable. One woman described the inner turmoil the activities of the protesters evoked for her:

> This one night . . . I'd walked a client up to her car, and it was like the end of the night. . . . And I walked over the hill . . . and there they were. And I just had this, like, *panic*, you know? This complete . . . feeling of panic. And I was just *over* it that night, just totally over it. Like they had gotten under my skin, and that was absolutely the worst thing. . . . I remember those nights, I would just get in the car and get on the

Interstate, and I'd roll up my windows and just scream. Just scream. You know, you do this whole job of like, protecting the clients—but who's protecting you? . . . I mean, it's just like this bully in the class-room; you don't want to let them know that they're bothering you. You know, don't—don't cry in front of the bully.

Managing anger remains a constant challenge for TWC workers, espe-cially because antis are a forceful reminder that women are not safe or secure in the public realm. TWC women repeatedly likened the antis' treat-ment of women (themselves and clients) to sexual assault or rape. But participants also repeatedly express their belief that the antis are entitled to their views, however distasteful, untruthful, or dangerous clinic workers may find them to be. They say they object not to the views of the antis so much as to their hostile treatment of women. As one worker said: "I can really respect the other side of the issue . . . because I was in that dilemma myself [of feeling anti-abortion sentiments]. And it's not like I can't see the other side. It's just when they lose that rational ability to think and talk about it, and it becomes this other, just obsessive thing that they're doing. . . . Just crazy, and *scary* crazy." As participants reiterate their be-lief that anti-abortionists are entitled to believe anything, however warped, they also come down against the moral relativism that undergirds their own abstract notion of free speech. TWC women are angry at *both* the substance of the antis' views and the tactics they use to make their views known. They are enraged that the antis remain impervious to feminist truths while workers feel perpetually vulnerable to antis' attacks.

TWC workers are all subject to antis' verbal harassment because until they are recognized as staff, they are considered by OR members to be potential clients. Once the antis learn who workers are, their assault changes but does not end. The litany addressed to staff members ranges from vehement accusations ("Murderer!" "Baby killer!") to a more plain-tive rhetorical interrogation: "Why do you want to kill babies?" "Why don't you get another job?" The antis also employ religious scripts similar to the ones they use with clients, telling staff members they will "burn in hell" or, alternatively, adopting a friendlier tone and claiming to "pray for" workers' souls.

The antis reserve a specialized script for minority women; according to one worker the protesters, who are overwhelmingly White, attempt to engage with African American women by focusing on their race:

Well, being a Black woman, the way the protesters handle me, I think, is a little different . . . from the way they handle other women . . .

who are not of color. They tend to use my history to try to slash out at me. . . . They always say things like, "The Reverend Dr. Martin Luther King would be very upset because you're creating genocide on your people." . . . They try to make me feel responsible for my whole race of people, as opposed to things that they would say to a woman who's not of color. . . . I don't know if they think that women of color don't care about what happens to themselves, but [they think] we care more about what happens to our people. So they . . . try to lay a bigger realm of guilt on me. . . . If I go in there and have an abortion, I'm gonna just stop the whole Black race. And that's basically how they say it.

Another African American worker relates a similar experience: an anti singled her out, saying, " 'See those two little Black boys over there? Their mother didn't have abortions.' And I can't tell you on how many levels I was enraged by that statement."

Black and White workers alike believe antis are so ignorant that they have no idea they are being racist in such encounters but, rather, seem to feel that particularized treatment demonstrates a sensitivity to issues of race. But this specialized rhetoric, like the antis' assaults in general, works only to infuriate staff members; in fact, many women say they feel such impassioned hatred toward the antis that their feelings themselves become stressful, and they talk about their attempts to gain control of emotions that seem overwhelming. In the words of one TWC worker: "It's disgusting. You feel soiled and gross and emotionally raped that you've been made to feel this way. It makes you face a lot of things about yourself—that we're not, you know, intrinsically all that different. I mean, that same kind of gross disgusting stuff that they feel is what I felt for them at that moment, . . . I was capable of that same kind of hatred."

TWC workers say they dislike responding with such hatred toward other human beings, especially other women. (Roughly half of the demonstrators I've observed are women, but most of the leaders are men.) Hatred does not play a part in the feminist ideals these women believe in; hatred in feminist and pro-choice rhetoric, they say, is really the other side's forte. Hatred for the antis feels productive at times only in the sense that it seems a step above hopelessness. Hatred infused by anger takes energy and becomes emotionally exhausting, adding insult to injury, because the women already experience their work as draining. Yet anger fuels motivation, even as it frustrates it. Workers struggle to hold on to their anger without letting it overwhelm them or make them feel guilty. The woman just quoted

elaborated on the positive aspects of anger and animosity, even visceral
hatred, but talked in a circle, ending as she began with unresolved ambivalence: "You just have to get comfortable allowing yourself to feel it. Women
are just, you know, we're not allowed to be angry. We're not allowed to
be bitchy. We're not allowed. And allowing yourself to do it, and feel it,
as long as you don't act on it [is necessary]. . . . As long as I don't act
on the feeling of wanting to tear one of their limbs off and beat them to
death with it, you know? As long as . . . I don't level a good drop-kick to
their head, you know? . . . Who wants to feel that kind of anger and gross
disgusting stuff?"

This woman, like many of her co-workers, at once feels entitled to, re-
sents, and regrets her own anger. Although TWC women believe their anger
is justified, they know that in our culture women's anger is considered un-
seemly. They find few ways to demonstrate their anger productively and no
way to purge themselves of it absolutely. They speak of attempts they made
to "deal with" anger and hatred, both through the tight-knit community
of TWC and alone, both by confronting the antis and by ignoring them.

Most say that though they may have interacted with antis at first, they
found there was little to be gained from any interaction. They explain
their efforts to ignore the protesters as an attempt to preserve their own
well-being. Workers describe their attempts to communicate or to achieve
common ground with the antis as ineffectual. Most interchanges become
sarcastic or angry on one or both sides. One woman, an actively religious
Christian, described the "last" time she had spoken to the antis:

> It was the feast of St. Mary. . . . So I had left work and gone to church
> during lunch and then I was on my way back in. And it was these
> assholes out front again, talking to me. . . . "Oh, if you *only knew*
> how much Jesus loves you." And I said, "I am *sick* of your arrogance!
> You don't *own* God! And it may interest you to know that I just got
> back from church," and I *wanted* to say, "—so fuck off!" . . . They
> said something like, "You may *think* that you know Jesus, and dah
> dah dah," and I just kept walking at that point. Because I wasn't there
> to dialogue with them. I just needed to tell them that they don't own
> God. And even though they couldn't *hear* that from me, I still just
> wanted to say it, even though I knew it wouldn't make any difference.
> So it made a difference to me.

Despite their beliefs that the attacks on them are ungrounded and ridicu-
lous, workers still feel accused, and feeling accused makes them want to
respond. Though workers usually described ignoring the antis as a posi-

tion of strength, they also expressed ambivalence, as with their anger and hatred. TWC workers feel that if they ignore antis' provocations, their stance may be mistaken for passivity, as if they have no words with which to fight. And thus, they explain that ignoring the protesters, though sensible, may not always be what they do. A few workers said they continued to engage in conversations with the antis in order to let off steam.

More commonly, clinic workers joke loudly with each other or with clinic escorts. Sometimes they comment on the antis' paraphernalia: "Oh, you brought my favorite sign today!" or, about the little plastic fetuses antis often hold in the palms of their hands during prayers: "Wouldn't they make nice earrings!" The women mentioned collectively engineered jokes made at the expense of the antis as the most productive means of retaliation. Their favorite began one day when, after several hours of protesting, only a handful of antis remained outside the building, all of them men. One of the clinic workers brought out a ruler and a large handprinted sign that read "Small Penis Contest," and posed next to the group of men while another took pictures. Mimicking the protesters' wielding of signs and their shaming techniques greatly amused clinic workers. But although incidents like this one help to diffuse the hostility the staff feels and to reinforce a sense of solidarity against the enemy, they are not enough so long as the antis and the threat they represent remain.

All workers, however remote their job responsibilities are from the performance of abortions, have been subjected to shouted insults or affronts, bomb threats, and vandalism both of the clinic and of their personal property. Many participants spoke of their attempts to protect themselves from this sort of invasive assault: some have unlisted phone numbers; some say they avoid discussing their work with people they don't know well; most describe being more attentive to who is around them when they are out alone, especially in transit between work and home.

Feminism and (F)utility

Interaction with anti-abortionists strengthens the determination of TWC staff to preserve procreative freedom, and has made those who stayed after 1988 feel more committed to their work. But this interaction also makes workers feel marginalized *because* they are feminist. Even though most people are not members of OR, or even anti-choice, TWC staff see the anti-abortion movement's rhetoric and stance as having made an indelible mark on mainstream Americans' thinking.

Already, anti-abortion activities have resulted in the curtailment of abortion services across the country and enormous cuts in both public funding (Medicaid now covers abortions in only a handful of states as a result of the 1976 Hyde Amendment) and private support. Susan Faludi gives evidence of this trend: "In 1988, United Way stopped funding Planned Parenthood, and in 1990, under pressure from the Christian Action Council, AT&T cut off its contributions, too (after twenty-five years), claiming that shareholders had objected to the agency's association with abortion— even though 94 percent of its shareholders had voted in favor of funding Planned Parenthood" (1991, 418). TWC women have plenty of evidence of the danger to women's procreative freedom, including the imposition of restrictions such as parental notification, parental consent, and waiting periods in various states; the reduction of Title X funds during the 1980s (Wattleton 1990, 269); dramatic increases in clinic bombings, bomb threats, and vandalism in the mid-1980s (Staggenborg 1991) and again in the early 1990s; and a dearth of doctors who are willing to perform abortions. TWC women's direct contact with antis makes them profoundly aware of the danger women face, danger they feel the general public does not perceive or does not care about *because* it accepts anti-abortionists' terms for framing the debate over abortion.

Participants share a core ambivalence about the future: their cynicism, anxiety, and sense of futility about the "chipping away" of procreative freedom coexist with an optimism that the feminist conception of women's "wholeness" will prevail. TWC workers' experiences during the conservative era of the 1980s fuel resistance, even as they result in emotional exhaustion. A new—or revived—radicalism burgeons in these women's outrage as they struggle to attain emotional equilibrium. They question the effectiveness of democratic means of achieving political change but want to believe that the democratic process works. They are ambivalent about the liberal ideology that frames the legal right both to abortion and to freedom of speech, torn because of their belief in feminist absolutes that attest to women's integrity and worth. Their radicalism is tempered by their feelings of powerlessness and vulnerability; they know that, practically, daily survival must take precedence over revolutionary ideological change. TWC workers' contact with anti-abortion opposition has taught them that frustration, ambivalence, anger, and commitment are all integral to feminist work in an antifeminist environment.

PART V

Social Movement Strategies:
Differences between
Organizations

CHAPTER 17

The Organizational Basis of Conflict in Contemporary Feminism

■

CAROL MUELLER

Increasingly, scholars have attempted to explain the course of the contemporary women's movement in terms of the internal conflicts of its first few years and what these conflicts have meant for the "identity" of the movement (Echols 1989; B. Ryan 1989, 1992). More specifically, these early struggles have been seen as destructive in their consequences for the course the movement has taken. Yet at the same time there has been an attempt to look to external controversies, such as the campaigns for the ERA and for the defense of abortion rights, as positive sources of a more unifying identity that might somehow hold the movement together (see esp. B. Ryan, 1992). Although these attempts to seek out the larger significance of the sometimes fierce battles—both internal and external to the movement— are certainly welcome, the efforts to date have failed to explore the differences among types of conflict orientation and the organizational context within which conflict occurs.

Descriptive as well as analytic accounts of contemporary feminism have acknowledged a high level of conflict, but there has been only modest attention to the dynamics of conflict in social movement theory. Zald and McCarthy (1987, 178) note in an account of "competition and conflict among social movement organizations," that "both economists and sociologists have a bloodless conception of interorganizational relations." Despite the shared goals that characterize organizations within a social movement, they "may wish death on one another; they may want to absorb the other, take over its domain, squash the competition." Assuming that shared goals lead to consensus, observers often ignore the existence of conflict between organizations or among organizations or groups that make up a social movement. Conflict is expected, of course, between the social movement and relevant actors external to the movement, most notably, agents of the state and countermovements. Although recent attention has focused on the "professionalization of reform" (McCarthy and Zald 1973) and "consensus movements" (Lofland 1989; McCarthy and Wolfson 1992), conflict is a necessary condition for the massive mobilizations that distinguish social movements from conventional politics (Schwartz and Paul 1992). Social movement scholarship that does emphasize the role of conflict has concentrated on its importance for mobilization (Lo 1992; Schwartz and Paul 1992) or its strategic outcomes (Piven and Cloward 1977, 1992; Gamson 1990). There has been little interest in the sources, the types, or the nonstrategic consequences of conflict.

This chapter suggests some possible questions that might fruitfully be addressed by a more thorough examination of conflicts in the contemporary women's movement. More specifically, it considers variation in the organizational sources of both internal and external conflict in terms of the distinctions between mass-based, formal organizations like the National Organization for Women (NOW) at one extreme and informal collectives or small groups at the other. These two ideal types of organization engage differently in external conflict and respond differently to internal conflict. Lying between the two extremes are the service organizations that share characteristics of both organizational types and respond differentially to both types of conflict. I link the two forms of conflict by examining the differential impact of "recruitment effects" resulting from external conflict. In making these distinctions, my interest is in laying out some of the issues involved in advancing our understanding of the organizational base of social movement conflict. The purpose of such an exposition is more to raise questions than to provide answers as to why the movement has taken the course that it has. Other contributions in this volume provide rich examples of many of the issues discussed here.

I begin with a brief overview of two basic types of conflict that have characterized modern feminism, distinguished by their internal or external orientation to the movement.

Conflict and the Women's Movement

The widely publicized external controversies for which the movement is best known have been battles between feminists and antifeminists over the Equal Rights Amendment (ERA) and abortion rights. Each of these issues has been associated with what has been called "liberal," "reform," or "equal rights" feminism, although in both cases the threat of losing rights has drawn together feminists of all persuasions (Petchesky 1982; Z. Eisenstein 1993). Both issues have served as ongoing sources of conflict between the women's movement and an aggressive countermovement that received increasing political and state support over an extended period of time. The two issues reached public awareness at about the same time in the early 1970s. The ERA passed both houses of Congress and went to the states for ratification in March 1972. A year later the attention of the country was drawn to the landmark Supreme Court decision *Roe v. Wade*, which established a woman's constitutional right to an abortion. Both issues served to galvanize a New Right political movement to defend the traditional, patriarchal family (Petchesky 1982). By the end of the decade the New Right had managed to undermine the political basis of feminist support in both houses of Congress and the White House which in the early 1970s had contributed to the landmark legislative victories for women (Hixson 1992). This highly successful countermovement was eventually able to forestall ratification of the ERA (Boles 1982) and to erode the right to abortion through denial of public funding and increasing restrictions on access. The anti-abortion countermovement became still more aggressive with the advent of direct action tactics in the early 1980s, followed by the creation of Operation Rescue, a national organization devoted to a campaign of civil disobedience, clinic bombings, and mass arrests (Ryan 1992, 144–52).

What is noteworthy for present purposes about these external conflicts is their organizational base in the women's movement. Both passage of the ERA and protection of reproductive rights were political campaigns conducted by large, mass-membership organizations. Despite the variety of groups that finally came together in support of the ERA during its last year, the eleven-year campaign was primarily an effort by coalitions of formal organizations. In fact, Eleanor Smeal, then president of NOW, argued that the ERA campaign was responsible for building the mass membership and filling the coffers of the organization (Boles 1982). Although the feminist campaign for abortion was always more diverse in the variety of groups and organizations supporting it (see Staggenborg 1991), it was primarily a campaign run by the National Abortion Rights Action League (NARAL), a mass-membership organization with a professional cadre of feminist leaders (McCarthy 1987; Gelb 1989). By the time the Supreme Court heard *Webster v. Reproductive Health Services of Missouri* in the spring and summer of 1989, a coalition including mass-based organizations such as NOW, Planned Parenthood, NARAL, the Committee for Abortion Rights and against Sterilization Abuse (CARASA), and other feminist groups had organized a campaign of marches, counterprotests, pickets, telephone calls, and supportive litigation to protect *Roe v. Wade.*

While mass-membership organizations tried to defend reproductive rights in the courts, the legislatures, and the streets, women's health clinics operated on a local basis, making abortion services available in practice and dealing on a very personal level with the daily possibility of face-to-face encounters with the direct-action anti-abortion tactics of the pro-life countermovement (Ginsburg 1989). To the extent that the abortion issue has been associated with providing services to the public, the controversy has extended to these sites in highly emotional confrontations occurring on a continuing basis for over fifteen years; see the chapters by Simonds (16), Morgen (15), and Hyde (20). Of the thousands of women's health clinics that came into existence during the 1970s, a majority had become targets of the pro-life movement by the mid-1980s.

Although observers of the contemporary women's movement may find these external struggles between feminists and antifeminists more familiar, internal disputes have been no less important. Within the movement, veterans still carry the scars of the deadly internecine battles of the late 1960s and early 1970s when "politicos" fought against "radical feminists," lesbians against heterosexuals, and radicals of all persuasions against liberal reformers (see accounts of these clashes in Freeman 1975; Echols 1989). The clinics have also been sites of intense internal contention among staff and clients because of differences in race, class, ideology, and sexual preference (Albrecht and Brewer 1990). More recently, pornography, sexuality, and spirituality have served as the basis for overt conflicts. Race and class have also emerged much more dramatically as sources of controversy. Throughout these struggles, the collective identities associated with feminism have been transformed and reconstructed again and again (see Hirsch and Keller 1990; B. Ryan 1992).

The movement faced early, though muted, conflict over the multiple identities that differentiated women who considered themselves feminists —most particularly, race and class. The predominantly white and middle-class membership of the early movement led to charges of elitism based on race or class, despite the participation by many of these members in the civil rights movement and the New Left (see hooks 1981; Giddings 1984; Buechler 1990b). Opinion polls, however, showed higher support for feminist issues among women of color than white women, and they too organized (Ferree and Hess 1985; Klein 1987). On the basis of the specificity of their oppression as women of color, African American women founded the National Black Feminist Organization in 1973; Latina women organized as early as 1972 in the National Congress of Puerto Rican Women and the Mexican American Women's Association in 1974 (Ferree and Hess 1985). Working-class women formed local groups such as the Berkeley Union Women's Alliance to Gain Equality (Union WAGE) in 1971 and the National Coalition of Labor Union Women (CLUW) in 1974. Despite these early signs of tension, it was only in the late 1970s that a heated debate over racism in the movement became widespread (Joseph and Lewis 1981; Moraga and Anzaldua 1981).

During the 1980s, women of color created a feminism that reflects the interaction of gender with race and ethnicity (Hull, Scott, and Smith 1982; Chow 1987). Although some women of color advocate coalitions with primarily White feminist organizations as a way of preserving differences among women while pursuing common interests (see Joseph and Lewis 1981), such coalitions have often been criticized as serving only the interests of their majority white members (Giddings 1984). In a continuing atmosphere of distrust, explosive face-to-face confrontations over race recur, for example at the annual meetings of the National Women's Studies Association (NWSA). Although NWSA attempted to recognize race and class concerns by giving minority caucuses disproportionate representation, a personnel issue led to a walkout by the Women of Color Caucus at the 1990 conference, the eventual resignation of the national staff and cancellation of the 1991 meeting, and subsequent efforts to create a new structure (Leidner 1991, 1993; B. Ryan 1992).

A major difference between the intramovement conflicts of the early years and those of the 1980s is the site or location at which the struggle occurs. Much of the early intramovement controversy took place within small groups and collectives. Although this wing of the movement has been variously characterized in terms of age and style ("the younger branch," Freeman 1975) and of political ideology ("women's liberation," Hole and Levine 1971; Carden 1974; Cassell 1977; and "radicals," Deckard 1975), the theme that is most pervasive refers to its organizational form. Ferree and Hess (1985) identify a "bureaucratic strand" and a "collectivist strand" as the basic distinction between the two branches of the movement. Although there were internal struggles within the mass-membership organizations (such as NOW) over the issues of ERA and abortion, lesbianism and minority rights (see Freeman 1975), these debates seem to have had fewer long-term repercussions than the bitter battles waged in collectivist groups.

Much of the intramovement conflict in the 1980s over issues of pornography, essentialism, and spirituality also occurred in a small-group context. The best documentation on the sites where issues were raised by women of color, however, suggests that they were organizations that deliver some kind of feminist service, such as health clinics, shelters, and women's studies programs. To what extent there was serious conflict within women's studies programs on college campuses is unclear, but there is no doubt that the annual meetings of the NWSA was one of the major sites where clashes occurred over race, ethnicity, class, and sexual preference.

The Effects of Conflict

Although new issues as well as old continue to divide feminists, I argue that the consequences for the movement vary depending on the organizational site of the conflict. The mass-membership organizations appear to have a unique advantage in dealing with intramovement conflict because of their rule-generating capacity. I also argue that conflict in the small groups is more likely to lead to factionalism and disintegration but that major theoretical contributions are sometimes made in the process (see Snow et al. 1986). Service-provider organizations, to the extent that they have bureaucratized, tend to have the moderating potential of formal rulemaking to fall back on, but their local, personal, daily interactions tend to heighten internal tensions as in the collectives from which they often developed.

In developing this argument, I take two clusters of variables from the previous discussion: organizational form and conflict orientation. Three typical organizational forms can be identified: (1) formal, social movement organizations are professionalized, bureaucratic, and inclusive in making few demands on members; (2) small groups or collectives are informally organized and tend to be exclusive in requiring large commitments of time, loyalty, and material resources from members; (3) service-provider organizations are a mixed form with characteristics of both types to varying degree. These organizational forms, differentiated by the degree to which "feminist" organizational principles of democratic participation are practiced (see Martin 1990b), combine and recombine in a variety of structural configurations ranging from coalitions (see Staggenborg 1986; and Arnold, Chapter 18) to complex social movement communities (Buechler, 1990b).

Conflict modes are differentiated by whether hostilities are oriented internally toward members or other movement organizations, or directed externally to a countermovement, the state, or civil society. While there are many possible relationships between external and internal conflict, one in particular suggests the possible importance of their combined effects. Conflict theorists have generally maintained that external hostilities will minimize internal strife within organizations because they heighten solidarity in the face of a common threat, create a common combat-oriented culture, and legitimate hierarchical divisions of labor. Though this no doubt occurs, experiences in contemporary feminism suggest that there may be other, more subtle, and yet highly disruptive, consequences of external contention. One of the most important can be characterized as the "recruitment effect" of external conflict on internal conflict. Whether offensive or defensive, from the perspective of the social movement organization (SMO), conflict heightens arousal in relation to the values under attack and pressures fence-sitters to take a position; that is, it polarizes attitudes and increases pressure toward action by raising the stakes (see Coser 1956; Coleman 1957; and Kriesberg 1973). In the process, an appealing social movement is likely to be inundated with new, raw recruits. Freeman (1975), for instance, points to the large number of women seeking to join chapters of NOW across the country after the national Equality Day marches and demonstrations of August 1970. A similar tide of new recruits sought out and transformed Students for a Democratic Society (SDS) following the first anti-Vietnam War demonstrations of April 1965 (see Gitlin 1980). The last-gasp campaign for the ERA brought in droves of recruits in 1979–82, and the Webster decision led to massive numbers of new recruits concerned about reproductive rights in the early 1990s. Although the recruitment effect guarantees some instability and internal conflict for all SMOs, the seriousness of the consequences appears to be strongly dependent on organizational structure. Let us explore these effects for each of the three organizational types.

THE SMALL GROUPS

Regardless of ideology, most small groups handle their internal affairs through informal understandings that are developed out of the common experiences of group members. Given enough time and stability of membership, such organizations usually develop a division of labor, leadership, and accepted procedures for making decisions that help them to survive. When small-group structure is coupled with an ideology of participatory democracy that encourages a mistrust of tradition and makes claims for the

equality of all members' experiences and skills, survival becomes considerably more problematic. External conflict coupled with a strong recruitment
effect can be devastating for small-group SMOs.

Social movements scholars usually argue that factionalism increases with
the heterogeneity of the social group making up a movement (see, e.g., Zald
and McCarthy 1987). Yet though the small-group branch of feminism in
the late 1960s and early 1970s was notably homogeneous in age, class, and
race (see esp. Echols 1989), it was also highly prone to factionalism. Not
only did New York Radical Women (NYRW) split off into action groups
such as WITCH (originally, Women's International Terrorist Conspiracy
from Hell) in the winter of 1968–69; it also spawned the New Women, who
wanted to organize traditional, working-class women. Eventually, NYRW
"seeded itself" in groups such as Redstockings, the Feminists, and New
York Radical Feminists—all of which had also disintegrated organizationally by 1970. Although NYRW is the best known among these groups,
because of the fame of the individual feminists who belonged to it, similar
processes of factionalism occurred in small groups throughout the country.

Despite the large literature on the small-group branch of feminism, a
preoccupation with internal conflict has distracted attention from the repeated encounters between representatives of the small (and usually radical) groups and the state or civil society in the first ten years of second-wave
feminism (see Freeman 1975; Cassell 1977). Because these external conflicts
occurred in a highly dramatic public format, the simplistic messages they
inevitably conveyed had the unanticipated consequence of recruiting large
numbers of new members sympathetic to that message but lacking the experiences of the founders. Thus, the informal understandings that usually
enable small groups to survive were lost, and differences were fought out
on the basis of constantly changing ideological positions.

The small groups cast aside as dehumanizing the protections of formal
bureaucracies as well as their constraints. They embraced the philosophy of
participatory democracy developed in the early days of the Student Nonviolent Coordinating Committee (SNCC) by Ella Baker and passed on to SDS
during the 1960s (Miller 1987; Mueller 1990). Participatory democracy was
early institutionalized in the form of "consciousness raising" (CR), which
became one of the distinguishing characteristics of the small groups. By
emphasizing the centrality of empowering all women through democratic
practices, the protections of agreed-upon rules for determining leadership
and a division of labor were abandoned in favor of the spontaneous expression of feelings and emotions. CR provided an ideal environment for

exploring the personal roots of oppression (see Taylor, Chapter 14), but it offered none of the procedural safeguards against factionalism that the mass-based SMOs were able to develop.

FORMAL SOCIAL MOVEMENT ORGANIZATIONS

The formal SMO is far more likely than the small group to carry on campaigns or actions that extend over many years. Engaging in long-term conflict is made possible by the longevity associated with its organizational structure (see Staggenborg 1986). Because the external conflict that engages a formal SMO is more likely to be protracted struggle with a countermovement than the sporadic protest demonstrations, marches, and guerrilla theater staged by small groups, it has an even greater capacity to polarize attitudes and galvanize action. Thus, a recruitment effect may send dozens or hundreds of new members into small groups but tens of thousands into the local branches of the formal, national SMOs. Yet the recruitment effect's potential for provoking internal conflict appears to be considerably less for the formal SMO.

Despite the organizational strains placed on the infrastructure of the fledgling NOW organization with the influx of new members after Equality Day in 1970 (see Freeman 1975), the recruitment effect of the demonstrations seemed to produce few new sources of internal conflict. Nor does the existing literature give evidence of internal conflict resulting from the massive infusion of new members during the ERA campaign of the late 1970s and early 1980s. Rather than provoking the factionalism that the small groups experienced as an internal consequence of external strife, the STOP ERA campaign led by Phyllis Schlafly led to unprecedented growth in membership and financial resources (Boles 1982). Membership grew from several thousand in 1970 to over a quarter-million at the height of the ERA campaign. Despite a slight decline in membership after the second deadline ran out in 1982, the external conflict generated by the opposition of a strong countermovement clearly contributed to growth rather than decline for the organization.

The processes by which formal social movement organizations, such as NOW, absorbed these massive numbers of new members without destructive internal dissension is not altogether clear, but the methods used by other mass-membership organizations in dealing with internal disputes suggests that the bureaucratic capacity for generating formal rules has the potential for defusing highly explosive sources of internal conflict. More focused research on this issue may reveal how this occurs. The most important factors may be the institutionalization of organizational experience in criteria for leadership succession, specified terms of office, and accountability in the structure of decision-making.

For instance, at its founding conference in July 1971, the National Women's Political Caucus (NWPC) pledged to oppose "racism, sexism, institutional violence and poverty through the election and appointment of women to public office, party reform, and the support of women's issues and feminist candidates across party lines." NWPC gambled that a strategy of inclusiveness would prevent charges of elitism or marginality without splitting the caucus into warring factions. The first attempt to put this statement of purpose into practice was the appointment of women of color to its Policy Council in 1971. In addition to White media stars such as Betty Friedan, Bella Abzug, and Gloria Steinem, the council included Dorothy Height, president of the National Council of Negro Women; Fannie Lou Hamer, Mississippi Freedom Party; Cecelia Suarez and Lupe Anguiano, Chicana activists; and Evelina Antonetty, Puerto Rican activist. The NWPC also initiated procedural innovations and recognized legitimate interest groups. Fears of domination by feminists from the Democratic Party were addressed by appointing more Republicans to the Policy Council. By 1973 procedural accommodations included a rule requiring some party balance in electing members at-large to the steering committee. Bylaw changes enacted in 1975 required that one national vice-chair be from a major political party different from that of the chair. In addition, Democratic and Republican task forces were developed. Caucuses of Blacks, radical women, and young professional women had emerged at the first organizing meeting in 1971; and by the late 1970s NWPC had given permanent representation on its steering committee to Blacks, Chicanos, Puerto Ricans, Native Americans, Asians, lesbians, and "the Capital Hill Caucus" (Feit 1979, 199). Each interest or identity group had one representative except Blacks and lesbians, which each had two. Bylaws also mandated that at least half of the highest officials be members of ethnic minority groups. Although dialogue between identity groups was frequently at a high emotional peak, it was sustained within a single organization through the flexible adaptation of procedural rules of representation. Such procedures do not preclude factionalism, but procedural flexibility offers an option not available to groups organized along the nonbureaucratic lines of the early forms of participatory democracy.

SERVICE ORGANIZATIONS

In offering services to the public, local feminist service organizations—health clinics, shelters for battered women, abortion referral networks, women's studies programs, and feminist cultural events—are much more exposed to ongoing, day-by-day encounters with the state, civil society, and countermovements than either formal SMOs or small groups; both of the latter have more discretion in picking the time and site of external encounters. Although exposure to the public helps to fulfill feminist service goals, it also creates a unique vulnerability. The considerable operating expenses of shelters and health clinics puts them at risk of recurring budget crises and harassment from state and private funding agencies (see Hyde, Chapter 20). Offering services to the public also places the organization under the regulatory authority of the state and, like the search for funding, subjects its internal practices to external examination and judgment (see Matthews, Chapter 19).

In face-to-face encounters with an external adversary at the site of service delivery, there is the potential for the identity creation processes described by new social movement theorists such as Melucci (1989), scholars in the symbolic interaction tradition such as Gerson and Peiss (1985), and those who draw on both traditions (Taylor and Whittier 1992). Observers such as Morgen (Chapter 15), for instance, refer to the unifying sense of community that results from day-to-day encounters with "pro-life" forces and from recurring financial crises. This sense of community implies a deeper emotional involvement and density of relationships than any but the most central activists can experience in the mass-based social movement organizations such as NOW and NARAL (see McCarthy 1987). Service providers have far more intensive experiences of externally oriented conflict because it is personalized by the intimate nature of face-to-face encounters (see Simonds, Chapter 16).

Because of their responsibility for providing services to the public, feminist service organizations have tended to formalize their structure and employ professional staff to secure a more reliable financial base while maintaining a feminist or antibureaucratic set of values to varying degrees (for a survey of this literature, see Martin 1990b). Because of ideological commitments to equality, empowerment, and democratic participation, service organizations often maximize the role of volunteers as well as professional staff in decision-making. Because of the same principles, they seek to serve a wide clientele of women and to employ women from all walks of life. The result, however, has frequently been open or suppressed conflict across boundaries of race and class and between volunteers and professional staff. Though much of the controversy experienced by service organizations derives directly from external countermovements such as the New Right or the anti-abortion movement, these external pressures may come on top of internal cleavages over prior identities, which bring their own share of conflict and division. Morgen (Chapter 15), for instance, found that the fifteen low-income women employed through a CETA grant by a feminist health clinic discovered racism, homophobia, and class prejudice among their feminist sisters, while the latter experienced pain, defensiveness, and shame regarding their own privileges.

Conclusion

The foregoing discussion has suggested that both external and internal conflict are endemic to the multiple organizational forms of the contemporary women's movement. The two types are sterotypically characterized as "good" conflict and "bad" conflict. The former is considered goal-oriented and directed against the opponents of the movement; the latter is seen as nonstrategic and oriented to internal movement power struggles directed by one group of feminists against another. Moreover, the two types of battles are often discussed as if they occurred in only one organizational form and not others. External conflicts are most often associated with the major, formal social movement organizations; internal conflicts are usually regarded as the restricted province of the small consciousness-raising groups.

A more careful examination of the history of the contemporary movement indicates that both conflict orientations are found in all three types of feminist organizations. Whether one form of discord is better for the movement than the other is largely a question of which outcomes are given preference. The consequences of the two types are very different, however, depending on the organizational context. In small, informal groups, mediating factors such as the "recruitment effect" of externally oriented conflict can lead to heightened internal conflict, followed by factionalism, particularly if organizational ideologies give new members equal standing with older, more experienced ones. In dealing with recruitment effects, the rulemaking capacity of formal SMOs gives them an advantage not available to groups that are informally organized. Thus, with regard to surviving external and internal conflict, the formal SMO seems to have the advantage.

Staggenborg (1989) has indicated, however, that more informal structures are better sources of innovative tactics and strategies. Though Staggenborg attributes these outcomes to differences in organizational structure, the arguments developed here suggest that they may be a result of the processing of conflict as well. The internal dissension that leads to factionalism and dissolution in small groups may also provide the impulse for theoretical generativity around competing identities. Much theoretical work on the intersection of gender, race, and class, for example, has been generated in reaction to the experience of conflict over these issues.

The service organizations share some organizational qualities of both the larger and smaller groups. To the extent that they became professionalized and bureaucratized, they are more likely to follow the model of the formal SMOs; to the extent that they rely on volunteers and try to create a "prefigurative" feminist community, they have tended in the direction of the small groups. This latter tendency is allayed somewhat by the continuing need to provide services. Robin Leidner's (1991) studies of the NWSA provide the most dramatic recent examples of how the two tendencies interact.

Discussions of social movement conflict that focus on either internal or external orientations alone will inevitably miss the relationships between the two. Although internal differences can always be expected to provide sources of conflict, the presence of a strong but not overpowering opposition—whether from a countermovement or the state—seems to overcome competing identities and create a sense of unity. To the degree that external conflict is intense and personal, these bonds may deepen to community. To the degree that the threat seems overpowering, both community and commitment may be destroyed. Although internal conflicts are almost invariably destructive of individuals, they sometimes provide occasions for organizational learning and cultural generativity that benefit the movement as a whole. In many important respects, a conflict-free movement would cease to move at all.

CHAPTER 18

Dilemmas of Feminist Coalitions: Collective Identity and Strategic Effectiveness in the Battered Women's Movement

■

GRETCHEN ARNOLD

Organizational issues concerning structure and process have been both a locus for innovation and a source of dilemmas for the contemporary women's movement. Whether at the broader level of movement structure—such as in networks and coalitions of various movement actors—or at the level of individual organizations, feminists have been concerned with the form they give to their organizations.[1] In certain feminist circles the development of alternative organizational forms has been valued as an expression of feminist politics (Freeman 1975; Simon 1982; Schlesinger and Bart 1983; Ferguson 1984; Riger 1984; Baker 1986; Leidner 1991; Taylor and Whitter 1993). Precisely because of their politically symbolic importance, issues concerning organizational structure—including the internal distribution of power and control, the division of labor, and decision-making rules (Martin 1990a)—have time and again been the rocks upon which feminist groups have been shipwrecked (Riger 1984). My study of the battered women's movement provides insight into why such organizational issues have been particularly difficult for feminist coalitions to handle.

In order to coordinate their actions in pursuit of a common goal, participants in social movements develop more or less persistent organizational connections (Melucci 1989). Activists in the battered women's movement have most often chosen to form coalitions for this purpose.[2] The wide range of ideological positions among feminists in this movement (Schechter 1982; Dobash and Dobash 1992), a diversity characteristic of the broader women's movement of which it is a part (B. Ryan 1989, 1992; Freeman 1975; Buechler 1990a), seems to make coalition the ideal format for uniting the various movement actors in collective efforts to achieve concrete goals

(Bunch 1987). As a supra-organizational form, a coalition enables distinct parties to mobilize around common concerns while preserving separate political and organizational identities. Coalitions do not require ideological agreement among members but instead rely on an overlap of interests (Ferree and Miller 1985). Yet as Suzanne Staggenborg notes in her study of pro-choice coalitions (1986), effective "coalition work" among diverse groups is notoriously difficult to achieve.[3] Staggenborg traces the difficulties of coalition work to the external and internal pressures experienced by all organizations, including resource availability and the maintenance needs of the member organizations. Here, however, I argue that a unique source of the difficulties in sustaining coalitions among feminists is a contradiction between the structural features of coalitions and the organizational requirements of some feminist ideologies.

Like the New Left activists who preceded them (S. Evans 1979; Breines 1989), many feminists have considered organizational form to be more than just a means to an end (see Echols 1989). They have viewed the design of an organization's structure as an opportunity to practice what Wini Breines (1989) calls prefigurative politics: that is, as a way to embody the movement's vision of the ideal society in its practices. Socialist and radical feminists have argued that the oppression of women is built into the very structure of our social institutions (Taylor and Whittier 1993); on this account, a central part of the feminist political program is to create alternative organizations whose internal framework serves as a model to challenge these oppressive structures (Ferguson 1984; Riger 1984; Baker 1986). This is why many feminists have tried to avoid traditional hierarchical organizational forms in favor of more democratic and egalitarian ones.[4] But the prefigurative requirement to embody normative ideals in an organization's structure, I argue, is in direct contradiction with the politically neutral format that is the hallmark of coalitions. In the case study at hand, the tension generated by this contradiction surfaced as a conflict over what initially appeared to be a trivial issue but quickly threatened to undermine the coalition itself.

The empirical material for this analysis is drawn from my case study of these issues in the battered women's movement in St. Louis. For two years (1988 to 1990) I was a participant observer of the activities of the local social movement community which (following Buechler 1990a) I defined as all those groups and individuals who identified their goals with the preferences of the battered women's movement and attempted to implement those goals. I was first a volunteer and then a part-time paid staff person at one of the local organizations for battered women. I was the organiza-tion's sole representative to the coalition that I analyze here, which formed immediately after I was hired; I was involved in it from the beginning but was not one of the initial organizers. Throughout the period, I was open about my dual role as movement participant and social researcher.

Although popular perception often equates the battered women's move-ment with shelters for battered women, shelters were not the only orga-nizations involved in movement activity in St. Louis. In addition to three shelters, six other organizations made up the local movement community: two women's organizations devoted primarily to counseling victims of wife abuse and other kinds of violence against women; one men's collective whose purpose was to end violence against women, largely by counseling men who battered their wives; one program established to provide legal advocacy for battered women; and two victims' service organizations with close connections to local prosecutors' offices that served battered women and victims of other types of crime. All these organizations were involved in the coalition for the duration of my study. The local battered women's movement community also included a number of women who had at one time worked in one of the organizations but no longer did so at the time I conducted this study. Some of these women participated in coalition meetings.

In addition to the participant observation, my research included a re-view of documents from local battered women's movement organizations as well as nationwide movement publications, and interviews with nineteen local activists in the summer of 1990. I obtained the quotations reported here from these documents and interviews.

The Battered Women's Movement in St. Louis, Missouri

When I began my study in 1988, several of the more experienced activ-ists complained to me that the battered women's movement community in St. Louis was fragmented and politically powerless. As in the emergence of the battered women's movement as a whole (Schechter 1982), separate individuals and institutions had, over a period of years, developed local programs to provide shelter and other services to battered women in crisis. Established in isolation from one another, the organizations had grown and operated with little or no cooperation among them.

According to these activists, much of the disunity within the local move-ment community stemmed from disputes concerning ideology, goals, and programs for change. I use the term "ideology" to refer to the set of political beliefs and values on the basis of which individuals interpret conditions and events. Mirroring the movement as a whole (Schechter 1982; Dobash and Dobash 1992), the battered women's movement in St. Louis was roughly divided into two camps. The most fundamental difference between the two camps concerned the degree to which each challenged the social and economic system of gender inequality that supports violence against women.[5] Those whom I refer to as moderates advocated goals and programs that only indirectly challenged the patriarchal system of power relations. The moderates' goal was to help women who were currently being battered to end the violence in their lives by providing them with services (shelter, police protection, legal aid, counseling, and so on). They tended to establish and evaluate programs for battered women primarily in terms of their strategic effectiveness for delivering services, and to align with conventional social service institutions. They expressed little if any interest in working with other grassroots groups—even other battered women's organizations—to pursue collective goals.

The more radical activists advocated fundamental change in the social and material conditions that support male domination and violence against women. They held that battered women's movement programs should foster alternative feminist communities based on grass-roots, self-help activity, both to challenge existing social relations of power and to enable women's own self-empowerment and autonomy. The radicals articulated multiple demands, including not only improved services for battered women but also economic equality for all women and an end to the racism, anti-Semitism, and homophobia from which women suffer. As part of this broad-based program to improve the condition of all women, the radicals advocated and actively sought alliances with other dispossessed social movement groups.[6]

Before 1988 the moderates and radicals in St. Louis had tended to regard each other with scorn. One activist from the radical camp described what she saw as the moderates' skepticism about the broader, and more nebulous, social change goals of the radicals: "The folks at [the Jane Doe shelter for battered women] have never been particularly interested in networking or whatever. . . . It's a very different vision [of what the work is all about]. It's like [they think], 'Oh, these [radical] people go to these [community-wide] meetings and they yell and scream, but we just go in there every day and *we do our work, we get it done and we do it well.*' And there's no 'big picture' at all." The difference between the groups as she described it concerned the breadth of their visions: the moderates focused more narrowly on providing services efficiently and effectively; the radicals also sought broader changes in the "big picture" of the gender inequality that supports the abuse of women.

In the fall of 1988 some of the radical activists were expressing both privately and publicly the need for better communication and cooperation among local battered women's movement groups. Until that time, the only successful collective actions they had undertaken concerned the passage of Missouri's Adult Abuse Law in 1980, and even that work was done within the context of statewide rather than local cooperation. With this exception, each agency's activities had been unilateral. Communication was minimal and unsystematic, and workers at any given agency often did not know what programs or services the others provided. Friction arose when invariably some projects overlapped or competed. By the time of this study, such competition, coupled with ideological and various personal conflicts between individual activists, had generated an atmosphere of bitterness and distrust.

The stage had been set for greater cooperation, however, by the increasing amount of advocacy work undertaken by activists in St. Louis between 1985 and 1988. One local movement leader described the change in activists' priorities this way:

> One of the things that I've seen happen just over the last three to five years is . . . an incredible increase in the language of advocacy in our local programs, and even five or six years ago most of what we were doing was trying to fit into funding proposals that were talking about counseling. . . . I don't think it's been a directed response, where all of us came together and said, "Hey, we need to do this," but I think it's really been a good change that's happened in most of our programs. People are talking much more about advocacy and spending much more of their resources on court advocacy and system advocacy than we were even a few years ago.

Battered women often need multiple kinds of assistance, some of which go beyond the capacities of shelters or other programs to provide. They need financial help from the government (usually Aid to Families with Dependent Children, AFDC), subsidized low-cost housing, and physical protection by the police and courts. Because poor women and women in crisis are often unable to marshal the necessary resources to negotiate on their own behalf for such assistance, battered women's program staff often advocate for them with public agencies. Whereas conventional social service delivery focuses primarily on individual clients and their personal problems, advocacy work forces the activist to look beyond the individual woman to her surrounding social context, a kind of activity that itself has a political dimension (Farris 1988). It calls attention to the institutional structures that perpetuate the oppression of certain groups of people. For example, advocacy with the local housing authority on behalf of battered women seeking low-cost housing reveals the barriers women face when trying to separate from an abusive partner. Not surprisingly, the advocate's negotiation and political bargaining on behalf of individuals often becomes bargaining on behalf of entire groups of people to change institutional policies and decision-making procedures. In this way, advocacy allows service providers to develop a critical political consciousness and to take a more activist stance toward the state.

In January 1989 a mini-conference organized by the local men's collective on the topic of men's role in the battered women's movement provided a forum in which local activists talked about the necessity for the local programs "to be working cooperatively to best serve the needs of women." In particular, according to the conference minutes, they discussed the need for "mechanisms which are inclusive of all of the actors in the DV [domestic violence] community by which we can work together . . . on macro issues (community education, police training, legislation, etc.)." All the local battered women's organizations had participated in a task force formed in the fall of 1988 to produce a community awareness program during Domestic Violence Awareness Month in October,[7] and some activists now proposed transforming this task force into a more permanent coalition organization. The coalition was to be clearly circumscribed in structure and scope, as a memo from one of the organizers to potential participants indicates: "The Task Force generated so much creative energy from the October activities that we decided to keep on meeting and taking on time limited, community awareness projects."

In February 1989 the proponents succeeded in forming the coalition, which they named the Alliance to End Violence against Women. In the beginning the group saw itself as a coalition of service providers. Its founders had conceived of the organization as a means of broadening community education—for example, by sponsoring speakers, passing out literature, and organizing media events to inform the public about wife abuse and about the local battered women's organizations. The participants agreed during the first two meetings, however, that this heightened community awareness would probably lead to an increased demand for services for which, all concurred, their organizations would be responsible. So they agreed to add service provision issues to the group's mission, including the coordination of member organizations' existing services and the development of new ones to fill in the gaps. At the third meeting, much to the surprise of the seasoned, more radical activists, participants voiced support for expanding the goals of the organization even further to include political action. Some of the radical activists had privately told me that they did not want the Alliance to limit itself to education and service provision. They wanted the group to undertake community organizing and provide leadership by taking a public stand on a variety of issues that affect women's lives, including economic and racial/ethnic discrimination and homophobia. Because they had not expected that the more moderate members would consent to such a broadening of the group's goals, however, they had not broached the topic of political activism at the earlier meetings. When one of the moderate members proposed adding political action to the group's mission, they happily agreed.

The mission statement for the Alliance that was composed during the third meeting, then, included not only the conventional moderate concerns for enhanced service provision and community education but also the proposal for political action usually favored only by the more radical activists: "To end violence against women and their children in the St. Louis metropolitan area by organizing public awareness events, increasing and strengthening services, and engaging in political action." The statement was written in terms general enough that all the participants could agree on its three components. Everyone recognized a common interest in trying to improve services for battered women by coordinating their individual programs and sharing information about community resources. Moreover, gaps in the area's services and problems with local public institutions had been brought to light by activists' advocacy efforts. Systematically inappropriate police responses to domestic violence calls were known to everyone, and each agency was engaged in its own struggle with police to get more effective enforcement of the Adult Abuse Law. Consensus on the need for a collective effort to change the police department's policies and procedures was easy to obtain. In fact, it was agreement on these latter issues that had led to the addition of "political action" to the group's mission statement.

The Alliance worked smoothly for the first six months. The group's actions stayed within a politically narrow range, and none of the small projects and fund-raising events they undertook was controversial for either the moderate or the more radical activists. Staff from member organizations cooperatively conducted a training seminar about battering for professional counselors and chemical dependency workers. In addition, the Alliance was asked by the state attorney's office for the St. Louis Circuit Court to provide input on implementation of a new "pro-arrest" police policy in the city, and the group formed a subcommittee to respond (although once it was formed, this committee operated independently). The Alliance also served as a forum for sharing information among the member organizations, as well as a context for activists to get to know one another personally and professionally.

After six months, however, the early success of the Alliance was shattered when the organization ran into a symbolic issue that divided the members. A dispute arose over the design of a greeting card that a local artist offered to donate to the Alliance to use for fund raising. The cover design was to be a graphic depiction of the group's activities in helping battered women, and it would show women together in a mutually supportive posture while children played nearby. Dissension arose over whether or not to include a man in the scene. The disagreement became highly charged and emotional, with some members adamantly in favor and others adamantly opposed.[8]

The greeting card art was supposed to be a graphic symbol representing those who belonged to the Alliance. The moderates argued that since representatives from the local men's collective were active members of the Alliance, the scene should include men. They were concerned not to exclude or alienate anyone who had been participating in the group. In contrast, the radical activists wanted the Alliance to reflect their political interpretation of the battered women's movement. In their view, any role men might have (itself a topic of ongoing debate) should be peripheral, given the movement's woman-centered philosophy; therefore, men should not be in the picture. When the participants were unable to agree about the greeting card design, the artist withdrew her offer, and the issue was dropped.

The same debate surfaced a few months later when the Alliance tried to set formal guidelines concerning membership and decision-making processes. Adopting a liberal position supporting the right of all groups to participate and all interests to be represented in decision-making bodies, the moderate members advocated opening membership to anyone who desired to participate. The radical members wanted restrictions on who could attend meetings and have decision-making power. Radical activists in the battered women's movement argue that the movement must "take its lead" from battered women themselves, not from social service professionals. Within individual service programs in St. Louis, partisans of the radical position often adhered to this principle by making concerted efforts to hire formerly battered women as staff. In practice, however, they sometimes hired people with academic credentials or state certification if those persons also held a feminist analysis of battering and a commitment to helping battered women. They recognized that in some respects it was a benefit to have credentialed staff; for example, it could enable the organization to obtain internship students from local colleges to do volunteer work.

Another way these programs tried to integrate formerly battered women into the movement was through the extensive use of volunteers, as one radical activist explained: "If you have a strong volunteer program, then you're likely to have a lot of formerly battered women who are part of that volunteer component, and so you have a way to bring that energy into the [service organization] on a regular basis. [A volunteer program] also, I think, helps . . . because you don't have such a split between those who are providing services and those who are receiving services. A strong volunteer program acts as a buffer between professional staff and those who receive the services." The more radical members argued that the best way for battered women to be represented in the Alliance was to restrict membership—or, at the least, decision-making power—to representatives from the local battered women's service organizations that had direct and ongoing contact with battered women. This position automatically precluded men, non-movement social service professionals, and even former staff of battered women's organizations from wielding power in the Alliance.

After two conflict-ridden meetings, participants agreed on a tentative— and vague—compromise in which membership would be open to anyone, but decision-making power would be restricted to the representatives of the local battered women's organizations, using a modified consensus format.[9] They reached even this agreement only on the condition that the decision would be reviewed after six months. A few of the moderate members who were no longer affiliated with any one battered women's organization expressed dismay at being excluded from decision-making and dropped out. Several other moderate members indicated their lack of patience with long, drawn-out debates that they considered peripheral to their "real" work of serving battered women; if the time they spent in Alliance meetings was going to be wasted in ideological disputes, they would withdraw.

To prevent further loss of members, the group retreated to its earlier position of limiting its range to practical projects. Minutes from the subsequent meeting make this point: "There was a positive discussion on where members would like to see the Alliance 'go from here.' Generally, members at this meeting were discussing the idea of 'letting go' of membership issues, format issues and the related and were wanting to get back on track of really focusing on *Projects that enhance community awareness*. What was felt was needed was a good turnout at the next meeting to start progress on more 'projects' that are time limited and utilize people's positive energy." From then on, the continuing participants ignored their decisions about membership and decision-making procedures and made no further reference to either issue.

Coalition and Conflict

At first glance, the depth of conflict over the greeting card and the subsequent membership and decision-making guidelines appears puzzling. The group had already navigated the potentially treacherous waters surrounding the writing of a mission statement and for months had been able to agree on joint projects. By comparison, one would have expected decisions concerning the organization's internal structure and membership to be of minor importance. But the participants' stands on these latter decisions were significant because they reflected a concern with the symbolic representation of the group's collective identity.

A number of social movement theorists have claimed that for activists in many contemporary social movements, organizational form is not solely a means to an end but is itself integral to the construction of a sense of "we" among participants. On this account, the type of organizational structure that a social movement adopts embodies its members' collective identity and the meaning they attribute to their actions (Donati 1984; Gundelach 1984; Melucci 1985, 1989). This was the issue at stake in the Alliance conflicts. The activists recognized that the greeting card art would be a representation of how they saw themselves as a group, of who belonged and who did not. Similarly, membership and decision-making guidelines would delineate the moral boundaries of the group, the principles that would underlie leadership and the exercise of power in the organization.[10]

But coalitions have particular difficulty resolving conflicts over collective identity. As Buechler (1990a) argues, group identity is inextricably intertwined with political ideology in social movements. Ideologies help constitute the groups that become involved in movement activity, and shared ideology provides the sense of collective identity that is a prerequisite for collective action. Yet the St. Louis activists chose a coalition format precisely because it did not require them to reach ideological consensus. Coalitions bring together ideologically diverse parties who maintain their separate identities. This contradiction between ideological diversity and organizational unity, however, need not be an obstacle as long as the coalition deals with issues that require only a superficial consensus.

The Alliance members had adopted this strategy early on. In different ways, the group's activities concealed the ideological divisions between the moderate and the more radical activists. Proponents of these two camps circumscribed the organization's activities, undertaking only the "time limited, community awareness projects" that its founders had proposed and thus largely circumventing the need for the group to take a public stand on political issues that might be opposed by some members. They wrote their mission statement in abstract terms that enabled them to avoid conflicts involving ideological matters. The group's stated commitment to "ending violence against women and their children" and even "engaging in political action" was broad and general enough that individual members could interpret it as consistent with their own ideological positions. Such a strategy often enables coalition members to establish the trust they need to work together (Ferree and Miller 1985).

But when the Alliance addressed the organizational issues of membership and decision-making, the prefigurative interpretation of these issues favored by the radicals forced the underlying ideological disagreements out into the open. For the radicals, the Alliance's internal structure had to embody their vision of empowering battered women. They argued that battered women, or at least those who most closely represented those women's interests and views, should have control over the decisions and direction of the organization, thereby excluding men and anyone else who was not currently working directly with battered women. The moderate activists adopted a liberal view of the organization as essentially instrumental: that is, as primarily a means to improve service provision for battered women. From this perspective, the broader and more diverse the membership base, the greater the group's potential power would be. Consistent with the spirit of coalition politics, the moderates were ready to welcome anyone whose interests coincided with those of the group. This conflict could not be resolved without engaging in further debate about ideological issues, which would alienate some of the moderate members. One option was to retreat from the dilemma without solving it, leaving the organization unable to deal with any but the least controversial issues. This is what the Alliance members chose to do.

Conclusion

The negative repercussions of ideological divisions within the women's movement have been downplayed by some analysts. For example, Jo Freeman minimizes the importance of ideological differences between feminist groups, arguing that in the end their goals for social change are substantially the same. Freeman, who applied the terms "older" and "younger" to the two different branches of the early contemporary women's movement, has argued that "the terms 'reformist' and 'radical' by which the two branches are so often designated are convenient and fit into our preconceived notions about the nature of political activity, but they tell us little of relevance. In fact, if an ideological typography were possible it would show minimal consistency with any organizational characteristic. . . . Structure and style rather than ideology more accurately differentiate the two branches, and even here there has been much borrowing on both sides" (1975, 50–51).[11]

Freeman deemphasized the role of ideology when activists in the two branches of the movement adopted different organizational structures, arguing instead that "two distinctly different kinds of experience have, in turn, largely determined the strategy of the two branches, irrespective of any conscious intentions of their participants" (1975, 51). But in this case study, I found that differing ideological positions of the liberal and radical feminists led to conflicts over structure and the near breakup of the coalition.

In the final analysis, a coalition that includes ideologically disparate groups or individuals may be incompatible with the prefigurative requirements of much socialist and radical feminism. It is impossible to fulfill such requirements in an organizational form that presumes its members are ideologically diverse and self-interested. If an organization's structure is to embody the normative ideals of a social movement, then those who design that structure must agree on what those ideals are. This is not to say that ideological consensus on the meaning and goals of the movement will preclude disagreement about specific rules and procedures, but rather that the debate will be carried on within a context of shared assumptions and ties of solidarity that may sustain its members' commitment to the group during such conflicts.[12] Since coalitions lack such a context of normative agreement, debates over issues such as membership and decision-making rules, which draw upon underlying ideological positions, may serve to divide the group's members and threaten the organization's continued existence.

In their efforts to hold the group together, the St. Louis activists avoided discussing these underlying disagreements, both before and after the conflicts erupted.[13] But this strategy is not neutral toward the two factions involved. By avoiding confrontation, the radical members effectively opted for the moderates' interpretation of the organization as a coalition of service providers. This, in turn, limited the group's undertakings to a relatively narrow range of community awareness and service-oriented projects. Within this framework the radical activists could not provide local leadership on a variety of issues affecting women's lives. To do so would have required a collective inquiry into the group's political principles and a deepening of their collective interpretive framework, which may well have alienated the more moderate members of the group. Not to do so, however, ran the risk of losing the commitment of the more radical members.

I do not conclude from this case study that coalition as an organizational form should be abandoned by the women's movement. Coalitions can be useful vehicles for undertaking collective action by feminist groups where their perceived interests coincide on particular issues and for limited periods of time. Coalitions can be particularly successful in defending against a common threat or taking advantage of an exceptional opportunity.[14] But the experience of the St. Louis Alliance to End Violence against Women illustrates that tensions and conflicts over issues of organizational structure are likely to emerge in any sustained coalition of feminists.

Notes

1. This concern with organizational form is shared by activists in many contemporary social movements. For analyses of this phenomenon from the perspective of what has been called "new social movement theory," see Donati 1984; Gundelach 1984; and Melucci 1985, 1989. For an overview of the new social movement theory approach, including its emphasis on organizational form, see Cohen 1985 and Klandermans 1989.

2. At the time of this writing the movement has one nationwide organization, the National Coalition Against Domestic Violence, established in 1978; fifty-two state coalitions (some states have more than one); and countless local coalitions of groups formed to address issues of wife beating.

3. The National Coalition Against Domestic Violence, for example, appeared ready to collapse in 1991. It was revived, but innumerable coalitions on the state and local level have not survived.

4. For an account of how activists have attempted to implement this principle in battered women's shelters, see Ridington 1977–78; Warrior 1978; Ahrens 1980; Schechter 1981, 1982; Clifton 1985; N. Davis 1988; and Murray 1988.

5. Steven Buechler (1990b) argues that the degree of radicalism of a social movement can be conceptualized in terms of the extent to which the movement challenges a system of power relations: movements that fundamentally challenge such systems are radical; those that tangentially challenge such systems are moderate.

6. Although there are a number of parallels between the moderate-radical split I describe in St. Louis and the generally accepted liberal feminist–radical feminist distinction, there are enough differences to make the latter ideal types misleading in this instance. For example, in her account of the early radical women's movement in the United States, Alice Echols (1989) argues that radical feminists typically refused to have anything to do with established political authorities; the radicals in my study were indeed suspicious of the ability of liberal institutions (especially the state) to coopt dissent, but they did work with and take money from the authorities when they thought doing so would help battered women. The radical activists in St. Louis more closely fit Alison Jaggar's (1983) category of socialist feminist in their advocacy of women's reproductive freedom, workplace equality, independent women's organizations, and political unity among oppressed groups, though they stopped short of advocating the revolutionary overthrow of capitalism. As an alternative to the three-part model of liberal, socialist, and radical feminism, I think that Buechler's (1990b) conception of movement radicalism (see note 5) provides a more accurate distinction among the social movement activists in this study.

7. Domestic Violence Awareness Month was created in the early 1980s as a direct result of the efforts of the National Coalition against Domestic Violence.

8. The issue of men's membership is a very old one in the feminist movement as a whole. Ferguson (1984), for one, argues that only women can make a feminist organization. For a review of how the issue has been addressed by different feminist groups, see Martin (1990b).

9. The decision-making model agreed to was called "Martha's Rules" (an alternative to Robert's Rules of Order), developed by Martha's Housing Co-op for Families in Madison, Wisconsin; for a description, see the article "On the Bias" (1986). I describe the Alliance's compromise agreement as vague because there were participants whose decision-making status was left unclear, including those from the local men's group and at least one other person who intended to start a shelter but hadn't done so yet.

10. The anguish expressed during the debate was consistent with the emotional commitment that people have to social identities they consider important. For an excellent analysis of social identity and its emotional component, see Cancian 1975.

11. Freeman (1975, 50 n. 22) notes that she is using "ideology" in a narrow sense "to refer to a specifically feminist belief system [that is, participants' positions on the major feminist issues] rather than a general world view on the nature of politics and society."

12. Echols (1989) shows that even fundamental ideological consensus may not be enough to hold groups together in the face of disagreements concerning organizational structure.

13. John Rawls (1993) calls this strategy "the method of avoidance": in order to maintain an overlapping consensus in pluralist societies, "contentious issues" are simply not discussed.

14. Indeed, Staggenborg (1986) has noted that coalitions are most likely to form when either environmental opportunities or threats emerge.

CHAPTER 19

Feminist Clashes with the State: Tactical Choices by State-Funded Rape Crisis Centers

■

NANCY MATTHEWS

Feminists made a unique contribution to the anti-rape movement in their broad analysis of sexual violence as a product of male dominance and gender inequality which ultimately can be eliminated only by transforming gender relations. The feminist anti-rape movement generated new ideas and expertise that have been partially incorporated into popular culture and professional knowledge.[1] The movement also changed rape legislation in almost every state and gave rise to a new kind of organization: the rape crisis center.

Rape crisis centers (RCCs) vary in organizational form. Gornick, Burt, and Pittman (1985) analyzed RCCs in terms of nine dimensions, the four most salient being (1) the priority placed on direct services versus community education and activism; (2) the comprehensiveness of direct services; (3) the degree of "political," "feminist," or "social change" orientation in a center's community education and action; and (4) the center's degree of independence or autonomy. While some RCCs are autonomous, many are affiliated with feminist or other kinds of organizations (U.S. Department of Justice 1975; Gornick, Burt and Pittman 1985; Harvey 1985; Byington et al. 1991; Koss and Harvey 1991). Because RCCs vary in the extent to which they have a movement identity versus a social service agency identity, they may variously see their agenda in terms of feminism, crime victims' rights, or therapeutic and social services (Burt, Gornick, and Pittman 1984; Gornick, Burt, and Pittman 1985). Finally, RCCs vary in their willingness to accept state funds and the restrictions that accompany them.

In the 1980s, RCCs became increasingly reliant on state funding, which enabled them to survive and pursue their service agenda but also compromised their pursuit of a feminist agenda. The relationship between RCCs and their funding agencies is one point at which organized feminism confronts the state. Social movement organizations often make demands on and can win benefits from the state (Tilly 1978; Gamson 1990; Tilly and Gurin 1990); the state funding that allows many RCCs to survive is such an example. Even after they achieve institutionalized funding, however, the relationship remains contingent. It may be cooperative, adversarial, or a mixture of these; it may change over time; and it can vary among organizations at the same time (Gornick, Burt, and Pittman 1985; Martin et al. 1992; Matthews 1994). As the social movement organization struggles to pursue its goals, conflict with the state may arise. How organizations deal with such conflict is the focus of this essay.

To analyze the dilemmas that feminist movement organizations confront in dealing with the bureaucratic state, I focus on RCCs with a social movement identity. I look at relationships between RCCs in California and the state agencies that supported them in the 1970s and 1980s. Although these RCCs appeared to have established a cooperative relationship with the state, conflict continued. When state requirements conflicted with an individual center's sense of mission, goals, and ways of doing things, the center made tactical choices about how to respond. By examining several clashes over organizational structure, rules, and procedures, I identify three patterns these tactics fall into: overt opposition, apparent accommodation, and active engagement. Employing such tactics, RCCs struggled to maintain their autonomy and define the work they had set out to do, accepting or eschewing state funding and other support in the process.

The state is composed of numerous organizations operating at different levels, with varying purposes, and therefore should not be treated as a unitary or fixed entity (Alford and Friedland 1985; H. Eisenstein 1991a). Moreover, the policies and politics of state agencies change. At one point an agency might support a particular program that it had not supported before, or a program might be transferred from one agency to another; for example, rape crisis program funding in California was passed from the Department of Social Services (DSS) to the Office of Criminal Justice Planning (OCJP) in 1979. These variations suggest the usefulness of conceptualizing the state "not as an institution but as a set of arenas; a by-product of political struggles whose coherence is as much established in discourse as in shifting and temporary connections" (Pringle and Watson 1990). Reinelt (Chapter 6) similarly treats the state as a "terrain of political activism" on which activists engage. I use "the state" as a shorthand reference to this arena as it is temporarily constituted in particular historical moments by actual state organizations. The executives and managers in these state organizations wield a great deal of power through their decisions about government programs and control of resources, but they are also responsive to pressures from "contenders" (Tilly 1978; Gamson 1990) in the arena. In this case, the contenders are feminist RCCs.[2] I am interested here in the tactical choices these contenders make in relation to centralized state agencies.

In 1988 and 1989 I conducted a comparative case study of six anti-rape movement organizations in Los Angeles. Three of these started between 1972 and 1976, another in 1980, and two in 1984. All these RCCs identified their mission more broadly than providing services to victims. Some were descendants of early feminist collectives; others more closely resembled mainstream social service programs but nonetheless identified with the activist social change agenda of the anti-rape movement (cf. Gornick, Burt, and Pittman 1985).

I conducted thirty-six interviews with participants in the six RCCs—including leaders, volunteers, and staff members from different time periods for the older centers—and with members of the California OCJP's Sexual Assault Program, which in 1980 became the primary source of funding for five of the six. I also use data from documentary sources, such as minutes of meetings, and published accounts of RCC experiences in California (see Matthews 1994).

Historical Background

Nationally, the anti-rape movement emerged in 1970 out of collectivist feminist organizing. Within a few years RCCs had multiplied and diversified (New York Radical Feminists 1974; Largen 1981; Gornick, Burt, and Pittman 1985). By 1973 the National Organization for Women had a Rape Task Force (U.S. Department of Justice 1975), and members of the movement had begun to work for legislative change.

Women in the early RCCs were often critical and suspicious of the state (New York Radical Feminists 1974; U.S. Department of Justice 1975). Politicized counterculture women in the early 1970s saw firsthand the repressive character of the state in police treatment of radical activists in the student, civil rights, and peace movements. They worried about being subjected to "scrutiny by the FBI, the CIA, or the police" (U.S. Department of Justice 1975, 126). Activists' experiences and observations of the ridicule and hostility that police and prosecutors directed at women who tried to make rape complaints further strengthened their opposition to the state. Radical activists in the anti-rape movement often saw their rape crisis work as an alternative to mainstream institutions such as the criminal justice system.

Over time, rape crisis work spread beyond the countercultural, collectivist feminist milieu and was taken up by more mainstream women who, while critical of institutional handling of rape, were more willing to work with and reform mainstream institutions. Even radical activists shifted their emphasis away from political action and toward direct service provision and advocating on victims' behalf in hospitals, with the police, and in the court system (Burgess 1985; Gornick, Burt, and Pittman 1985).

THE EARLY LOS ANGELES RCCS

Feminist activists from two autonomous women's centers founded the Los Angeles Commission on Assaults Against Women (LACAAW) in 1973, after about two years of ad hoc work as an anti-rape squad. A network of social work professionals in several community agencies established the Pasadena YWCA Rape Hotline in 1974. Latinas involved in social work and community activism started the East Los Angeles Rape Hotline (ELARH) in 1976; one of its founders had been active in LACAAW but wanted to establish an RCC to serve Spanish-speaking and bilingual women in the city.

Although founded in a common time period, the three groups developed different approaches. The primarily White and politically leftist feminists who founded LACAAW drew on collectivist organizational ideals and were suspicious of the state and law enforcement. The group experienced the classic problems with collectivist feminist organization, including time-consuming and wearing consensus decision-making, personalized resentment of informally emerging leadership, and conflicts over values (see Freeman 1975; Rothschild-Whitt 1979; Ferree and Hess 1985; Rothschild-Whitt and Whitt 1986; Echols 1989). And because its ideological commitment to collectivity challenged mainstream organizational structure, LACAAW confronted serious conflicts when it stepped into the arena of state funding.

The Pasadena YWCA hotline founders were employed at the YWCA, Planned Parenthood, and a hospital. These women had access to and resources for influencing the institutions already involved with rape victims, including hospitals and the police, and were less ideologically opposed to the state than the LACAAW activists. The Pasadena organizers paid less attention to creating alternative organizations than to connecting with existing networks of service provision and to creating new services where necessary.

The Latina founders of the ELARH were professionals with similar connections and concerns as members of the Pasadena network, but they were also activists who had a critical political analysis rooted in La Raza[3] and feminism. They developed bilingual and culturally appropriate rape crisis services to further the empowerment of their communities, broadly defined.

THE LATER LOS ANGELES RCCS

The San Fernando Valley Rape Crisis Service (SFVRCS) started in 1980 with an emphatically radical feminist and anti-statist political perspective. Its founders were critical of the older organizations for having become too mainstream, and they attempted to maintain a collectivist style of organization despite the changed political environment. SFVRCS operated from 1980 to 1986 but, unwilling to make the compromises that went with OCJP funding, did not survive.

Two additional RCCs that began in the 1980s were the Rosa Parks Sexual Assault Crisis Center and the Compton YWCA Sexual Assault Crisis Program. They were founded with grants from the OCJP to bring rape crisis services to "underserved" areas, including the predominantly African American communities in Los Angeles.[4] The Martin Luther King Legacy Association (the local branch of SCLC, the Southern Christian Leadership Conference) and the Compton YWCA responded to a call for proposals from the OCJP in 1984. Unlike those established during the 1970s, these RCCs were closely linked with community and grassroots victims' groups whose focus was protesting violence in general, rather than violence against women as a manifestation of sexism.

The Rosa Parks and Compton RCCs were bureaucratized from the start and, having been founded with state money, were less inclined to be immediately oppositional toward the state. As I discuss elsewhere, however (Matthews 1989), operating in poorer communities that lacked other resources made broad demands on them. They did work that was not "accountable" to the state because it did not fit into the categories for which the organization was funded. For example, getting a victim and her children fed because they were hungry and helping a victim find shelter were not services for which the RCCs were funded but were often provided nevertheless, because only by addressing these immediate needs could they provide the rape crisis services that *were* funded. Such dilemmas created conflict with the state over the funding formula and definitions of rape crisis work.

Conflict with the State and Tactical Choices

The state and RCCs agree that rape crisis work should be done, but they differ over *what* the work is and *how* it should be done. In the interview participants' discourses about the meaning and necessity of organizational rules and procedures, the taken-for-grantedness of hierarchical structure, and their priorities in anti-rape work, I discovered numerous conflicts. Rape crisis centers' increasing reliance on state grants created a new structural relationship to the state as they struggled to maintain a feminist agenda while accepting state funding.

The three kinds of tactical choices RCCs made when conflict arose with state funding agencies—overt opposition, apparent accommodation, and active engagement—may be best thought of as a web of practices or "tactical repertoire" (Snow and Benford 1992) that organizations adopt at different times. The choice of action draws on general ideological histories but is also contingent on more immediate factors. Each of these tactical choices reveals the adaptability of RCCs in their encounters with the bureaucratic state and the state's superior control over how RCCs organize their work.

OVERT OPPOSITION

Overt opposition, which may be proactive or reactive, involves a dynamic in which the state tries to control or limit RCC action or the RCC reacts uncooperatively to a requirement of the state. When the OCJP program was established, early grants made before administrative requirements and guidelines were in place were based on sketchy proposals. Formal requirements were soon instituted, however, and some groups balked at meeting the new record-keeping and data-collection rules. Santa Cruz Women Against Rape (SCWAR) resisted this requirement openly, refusing to include what the OCJP considered adequate data in its quarterly reports (Mackle et al. 1982). As the Sexual Assault Program (SAP) manager explained:

> Santa Cruz . . . refused to submit data to us, information on their activities. . . . The Santa Cruz center, which was an ultra-feminist organization, felt that that was politically incorrect to collect that data. . . .

It had to do with making those kinds of distinctions between people and even asking people if you were in a certain [racial category]. . . . Our position was *if* the information should come naturally during a crisis call, record it. . . . If you don't know, check "unknown." . . . But they [SCWAR] felt philosophically, and this is an example of the intransigence, . . . [that] it was incorrect to collect data on minorities, and so they refused to do it.

SCWAR members protested by filling in all the forms they objected to with "unknown." Although this was technically acceptable, in the eyes of the program manager they went too far by doing it routinely. After several months of argument on both sides, the OCJP withdrew its funding in 1982.

SCWAR's loss of funding led to substantial concern at other centers about what the boundaries were in collecting data. Many saw the issue as one of control by the state for potentially repressive purposes. OCJP's action effectively deterred overt opposition to such requirements by other centers, but the issue of what data are collected, how thoroughly, and for what purposes continues to be a point of contention between RCCs and the state agency.

Refusal of funding that is too compromising is a proactive form of opposition. In the 1970s the federal Law Enforcement Assistance Administration (LEAA) offered substantial funding, but many RCC activists saw law enforcement money as especially co-optive and at odds with their agenda (U.S. Department of Justice 1975). Law enforcement represented the most obviously repressive arm of the state, and the LEAA requirement that victims report their rapes to the police conflicted with RCCs' principle of empowering women by allowing them to decide for themselves whether to use the criminal justice system (Schechter 1982). In LACAAW the question of LEAA funding led to the first split in the organization. An early activist recalls the dynamics that led to the group's refusal to ask for it:

The line [had been] going for about a year on a hand-to-mouth kind of basis, writing proposals to whoever we could find to write them to. We tried the city, and we tried foundations, but when it came to submitting a proposal to the Law Enforcement Assistance Administration, which was a very likely source of funds for us, the membership of the Commission [LACAAW] divided right down the middle. . . . We never did apply for that money. . . . We saw ourselves as . . . an alternative to criminal justice system involvement for rape victims, because the criminal justice system was doing so badly, and . . . the issue was that if we took money from the criminal justice system [then] we would have to participate in that system. And in fact, most of the LEAA money had with it as a requirement . . . that whatever victim uses the services make a police report. And at that time we were advising women not to.

Later, the San Fernando Valley Rape Crisis Service, the RCC started in 1980, eschewed OCJP funds for similar reasons, and although it survived without them for six years, lack of resources and internal conflicts eventually led to its demise.

Such forms of overt opposition are rare because the price paid is high. Some organizations collapse; others lose members or divide. RCCs that choose this tactic never do so lightly, and the controversy generated within the organization adds to the strain of lost funds.

APPARENT ACCOMMODATION

Apparent accommodation involves adjusting RCC practice so that it conforms or appears to conform to state rules. I term it "apparent" because it includes surreptitious or covert resistance to the rules, which may be occasional or routine.[5] This kind of resistance provides an alternative to the risks of overt opposition.

RCCs that were structured as collectives initially found that operating hotlines and related services entailed demands that were not always compatible with collectivity. Even small amounts of funding from state sources obliged groups to orient their work differently. For example, the California Department of Social Service (DSS) grants required considerable work for a modest amount of money. One ELARH staff member described the requirements:

> The first grant that we got for $5,000 from the Department of Social Service, . . . we had to provide the twenty-four-hour hotline coverage, . . . and we were expected to provide advocacy, you know, going out and meeting clients at the hospital or the police station and providing the crisis intervention. That was . . . implied and later on it became an actual requirement. And not only having to provide these services twenty-four hours a day, but also having to do community education. . . . A lot was expected for the very little money that we received, and we thought we were doing great to get a $5,000 grant.

Though most of those activities were goals of the organization anyway, the volunteer-based group was necessarily flexible in the extent to which the goals were met. Having a state grant, however, created pressure to meet the required standards whether the additional resources were adequate or not.

From 1976 to 1978 LACAAW received National Institute of Mental Health (NIMH) funds that enabled it to hire more staff, but the support brought new requirements that led to internal conflicts. A participant from that period recalls how the grant led to greater rationalization and formalization of the center: "So we really got structured, because it was a research and demonstration center. . . . We had an obligation in terms of products that we had to develop—training manual, educational manual—[we had to] develop the program, and then evaluate them. So we went through kind of a formal process of development, using the expertise of the people at the Commission [LACAAW], building on what they were already doing." In addition to demanding new products, the grant brought in new personnel, which changed the way coordinating work was done. Integrating the new staff and other resources put new demands on the existing informal collectivist structure:

> All of a sudden there were five new staff people at the Commission. You know, [the early volunteer codirectors] had just been working it out on their own. They did as much work over phone calls in the middle of the night as they did anywhere else, and all of a sudden there was money for rent and there was an office to relate to, to take care of, to staff. . . . The change was very hard. . . . Well, we set ourselves up as a collective. Everybody made the same salary, everybody made decisions together. . . . There was a whole process of trying to develop a decision-making process which included hotline volunteers as well as staff. It meant that every discussion was agonizing.

These new conditions exposed the disjuncture between the ideal of collectivist organization and the reality of concentrated informal leadership. Nevertheless, LACAAW members attempted to accommodate the demands of the funding while still retaining a collectivist, feminist structure.

About the same time, funding also became available through the Comprehensive Education and Training Act (CETA) which could be used to hire staff. But CETA, officially a job-training program, required that someone supervise and train CETA employees, which conflicted with LACAAW's collectivist structure. Furthermore, individuals who qualified as CETA trainees were not necessarily committed to the goals of the RCC, which created friction. A participant describes the disjuncture between the mainstream CETA program and LACAAW's goals as a feminist collective:

> Under the requirements of the [CETA] program, they had a certain way of defining "work." It didn't match what we did as an organization. . . . We were having to structure an "employment experience" for people who . . . got these jobs mostly, theoretically, because they needed that training. And that training was supposed to lead them into some mainstream employment. And neither did most of the applicants that we got for these CETA positions have any notion of what this "feminist" business was all about. . . . [Moreover] somebody had to be a supervisor: there *had* to be a boss. Somebody had to do the paperwork and sign off on this person's work, okay? Everybody who had been there before was doing it out of the dedication and commitment that comes out of being a feminist and wanting this service to take place.

Obviously, the addition of new, untrained staff was problematic for both the CETA workers and their "supervisors." Managing their integration produced a clash between collectivist and bureaucratic principles and created instability in LACAAW.

This conflict was resolved without overt resistance on LACAAW's part. Adopting a tactic of apparent accommodation, the RCC began to recruit first on the basis of commitment to anti-rape work and *then* on a determination of whether the candidate could qualify as a CETA worker. Excluding workers on the basis of their political commitments violated the rules governing such state-funded hiring, but the RCC was able to appear to follow the rules by finding workers who did meet the CETA standards. Ironically, however, new conflicts arose between old leaders and new paid staff members who also had anti-rape movement backgrounds. Eventually, older leaders left LACAAW.

It was not the state requirements per se, but the lack of fit with LACAAW's alternative organizational structure that produced conflict. By contrast, ELARH used CETA trainees without problems. Its CETA workers entered a community center that was managed by one of ELARH's founders, which provided a ready-made bureaucratized structure with acknowledged lines of authority and expectations for work, as well as procedures for monitoring work and keeping records. By locating the CETA workers at the community center rather than directly at the RCC, ELARH avoided the additional burden of reproducing such a structure in their own organization.

State funding thus offered both these organizations additional support for their work but also produced unanticipated organizational stress in meeting the terms that went with funding. Because the benefits were substantial, both organizations tried to accommodate the new rules but also creatively bent the rules to fit their own needs.

ACTIVE ENGAGEMENT

Active engagement involves attempts to intervene in the state either proactively or reactively to change its policies. Many RCC activists who were critical of the OCJP urged the agency to accommodate the RCCs rather than force the centers to conform to OCJP requirements. One example of this tactic was the effort to change the funding formula the OCJP used to determine grants to RCCs. The SAP manager explained that the formula depended on the number of *new* victims served: "Since funding started, . . . it's always been based on the number of new victims the agency saw or provided services to." A formula based on the number of new victims served in crisis intervention was a problem for less-established centers, for those that needed to spend more time introducing their services to the community through education, and for those that did more follow-up with victims because of the shortage of other services in their communities. It also hurt RCCs whose clients had multiple problems, such as homelessness, poverty, or drug use, since these centers needed to spend more time with each client.

Many Los Angeles RCC activists viewed the funding formula as an issue of equity among centers. In their view, some centers were unfairly disadvantaged. In 1983 members of the Southern California Rape Hotline Alliance protested that the formula created structural impediments to serving women of color (Alliance minutes). In 1988 the Compton RCC director explained to me how this continued to be a problem with reference to the African American community: "It takes time for people to have . . . trust and faith. . . . I think that in a few years our community will reach the heights of where rape and sexual assault is on the agenda and we won't take it anymore, and we'll have a lot more support in that area. But at this point, I would say, we're still working on awareness. . . . It takes time to educate a community." Community education, including consciousness raising about sexual assault and prevention education, is crucial to RCCs because it lays the groundwork for the services they provide. RCC activists felt that the formula based on the number of new victims differentially affected their centers, depending on the kinds of communities they served. RCCs serving a broad population were more likely to be able to reach enough new clients to meet the requirement for their grant, even if they were frustrated about not being adequately funded to do community education. For RCCs whose mission was to serve special populations, problems of establishing awareness and trust in the community could make it difficult to assist enough victims to justify an adequate grant.

The OCJP gave "special emphasis" grants to some centers for underserved, high-crime areas, but although these supplements helped, the funding formula remained problematic overall. Several RCCs lobbied to change the formula. In 1988 the then-new second manager of the OCJP Sexual Assault Program recognized the need for change and identified criteria other than number of new victims that RCC activists had proposed:

> [Funding] could be based on *all* of the mandated services, as opposed to *one* of the mandated services. The services are crisis intervention, follow-up counseling, in-person counseling, advocacy, accompaniment, information-referral for the community that calls in, and community education. They're required to do all those services. The funding is now on one of those services, crisis intervention, which means new victims served. That's capturing the number of new clients to the agency. . . . Part of the feeling of the [ad hoc] committee [studying the funding formula] is that the range of follow-up services maybe should be taken into account, because they're required to provide those services.

RCC representatives on the ad hoc committee actively lobbied the OCJP to change rules that affected their work, an approach the OCJP manager preferred to overt opposition. It is unclear, however, whether this tactic was any more effective at getting results. In 1992 an associate director at LACAAW said, "Nobody really knows what [the funding formula] is based on." She recalled that the OCJP conducted a survey in 1988 about the number of people served in all their various activities, but she was not sure whether all of these were weighed in determining the size of operating grants.

Conflict over the funding formula was a struggle over priorities and conditions of doing rape crisis work. The formula affected the quality of services and the types of activities centers could legitimately emphasize. The formula gave short shrift to prevention education, which is the main vestige of the movement's early feminist political agenda (Burt, Gornick, and Pittman 1984).[6] Educational programs in schools and other community settings offer the potential to change gender relations so that sexual assault can be reduced, not just treated.[7] Education is essential in communities where the idea of sexual assault services must be legitimized before victims will use them, especially in communities that are reluctant to discuss sexual assault, as the director of Compton RCC pointed out. Asian, African American, and Latina activists have developed special approaches that are sensitive to their communities (Rimonte n.d.; Kanuha 1987; Lum 1988). Without such customization, sexual assault crisis services may be viewed in some communities as a form of colonization by the white, middle-class social control establishment. The funding formula and its minimal emphasis on education signals that the OCJP generally favors treatment over prevention.

Active engagement tactics are more available to activists as they become legitimate participants in the political arena. Their merits include relatively low risk and the possibility of having substantial influence on policies. Entering political dialogue through lobbying and committee work do not guarantee effectiveness, however, as RCC activists involved in the funding formula debate discovered. Indeed, one of their purposes was to increase the emphasis on prevention education, but since 1990 the OCJP has reduced its support for such activities, including child abuse prevention and self-defense programs.

Some RCC activists used this tactic selectively on issues they felt strongly about or in areas where they saw some possibility of changing OCJP policy. Others adopted it as a general strategy, hoping that engaging in conflict in a cooperative "through the channels" manner would pay off. Doing either of these has organizational costs, as staff time is spent on negotiating with the funding source rather than doing other work.

Conclusion

Rape crisis centers and their state funders rarely saw eye to eye about rape crisis work. Negotiating how to do the work in the context of the bureaucratic state led to conflicts over organizational arrangements, rules, and procedures. Occasionally, RCCs opposed the state overtly, but such an approach undermined their goal of getting support for service provision and social change work; they risked losing funding or even collapsing as an organization. More often, RCCs conformed, or put on the appearance of conforming, to state requirements that conflicted with their goals and vision. The benefits of such accommodation may have seemed compelling at the time but carried unforeseen costs. RCCs sometimes actively engaged with the state, using their access and political skills to try to produce changes in policy. Although this may seem the least risky choice, it absorbed significant organizational energy into political and bureaucratic processes.

The RCCs' tactical choices depended on the environment, local and extra-local, immediate and historical. Women who were situated differently by race or class and women who held different ideological views chose different tactics. The women of color in this study were usually less contentious in relating to the OCJP because their jobs originated with state funding. Although critical of state policies, they related to the state like the moderate White women who had a positive view of what could be accomplished by cooperating with the state. Other White women viewed their work in a rape crisis center as a socially relevant job demanding that they take principled stands on rape and social change, even when such stands were organizationally risky.

These conflicts between RCCs and state agencies provide a window of understanding into feminism vis-à-vis the state (see also Eisenstein, Reinelt, Spalter-Roth and Schreiber, Chapters 5, 6, and 7). California's steadily increased funding for rape crisis work during the 1980s highlights what can be accomplished through women's movement work in the state arena.[8] But state agencies reformulate demands into issues they are willing to address. In response to the anti-rape movement the state changed its approach to the problem of sexual assault and supported a new right to treatment for victims, but it provided little support for activities that might alter social relations more fundamentally. As RCCs became institutionalized, more mainstream points of view on the issue gained prominence, and the feminist analysis of rape as a problematic gender issue became a less central theme in rape crisis work. Yet without state funding, more of these centers would have collapsed and disappeared. Although neither the state nor the RCCs are entirely satisfied with their relationship, they tolerate each other because each needs the other for its own ends: the state to provide newly legitimized services to rape victims; the RCCs for the resources to survive.

Notes

1. The specter of "date rape" has had a lot of recent exposure in the mass media, including television movies, news programs, and mass-circulation magazines. "Rape trauma syndrome" has gained legal and professional recognition because rape crisis workers have discovered and documented the patterns of reaction that survivors of sexual assault experience (Burgess and Holmstrom 1974).

2. Other recent research on RCCs addresses their relations with the local face of the state, such as prosecutors' offices (e.g., Gornick, Burt, and Pittman 1983; Martin et al. 1992).

3. La Raza, the broad movement among Chicanos, Mexicanos, and other Latinos for civil rights and cultural self-determination, paralleled the African American movements for civil rights and Black power in time but was centered in the southwestern United States. Among other issues, La Raza has championed immigrant rights (especially those of farm workers) and bilingual education, and fought racist police brutality. Chicanas, Mexicanas, and other Latinas have fashioned a particular expression of feminism out of their experiences (see, e.g., Anzaldua 1990).

4. Few Black women were involved in the anti-rape movement in its early period, largely because of the historical relationship between racism and rape in the United States, Black women's involvement in other causes, and their general alienation from the predominantly White women's movement (A. Davis 1981; Giddings 1984; Matthews 1989; Collins 1990).

5. Covert resistance, which from the state's point of view is rule violation, is revealed to researchers only when a certain level of trust is established. I found the pattern common enough that it influences my analytical categories, especially because I assume that not all my informants would have been willing to share such risky information, and thus this tactic may be even more common than I was told. The description of such action is an example of the "guilty knowledge" researchers acquire. It influences our overall conceptions of social processes, but analyzing it fully in public settings is difficult because doing so puts informants at risk.

6. As Burt, Gornick, and Pittman (1984) point out, not all prevention education explicitly relies on a feminist analysis of rape.

7. Volunteer training is another venue for feminist education, as the forty hours of training mandated for RCC advocates in California includes intensive consciousness raising about not only sexual assault but gender inequality, racism, homophobia, ableism, and related topics.

8. This trend reversed in the early 1990s, when a state budget crisis led to cuts in RCC grants in California.

CHAPTER 20

Feminist Social Movement Organizations Survive the New Right

■

CHERYL HYDE

Throughout the 1980s the health and direction of the U.S. women's movement was debated widely. Was the movement adrift or dead? Had movement activists lost touch with the "average American woman," failed to articulate a meaningful vision, provoked antifeminist backlash? One factor that contributed to such speculation was the rise of the New Right. Feminist supporters and opponents generally agreed that New Right successes placed the women's movement on the defensive. Although the actual damage is difficult to ascertain, by most accounts feminists witnessed erosion of hard-won gains and fought to retain victories once believed secure (see, e.g., Ferree and Hess 1994).

This essay examines the responses of feminist social movement organizations (FSMOs) to antifeminist strategies orchestrated and executed by the New Right. I identify the different survival paths of nine FSMOs and suggest some reasons for and consequences of their strategic decisions. I also hope to shed light on some of the battles that grassroots feminists waged against New Right proponents during the 1980s.

New Right Mobilization and FSMO Responses

The growth and success of the women's movement during the 1970s greatly contributed to the rejuvenation of right-wing activism. Outrage over such events as the 1972 congressional passage of the Equal Rights Amendment and the 1973 *Roe v. Wade* decision legalizing abortion, combined with a general perception that the moral fabric of America was eroding, provided the emotional fodder for the New Right's rise. The speed of its mobilization can be attributed to three factors: reactionary ideology that primarily emphasized patriarchal authority relations; an organizational infrastructure that facilitated resource, constituency, and leadership development in secular conservative organizations and fundamentalist or Catholic churches; and a wide-ranging strategic action repertoire that included lobbying, media and direct mail appeals, evangelism, Political Action Committee (PAC) mobilization, candidate targeting, protest activities, and violence (Hunter 1981; Viguerie 1981; Hill and Owen 1982; Conover and Gray 1983; Paige 1983; Rusher 1984; Klatch 1987; Hyde 1991).

Much of the New Right's agenda was in keeping with the Reagan-Bush presidential platforms. Leaders of various New Right organizations filled high-ranking positions in these administrations. Issues such as the elimination of legalized abortion were advanced by both presidents. Recognized conservatives were appointed to the Supreme Court and federal bench. Even when not explicitly advancing New Right causes, Presidents Ronald Reagan and George Bush tacitly condoned many New Right activities (Abramovitz 1982; Bawden and Palmer 1984; Braun 1984; F. Davis 1991; Faludi 1991; Hyde 1991; B. Ryan 1992). This alliance with the state fostered New Right growth and viability.

It is important to understand that little common ground exists between feminism and the New Right. Views on the family, gender roles, and moral development were and are diametrically opposed. The New Right framed feminism as an attack on the traditional family, an attack that necessitated a large-scale response. New Right actions were "direct measures of the patriarchal resistance to the goals of women's liberation" (Barry 1983, 60).

To explain the different ways in which the FSMOs negotiated the hostile environments generated by the New Right, I identify five organizational survival paths, based on FSMO analysis of and responses to New Right strategies.

1. Minimal response: There is little analysis of the New Right and only sporadic counteractions; the organization does not use the opposition to mobilize on behalf of itself or the movement.

2. Service agency development: Analysis of the New Right focuses on threats to the fiscal health of human service and welfare organizations; responses promote organizational professionalization, the pursuit of "nonfeminist" resource providers, and coalitions with civic, business, and human service sectors rather than with other movement groups.

3. Grassroots agency development: Analysis underscores the danger of the New Right to women and other oppressed groups; responses combine

professionalization and cultivation of nonfeminist allies and resource providers with attention to service accessibility, community education, and coalition building with feminist and other movement groups.

4. Grassroots movement development: Analysis focuses on the New Right as a danger to women and other oppressed groups; strategies center on broadened service availability to underserved populations, community education and outreach, and cultivation and diversification of political community ties; the organization largely forsakes identification as a human service agency.

5. Proactive mobilization: This response incorporates the analysis and community-oriented strategies of the grassroots development trajectories and exploits the presence of the opposition to advance and expand the movement's base through direct-action strategies.

I argue that these FSMO analyses and responses, which place each organization on a distinctive survival path, are shaped largely by the combination of three factors: the feminist ideological frame(s) that guided organizational vision and action; the nature of the organization's environmental linkages; and the type of New Right strategy.

My FSMO sample comprises three National Organization for Women (NOW) local chapters—Midwest NOW, Northwest NOW, and South NOW; three health centers—Community Health Center (CHC), Cooperative Health Project (CHP), and Self-Help Clinic (SHC); and three antiviolence crisis centers—Domestic Violence Project (DVP), Multipurpose Crisis Center (MCC), and Sexual Assault Crisis Center (SACC). These organizations represent the three key feminist concerns of the 1970s: passing the Equal Rights Amendment (ERA), securing reproductive rights, and ending violence against women. All three issues were primary targets of the New Right, and all nine FSMOs contended with New Right actions.

The FSMOs vary by region, size, service or action emphasis, structure, year founded, governance, and degree of volunteerism. Members viewed all these organizations as feminist. Six of the nine provided services that were understood as the primary expression of their feminist politics. The other three, all NOW chapters, considered the protection of feminist services a primary goal. Their combined properties make each FSMO unique, but two factors were crucial in how they developed in the 1980s. I argue that each FSMO's *ideology* and *environmental relations*, both of which were in place before their interactions with the right wing, were key to how that organization understood and countered New Right actions.

FSMO *Ideology and Environmental Relations*

An organization's ideology transmits basic values and visions, frames appropriate problem analyses and interventions, fosters membership recruitment and solidarity, and suggests strategic responses to environmental forces. Ideologies are conveyed explicitly through public statements (such as manifestos) or implicitly through governance mechanisms, rituals, rhetoric, and technology (Ahrens 1980; Beyer 1981; A. Meyer 1982; Riger 1984; Hyde 1992). Ideology is a crucial element in the identity of the participants and of the organization as a whole.

The organization's linkages with the environment indicate, in part, how that particular group strives for credibility. Credibility refers to the legitimacy, plausibility, or reliability of an organization as conferred by some essential actor(s) (individuals, groups, organizations). Being viewed as a credible organization is necessary to gain resources in the form of money, status, personnel, and coalition allies. An organization strategically negotiates its environment in order to build credibility with the actors critical to its survival (McCarthy and Zald 1977; Zald and McCarthy 1980; Freeman 1983; Garner and Zald 1983; Staggenborg 1991). Table 20-1 summarizes the ideological frames and select environmental relations for the nine FSMOs.

The feminist movement produced a wide range of ideological frameworks that explain the nature of women's oppression and guide strategies for social change. These ideologies, when applied to organizational contexts, suggest certain "imperatives" for goals, processes, and products (Gould 1979). Three feminist ideological frameworks, broadly defined, are found in this FSMO sample: liberal, socialist, and cultural. Liberal feminism assumes that sex role socialization is the root of women's oppression; therefore, the remedy lies in the end of such stereotyping, as well as in the removal of structural barriers that prevent equal opportunity. Socialist feminism seeks to eliminate both gender and class oppression through revolutionary change, since it sees women's subordination as due to the intersection of capitalist and patriarchal systems. Cultural feminism, sometimes called radical feminism, contends that the subordination of female nature and the devaluation of female attributes are the reasons for women's oppression; the solution lies in the establishment of woman-centered institutions that provide refuge from patriarchy and affirm women's ways (Riger 1984; Ferree and Hess 1985; Weil 1986; Alcoff 1988).

TABLE 20-1

FSMO FEMINIST IDEOLOGIES AND ENVIRONMENTAL RELATIONS

FSMO	FEMINIST IDEOLOGY	ENVIRONMENTAL RELATIONS
Antiviolence		
DVP	liberal, sex role socialization	oriented to national movement; local linkage with legal, human service, health agencies
MCC	cultural	hub of community feminist activities
SACC	liberal, sex role socialization	oriented to national movement; local linkage with legal, human service, health agencies
Health		
CHC	socialist	tied to international liberation and national health movements; strong local connections with variety of movement groups
CHP	socialist	strong ties to national women's health, pro-choice movements; local ties to variety of movement groups
SHC	socialist and cultural	strong ties to international women's health movement; key member of national feminist health network; member of national and state pro-choice coalitions; few local linkages
NOW Chapters		
Midwest NOW	liberal, equal opportunity	oriented to national NOW; spark for local feminist organizations; local linkages diminished over time
Northwest NOW	liberal, equal opportunity	broke from national NOW; strong local ties with variety of movement groups
South NOW	liberal, equal opportunity	distant from national NOW; ties to local political and civic groups

All three NOW chapters espoused liberal ideologies, with emphasis on discrimination and the need for equal opportunity. Activities in these FSMOs focused on sex equity in public school systems, the end of bias in the insurance industry, and gender-neutral newspaper employment ads. From the late 1970s until 1982 their primary issue was the ratification of the ERA.

Two of the antiviolence projects, the Sexual Assault Crisis Center and the Domestic Violence Project, also embraced liberal feminism but downplayed public articulation of a liberal feminist framework. Their emphasis was on sex role socialization as the cause of violence against women. Both organizations connected gendered violence and mental health, illustrated in this excerpt from a 1980 SACC grant proposal: "The underlying philosophy of this approach [advocacy for victims and public education] is that real prevention happens when positive and healthy male and female self images develop from childhood. . . . SACC views rape and other forms of sexual assault as a mental health problem. . . . The rapist experiences a severe mental health problem. . . . He is an individual whose inability to deal effectively with his particular life stresses has forced him finally into an acute crisis of his own which finds its vent through violent sexual behavior."

All three health centers conveyed, quite publicly, a socialist feminist view that was infused throughout the organization. For example, one claimed: "We are in the process of struggling through an anarchist/socialist/feminist analysis and applying that to the functioning and structure of the clinic. . . . Our commitment to women's health care comes from the fact that in medicine, as in most aspects of our culture, women are treated like second-class citizens" (CHP newsletter, 1978). Members viewed their organizations as vehicles for revolutionary change, as distinguished from just working within the system. Their core strategy was self-help health care, which was oriented to the education, consciousness raising, and empowerment of the consumer.

Cultural feminism was predominant in one antiviolence project (MCC) and visible as well in one of the health centers (SHC). This framework emphasizes woman-only sanctuaries, as in this example: "[Our state's] women need a shelter. The struggle to empower women and to maintain a safe refuge that can provide women the space to find their own power is vital to social change" (MCC, 1980 grant application). Another core theme within cultural feminism is that of entrepreneurship, manifested in the delivery of services by and for women. This resulted in an interesting, and uneasy, ideological melding in the SHC. Cultural feminism, as operationalized in this clinic, emphasized leadership recognition and pro-woman business values, themes that were antithetical to the socialist feminism that this organization also endorsed.

The FSMOs' environmental relations were influenced by these ideological frames. For the purposes of this analysis, I focus on movement and community linkage along two dimensions. First, organizations' varied in forming linkages primarily with feminist or other movement groups as opposed to nonfeminist organizations. Second, their ties differed in being primarily local or national.

The three health centers, the three NOW chapters, and the Multipurpose Crisis Center developed linkages largely with feminist or social movement (for example, civil rights, peace, anti-draft) organizations. To varying degrees, these FSMOs viewed themselves as actors in larger social change efforts. In contrast, the Sexual Assault Crisis Center and the Domestic Violence Project focused on cultivating linkages with law enforcement, health and mental health, civic and business organizations. At times they eschewed feminist ties. From their founding, these two FSMOs viewed themselves as human service more than social change organizations.

The Multipurpose Crisis Center and the South NOW chapter, while affiliated with relevant national movements, exhibited the strongest localized identity. In both cases, these organizations were viewed as the primary feminist organization in their communities. The Sexual Assault Crisis Center and the Domestic Violence Center also had strong local ties, but theirs were with nonfeminist organizations. Their relatively weak feminist identity expressed itself solely through memberships in state and national antiviolence coalitions. The Cooperative Health Project, the Community Health Center, the Northwest and Midwest NOW chapters had identified at their founding with national and international women's health and women's rights movements. Yet by the late 1970s, each had developed strong ties with its local community, and Northwest NOW went so far as to attempt to sever ties with national headquarters. The Self-Help Clinic continued to view itself primarily as a member of state, national, and international feminist health movements. Only after the New Right began its assaults did this organization purposefully cultivate local affiliations.

Differences in these ideological commitments and organizational linkages do not fully explain the variations in strategic responses to New Right actions. A third factor is the kind of New Right activity experienced by each FSMO. Each type of attack, individually and in combination with others constituted different dangers and possibilities for the FSMO, to which it responded in a distinctive fashion.

New Right Actions against the FSMOs

The three types of New Right strategies experienced most often by the nine FSMOs were *resource withdrawal*, actions that eliminated or restricted funding opportunities; *legislative activities*, campaigns that shaped or influenced the legal status of women on local, state, or national levels; and *direct actions*, protest activities, usually on the grassroots level—marches, rallies, demonstrations, pickets, sit-ins, and acts of violence—aimed specifically against the FSMO or other community organizations. I offer an illustrative summary of these activities with the intent of conveying New Right tenacity, the general climate of anxiety and defensiveness generated by the New Right, and the disabling impact of the New Right–state alliance.

RESOURCE WITHDRAWAL

Within the first year of the Reagan administration, key federal programs upon which FSMOs depended for fiscal resources were drastically cut or eliminated. Of particular consequence for FSMOs with staff was the elimination of Comprehensive Employment and Training Act (CETA) and Law Enforcement Assistance Administration (LEAA) grants. All but two of these FSMOs (Midwest and South NOW chapters) lost CETA workers during 1980 and 1981. The antiviolence groups also lost their LEAA funds, and the Multipurpose Crisis Center closed during most of 1981 while its members planned a new course of action.

Regional New Right resource initiatives also harmed the FSMOs. A sweeping tax reduction measure dramatically affected the Community Health Center. This reduction, combined with the election of conservative county commissioners, resulted in a substantial loss of county revenue between 1980 and 1982. The insurance provider for the Cooperative Health Project deemed the regional climate so fiscally unstable that it dropped its coverage of the clinic. Members of all nine FSMOs reported difficulty in local public fund raising. They attributed this to antifeminist and anti–human service sentiments, as well as a poor economy.

LEGISLATIVE ACTIVITIES

These New Right campaigns targeted issues that shaped or influenced the legal status of women. The New Right opposed ratification of the Equal Rights Amendment, reproductive choice, and gay rights. The anti-ERA strategies, which occurred until 1982, consisted of attempts to rescind the ERA in ratified states and to block its passage in unratified states. Northwest NOW and Midwest NOW were in ratified states, and consequently, national (rather than local) campaigns for passage influenced these chapters. South NOW was in an unratified state (deemed hopeless), but ERA organizers viewed the neighboring state as essential and winnable.

During Reagan's first term, countless "Human Life" and "Family Protection" measures were proposed. The intent of these efforts was to criminalize abortion and reinstitute "traditional" (patriarchal) values in families, schools, and places of employment. Of particular concern for some FSMOs were anti-choice legislative strategies centering on two issues: banning Medicaid payments for abortion, and passing restrictive ordinances on abortion clinics. In both cases, the New Right attempted severe restriction of access to abortion at the state and local levels. Midwest NOW, the Cooperative Health Center, and the Self-Help Clinic were in states that were either contemplating or instituting Medicaid bans. The South NOW chapter's community debated and passed an ordinance (later overturned in court) that set restrictive licensure measures for local abortion clinics. Early in its history CHC lost its abortion clinic license and was briefly shut down by the state. When it reopened several months later, clinic participants decided to offer abortion-related counseling but not abortion services. This decision perhaps spared the center direct attacks by the New Right.

The anti-gay rights campaigns focused on explicitly allowing employment discrimination and preventing AIDS-related treatment and education. The state and city in which Northwest NOW is located had anti-gay employment ballot referenda. The state in which the South NOW chapter is located refused to pass safer-sex curricula for public schools. Most notably, fundamentalist Christian groups attempted legislative blocks of HIV counseling and community educational services in the areas served by all three health clinics.

DIRECT ACTIONS

The most virulent antifeminist right-wing activities were the direct-action campaigns against abortion clinics. Indicating the generally hostile climate all nine FSMOs faced, New Right forces harassed at least one family planning or women's clinic in each of their communities. The Northwest and South NOW chapters were in areas that witnessed dramatic clinic violence; in both cases, local clinics were picketed, vandalized, and fire-bombed.

The New Right picketed the Cooperative Health Project on a regular basis during 1982 and annually on the *Roe v. Wade* anniversary. Picketers harassed and "counseled" patients, prevented them from parking near the clinic, and drove up and down the street with a bullhorn condemning workers and patients as sinners. The Self-Help Clinic was subjected to harassment which peaked during 1985 and 1986. The clinic was picketed daily (protesters usually numbered fifty but on some occasions were close to two hundred). The picketers harassed patients, verbally badgering, physically intimidating (by surrounding or restraining), and taking photographs of them. They blocked access to the clinic through sit-ins. They vandalized the property, attempted invasions, and made bomb threats. The formidable right-to-life leader Joseph Scheidler, one of the founders of Operation Rescue, targeted this FSMO for closure.

Through the use of fear and intimidation tactics, in combination with highly emotional pleas for support, the New Right had a chilling impact on feminism and its allies. The right wing legitimated or reinforced conservative and reactionary forces, such as the medical establishment, which in turn often opposed the FSMOs. Given such opposition, FSMO activists needed to develop strategies for survival. These choices resulted in different paths of organizational development.

FSMO Survival Paths

FSMO responses to these New Right threats ranged from relative inactivity to highly creative and aggressive counterattacks. All nine FSMOs offered at least some active resistance. All sponsored rallies and educational forums on such issues as reproductive rights (particularly access to safe and legal abortions), ERA ratification, and the consequences of domestic budget cuts. Through newsletters, membership letters, and newspaper articles, these organizations alerted and urged their constituencies to oppose New Right efforts such as the Human Life Amendment, the Family Protection Act, parental notification of minors (for abortions), the elimination of family planning funds, the Robert Bork nomination to the Supreme Court, and mandatory AIDS testing and quarantine. Often, these feminist counterstrategies were well orchestrated initiatives that connected the FSMO with other community groups and agencies.

FSMO characteristics (ideology and environmental relations), together with the kind(s) of New Right attacks they faced, however, produced differing survival strategies in these nine organizations. In general, those that had liberal or cultural ideologies, had formed weak ties to feminist or other local movement organizations, and had experienced primarily fiscal attacks either were relatively inactive or pursued agency development strategies. Conversely, FSMOs that had a socialist ideology, had formed strong local social movement ties, and had experienced a mix of New Right actions, particularly direct actions, pursued grassroots development or proactive mobilization strategies. I summarize the FSMOs' analyses of and strategic responses to the New Right activities along the five paths I have identified, ordered from least to most confrontational.

MINIMAL RESPONSE

Midwest NOW exhibited the least engagement with the New Right, in part because there was infrequent New Right activity in that chapter's community. Quite simply, the right wing was not viewed as a serious threat. In addition, this FSMO's lack of activity stemmed from a relatively weak feminist identity. The chapter's ideology, as translated into its programs, emphasized the importance of women's access to the business world: for example, offering a forum on making "smart" investments.

Some disgruntled members suggested that the chapter was "out of touch" with the salient feminist issues of violence, reproductive rights, and poverty. In essence, these members deemed the organization classist and racist. As one of them explained: "They [the leadership] always whined about why women of color didn't get involved. When I pointed out that 'we're a White, middle-class chapter doing White, middle-class issues,' they didn't get it. I said we needed to do things that would appeal to low-income women and women of color. . . . The members are either married and not working or are working and making money. Very well off. I think the chapter is seen as the Junior League of political activists. . . . I never perceived the chapter as active in the community. I think many people didn't" (interview). This orientation resulted in weak ties to other movement organizations and a general lack of credibility in the community. Moreover, the chapter was not the only feminist organization in its community; interested activists could and did go elsewhere. Midwest NOW's exclusive ideology and weak ties meant that it could not act as a leader against right-wing threats. The chapter's ERA efforts (fund raising for ERA "missionaries"), reproductive choice celebrations (cosponsoring rallies), and occasional newsletter articles condemning the New Right derived largely from national NOW's policies.

SERVICE AGENCY DEVELOPMENT

The Sexual Assault Crisis Center and the Domestic Violence Project survived by increasingly emphasizing their identities as human service agencies. Both organizations enhanced their linkages with nonfeminist organizations. Cultivation of these environmental relations was part of a larger survival strategy of presenting a "professionalized image" to solicit financial support and solidify mainstream legitimacy: "We are writing to approximately 200 major corporations advising them about who we are and telling them of our expertise in intervening in family violence. . . . Technical assistance and materials will be free, but we will charge corporations for training. I see this as an opportunity to get DVP's name into the corporate sector and enhance our credibility" (DVP director's report, August 1984).

This approach made sense for both organizations, since their encounters with the New Right were fiscally based. Neither FSMO was embedded in its local feminist or movement communities, and neither one developed such connections for the purposes of political solidarity. In keeping with their liberal feminist frameworks, the primary concern was the protection of services that aided victims and educated the public regarding victims' rights and the need to end sex role socialization. Maintaining services was an orientation that fostered their ties to civic groups, hospitals, law enforcement agencies, and businesses.

GRASSROOTS AGENCY DEVELOPMENT

The Multipurpose Crisis Center and the Self-Help Clinic, in keeping with their shared cultural feminism, emphasized entrepreneurial strategies such as professionalized images, business management practices, and diversified funding. These actions fostered an agency identity. Unlike SACC and DVP, however, MCC and SHC viewed the New Right as an explicit threat to women. In response, both promoted grassroots feminist and other movement ties.

MCC's version of cultural feminism was consistently conveyed through repeated dedication to its self-definition as a women's refuge. Participants emphasized the necessity of "women-only space," even when this stance jeopardized funding as a result of refusing to allow men on the advisory board. This FSMO did not, however, engage in mobilization activities. It experienced only fiscal attacks by the New Right and, like SACC and DVP, did not view movement-based coalitions as a viable counterstrategy. To address its fiscal vulnerability, it diversified its funding base, with particular emphasis on obtaining money for drug and alcohol treatment. Though necessary to preserve positions and services, this strategy shifted the mission of the center from a specific focus on violence against women to one that linked family violence with substance abuse. As the director noted, "The center has devolved into an agency. My own job has become that of a paper pusher, always pursuing grants" (interview).

Given its unique mix of socialist and cultural ideologies, SHC condemned the New Right and the state as clear enemies of women and disenfranchised groups. Because its clients and staff were under direct attack, the organization responded in rhetoric and action. Staff engaged in a variety of mobilization strategies, including localized cross-movement coalition building, designed to contain New Right damage. For example, the clinic organized the other clinics in the area to hire a private detective, who reported on the plans of local right-to-life organizations.

In addition to these countermobilization efforts, SHC also sought to professionalize its image in order to compete more effectively with other health clinics and to be more attractive to resource providers: "In an effort to increase our business, we changed the structure of our Well Woman clinic. Women can now come on Mondays and Wednesdays and are seen on an individual basis by a health worker and nurse practitioner [rather than in a group self-help session]. It seems as though more women are coming for services, and they are definitely here for a less amount of time, but we recognize the amount of [political] 'turf' we have given up to increase our business" (clinic team report, 1985). This strategy suggests the influence of cultural and entrepreneurial definitions of feminism on the center's operations, as well as its fiscal vulnerability in a very hostile environment.

GRASSROOTS MOVEMENT DEVELOPMENT

The Cooperative Health Project and the Community Health Center, unambivalently socialist in perspective, also unambiguously excoriated the New Right for its danger to women, gays, people of color, and the poor. As they saw the situation: "Reagan is hazardous to your health. The current administration is jeopardizing the health and livelihood of millions of people both in the U.S. and abroad. From the Human Life amendment to nuclear development, basic human rights and respect for the individual are being threatened and ignored. The strong connections between the eradication of social services, increased defense spending and military intervention in foreign countries can no longer be passed off as speculation" (CHC newsletter, 1981).

Like SHC, both these FSMOs used the threat of the New Right to expand grassroots ties and mobilize counteractivities. Unlike SHC, they did not also try to "professionalize." There is little evidence to suggest that members reframed the identity of either organization to that of an "agency." Even though there were concessions to the demands of regulators such as insurance providers and medical review boards, neither FSMO softened its stance as a movement organization. Both organizations used their socialist feminism and their existing community linkages to advocate mass-based social change by organizing across race and class lines. For example, CHP developed a community-based "scholarship" fund so that low-income women could obtain gynecological and abortion services; CHC became an integral part of a community coalition that sought amnesty, decent living conditions and health care for undocumented workers in its area. CHC itself provided health care services to these immigrant workers and their families at below market rates.

PROACTIVE MOBILIZATION

Northwest NOW and South NOW used the presence of New Right forces to expand their base. Both chapters demonstrated that "mainstream feminism has the potential for radicalism" (Z. Eisenstein 1981, 3). The breadth and intensity of New Right attacks in their locales provided a clear target for mobilization, and each saw its role as providing leadership in the resistance. The community ties these chapters had already developed during ERA work anchored the localized feminist expansion: "We are pleased that National NOW and civil rights groups have spoken out against the Bork nomination loudly and swiftly. . . . As for our local work on this issue, we are getting together with other women's, civil rights, pro-choice, and labor groups to come up with an effective local strategy" (Northwest NOW newsletter, 1987).

This community niche, in turn, solidified their feminist identity and radicalized the chapters. As one member of South NOW asserted, "Yes [the chapter is feminist], because it is the biggest threat in town. We're the only organization that takes on women's issues. The only radical game in town. It's the threat that makes us feminist" (interview). For Northwest NOW, association with other organizations, especially ties with the radical peace and civil rights movements, fostered innovations. For example, the chapter instituted educational and consciousness-raising sessions for actual and potential members as the means of keeping the danger from the New Right and the necessity of feminism in the foreground. In both chapters, the needs and conditions of the local communities took precedence over national NOW's agenda.

Implications and Conclusions

New Right attacks on feminist movement organizations in the 1980s suggest that environmental stress generates strategic responses anchored in preexisting organizational properties. Although such organizational identities do not necessarily become more pronounced, they have subtle but far-reaching effects on the totality of organizational development. Under attack, feminist organizations did not create entirely new missions or operations, nor did they deviate substantially from their founding characteristics. All the FSMOs in this sample mounted some resistance to right-wing actions. Despite this commonality, it also was apparent that the particular survival paths adopted by the FSMOs varied widely.

No one survival path emerged as the most successful or frequently followed in this sample. There was a continuum of responses from largely inactive to assertively proactive. While "prevailing wisdom" often holds that encounters with oppositional forces will result in co-optation or professionalization, only a few organizations exhibited such tendencies. In two instances (DVP and SACC), the professional agency image was in place early in their development and thus could not be considered a transformation for the purposes of survival. Perhaps more interesting were those FSMOs that maintained and enhanced their grassroots, action-oriented identities. These organizations used the presence of the New Right to extend an activist stance within their communities, a stance that also facilitated their survival. Such a strategy runs counter to the conservatization scenario, which expects all social movement organizations to become less radical over time, particularly when under attack.

This analysis highlights the significance of ideology as a movement organization property, a characteristic often overlooked in the resource mobilization paradigm. Founding feminist ideologies shaped the provision of services, the preferred linkages with the environment, and the analysis of the New Right threat. The ideology helped set the organizational course. In turn, environmental linkages supported or enhanced ideological tendencies. Considerable contact with hospitals and law enforcement agencies, for example, was likely to result in greater comfort with or acceptance of mainstream views. It appears to be the interaction between ideology and environment that is important in producing an organizational identity, and this self-concept shapes the types of responses that a group can make to threats.

Also important in determining the survival pathways that were chosen was the type and intensity of New Right opposition. Fiscal attacks were usually countered by agency-oriented responses. Legislative attacks encouraged consideration of some collective actions. Direct attacks demanded ongoing resistance and made for a high level of mobilization among allies as well as in the organization itself. Antiviolence organizations did not experience direct actions, which may explain their more low-key strategies. The most proactive and transformative strategies were followed by the organizations in localities that experienced the most intense level of attack. These FSMOs, however, were not themselves the objects of attacks; they organized in defense of other community organizations under siege, a strategy that flowed from their transformative ideology and embeddedness in the movement community. The most severely stressed organizations devoted their resources to survival; it was their allies who had the ability, inclination, and resources to mobilize resistance actions.

Connecting ideology, environmental relations, and types of attack with survival options suggests the importance of a longitudinal and broad-network lens in studying movement development. A longitudinal perspective matters because the organizations built upon their founding characteristics to guide their later strategic planning. Attention to broad networks, rather than single social movement organizations, is also crucial because groups rarely functioned in isolation. The extent of isolation or embeddedness of any SMO is a key factor in explaining the resources and strategies it employs in any given situation. As this analysis has shown, the ways in which an organization develops and articulates its identity, interacts with the community, and positions itself in terms of resource flow and conservation cannot be understood without knowledge of its history and community niche. Most of these FSMOs understood that isolation would result in vulnerability; even in "good" times, they actively cultivated certain linkages. Those that connected with other social movement organizations were the ones most likely to sustain a transformative focus. By capturing the historical and contemporary ties to the local movement community, one may gain a clearer understanding of what sustains grassroots radicalism.

This story of surviving the New Right rests on identities and alliances, as well as threats and resources. Each feminist movement organization, with its unique configuration of characteristics and position in the environment, responded as best it could. The nature of that environment and the organization's analysis of it played a critical role in determining FSMO survival. There was, consequently, a diversity of responses. Yet in the end, what is most remarkable is that all these organizations did resist—and all survived.

Note

Acknowledgments: This analysis is part of a larger research project: an investigation into the impact of the New Right on change in feminist social movement organizations from 1977 to 1987 (Hyde 1991). I thank Myra Marx Ferree and Patricia Yancey Martin for their suggestions and assistance.

CHAPTER 21

Confrontation and Co-optation in Antifeminist Organizations

■

SUSAN MARSHALL

The well-being of the contemporary feminist movement has increasingly engaged public interest, judging by the popularity of books claiming that feminism is either dead, ailing, or seriously off track (Hewlett 1986; Kaminer 1990; Faludi 1991). Perhaps inspired to self-examination by commemoration of a full generation of renewed feminist mobilization, the defeat of the Equal Rights Amendment, or the imminent loss of reproductive rights, feminist scholarship has likewise produced numerous volumes taking stock of the women's movement (Katzenstein and Mueller 1987; Tilly and Gurin 1990; Boles 1991a). Many of these assessments adopt a comparative approach, but one group rarely utilized in comparative analyses of the women's movement is the opposition. The omission of antifeminism derives in part from the general assumption that countermovements are reactive phenomena with little impact on the careers of social movements.

The prevalent appraisal of antifeminist organizations stereotypes them as static, dedicated to maintaining women's traditional place within the home, and opposed to all changes in women's roles. Such simplistic analyses hinder scholarly assessments of the structure and political agenda of antifeminism, which scored major victories in the 1980s. This essay posits a mutual interaction between the feminist movement and its countermovement. It examines two of the largest antifeminist organizations, Eagle Forum and Concerned Women for America, both of which have a predominantly female constituency and leadership. Examination of their monthly publications demonstrates that antifeminism is by no means a static or single-issue movement; rather, its ideology and goals have changed to resemble its declared enemy. Since organizing in the 1970s, antifeminism has attempted to demonstrate greater support for American womanhood than the women's rights movement. This research suggests that antifeminist organizations challenge feminism on issues of perceived vulnerability and selectively appropriate feminist successes. Antifeminist tactics of confrontation and co-optation reveal the perceived strengths and weaknesses of the feminist movement and underscore the need for dynamic analyses of movement and countermovement interaction and for candid and thorough feminist appraisals of the female opposition.

Antifeminism in Scholarly Perspective

Studies of the impact of feminism on American culture and politics have tended to ignore the influence of the antifeminist movement. For example, examinations of the popular diffusion of feminist ideology (Mueller 1987; Katzenstein 1990; Sapiro 1991) tend to contrast "feminist" with "traditional" gender-role attitudes and beliefs about equality. The effects of antifeminist mobilization on women's attitudes are rarely mentioned, although numerous studies examine the impact of the religious New Right on public opinion (Himmelstein and McRae 1984; Hertel and Hughes 1987; Sigelman, Wilcox, and Buell 1987; Wilcox 1987). Other research investigates the influence of the feminist movement on electoral politics and social policy (Freeman 1987; Gelb and Palley 1987; Mueller 1988; Jennings 1990) but pays scant attention to the political competition between feminism and antifeminism. A third group of scholars (Ferguson 1984; Martin 1990b; Schlozman 1990; Boles 1991b) variously compares attributes of feminist organizations with capitalist bureaucracies, occupational organizations, and public interest groups but not with antifeminist organizations.

Given the volume of comparative analyses of contemporary feminism, the relative dearth of research comparing feminist with antifeminist movements and organizations is somewhat surprising (but see Boles 1979; Conover and Gray 1983; Ferree and Hess 1985; and, on the abortion issue, Luker 1984; Staggenborg 1987a; Ginsburg 1989). Women's antifeminism has been the focus of a few studies (Marshall 1985, 1991; Chafetz and Dworkin 1987; Klatch 1987), but social movements research has generally bypassed the topic. A partial explanation for this imbalance is that social movements receive considerably more scholarly attention than countermovements (but see Mottl 1980; Lo 1982) because countermovements tend to be characterized simplistically as static, particularistic, and single-issue, while social movements are viewed as dynamic and complex. When antifeminist movements are implicitly contrasted with feminism, they understandably provoke less scholarly interest. These assumptions in social movements research partly explain not only the disparity in research quantity between the two contesting groups but also the analytical perspective of most research on antifeminism. Without further probing, antifeminism is generally stereotyped as opposed to all proposed feminist changes in women's roles and focused exclusively on upholding the traditional place of women within the domestic sphere (Chafe 1972; Chafetz and Dworkin 1987; McAdam, McCarthy, and Zald 1988; Marshall 1989).

Recent developments in social movement theory suggest a more complex relationship between initial movements and their countermovements, with implications for the study of antifeminism. Emerging from the resource mobilization perspective, for example, is a broader conceptualization of rhetoric, which has previously been used primarily as an indicator of group ideology and individual motivation for recruitment. But rhetoric is also a tactical resource, shaped not only by the ideology of its committed constituency but also by competition with adversaries and the pressures of public opinion, the state, and other third parties (Ferree and Miller 1985; Snow et al. 1986; Turner and Killian 1987). A second contribution of resource mobilization theory is a more dynamic approach to social movements, turning greater attention to movement careers than to origins, and to the various organizations' ongoing interactions between movement and countermovement, and between external constituencies with the potential to influence movement outcomes (Gale 1986; Zald and McCarthy 1987; Zald and Useem 1987).

These revisions of social movement theory have implications for a reconsideration of contemporary antifeminism and its representative organizations. Acknowledging some flexibility of antifeminist organizations to respond to altered opportunities and challenges, the following analysis is based on the premise that studying the shifting patterns of antifeminist attacks and concessions may contribute useful insights about the feminist movement itself.

Organizing Antifeminism

NONDEMOCRATIC STRUCTURE

A distinguishing feature of antifeminist organizations is their nondemocratic structure. Phyllis Schlafly founded Eagle Forum; Beverly LaHaye founded Concerned Women for America (CWA); and both women are essentially presidents for life. There are no specified terms of office, no elections, no provisions for the transfer of power, and no organizational mechanisms to challenge the existing leadership. Nor is there evidence that members are dissatisfied with the existing structure. Both leaders are regarded as heroic figures within their respective organizations, and personal loyalty to them is used to sustain group commitment and unity. Both organizations cultivate this charismatic authority through syndicated weekly radio programs, hosted by Schlafly and LaHaye, which address current issues and exhort listeners to activism.

Although the two organizations share these leadership traits, their other characteristics diverge. CWA has a somewhat more bureaucratic structure, evidenced by its more elaborate division of labor: a national board of directors, paid legal staff, and hierarchical organization into areas, districts, and local chapters. Eagle Forum seems to operate without such an extensive formal structure, protecting the identities of its constituency and cultivating an image of spontaneous protest as testimony to the rightness of its cause. The contrast between the two organizations is apparent in their respective newsletters: *Family Voice* has numerous departments, an editorial staff, and featured writers with bylines, whereas each issue of the *Phyllis Schlafly Report* appears to be the product of a single author focusing on a single topic.

THE BROADER AGENDA

Mottl (1980, 622) argued that a definitive feature of countermovements is "the use of a single idea as an ideological lever for the mobilization of disparate constituents to preserve the status quo." Antifeminism has often been used to illustrate this principle of particularistic, single-issue politics. For example, Chafe (1972) identifies the prevalent argument of antifeminism since the mid-nineteenth century as the demand that women remain in the home in order to preserve the traditional family. My analysis of Eagle Forum and CWA, the two largest contemporary antifeminist organizations, suggests that this assessment is overly simplistic. The agenda of both groups is far broader than antifeminism; in fact, women's issues do not even predominate in their literature.

Phyllis Schlafly, long active in Republican Party politics, began the STOP ERA movement in 1973, the year after Congress passed the Equal Rights Amendment, and she incorporated Eagle Forum in 1975 (see Felsenthal 1981; Marshall 1991). Although many of its resources were focused on the

ERA throughout the 1970s, Eagle Forum was never a single-issue organization. Its broader conservative agenda not only mobilized a large constituency to battle the Equal Rights Amendment but also facilitated a smooth transition after the ERA's defeat in 1982. By this tactic, Eagle Forum not only prevailed but prospered after achieving its original goal and thus avoided the common crisis faced by many single-issue organizations—including, ironically, the suffrage movement, which collapsed into factions after gaining the vote for women. Moreover, this multiple-issue orientation serves the antifeminist cause very well, for Eagle Forum maintains ties to a conservative constituency that can be remobilized quickly into STOP ERA groups. For example, after the defeat of the federal amendment in 1982, state referenda were placed on the ballot in Maine (in 1984) and Vermont (in 1986); both were defeated, in part by the active opposition of Schlafly's organization. More recently, Schlafly appealed to her "Eagle Friends" to help defeat "the fraudulent ERA" in Iowa in 1992 (Eagle Forum correspondence, December 1991).

Currently, antifeminist themes occupy slightly more than one-third of Eagle Forum's monthly newsletter. Women's issues are not the most frequent topic in the *Phyllis Schlafly Report*; children's education fills over 40 percent of its contents. Although this focus on education might be interpreted as maximizing and reinforcing women's traditional motherhood role, it is much more. The ideological agenda of the New Right is to retake control of society's moral values and eradicate liberalism's appeal as a social and political doctrine; to this end, Eagle Forum also publishes the monthly *Education Reporter*. The major grievance expressed concerning public school education is curricular, objection to the teaching of anti-family values as reflected in such matters as "contraceptives, homosexuality, incest, and sexual deviations without parental consent or interference" (*Phyllis Schlafly Report* 1991d). Schlafly, who taught her own six children at home, decries the replacement of the basic skills curriculum by what she calls "group therapy," meaning the teaching of liberal values and individual decision-making over clear statements of right and wrong (*Phyllis Schlafly Report* 1989b). She frequently attacks the "ultra-left" agenda of the National Education Association (NEA) and the "politically correct" multicultural revisions of college curricula.

Schlafly regularly promotes other New Right issues, such as withdrawal of federal funds for "pornography" through the National Endowment for the Arts, increased tax exemptions for families with dependent children, and opposition to parental leave and subsidized day care. Consistent with the right-wing tradition of militant anticommunism, Eagle Forum opposes U.S. aid for the former Soviet Union and repeatedly warns about the dangers to national defense of American demilitarization. Surprisingly, despite its pro-life position, abortion is not heavily emphasized in Eagle Forum literature, perhaps because that issue is well covered by religious organizations in the New Right constellation.

Concerned Women for America (CWA) is one such organization. It was founded by Beverly LaHaye in 1979, reportedly after she heard Betty Friedan's "anti-God, anti-family rhetoric" in a televised interview and became infuriated at Friedan's claim to speak for American women (CWA n.d.; see also Marshall 1991). In contrast to Schlafly's extensive background in conservative politics, LaHaye's activist origins are religious. With her husband, New Right minister Tim LaHaye, she founded Family Life Seminars in the early 1970s, which led to a mail-order ministry and a popular Christian sex manual for married couples (Paige 1987). CWA has built on this religious base and moved its national headquarters from San Diego to Washington, D.C., in order to lobby the federal government more effectively.

CWA concentrates primarily on two issues, abortion and parental rights in public schools. Unlike Eagle Forum, CWA is working to reinstate prayer in the public schools. Whereas Eagle Forum relies heavily on grassroots lobbying and letter-writing campaigns, CWA tactics also include legal challenges to the separation of church and state. It retains a staff of attorneys who file lawsuits with other New Right organizations petitioning for "religious freedom" in the public schools and supporting "pro-family" restrictions on contraception and abortion. Through its grassroots network of prayer and action chapters, CWA organizes national boycotts of companies sponsoring "anti-Christian" television programs, as well as letter-writing and phone campaigns to defeat legislation (CWA correspondence). Its *Family Voice* newsletter lists monthly topics for prayer and action, and LaHaye reportedly credited the defeat of the ERA to the weekly prayers of CWA chapters ("Abortion: Right, Left" 1989). As a religious organization, CWA devotes more space than Eagle Forum to political campaigns to restore morality, such as its anti-homosexuality crusades. It also regularly monitors feminism through "Feminist Follies," a feature in its monthly newsletter.

For both organizations, opposition to feminism constitutes part of a larger conservative agenda that opposes government spending, supports a strong defense, condemns media and school promotion of individual decision-making, and favors reinstitution of absolutist moral principles.

My study suggests that women's issues are not central to the antifeminist agenda, in contrast to that of feminist organizations, for whom women constitute the major focus. This distinction in pro-woman stance is symbolically illustrated by contrasting the titles of the National Organization *for Women* and Concerned Women *for America*.

Dynamics of Movement Competition

CONFRONTATION

Eagle Forum and CWA intensely scrutinize the opposition for any sign of feminist weakness they can exploit. The *Phyllis Schlafly Report*, for example, reports gleefully the results of the latest public opinion polls finding weak support for feminism, cites Susan Faludi's thesis in *Backlash* (1991) as proof of an antifeminist victory, and even touts television reporter Connie Chung's attempts at motherhood as an example of the rejection of feminist careerism. CWA's "Feminist Follies" column consists solely of short quotations lifted from feminist publications. Feminist support for lesbian and abortion rights is a frequent "Follies" theme, and although many excerpts appear to be selected for their shock value, even Hillary Clinton's statement that she "could have stayed home, baked cookies, and had teas" led one month's column (*Family Voice*, May 1992). The National Organization for Women (NOW) is carefully monitored, its "radical" and "anti-religious" resolutions translated for the antifeminist readership (*Family Voice*, March 1992; *Phyllis Schlafly Report* 1990, 1991f).

In contrast, feminist newsletters rarely mention the female antifeminist movement; they are far more likely to target the predominantly male Congress than other women as opponents. The difference in tactics between feminists and antifeminists suggests an interesting contrast between movement and countermovement; their claim to be "the women's movement" perhaps constrains feminist organizations from engaging directly in battle with female antifeminist organizations, whereas the opposition has more to gain by publicizing examples of women breaking rank. Moreover, feminists are more likely than antifeminists to make their internal ideological conflicts public and to engage openly in self-criticism. These are ideological and organizational differences between the two movements, but it is probably also an antifeminist tactic to portray a united front in order to support its claim of representing the majority.

In addition to the opportunistic assaults on feminism that derive from constant monitoring antifeminist organizations repeatedly target certain themes in their strategy to undermine support for feminism. Perhaps most important, the battle with feminism is openly joined on certain issues and conceded at others. In some cases the antifeminist movement has actually altered its position through time to a profeminist stance, although it is never labeled as such. As Turner and Killian (1987, chap. 16) suggest, countermovement ideology will respond militantly to perceived weaknesses in the initial movement but "will adopt popular elements of the initial movement's ideology as its own" when they prove useful to its own agenda. These patterns of confrontation and co-optation provide insights into the weaknesses and strengths of the feminist movement derived from the scrutiny of its opposition.

One contested issue concerns which side best represents the interests of American womanhood. As the story of the founding of CWA illustrates, part of the antifeminist movement's raison d'être is to demonstrate that it is more pro-woman than feminism. Several rhetorical tactics are used to reverse public identification of feminism with women's rights, the most basic of which is the almost exclusive use of the label "feminism" rather than "women's movement." Phyllis Schlafly in the 1970s favored the term "women's libbers" (Schlafly 1977), and although she has since dropped that appellation, she occasionally refers pejoratively to the "feminoid" opposition (*Phyllis Schlafly Report* 1991c). These terms are designed to imply that feminists are extremists, "out-of-touch," their values "more and more skewed" (Hutchens 1992) and perhaps not fully human. The logo of CWA's "Feminist Follies" is a cartoon woman, sloppy and straggly-haired, with her fist raised in the air, a stereotypical portrait of the feminist as unfeminine.

A second strategy for undermining the women's rights movement is to challenge its notion of rights. Schlafly puts it bluntly: "When feminists talk about 'women's rights,' they don't mean fair treatment for women in jobs, school, or home" (*Phyllis Schlafly Report* 1991f). The catchword most frequently used to describe the feminist agenda is "gender neutral." This term carries a double meaning, referring to both the lesbian stereotype and the view that feminists harm women by working to eliminate differences of treatment between the sexes, implicitly ignoring the fact that pregnancy and motherhood are not gender-neutral situations (*Phyllis Schlafly Report* 1991b). For example, the stress that the Gulf War placed on women soldiers with young children was highlighted by both organizations, complete with anguished vignettes of maternal separation and child trauma (*Phyllis Schlafly Report* 1991a; Donnelly 1991).

A third tactic of the antifeminists is to portray feminists as a group of selfish, elite women ("yuppies"), while painting themselves as champions of the underdog and appealing to working-class resentments. For example, Schlafly contends that women officers push the goal of equal treatment for military women at the expense of "enlisted women who lack a college education" (*Phyllis Schlafly Report* 1989a, 1991a). Establishing federal policies to break the so-called glass ceiling is viewed as unfair to "the wives of the men who would be the losers in a system of Affirmative Action Quotas for executive women" (*Phyllis Schlafly Report* 1991c, 1991f). Successful women such as U.S. Supreme Court Justice Sandra Day O'Connor and Professor Anita Hill are chided for "whining" about past grievances while holding prestigious professional positions that testify to the fairness of the American system. More generally, Schlafly states: "Feminism is not about achievement for women" but rather about giving power "to their own little coterie of doctrinaire feminists" (*Phyllis Schlafly Report* 1990). The rhetoric of antifeminism almost exclusively portrays the enemy as wealthy and elitist, from yuppie couples forcing single-income families to subsidize day care benefits only the former would enjoy to rich homosexuals imposing their sexual agenda on the American people.

These references to feminist elitism have multiple meanings: they appeal to class resentments, undermine feminist claims to represent the majority of American women, and attack the feminist view of woman as victim. Significantly, antifeminist literature never criticizes feminists on the issue of race. If we accept Turner and Killian's (1987) thesis concerning countermovements, these findings indicate that antifeminists have taken specific aim at some weak spots in the feminist arsenal. Issues of sexuality, elitism, equality versus difference, and universal victimization have all dogged the contemporary feminist movement and been topics of scholarly debate (see Elshtain 1981; Friedan 1981; Stacey 1983; C. Epstein 1988). More puzzling is that despite the defeat of the ERA, the erosion of reproductive rights, and the plethora of public opinion polls demonstrating public ambivalence if not outright hostility to feminism, the rhetoric of the antifeminists implies that they, not feminists, are the underdog.

CO-OPTATION

One reason for this apparent paradox is that despite the defeat of the Equal Rights Amendment, a profound feminist-inspired change has taken place in women's labor force participation since the 1970s, the largest increases being in the employment of mothers with young children, the group strategically most important for upholding women's traditional familial role. This trend has forced a noticeable shift in the rhetoric of antifeminism. Eagle Forum, for example, has been forced to moderate its opposition to women's employment, while continuing to bestow its annual full-time homemaker awards. The following statement illustrates Eagle Forum's position: "Today, women are looking for a mommy track so they can spend time with husband and babies, for sequential careers in which business or profession comes only after they've raised their children, and for family-friendly workplaces to accommodate the new traditional woman" (*Phyllis Schlafly Report* 1990). This is not a feminist position, but neither does it fit the traditional stand against women's employment. Similarly, Eagle Forum has expanded the number of acceptable military roles for women but draws the line at women in combat, claiming to represent the best interests of those women pursuing a "serious military career" (*Phyllis Schlafly Report* 1991b). Rather than outright opposition to women leaving the home, the antifeminist movement is now trying to accommodate the two roles in ways that contain the disruptive effects of women's employment, protecting not just the traditional family but also its own ideological integrity. Home-based employment and late childbearing are two concessions made by Eagle Forum to women's dual orientations (*Phyllis Schlafly Report* 1992).

While continuing to reject feminism outright, antifeminist organizations nonetheless have appropriated some of its liberal rhetoric. For example, CWA refers to its litigation to reinstate the Bible in public schools as "equal access" cases (Sekulow 1991), and Eagle Forum denounces the "feminist censorship brigade" for promoting the usage of Ms. rather than the traditional titles of Miss and Mrs. (*Phyllis Schlafly Report* 1990). Progressive and conservative labels are sometimes reversed; for example, Eagle Forum called the proposed family leave legislation an "outdated notion" whose "time is past" because computer technology has made it possible to work at home, because workers are more concerned about other employment issues, and because such cradle-to-grave policies have been repudiated with the global decline of socialism (*Phyllis Schlafly Report* 1991c). Following the controversy over the confirmation hearings on Clarence Thomas's appointment to the U.S. Supreme Court, Schlafly adopted the rallying cry of Professor Anita Hill's supporters and declared, "Feminists just don't get it" (*Phyllis Schlafly Report* 1992). Claiming that the majority of Americans disagreed with Anita Hill's testimony on the basis of "truth" and "fairness," Schlafly adeptly appropriated feminist rhetoric while repudiating its content.

In addition to the use of popular feminist catchwords, both organizations have adopted positions strikingly similar to their opposition on certain issues. While maintaining that Hill was a "spiteful liar," Schlafly nonetheless moved away from her former stand that "sexual harassment is not a problem for the virtuous woman" to recognition that it does occur ("Asking for It" 1981; *Phyllis Schlafly Report* 1991e). Eagle Forum has criticized pornography for exploiting women, taken a stand against date rape similar to that of feminists, and provided a quasi-feminist critique of the prevalence of anti-woman rape myths in daytime soap operas (*Phyllis Schlafly Report* 1984, 1989c). CWA has based its opposition to the "abortion pill" RU-486 not on the organization's traditional protection of babies but on women's health, focusing on the pill's painful procedure and dangerous side effects (Berkebile 1992), perhaps in an attempt to co-opt feminist successes in the women's health care movement. Adjusting to their new woman-centered position, both groups increasingly shift the dispute with feminists from ends to means.

A final area of the antifeminist movement's accommodation can be seen in its reconsideration of feminist criticism of male dominance. Whereas her earlier writings were filled with scathing descriptions of man-hating feminists, Phyllis Schlafly now goes so far as to attempt to understand the so-called feminist grievance against men by charging that male "left-wing intellectuals" treated their wives like "unpaid servants," citing Ibsen's exploitive relationships, Tolstoy's refusal to treat women as "serious, adult, intelligent" human beings, and Picasso's misogynous paintings (*Phyllis Schlafly Report* 1989). The recognition that women can be abused in marriage and the proclaimed sympathy for a feminist viewpoint is new, but Schlafly is careful to criticize individual men rather than the institution of marriage.

This criticism includes castigating politicians and businessmen with sexually demeaning epithets for acceding to feminist demands. Schlafly does not adopt a deferential posture toward men; in fact, she probably goes further than feminists in excoriating those who fail her. For example, she has referred to male supporters of affirmative action for women as "obsequious" and "wimps," described the U.S. military as "hen-pecked" and a "lap dog" for allowing the deployment of mothers to the Gulf War, and called upon former Defense Secretary Dick Cheney and the American military to "stand up and be men" and "never again send mothers off to war" (*Phyllis Schlafly Report* 1989a, 1991a, 1991c). These signs of frustration with the state and business communities do not fit their ladylike stereotype and further suggest that antifeminists may feel that they have won the battle of the ERA but somehow lost the war.

Conclusion

This essay has applied insights from social movement research on countermovements to the study of contemporary antifeminism. Using the publications of Eagle Forum and Concerned Women for America, I conclude that antifeminist movements are neither single-issue nor static. They differ from their feminist adversaries in being less focused on women's advocacy and less democratic in organizational structure. Nonetheless, antifeminist organizations are engaged in intense competition with the initial movement, and their patterns of confrontation and co-optation suggest areas of feminist vulnerability and strength. For example, antifeminists challenge the feminist movement on controversial questions of sexuality, gender differences, elitism, and the feminist label itself, but in other ways they seem to judge the feminist movement as stronger than do the general public and mass media. While they continue explicitly to oppose feminism and to pursue goals directly at odds with those of the feminist movement, these antifeminist organizations nonetheless have shifted on some key positions, such as women's employment, to resemble their declared enemy. I propose that such changes suggest acquiescence to the impact of feminist ideology on the lifestyles of antifeminism's female constituency, although antifeminist organizations are careful to obfuscate their conciliations to feminism by cloaking them in traditional rhetoric.

On the basis of these findings, I offer the following tentative observations about the interaction between social movements and countermovements. First, greater attention must be paid to the complexity and dynamism of countermovements. The fact that antifeminist organizations generally oppose change should not blind us to their own adaptations and transformations. Second, the constituencies of the competing groups may be a mediating condition in the mutual interactions between movement and countermovement. The fact that antifeminists are also women has allowed them to assault feminist vulnerabilities with an aggressiveness that might have backfired on male opponents. Conversely, the feminist movement's claim to be fighting for all women's rights has constrained its ability to confront directly the female countermovement's definition of the same issue. Third, the grounding ideology of countermovements should be distinguished from the strategic issues of rhetorical and tactical parrying. There is only so much flexibility in the movement-countermovement interaction. In this case, despite the fact that antifeminist organizations have co-opted elements of feminist rhetoric, their conservative world view has prevented them from employing (and perhaps even understanding) the basic feminist position of structural blame for inequality. Eagle Forum could go no further in its critique of men's oppression of women than blaming individual men for abusing individual women.

Finally, these results partially acquit the feminist movement of the criticisms leveled at it after the defeat of the Equal Rights Amendment. Antifeminist organizations, constituting a more formidable opponent than is generally recognized, played an important part in that defeat. Furthermore, equality may not have been a weakness of feminist rhetoric during the ERA ratification campaign, since it has been appropriated by the opposition. Careful attention to feminist arguments by antifeminists and their selective co-optation of successful arguments suggests that, ironically, the progress of the continuing struggle for women's rights may be more appreciated by its opponents than by many feminists.

PART VI

*Expanding the Scope
of the Political: An Inclusive
Vision of Success*

CHAPTER 22

Can Feminist Organizations Be Effective?

■

SUZANNE STAGGENBORG

The literature on feminist organizations is replete with examples of organizations that are torn apart by internal conflict, of leaders who are "trashed," and of groups that dissolve before accomplishing their goals. Such difficulties are certainly not unique to feminist organizations; New Left organizations struggled with many of the same problems (see Breines 1982; Miller 1987). They are of particular concern, however, given the commonplace feminist goal of fostering democratic and caring kinds of organizations that empower participants. Indeed, feminist organizations have been the main carriers of the "participatory democratic" mode of social movement organization since the 1960s, and feminists have been influential in spreading this form of organization to other movements with similar concerns, such as the antinuclear power movement (see B. Epstein 1991). Tales of infighting, marathon meetings at which nothing is decided, and other organizational disasters raise the question of whether these groups can be effective.

To answer this question, I begin with the definitions of success that have been employed by social movement theorists and some of the problems involved in assessing movement outcomes. Next, I examine the characteristics of feminist organizations that are related to their effectiveness. I then focus on a particular type of feminist organization for which effectiveness has been especially problematic: the informal, "radical" feminist organization. I compare organizations that have had problems accomplishing their goals with others that have enjoyed more success. I conclude that feminist organizations can be considered effective if a broad definition of movement "success" is adopted. At the same time, I specify some of the obstacles to success confronted by different types of feminist organizations.

Definitions of Social Movement Success

Surprisingly little attention has been paid to the outcomes of collective action and to the question of what determines success in social movements, despite its obvious importance. Gamson's *The Strategy of Social Protest* (1990; first published in 1975) continues to stand as one of the few empirical and theoretical treatments of the problem. The criteria of movement success employed in his widely cited work are (1) *acceptance* of a challenging group as a legitimate representative of a constituency by the target of collective action, and (2) *new advantages* won by a challenger. One issue in an evaluation of the usefulness of these criteria is the extent to which they capture a broad range of outcomes that advance the cause of a movement.

It is perhaps easiest to think about acceptance and new advantages in narrow political terms, as some of Gamson's examples suggest. When representatives of a challenging group are routinely invited to testify at congressional hearings, this is a sign of acceptance (Gamson 1990, 32). When a new law is passed, a new advantage has been won. The model suggested is that of "outside" challenging groups trying to gain specific policy outcomes along with "membership" in the polity (Tilly 1978).

Burstein, Einwohner, and Hollander (1991) adopt such a focus on political movements and point out that Gamson's criteria of success need to be expanded to take into account other aspects of the political process. Drawing on the work of Schumaker (1975) and Kitschelt (1986), they argue that in addition to acceptance (or, in Schumaker's terms, "access responsiveness") and new advantages (or "policy responsiveness"), success involves getting movement demands on the political agenda, getting new policies implemented, actually having the intended impact on an aggrieved population, and transforming political structures. (One might argue that these can be subsumed under Gamson's categories, but I think it is useful to elaborate these political and policy outcomes.)

Beyond expanding the definition of how success is achieved through the political process, we can also look at movement success in broader cultural terms. Although his work lends itself to a narrow political interpretation, Gamson makes clear that a number of different types of outcomes are included in his definition of success. For example, the target of collective action may be public opinion, and "acceptance" may occur when the public changes its view of the challenging group promoting the change (Gamson 1990, 33). The "new advantage" won by a challenging group may be a change in public values or practices (Gamson 1990, 35). In comments written for the second edition of *The Strategy of Social Protest*, Gamson (1990, 149–50) emphasizes the importance of the mass media and suggests that influencing the framing of an issue by the media is a kind of success.

Others have explicitly advocated that a broad definition of social movement outcomes be adopted in assessing the influence of social movements. Gusfield (1981) advances a "fluid" concept of social movements, which leads to concern with a variety of consequences of social movements beyond the achievement of programmatic goals. One consequence is the activation of a pool of people who can be drawn into subsequent movements. Another is the broader change in public and private values and meanings created by movements as new vocabularies and new ideas are introduced and disseminated, often by the mass media. In Gusfield's (1981, 326) view, movements affect far more people than those who participate in collective action, and they have cultural consequences beyond the impact of their organized and public activities.

Mueller (1987) is similarly concerned with the broader cultural outcomes of social movements, which she links theoretically to the political and policy outcomes of movements. She points to the development of a "collective consciousness" as one type of movement "success," which can then affect future mobilization and the ability to bring about political and policy outcomes. Some movements, like the women's movement, need first to challenge existing ideas, cultural practices, and means of socialization before achieving more substantive goals, and these outcomes should be treated as successes (Mueller 1987, 93). In place of Gamson's distinction between "acceptance" and "new advantages," Mueller (1987, 104 n. 2) proposes that success be measured in terms of "substantive reforms" and "outcomes that create resources for future mobilization."

Based on these and other discussions of the problems involved in assessing the effectiveness, success, or consequences of a social movement, three main categories of movement outcomes can be identified: (1) political and policy outcomes; (2) mobilization outcomes; and (3) cultural outcomes. The first category, perhaps the most straightforward, includes various steps in the process of bringing about substantive changes through the political system. The category of mobilization outcomes focuses on organizational successes and the ability to carry out collective action. Cultural outcomes include changes in social norms, behaviors, and ways of thinking among a public that extends beyond movement constituents or beneficiaries, as well as the creation of a collective consciousness among groups such as women.

Consideration of these different types of outcomes encourages a long-range, processual view of social movements. Because movements are characterized by multiple rather than single outcomes, an interesting question is how different outcomes are linked to one another. One type of success may have a bearing on another type, and outcomes occurring at one point in time affect future outcomes (Snyder and Kelly 1979). Rupp and Taylor (1987), for instance, show that the ongoing mobilization of the National Women's Party in the period from 1945 to the 1960s was quite important to the subsequent resurgence of the women's movement; in particular, it bequeathed the struggle for the Equal Rights Amendment, which provided a unifying goal that mobilized many activists in the 1970s and early 1980s. Mueller's (1987) work is important in revealing something about the process whereby political outsiders become insiders. She shows how the creation of a collective consciousness among women legitimated their political ambitions and led in the 1970s to the first significant rise in the number of women elected to public office—a result with important implications for future outcomes of the women's movement. Feminist organizations did not become important in providing resources for women candidates until the late 1970s, after the first round of "self-starters" had already gotten themselves elected.

Movements, then, can be successful in introducing new ideas and creating new social norms, and these outcomes may produce subsequent achievements. Moreover, this sort of cultural "success" can typically be attributed not to the actions of any one social movement *organization* (SMO) but rather to a less clearly defined *movement*. In assessing movement successes and their determinants, we have to live with the fact that we cannot stay solely within the bounds of that convenient unit of analysis, the SMO. Not only are some outcomes the product of less organized aspects of a movement, but some movement organizations have less distinct boundaries than others. It is important to look at variations in the characteristics of organizations and to understand groups as *movement* entities rather than only as organizations.

Characteristics of Feminist Organizations

Feminist organizations vary in a number of ways that are important to their effectiveness. Martin (1990b) argues persuasively that there are no essential characteristics of feminist organizations. Although some activists and scholars have viewed a collectivist or nonhierarchical organizational structure as the hallmark of a feminist organization, there are many organizations—such as the National Organization for Women—that do not have such structures but must surely be regarded as "feminist." Martin's proposal that a feminist organization be defined as one that meets any one of several criteria seems more useful.[1] In recognizing that there are differ-

ent types of feminist organizations, we can look at which types are most
effective in producing which kinds of outcomes.

Existing work suggests that there are two particularly important influences on the effectiveness of feminist organizations: (1) organizational
structure and (2) ideology and related goals. As Martin (1990b, 195) notes,
the main distinction that has been made with regard to organizational
structure is between organizations that are "collectivist" or "participatory"
and those that are "bureaucratic" or "hierarchical." Feminist ideologies
have been characterized in a variety of ways (see, e.g., Black 1989; Tong
1989), but one basic way in which feminist organizations vary is the extent
to which they adopt "radical" ideologies and goals (see Ferree and Hess
1985; Taylor 1989a). Buechler (1990a, 108) defines a "radical" movement
or SMO as "one whose ideology, goals and program pose a fundamental
challenge to a particular system of power relations."

The problems of "collectivist" organizations, which tend to have radical ideologies, are well documented (see, e.g., Freeman 1972; Mansbridge
1973; Riger 1984; Baker 1986; K. Hansen 1986). Feminist organizations
that stress collective decision-making and empowerment of individual
members often focus on group process at the expense of other goals. The
emotional intensity of interactions in such groups, and the level of commitment expected, lead to high levels of "burnout." The lack of an established
division of labor makes it difficult to complete organizational tasks, and the
refusal to recognize official leaders leads in many groups to unofficial domination by persons tied into friendship networks who lack accountability to
the group. Because of these and other internal conflicts, collectivist organizations often do not survive for very long.

Bureaucratic or formalized organizations, which are often assumed to
have less radical goals, tend to be more stable organizationally and better
able to bring about specific policy outcomes. Gelb and Palley show how
such organizations have been involved in bringing about change in several
areas of public policy. They argue (1987, 22) that groups such as NOW,
which have become increasingly hierarchical and professionalized, nevertheless "have not fallen prey to the perils of bureaucratization" predicted
by Max Weber and Robert Michels but "have remained agents for change
in the status of women in society even as they have worked to broaden
understanding for the goals of the movement." Others have similarly shown
how the women's lobby in Washington, made up of formalized movement
organizations in alliance with established organizations, has become increasingly effective (A. Fraser 1983; Costain 1988). There are, however,

limitations on the ability of these organizations to effect change, which can be attributed both to internal organizational features and to external political constraints.

The distinction between "bureaucratic" and "collectivist" feminist organizations has been useful in focusing attention on organizational as well as ideological differences in the women's movement. It is clearly inadequate, however, for the purpose of characterizing the range of structural dimensions of feminist organizations related to their effectiveness and elaborating the kinds of social changes that are achieved by different types of feminist organizations. Gamson's (1990) formulation is somewhat more helpful in identifying both centralization and bureaucratization as key characteristics related to success. In my own work (Staggenborg 1989) I have argued that an informal, decentralized structure makes organizational maintenance difficult but tends to encourage strategic and tactical innovation, whereas a formalized and centralized structure promotes maintenance while narrowing strategic choices. Other more specific features of feminist organizations, such as the way in which boards of directors are constructed and the nature of relations between staff and volunteers, can also be expected to influence various kinds of movement outcomes.

Among formalized organizations, groups that have grassroots components, such as NOW, need to be distinguished from others that are more strictly professional. NOW and other national women's movement organizations have succeeded and failed not only in achieving specific policy changes but with regard to all the kinds of political outcomes elaborated by Burstein, Einwohner, and Hollander (1991). Their achievements and inadequacies are related to their organizational structures as well as to external constraints, and some apparent "failures" are actually "successes" of a sort. For example, NOW has recently received a great deal of criticism, including some from other feminist organizations, for its proposal to create a third political party on the grounds that neither the Democratic nor the Republican Party adequately addresses the concerns of women and minorities. Although critics find the idea of a third party unrealistic, such a party might be successful in pressuring the major parties to address the issues it raises, if not in electing candidates (see Rothschild 1989). Whether or not such success is possible, the relationship between the strategic choice and NOW's organizational structure is of interest. For example, empirical research might show how grassroots activists influence NOW's strategies— and hence its successes and failures—and perhaps how the organization's structure discourages the kind of coalition work with other groups that might prevent such strategic choices.

Informal organizations, similarly, are not all "collectivist," and differences among such groups produce varying outcomes. Many are "radical" insofar as they seek fundamental changes in power relations, but they vary in both their ideologies and their structures. Looking at some differences among groups of this type helps to clarify the issues involved in assessing their impacts. Different types of informal and radical organizations do have difficulties associated with their organizational structures and ideologies, but they are also effective in ways that are generally not recognized.

Informal, Radical Feminist Organizations and Social Change

The organizations considered here are part of the "younger branch" of the women's movement (Freeman 1975), which some would argue no longer exists or has merged with the "older branch" of the movement (Carden 1977). This branch once included socialist feminist unions, most of which declined in the 1970s (see K. Hansen 1986), as well as radical feminist groups, a tendency within the women's movement that some claim has given way to "cultural feminism" (see Echols 1989). In a narrow sense, these groups can be considered complete failures because they had radical goals—such as changing the structure of capitalist and patriarchal society—but dissolved before achieving any of them. In a broader sense, however, they enjoyed a number of successes, albeit ones that are less easily measured than policy outcomes.

Take the case of the Chicago Women's Liberation Union (CWLU), a socialist feminist organization formed in 1969 and dissolved in 1977 (see Strobel, Chapter 10). Viewed as an *organization*, the CWLU enjoyed only limited success.[2] It established an office and provided some coordination of various activities of the Chicago women's liberation movement, but it also had serious problems. It had trouble integrating into the Union new people who wanted to become active; it was always short of money; its resources were spread so thin that many projects never got off the ground; and it was devastated by internal conflict. In evaluating the achievements of the CWLU, however, it is more useful to view the group as part of a *social movement community* (Buechler 1990b) than as a task- and goal-oriented organization.

When the CWLU was founded in 1969, the antiwar movement was in disarray, but the younger branch of the women's movement that emerged from it was flourishing throughout the country. Growth of the CWLU came quickly, as there was already a constituency eager to work on the burning issues of the women's liberation movement. In other words, the CWLU was not an organization in the position of trying to create a movement; there was no need for issue "entrepreneurs" to create grievances (McCarthy and Zald 1973, 1977). The constituents and the issues—the movement—were *there*; networks of women were already mobilized, and phone calls from other interested women poured in. The CWLU had only to find ways to harness the existing energy and excitement.

As a kind of movement center (Morris 1984) around which the small groups revolved, the CWLU was successful for a time in attracting many energetic activists to its work groups (which were more numerous and active than its "chapters"). The Union's informal structure and orientation to the movement community was important in allowing the group to reach women who were not necessarily "members." For example, in 1972 its Liberation School enrolled over 220 women in twenty classes, and the Action Coalition for Decent Childcare organized a public hearing attended by some two hundred people (Rothstein and Weisstein 1972). The CWLU was not able to sustain such levels of mobilization after the early 1970s, however, in part because the cycle of protest that generated the larger movement had declined.

Beyond its temporary capacity to act as the center for a vibrant social movement community, the CWLU was also "successful" in that it contributed to later rounds of feminist collective action in several ways. First, the organization created alternative institutions that endured beyond its own demise, including two women's health centers and the Health Evaluation and Referral Service (HERS). Beyond whatever cultural impact these alternative institutions had, they later played a role in the local pro-choice movement by bringing together persons in the left-feminist community interested in fighting threats to abortion rights. Second, the Union helped to develop a pool of activists who went on to participate in other existing organizations, such as NOW, or to create new organizations such as the Chicago Women's Health Task Force, a group that also became involved in abortion rights work (see Staggenborg 1991).

Work groups of the Union also created models for collective action that could potentially influence other groups. An organizer of the Liberation School talked of the project as "a new, woman-controlled approach to women's studies which we hope will provide a model for other institutions" (Rothstein and Weisstein 1972, 6). Although it is difficult to know what, if any, impact the Liberation School and many other CWLU projects actually had, one work group, the Abortion Counseling Service—better known as "Jane"—has achieved almost mythic stature within the women's movement. As a collective of women who started out providing abortion referrals and ended up performing abortions themselves before legalization in 1973, Jane was and still is seen as a model of feminist service delivery (see Bart 1987; Addelson 1988). Not only did Jane influence other projects in Chicago, including HERS and the women's health clinics, but some have suggested that the model will be copied by many if abortion is again made illegal (e.g., Van Gelder 1991); in fact, former Jane members were asked to speak at the National Women's Studies Association conference in 1990 for just this reason (Blakely 1990).

Finally, the ideology developed by the CWLU and other socialist feminist groups across the country continued to motivate and attract adherents in later years. This can be seen in the concern of the women's health and reproductive rights movements with issues involving both class and gender, such as sterilization abuse and public funding of abortions. In Chicago, both former CWLU members and new activists were drawn into the abortion rights movement in 1977 in response to a threatened cutoff of state funding of abortions, and again in 1980 in response to the closing of the Cook County Hospital abortion clinic, which served poor women.

Thus, a feminist organization that exerted little direct influence on public policy and accomplished none of its radical goals can be seen as effective if we take into account its mobilization outcomes and broader cultural outcomes. The legacy of the CWLU also calls into question assertions that socialist feminism is no longer influential in activist circles (B. Epstein 1991, 178–80; Buechler 1990b, 116–19). The CWLU is one socialist feminist organization that has influenced subsequent feminist concerns and produced alternative institutions and individual activists who carry on this tradition of feminism; it would be surprising if other socialist feminist groups did not have similar impacts.

The influences of such groups are no doubt neglected because of the many difficulties involved in tracing "fluid" kinds of outcomes of feminist organizations. It may not be possible to attribute some achievements to any particular movement organization, and it may be difficult to figure out what role, if any, movement activities played in producing a given outcome (a problem that also arises in assessing political and policy outcomes). The ideas of a movement, for instance, may spread, but how does this occur? Movement organizations may actively promote their positions through public education campaigns; actors outside of SMOs or movements may take up their ideologies; there may be larger social and political reasons why particular ideologies are accepted or rejected at different times.

In some cases, such as the reproductive rights movement that emerged in the late 1970s, it may be relatively easy to trace the roots of the movement to an earlier mobilization. In Chicago, women who had been members of the CWLU organized the Chicago Women's Health Task Force, and activists from that group formed Women Organized for Reproductive Choice (WORC). Some of the same individuals were involved in each succeeding organization, and there were clear ideological continuities. But even where there are direct links between organizations, it would be a mistake to think of the movement and its maintenance only in terms of its SMOs. Here, Buechler's (1990b) notion of a social movement community is useful in explaining the continuity in ideology and mobilization. It was the creation not only of a small organization called the Chicago Women's Health Task Force (consisting of fewer than twenty activists) that sustained socialist feminist activity in Chicago in the mid-1970s, but of a whole network of small women's health projects and alternative institutions such as HERS. Although many movement organizations were dissolving, there were events and networks that kept a social movement community alive.[3]

Thus, social movement communities operate to sustain movements and bring about social change in a number of ways. Even movements and movement organizations that seem to die out may be successful in influencing individuals or changing the collective consciousness of some group (McAdam 1988). For example, the reproductive rights movement of the late 1970s and early 1980s had a difficult time achieving its goals, and the Reproductive Rights National Network (known as R2N2), formed in 1978, dissolved in 1984 (see Staggenborg 1991 for details). Aspects of the movement, including its ideology, seem to have survived, however.

One of the new organizations that I discovered in researching the recent history of the pro-choice movement is a student-based organization called Students Organizing Students (SOS). I obtained some literature from the organization and later interviewed one of its staff members. I was interested to see that SOS's literature presented a perspective strikingly similar to that of the Reproductive Rights National Network. Both talk about the importance of abortion rights in connection with other health and reproductive rights issues, including sterilization abuse. In addition, SOS calls for "free abortion on demand," the very slogan used by the CWLU and other women's liberation groups before the legalization of abortion.

I asked the SOS staff member, a college student, whether she knew of the earlier reproductive rights movement, and she did not. Yet somehow the ideas of earlier movements and organizations were present in the literature of a student organization that was formed after the 1989 Supreme Court decision threatening abortion rights.

When this kind of outcome is taken into account, the hidden successes of feminist organizations become visible. On the other hand, informal organizations with radical goals do encounter real difficulties that should not be glossed over. Comparisons among feminist organizations are helpful in revealing the organizational characteristics that are responsible for both their successes and their failures. Here, I compare two reproductive rights organizations that are no longer in existence, the Reproductive Rights National Network and its Chicago affiliate, Women Organized for Reproductive Choice, with two other groups that have managed to survive, the National Women's Health Network and the National Women's Music Festival.

R2N2 was similar to the Chicago Women's Liberation Union in that it was able to grow quickly at a time when mobilization came easily. For the CWLU, the cycle of protest under way in the late 1960s generated activism; for R2N2, events in the abortion conflict in the late 1970s and early 1980s, including the cutoff of Medicaid funding of abortion and the election of Ronald Reagan, mobilized participants. Neither organization was able to endure for very long once these external impetuses disappeared. WORC did survive the demise of R2N2, remaining in existence until 1989, but for many of its years it was a very tiny organization held together in large part by one individual (see Staggenborg 1991). Although these organizations had some successes of the sort discussed above, they certainly did not accomplish their radical goals, and they had many organizational problems. What were the sources of these difficulties?

One obvious problem for groups with radical goals is that their aims are hard to achieve, and, in the absence of progress toward goal achievement, it is difficult to remain mobilized. Part of the dilemma associated with radical goals is tactical. The reproductive rights movement formed as a result of concern that the "pro-choice" movement had become completely reactive, responding in a narrow, single-issue manner to the New Right. Reproductive rights activists wanted to turn this situation around and, at least in the long run, advance a more comprehensive notion of reproductive "choice," one focused not only on abortion but on other issues—such as access to health care, employment, and day care—that are involved in making the decision to have a child a real choice for women. But reproductive rights groups had problems finding ways to advance this agenda and little or no success in achieving their goals in the late 1970s and early 1980s.

When asked about strategy, participants in such radical groups as the CWLU and R2N2 often talk of the consciousness-raising aspects of their activities. In explaining their early work on abortion rights, for example, a member of the CWLU commented: "[We] were doing political education about what people's rights in fact were. . . . We wanted a situation where abortion was not only available on demand, but ultimately where we had a health care system which did not allow profiteering on people's abortions, etc., etc., so it was couched in terms which would set up a debate which would allow all of these issues which we thought were consciousness-raising to be elaborated." One of the founders of the Reproductive Rights National Network explained in an interview that R2N2 intended to do "mass education" while groups like the National Abortion Rights Action League engaged in legislative lobbying and the like. R2N2 did hold some demonstrations and petition drives as a means of implementing this strategy, but it was difficult to keep them up indefinitely, and leaders became frustrated by tactical limitations. As my informant commented: "In general, R2N2 was not too innovative. The problem is that most of the fight is at the legislative level and we didn't want to get involved in that. So we concentrated on educational things . . . but it's really difficult to find an arena for R2N2's activity—so we ended up doing petitions, postcards as a means of educational outreach." Such activities may be successful insofar as they alter public opinion or create adherents for a particular feminist position, but it is extremely difficult to assess their impact. And without visible victories, it is difficult to keep supporters involved for long periods of time.

Feminist organizations with radical goals also try to achieve more concrete changes, but the political opposition they encounter creates tactical dilemmas. For example, Women Organized for Reproductive Choice continued in the 1980s to try to fight for poor women's access to abortions, particularly to reopen the Cook County Hospital abortion clinic, which had been closed in 1980. Because they could not alter the power structure in Chicago, they were unable to make any headway, and after a few years WORC simply ran out of tactics that could mobilize supporters in the absence of any progress toward victory.

Another difficulty for organizations like R2N2 and WORC is structural. Although R2N2's founders wanted to create a national organization that could coordinate local efforts and help build a larger movement, they were also wary of bureaucratic and centralized organizations. Consequently, they never tried to build a formalized organization with professional staff. Board members from local groups were supposed to provide leadership to the organization with assistance from one paid coordinator. The result was what a former board member called "the classic leadership problem" of feminist organizations. Because participants feared hierarchy, they failed to create an organization with a division of labor that would ensure that organizational tasks were completed and that persons with the appropriate skills were available.

The demise of R2N2 and other reproductive rights organizations cannot be attributed solely to their lack of formalized structures. Nevertheless, comparison with some other radical types of feminist organizations reveals that more formalized structures do promote longevity and do not necessarily preclude the empowerment of individual participants. The National Women's Health Network is an example of a national movement organization that has survived since its founding in 1975, despite ups and downs. Paid staff, first hired in the late 1970s, have been one important ingredient in the Network's survival. Staff members, together with national board members, have kept the organization visible and stable through the production of high-quality literature, through expert testimony to Congress, and through the generation of grant money. Direct-mail techniques, first used in the early 1980s, have generated members and additional funds. The NWHN has not had much success in activating a grassroots constituency, but it has remained alive by adopting a somewhat formalized structure (see Staggenborg 1991 for details). At the same time, the Network has continued to take positions that are radical in the sense that they challenge existing power relations in the health care system.[4]

The National Women's Music Festival (NWMF) is another type of feminist organization that has successfully employed a formalized structure without sacrificing feminist principles (Eder, Staggenborg, and Sudderth forthcoming). The organization was originally a feminist collective that began in 1974 to produce a women's music festival on the campus of the University of Illinois in Champaign. The festival was held annually until 1981; there was none that year because of the group's large debts and the unwillingness of the university to permit the festival to be held on campus any longer. In 1982 a group formed to revive the festival at Indiana University in Bloomington, where it has taken place ever since. The group that revived the festival also tried to operate as a collective but after a few years was again in danger of extinction. At this point a festival producer took charge and made the NWMF into a formalized organization with an intricate division of labor and clear chain of command. Although there have always been some internal conflicts, the structural changes appear to be responsible for the organization's ability to survive and, in recent years, to attract large numbers of participants.

The festival producer responsible for this accomplishment commented on the difficulties of the earlier collective in a 1991 interview: "The problem with this group—and the problem with consensus decision-making—is that *everyone* has to be involved in *every* decision and has to agree on all of it, and no one wanted to give away any power. Everyone wanted input into *everything*. So, we would have huge meetings that would take *forever* and we'd get a couple of decisions made and, you know, we were getting further and further behind because we weren't getting things done. No one would allow someone to go off and take care of something." Although there was no bureaucracy in the collective organization, power was actually more centralized there than in the more formalized organization that followed. When a division of labor was created, different women became responsible for overseeing different areas of the festival production—workshops, services, music, and so forth—so that although there is hierarchy within the organization, responsibility and decision-making power are more dispersed than they were in the collective.

When asked if she considered the NWMF a feminist organization, the festival producer responsible for its structure replied:

> Yeah, definitely. Well, because we empower people. I think that by the time anybody's worked with us for a year or two, they're not afraid of figures, they're not afraid of budgets, they know how to read one, they know how to put things together. Basically, I think each of them learns how to be a producer in their own right. Actually, what they're doing, if they're doing spirituality, or if they're doing the health series, they are actually producing a health series. . . . I think that the empowering, and allowing everybody on every level—that as soon as you take on responsibility, you get the power in order to deal with that responsibility and then the accountability. The power and responsibility and accountability—having all those together, I think that that's very feminist oriented.

Conclusion

Feminist organizations can be effective at the same time that they self-destruct as organizations and fail to achieve changes in public policy. Groups that are unsuccessful in terms of organizational maintenance and policy outcomes may be effective as the centers of movement communities and as the originators of cultural changes. Although the successes of many feminist organizations tend to be hidden, they are likely to have an impact on subsequent rounds of collective action. The women's movement is perpetuated not only by its movement organizations but also by its cultural achievements. As I have argued, these achievements include the creation of alternative institutions that serve as movement community centers, pools of activists who remain involved in movement activities, models of collective action that are employed by subsequent activists, and ideologies that continue to attract adherents.

Informal, radical feminist organizations that are committed to participatory democracy and to the empowerment of participants as well as to the achievement of more instrumental goals are often used as the standard for what a feminist organization is. They are also the subject of much of the debate regarding the effectiveness of feminist organizations. I have argued that the cultural outcomes often produced by such groups in lieu of substantive reforms must be taken into account in judging their effectiveness. At the same time, I have identified some of the problems of such groups, which stem from both their ideologies and their structures. Because they have radical agendas, some feminist groups have a difficult time finding specific targets and tactics; consequently, they have trouble producing the victories needed to keep supporters mobilized. And because their ideologies are radical, such groups are likely to meet with powerful external opposition. Internally, informally organized groups lack the division of labor necessary for longtime organizational maintenance.

In focusing on informal, radical feminist organizations, I do not mean to imply that the operation of more formalized and less radical movement organizations is unproblematic. Detailed empirical research is needed to assess the strengths and weaknesses of all kinds of feminist organizations and to specify the important dimensions on which feminist organizations vary. Comparing organizations with different types of structures and ideologies is particularly useful in identifying the sources of their successes and failures.

My analysis in this paper provides some direction for future study of the outcomes of feminist organizations. It suggests that feminist organizations need to be considered in the context of a larger social movement community. Movements consist not only of political movement organizations, but of individuals, alternative institutions, and ideas, which are often perpetuated beyond the lives of the organizations. Feminist organizations can be effective in a variety of ways; studies are needed of the processes whereby they have the effects that I have identified. Key questions include how social movement communities extend beyond the bounds and lifetimes of movement organizations; how alternative institutions function; how individuals are kept within community networks; and how the ideas of movements get disseminated. Among the detailed investigations needed for an understanding of the outcomes of feminist organizations are studies that trace the movement careers of individual activists; examinations of how alternative institutions created by movements function and how they affect subsequent collective action; and reports on the role of women's studies courses and other likely avenues for spreading feminist ideas and assisting new mobilizations.

Notes

Acknowledgments: I thank Myra Marx Ferree and Verta Taylor for helpful comments on an earlier draft of this essay.

1. Martin (1990b, 185) argues that "an organization is feminist if it meets any one of the following criteria: (a) has feminist ideology; (b) has feminist guiding values; (c) has feminist goals; (d) produced feminist outcomes; (e) was founded during the women's movement as part of the women's movement." I think these are useful criteria, although I would argue that feminist outcomes must be produced *intentionally*; one can well imagine an antifeminist organization that inadvertently produces feminist outcomes (e.g., by creating a feminist mobilization in response to its actions), but we would not want to call such an organization "feminist."

2. The CWLU was more successful than many other socialist feminist unions (see K. Hansen 1986), and the group did continually try to learn from past mistakes, as Strobel (Chapter 10) emphasizes. I stress the organizational problems of the CWLU somewhat more than Strobel does, in part because I have compared it with more formalized groups (see Staggenborg 1989), whereas she compares it with less structured groups.

3. In 1975, for instance, a socialist feminist conference was held in Yellow Springs, Ohio, even as many socialist feminist organizations were dissolving. Although the conference was divisive, activists from Chicago whom I interviewed recalled that Helen Rodriguez-Trias spoke about sterilization abuse at the confer-

ence and that her speech was an important impetus for the growth of the Committee to End Sterilization Abuse (CESA). The issue became quite important to the women's health movement in the mid-1970s and was linked to the abortion issue, particularly through the founding of the Committee for Abortion Rights and against Sterilization Abuse (CARASA) in 1977.

4. The goals of the National Women's Health Network and those of the Reproductive Rights National Network seem equally radical. The NWHN focuses more narrowly on the health care system, however, and this may also be a key to its success in that it does not have the same tactical dilemmas as R2N2 and WORC. Similarly, the National Women's Music Festival has radical goals but focuses on the task of putting on a festival.

CHAPTER 23

Doing It for the Kids:
Mexican American Community
Activists, Border Feminists?

■

MARY PARDO

Yo como madre de familia, y como residente del Este de Los Angeles, siguiré luchando sin descanso por que se nos respete. Y yo lo hago con bastante cariño hacia mi comunidad, y digo "mi comunidad," porque me siento parte de ella, quiero a mi raza como parte de mi familia, y si Dios me permite seguiré luchando contra todos los gobernadores que quieran abusar de nosotros. [As a mother and a resident of East Los Angeles, I shall continue fighting tirelessly, so we will be respected. And I will do this with much affection for my community. And I say "my community" because I am part of it. I love my *raza*, my people, as part of my family; and if God allows, I will keep on fighting against all the governors that want to take advantage of us.]

Esperanza Chacon

The parole office representatives they think it won't be long before the residents give up. I told him he would be hearing from us until it is moved. It is the little kids who suffer. . . . I'm sorry, I get emotional about it. It would be OK if it were a high school a block away. But kids in elementary school are still too young to defend themselves.

Gina Lucero

By mobilizing neighborhood action, Esperanza Chacon and Gina Lucero each passionately opposed a state-sponsored project that was imposed upon her community.[1] Esperanza Chacon is a Mexican immigrant woman and mother of nine who belongs to a group called Mothers of East Los Angeles (MELA). With the encouragement of a Catholic priest, MELA grew from a core group of about fifteen women to a network of over four hundred families that mobilized 4,000 people in opposition to the first state prison planned for a densely populated urban setting. The group later engaged in opposition to a toxic waste incinerator, established political ties with other environmental groups, and emerged as a permanent community voice. Gina Lucero, who helped to mobilize opposition against a parole office situated half a mile from an elementary school, is a native-born Mexican American woman living in a multi-ethnic, middle-class suburban neighborhood.[2] Her organization, Concerned Parents of Monterey Park (CPMP), succeeded in ousting the parole office and then dissolved, unlike MELA, which continues to address other community issues.[3]

How do the two cases of grassroots activism where women held central positions illustrate the relationship between women's political activism and gender relations? Differences and similarities tell us about how these women's social identity—which includes not only gender but also ethnicity, class, *and* community context—conditioned their community activism, their perceptions of social justice, and their resistance strategies. Institutions are indeed gendered, meaning gender is present in the processes, practices, images and ideologies, and distributions of power (Acker 1992, 567). Feminist critiques (Randall 1982; Sapiro 1987; Thiele 1986) thoroughly specify how political science assumptions exclude women's political participation by defining what is male as universal and by designating women's "natural" activities as irrelevant to a social or political explanation. Both assumptions imply a dichotomous relationship—women, family, and nature on one side, opposed by men, civil society, and politics on the other—and explain how it is that women's grassroots activism goes unrecognized as political.

Women predominated in both of the cases I studied, but can their groups be called feminist organizations? The answer depends on our definition. If attacking sex-based inequality defines the actions of a feminist organization, these groups are definitely excluded. If the definition of feminism includes implicitly feminist practices, however, we may consider these women "border feminists" (Saldivar-Hull 1991). Studies of women's community activism in the United States and in third world countries challenge definitions of feminism that exclude ethnic/racial and class identity. Just as feminists have critiqued male social scientists for building conceptions of the political on what men do, Black women and Latinas have criticized women's history and women's studies for building conceptions of feminism on the experiences of European American women; universalizing solely from their experiences shuts other women's struggles outside the conceptual framework (Lugones and Spelman 1983; Collins 1990; hooks 1990; Sandoval 1990).

Attempting to address exclusionary definitions, some Black women scholars have opted for alternative terms, such as "womanist," that allow for a holistic view of women, since race and class also shape the lives of *all women* (Gilkes 1980; Brown 1990). Third world women scholars, less concerned about changing terminology, have challenged feminists to "decolonize" their vision of social change and give up the search for the generic woman who has no particular identity in terms of race, class, and ethnicity (Spelman 1988). Decolonizing feminism means rethinking conceptual frameworks and political agendas and redefining and widening feminist terrain to include other bases of oppression such as race, class, and imperialism (Johnson-Odim 1991). The approach attempts to address two related tensions: retaining the term feminism so that women remain integral to the political context, and allowing feminism to address the issues of the majority of women in the world. Much as the explanatory power of male-centered concepts is weakened when they omit 50 percent of the population, feminist concepts are also weakened when they omit the other social categories, beyond gender, that structure women's daily lives.

In an effort to expand the boundaries of what can be claimed as a feminist organization, Martin (1990b) directs attention to the ideological claims and actions of women's organizations. An organization that may not identify with feminist ideology may have feminist values, goals, or outcomes. "Feminist outcomes" refers to women's transformation by participation in the organization. Transformation may include improved self-esteem or empowerment and political awareness. The notion of implicit feminist outcomes suggests that grassroots women's groups that do not explicitly identify themselves as feminist may nevertheless be considered feminist organizations.

Some Chicana feminists argue that Chicanas are at the "borders" of feminist conceptual frameworks and that their efforts to empower themselves within the material conditions constituted by ethnicity/race, class, and gender are best characterized by the notion of "border feminism" (Anzaldua 1987; Saldivar-Hull 1991). Testimonies by women prominent in Latin American human rights movements, rather than in narrowly defined feminist struggles, illustrate patterns of activism among women of color who enter political arenas and empower themselves and their communities (Barrios de Chungara 1978; Burgos-Debray 1987). In similar though less dramatic ways, grassroots Mexican American women activists in the United States also empower and redefine themselves when they become community activists.

Drawing on ethnographic methods, participant observation, and in-depth interviews carried out from 1987 to 1990, I followed two such cases of women's activism. The cases differed in magnitude, duration, and community involvement, but both provided an opportunity for me to see women community activists *in action* and draw useful comparisons between activism in suburban and inner-city communities. I asked the following questions: First, how did women explain their entry into the issue? Second, how did they mobilize others, and how did their mobilization efforts illustrate gender relations? Third, what strategies did they use to express community opposition? Fourth, what were the personal and public outcomes of their activism?

The Latino Eastside: Mothers of East Los Angeles

The 1984 decision to place Los Angeles County's first state prison in East-side Los Angeles occurred only after several other communities had rejected it (Arnold and Seiler 1984). The Department of Corrections justified the selection of the Eastside site by its proximity to the courts in downtown Los Angeles and accessibility to inner-city neighborhoods that would presumably facilitate inmate communication with family members (Blonien 1986).

Two years later, in 1986, the state proposed another undesirable project for the Eastside: a toxic waste incinerator. This incinerator would worsen the already debilitating air quality of the entire county and set a dangerous precedent for other communities throughout California. When Mothers of East Los Angeles, having already opposed the prison, took up the fight against the toxic waste incinerator, it became more than a single-issue group and began working with environmental groups around the state. Since its emergence, MELA has become centrally important in a network composed of grassroots activists, a select number of Catholic priests, and two Mexican American female political representatives: City Council-woman Gloria Molina and State Assemblywoman Lucille Roybal-Allard.[4]

The women's accounts of how the residents found out about the prison offered insights into the social relations in the community and showed the common sources of information, the women's relationship to the church, and the way they understood their opposition to the prison as part of their social responsibility. In the name of their organization, Mothers of East

Los Angeles, gender identity and the metaphor of "mother" as protector of the community ring out loud and clear. Not all women came to the issue as "mothers" or directly through the church, however; some were informed and recruited by neighbors and family members. Women entered into the struggle not only as good Catholics at Father John Moretta's behest but also as "good citizens."

MOBILIZATION STRATEGIES AND SOCIAL NETWORKS

The founding mothers began their mobilization efforts by informing *existing networks of people in the community*. Different segments of the community came together and pooled their resources. These included merchants, professionals, and extended families of participants—including the sons and daughters of men and women still living on the Eastside. One year later Mexican Americans who were not Eastside residents joined as individuals and as representatives of Chicano college student groups. The regional chapters of state and national organizations such as the Mexican American Political Association, the League of United Latin American Citizens, and the Mexican American Education Commission also endorsed and participated in protest marches (Shuit and Gilam 1986).

Father Moretta and as many priests as he could cajole into assisting announced the dates and locations of hearings and demonstrations from their pulpits and thus mobilized hundreds of people. Less formal information networks complemented the parish bulletins: information traveled by word of mouth through extended family and neighborhood shopping networks.

When I asked Dolores Duarte how she encouraged more people to participate, she reminded me that she comes from a large family, born and raised in Boyle Heights: "All my six sisters came to the marches with my mom and my brother. I have a sister who lives in Commerce, another one in Monterey Park, one in Hacienda Heights, and two sisters that live here in Eastside L.A. Then, my sisters started bringing their daughters to the marches." Some of her family members who no longer lived in the area were already commuting weekly to the Eastside from their suburban communities to attend church and visit their parents. They added participation in the demonstrations to their agenda.

At one point the women in MELA traveled to UCLA in West Los Angeles—quite a distance in mileage and traffic congestion—to join a student demonstration against ethnic discrimination on campus. I assumed that Chicano student groups and MELA supported each other on the basis of ethnic and class identity. This was partly true, but later I found out that several women in MELA had children or grandchildren attending UCLA; it was a combination of family and ethnic relationships that formed the basis of their social networks for political action.

At different times and in different situations, the women's activities and stories illustrated how they crafted oppositional strategies from their gender, ethnic/racial and class/community statuses and identities. This process is often referred to as the "intersection of race, class, and gender," but that description fails to capture the fluidity and dynamic nature of the MELA women's interpretations and actions. Social identity may be interpreted and used in innumerable ways; it is not predetermined. I have selected situations that show how the women creatively crafted expressions of identity and used them to confront the state's agenda. I also include the more subtle way they resisted the social identity that Father Moretta created for them—and successfully used—at the beginning of the mobilization.

LAS OBLIGADAS?

It was Father Moretta who named the group. After viewing the film *The Official Story*, about the courageous Argentine women who demonstrated for the return of their children, *los desaparecidos* (the disappeared) during a repressive right-wing military dictatorship, he transformed the Argentine name "Las Madres de la Plaza de Mayo" into "Mothers of East Los Angeles." Also following the example of the Argentine women, who wore white mantillas, Father Moretta bought yards of white cotton cloth and had it cut into scarf-sized squares for the women to wear during demonstrations. He believed that the name and the visual image of the women would generate empathy and support for the cause.

The hundreds of Mexican American women wearing white head scarves at the early Eastside demonstrations achieved the desired effect. Reporters who saw them immediately asked who they were and what they were about. The media's delight with the image of "ethnic" women wearing scarves seemed to be simultaneously a curiosity and a confirmation of the way they perceived the women of Eastside Los Angeles. As some of the women said, we look like "poor homebodies," or, as one woman laughingly stated, "We are supposed to be . . . *las obligadas*, the submissive ones."

This sort of wry commentary revealed the women's resistance to being identified as submissive housewives. Out of respect for Father Moretta they wore the scarves in the beginning, yet over the course of the five years from

1986 to 1990, the number of scarves worn on the head and tied under the chin declined significantly. One woman described her surprise at the contrast between what the pastor called a mantilla, which is a lace scarf, and these "pieces of white rag." Gradually the women began to balk at wearing them. Some would say it was "too hot" or they "forgot them," but their primary reason was that their identities as Mexican American women in the United States diverged from those of the Argentine women. As one participant said, "The idea came from women in South America" and made the demonstrators "look like a religious group to me and it really wasn't that." Another woman acknowledged that the scarves did attract media attention, but for her they held a significance different from what Father Moretta intended: "I used to rebel against wearing those white rags because frankly I associate wearing a scarf with doing housecleaning! I think the scarves are [meant as] a symbol that we are "homebodies" and [yet] we are a dignified people. Of course, the young girls don't like wearing them tied under their chins."

At the demonstrations I attended, I observed scarves worn in a variety of ways. Some of the young men and women twisted them and tied them across their foreheads as headbands. Others wore them around their necks or upper arms. One woman who did wear the head scarf interpreted the white as a sign of the fact that they were "protesting, but protesting peacefully." The women's varied responses to wearing the scarves expressed the difference between their identity and the identity of the Argentine Mothers of the Plaza de Mayo, and also indicated a latent feminist resistance to definitions of women as domestic and submissive.

PERSONAL AND PUBLIC OUTCOMES

The political work of core activists in Mothers of East Los Angeles generated changes in the activists themselves and in the community. The activists became recognized as "grassroots community leaders." In this sense, they took on a public presence and were the featured persons in many newspaper interviews and popular magazine articles (McDonald and McGarvey 1988, 245; Russell 1989, 127). They became a public resource for other organizations, parent education projects such as the Mexican Education Legal Defense and Education Fund (MALDEF), environmental groups such as Greenpeace, and local political representatives.

Whereas the fight against the prison engaged other Latino groups on the basis of ethnic and class identity, no groups of other ethnic background joined this grassroots battle. When the women took up the fight against the toxic waste incinerator, however, they joined other groups who opposed toxic waste landfills and incinerators. Greenpeace representatives attended some of the Eastside meetings, provided testimony at the hearings, and invited MELA to demonstrations organized in other working-class communities. In 1988 MELA traveled to Casmalia, a small town 150 miles north of Los Angeles, to join a demonstration for the closing of a toxic dumpsite. In turn, grassroots groups from small northern California cities with a large minority population—Kettleman, McFarland, Casmalia, Richmond—joined the march against the toxic waste incinerator led by MELA in November of 1988 (Christrup and Schaeffer 1990, 14–19). These combined efforts were eventually successful: after years of mass demonstrations, community hearings, and legal proceedings, the incinerator project was defeated in 1991 and the prison in 1992.

Esperanza Chacon and some of the other women who formed the core group of activists became leading spokespersons on many Eastside community issues. Because most of the women did not work for wages, they were able to attend daytime public hearings. Their children's schedules determined the time they could leave in the morning and the time they had to return in the afternoon. Thus, the MELA members retained a primary commitment to home and family but expanded their identities to include community activist and political change agent. The flexibility of the schedule that their mother-and-homemaker status entailed was used as a resource in their work as community activists and leaders.

In the course of attending meetings and public demonstrations, the women became increasingly critical of the state's practices regarding community notification. They established public identities and became personally empowered to speak out for community issues.

Suburban Monterey Park: Concerned Parents of Monterey Park

Counseling services for over 1,000 paroled felons were being provided in the office of an unmarked building located on the border of two adjacent, ethnically diverse suburban communities, Monterey Park and Alhambra. After two men assaulted and robbed a woman who lived a block away from the building housing the parole office, investigating police officers assured a resident that they would check out the description of the assailants with "the local parole office." When the residents made inquiries, however, officials of both cities denied knowledge of its existence before the incident.

Immediately after the assault, people in the neighborhood informed others about the parole office presence and residents formed the Concerned Parents of Monterey Park a few days later. The initial sequence of events spanned a weekend, from the assault on Friday to the first community meeting held in the Monterey Park City Hall on Monday. Six women and one man did the most work to mobilize the community: they offered accounts to local newspapers and at public hearings, and the women worked through their already established church affiliations, neighborhood watch groups, extended families, PTA, Girl and Boy Scouts, and Republican Party networks. Vilma Ruiz, one of the six core organizers, referred to the neighborhood groups as "branches in the community." In the beginning, women attendees outnumbered men by three to one.

MOBILIZATION STRATEGIES AND SOCIAL NETWORKS

During community hearings with city council members and the police department, women also outnumbered men in providing testimony. The predominance of women's testimony at public hearings speaks to their habit of "monitoring" the neighborhood for strangers and safety concerns (Suttles 1972). This may be interpreted as an outcome of women's greater embeddedness in residential communities. As mothers who are typically responsible for taking children from home to school and extracurricular activities, doing the shopping, and running other household errands, they keep "an eye out for strangers." The threat of violence against women also sensitizes women to observe their surroundings more carefully than men do.

The Concerned Parents of Monterey Park (CPMP) launched a community campaign to hold public hearings regarding the continued operation of the parole office. The debate between parole office representatives and the community group centered on whether the presence of the office was generating crime in the neighborhood. While the parole office representatives used police crime statistics to deny any connection between the parole office and crime, the residents began to construct a different scenario that relied heavily on the women's observations of daily life in the neighborhood. Almost all references to strange occurrences or unfamiliar people in the Highlands neighborhood that were attributed to the parole office clientele originated in a woman's observations or experience.

One Mexican American woman who lived about a block from the office nodded her head affirmatively when she reflected on her observations of the "weird people hanging around" the neighborhood grocery: "All of a sudden at the Hi-Ho Market—I go there a lot—I began to see [she hesitates, searching for the correct words], oh, men who, you know—without their shirts on, tattoos on their arms. They just looked rougher. And, I thought, where are these people coming from? They don't look like they could afford it here." Sandra Aguirre's description of the "weird" people focused on a particular clothing and grooming style rather than race or ethnicity. Since homes in the Highlands sell for over $300,000, she concluded from her observations that the men were not residents and did not belong. She identified "those who don't belong" by constructing an image of people who looked as if they could not afford the cost of middle-class housing.

The members of the group, who were mostly women, began assembling observations to serve as evidence of undesirable activity in the neighborhood: broken beer bottles in the school park, graffiti on walls, sleeping bags hidden under bushes, and teenage girls being offered rides by men who came out of the parole office (Kelley 1988). The women used their gender responsibilities as homemakers and mothers to monitor the community. They also used social-class identities to determine who belonged and did not belong in the area.

Throughout the community mobilization efforts, both women and men expressed concerns for family safety. Family safety unified men and women across ethnic/racial and immigrant/native-born divisions: By 1986 the ethnic and racial composition of Monterey Park had changed from a predominantly Anglo population (85 percent) with small Latino and Asian minorities to a majority and growing immigrant Asian population with an increased Latino and a decreasing Anglo segment.

The parole office struggle unified residents and facilitated cooperative action across ethnic, racial, and established resident–new immigrant lines. Children's safety motivated residents' concern. Residents referred also to the presence of ex-felons and the dangers of burglary and robbery. Gina Lucero, a Mexican American woman active during a year of community

meetings about the parole office vowed to keep on fighting. In these mobilization efforts, however, women's and men's contributions differed and
were interpreted differently.

"WOMEN DO THE DETAIL WORK!"

Within approximately one month, the protests of the Concerned Parents of
Monterey Park were channeled into a more broadly representative Citizens
Advisory Board, which met monthly. (The CPMP did not dissolve, but
thereafter it met irregularly, calling meetings only for specific purposes.) A
year later, in the summer of 1989, about two-thirds of the residents attending those meetings were women. As the formality of the group increased,
some of the women stopped attending, but they continued to participate
at the neighborhood level, activating letter-writing campaigns when the
board decided to use that tactic.

The Citizens Advisory Board included some residents, a pastor from a
local church, a Corrections Department representative, the police captain,
and an elementary school principal. Even though women had carried out
much of the work during the early weeks of neighborhood mobilization,
the primarily female board selected a Japanese American man as its chair.
According to one woman, "We needed a figurehead," and according to one
man, "It was either Richard or me, because we had the most experience
with this kind of thing [chairing meetings]." Some women saw the need
for a male authority figure to maintain focused discussions at the meetings. Melanie Hauser thought that Richard Kurumada was the best choice
because the women tended to digress from the issue: "It was kind of unani-
mous. We just sort of appointed him. He is a teacher at a school in L.A.
and he is very bright and vocal and he kind of pulls us together. We get
to talking and gossiping and we kind of get off the subject and he pulls us
back on the subject. You know how women are," she laughed. "We can go
in all directions."

Vilma Ruiz supported the view that a man should chair the board meetings; however, she distinguished between women's and men's ways of
contributing to community work: "The women have the patience. And,
generally, that is what it takes to sit down, take your time, and go more into
detail work like calling, doing the footwork, writing down everything, and
following up. It's time-consuming and I think it takes patience." In short,
though the women took initiative and responsibility, they did not accept
an identity as official leaders.

In general, women believed that men and women approached their work differently and took on different kinds of work. As the women saw it, men came in and made their statements and were heard. Women performed the detailed tasks that required patience and attention. The women who did the bulk of the mobilization did not work for wages. They discussed these differences but made no reference to any hierarchical relationship between women and men. They stated the differences in a matter-of-fact tone, without critiquing gender stereotypes.

A polite debate took place among board members over the kind of strategies to be utilized: confrontational and militant versus cooperative and civil. Some of the women believed that the formation of a Citizens Advisory Board composed of not only residents but also city officials and parole office representatives led to the exclusion of militant strategies: "In the beginning we wanted to picket and make a big deal out of it. The parole office people told us to keep it cool so we didn't stir up the people in Pasadena [where the parole office would be moved]. We didn't, and they [Pasadena community members] found out on their own. We listened to them, and on hindsight, we should have stuck to our gut feeling. I mean do it all the way." In a written statement submitted to the committee, Gina referred explicitly to the fact that the group did what the Department of Corrections asked: formed an advisory board, kept a low profile, and refrained from speaking to reporters or organizing protests. After staging just one small demonstration, which met with disapproval from Department of Corrections representatives, they agreed to keep quiet so the state could quietly relocate the parole office in Pasadena (a nearby suburb where there was no such office at the time) without fanfare or resident opposition.

PERSONAL AND PUBLIC OUTCOMES

Like the women in MELA, the women in CPMP extended their activity into the public sphere and extended the boundaries of their gender identities as wives and mothers. Their household responsibilities remained constant, but they became public community figures as well: they received media coverage in the local newspapers, and city council members and people in the community identified the core of women activists as contact persons in the neighborhood.

Only one of the women's husbands occasionally attended the meetings after the initial community hearings. I asked Vilma how her husband responded to her involvement. His reaction was mixed, she said, partly because he disapproved of the conciliatory tactics the group adopted and also because her involvement interrupted their family time: "He would just listen and give his advice to do it with a bit of splash. But when they had meetings on Sunday evening, he would give me some negative feedback and say that's when we watch *Sixty Minutes*, and he saw it was interfering with family togetherness." Vilma said she managed to get her children to help her fold flyers and pass them out so that the work became a family activity. She also arranged her activism so that it created no interference with her household responsibilities. After the formation of the advisory board, however, she no longer attended meetings because she returned to work at her full-time job.

Commonalities and Differences

The case study of suburban Monterey Park shows how a perceived threat to family safety drew together a diverse group of residents differing in ethnicity and race but sharing identity as middle class. The differences in cultural contexts affected displays of ethnic identity. The residents of Monterey Park assumed that placing a parole office in a middle-class suburban residential area was a mistake made by the Department of Corrections. They assumed that the mistake would be corrected when they called it to the attention of officials, so the group avoided using protest marches and militant tactics to reach their objective.

The strategy the women accepted reflects the social history and social class of the community, a multi-ethnic community without a long history of grassroots struggle. They worked closely with local representatives and followed their lead and definition of an appropriate strategy, conforming to the officials' desire to avoid controversy and publicity. The effectiveness of one or the other strategy is not the issue. The process they used to endorse this strategy over a more militant one is the story that illustrates the ways in which ethnic/racial identity, gender identity, and class/community identity direct and shape community activism.

The case shares commonalities with the Eastside Los Angeles case. In both, the women's location in the community enabled and motivated them to take a leading part in grassroots mobilization. They framed and legitimized their activism as being in their children's and families' interests and did not change their roles in the traditional household. Instead of challenging the gendered division of labor, they added new activities to it. In both communities women used their status and role as mothers to *legitimate* their activism. This public and political use of a legitimate private role deserves scrutiny. They did something deviant while remaining mothers; from a status that is private in the world's eyes, they engaged in political work that is public. They legitimized their public activism by making it an extension of the wife-and-mother role, including it in the traditional definition of family. Making public activism an extension of the traditional role would not jeopardize their traditional domestic arrangements.

How did the strategies of the two groups differ? In Eastside Los Angeles, MELA staged many collective actions and mass demonstrations; in Monterey Park the CPMP held orderly monthly meetings and took an accommodationist approach with city officials and representatives from the Department of Corrections. Not until the residents became frustrated did they choose to emphasize their point by mobilizing their one small, unrepeated demonstration, which for some of the core activists and most of the marchers marked their first collective action against a state decision.

The women's and men's work differed in each group; a gendered division of labor developed in both communities. In Eastside Los Angeles the women credit the Catholic priest and a male urban planner for inspiring, forming, and guiding them in their five-year resistance to the state's proposed prison. In Monterey Park the women mobilized, called people to remind them of meetings, took signatures, and transcribed the minutes of meetings from tape-recordings, but they perceived the chair and vice-chair, both men, as keeping them focused. In the CPMP as in MELA, women participated in greater numbers than did men.

Women in each group spoke of the knowledge they had gained from the experience of mobilizing around a contested neighborhood issue that brought them into a situation where they questioned and confronted state decisions. Their observations and political participation revealed to them the failings of the system and provided them with a view of how important their activism was in working toward more equity and justice. All gained a multi-dimensional and sophisticated understanding of political dynamics. They became public persons and, as such, new resources to their communities.

Within their material circumstances, women in both communities challenged the state's agenda for their neighborhoods. In the low-income neighborhoods they creatively fashioned scarce resources into tools of change through the use of family networks, ethnic identity, and the shared history of an oppressed community. In the suburbs, where lives are more privatized and "less explicitly ethnic," women shook loose from convention, though less dramatically, and glimpsed the power of questioning state projects in defense of their community's well being.

Conclusion

Although the women in the case studies neither self-identified as feminists nor challenged gender roles, the woman-centered basis for community mobilization constituted a border space for them to bridge so-called private and public spheres. The organization of their daily lives offered potentially powerful political networks. Women's activism was both constrained and enabled by their household responsibilities and activities as women and mothers. The cases illustrate how community activism can reinforce women's conventional self-definitions while extending and changing them at the same time.

How, then, do we classify these women's groups? They engaged in community activism; they used parenting and homemaking skills and redefined them as political skills; they transformed family, friends, and neighbors into networks for collective action. The community context conditioned the form the women's activism took, but the women themselves interpreted and constructed meanings of the notion "quality of community life," devising oppositional strategies with the resources at hand. From participation in neighborhood issues, women gained political awareness and improved self-esteem, outcomes that Martin (1990b) refers to as feminist. A broadened definition of feminism that tolerates some ambiguity makes room for conditions under which working-class and some middle-class women of color assert and empower themselves.

Instead of binary definitions of feminist and nonfeminist organizations determined by whether or not the group addresses issues of sex inequality, a multidimensional definition of feminist groups may provide for a more dynamic and contextual concept that involves class, ethnic, and gender struggles. If we open the borders of feminist frameworks and theories, we may broaden, strengthen, and enrich feminist political agendas and equate women's rights with other human rights.

Notes

Acknowledgments: Portions of the data in this chapter also appear in "Mexican American Grassroots Community Activists: Mothers of East Los Angeles," *Frontiers* 11 (Spring 1990): 1–7.

1. Because some activists did not give permission for their names to be used, I have employed pseudonyms throughout, save for public figures such as Gloria Molina, Lucille Royball-Allard, and Father John Moretta.

2. In respect for self-definition and in the interest of consistency, I use "Mexican American" in reference to the women interviewed who were born in the United States, "Chicana" for authors who self-identify as such, and "Latina (Latino)" as an umbrella term for Mexican Americans and Mexican and Central American immigrants. Chicana (Chicano) is a colloquial term, for Mexicans born in the United States; it is considered derogatory by some but since the 1960s has been used to signify ethnic pride and a commitment to civil rights and social change.

3. In 1990, MELA split into two separate groups, both of which continue to address quality-of-life issues in Eastside Los Angeles. Madres del Este de Los Angeles, Santa Isabel Parish, incorporated as a nonprofit group and as of 1994 was initiating community betterment projects such as infant immunization campaigns, student scholarships, and graffiti cleanup.

4. Gloria Molina served as a California assemblywoman for the 56th District in 1982–87; the first Mexican American woman Los Angeles City Council member, 1987–91; and, since April 1991, the first Mexican American and first woman Los Angeles County supervisor for the newly created First District.

CHAPTER 24

Women's Conceptions of the Political: Three Canadian Women's Organizations

■

LINDA CHRISTIANSEN-RUFFMAN

Politics appears to be stereotypically and numerically male. The fifty-two-seat provincial legislature in Nova Scotia, Canada, in the late 1980s had only one female member from each of the three political parties. The small proportion of elected women is typical. Historically, Langevin (1977) describes women politicians as "missing persons"; globally, a United Nations (1991) study found that in 1987–88 a mere 3.5 percent of the world's cabinet ministers were women; and many researchers have sought explanations for the low number and proportion of women politicians (in Canada, e.g., Vickers 1978; Brodie 1985; Megyery 1991; Arscott 1993).[1] Despite such institutional indicators of women's political absence, my research over the last twenty years finds that women are organized in groups to realize their political agenda. A broader analytical definition of political actions than is encompassed by formal electoral representation is required if the concerted activity designed by women's organizations to shape and alter the public realm is to be understood. Such a line of sight clearly shows that women have been active in politics.

This apparent contradiction between women's absence and women's presence in politics points to an underlying analytic problem in the definitions and conceptions of politics and the political. The issue for feminist scholarship is that the intellectual tradition has been shaped by male theorists who conceptualize male actors and focus on the patriarchal world (see, e.g., general critiques by D. Smith 1974, 1987; McCormack 1975; Eichler 1983; Christiansen-Ruffman 1985, 1989; Miles and Finn 1989). If, following Martin (1990b, 184) and Freeman (1979), we define a feminist organization as "pro-woman, political and socially transformational," what do we as feminist scholars mean by the term "political" and how can it usefully be conceived? I address these questions using a methodological strategy of "autonomous feminist theorizing": that is, grounding my search for theory in the actual ideas and practices of women.[2] First, however, I review the scholarly literature.

Scholarly Conceptions of Women in Politics

For centuries, politics has been considered by scholars to be the realm of men. Suffrage was declared to be "universal" long before women were allowed to vote. As Bourque and Grossholtz (1974) pointed out, the academic discipline of political science considered female participation an "unnatural practice." The first scholars to focus on women in politics acceded to the narrow version of the political realm. Because the concept of politics was centered in men's experiences, the activities of women— when they finally emerged as a focus of study—were not central conceptually; women's activities were treated only functionally (Okin 1979). For example, Collier (1974, 96) examined women as "social actors whose choices affect the options open to politically active men." Feminist scholars, though critical of biases in the literature, continued to use a narrow range of "malestream" political science concepts as their central analytic focus (see, e.g., Carroll 1979, 1980; Stacey and Price 1981; and Randall 1982, 1987).[3] Generally, scholars who did not ignore women in politics focused almost exclusively on women in political institutions—as politicians, delegates, or voters—and on the barriers to their political participation or efficacy (e.g., Brodie and Vickers 1982; Maille 1990; Bashevkin 1993).

The tendency to associate the political primarily, even solely, with actions undertaken within state structures and formal political institutions continues to direct most research on political participation.[4] Such a narrow focus, however, hides a vast range of political activity, especially that undertaken by women. For example, this incomplete conception of the political, which portrays the woman suffrage movement as a series of famous people and dates, does a disservice both to political analysis and to the activities of the many early feminists. Dates associated with suffrage are usually national, minimizing the many prior political struggles for the vote that took place at the local or municipal level in the 1880s (see, e.g., Edwards 1900) and that were, in fact, most significant to politics of suffrage and of social change (see Cleverdon 1950 for the most detailed description of Canadian suffrage). Moreover, the names and dates mislead readers, for they record men's activities and ignore the real political battles of women. By 1916 in Manitoba, for example, women had already staged their mock parliament, gained support of the opposition party, done their organizing, helped to undermine the party in power, and put together a coalition that enfranchised women in the province. January 1916 marks the date that male legislators agreed.

The importance of women's politics—and its ability to alter community definitions, to shift resources, and to change the public agenda—has been obscured by the institutional focus of political writers. This narrow perspective fails to illuminate the crucial role of community-based activism in creating collective wealth in the form of community and cultural institutions: schools, libraries, museums, theater groups, transportation systems, and sewers (Christiansen-Ruffman 1987). Even when focused on grassroots politics, the narrow institutional and patricentric conceptualization has misled scholars with an image of leadership that is blind to women's initiatives (see my critique in Christiansen-Ruffman 1982).

In a broader and reconceptualized view, political activity may be defined as the method by which citizens and diverse groups and organizations, including corporations, attempt to create what they envision to be the good society. In addition to both formal and informal mechanisms of power and authority, women's politics consists of organizing to change what needs to be altered and to preserve what works. The political resides not solely in the institutional realm of government but also in reform movements, in community activities, and in resource-based structures. Political action is not limited to politicians and voters; informal as well as formal organizations and individuals in many roles engage in political activities.[5]

This broader conception of politics was the theoretical and methodological foundation of a comparative collaborative study on Women's Involvement in Political Life in Canada (see CRIAW 1987; Vickers 1988). A nationwide sample of groups was selected that illustrated women's ability to create change at the community level.[6] The Nova Scotian groups selected in 1985–86 for that study are the same groups featured here. We chose them then because their activities exemplified diverse ways in which women were accomplishing political goals; they had been successful at "getting things done" in the public arena.

The three groups form a particularly interesting set for this conceptual exploration of politics for several reasons. They share a successful record of accomplishment but are diverse organizationally and in their specific forms of political action. Analytically, the rare presence of both individual and group data within a known community facilitates new forms of contextual analysis. Newly updated information (from 1986 to 1992) contributes a further longitudinal dimension. During recent analysis I discovered an anomaly that prompted this essay: namely, that members of two of the three groups selected to exemplify political success stories did *not* define their work as political when they joined or initiated their groups.

After describing and comparing the groups I report the results of qualitative analysis, conducted in 1992, of members' 1986 answers to questions about politics. This analysis discovers three concepts of the political and relates them to their groups' activities; clarifies why a majority of members did not, at first, consider their groups to be political; and considers some of the consequences of these political images. I then introduce the concept of a closeted women's political culture to explain the striking similarities in the political actions of these three organizations. The conclusion reflects the broad definition of politics suggested by feminist analysis in these groups and elsewhere.

Women's Politics: Three Groups

My analysis is based on case studies of the three women's organizations in Nova Scotia over almost a decade and on interviews with group members about their conceptions of politics. I describe the political and organizational activities of the MUMS (a low-income housing group), AANE (an Acadian group) and Pandora (producers of a feminist newspaper).[7]

HOUSING AND MOTHERS UNITED FOR METRO SHELTER (MUMS)

The metropolitan area of Halifax-Dartmouth in the early 1980s had a housing shortage with exceptionally low vacancy rates for low-income units. Nova Scotia's minister of housing, however, refused to acknowledge the housing crisis. In fall 1984 two residents of a shelter for battered women—Heather Schneider and May Spinney (now May Ocean)—decided to demonstrate against the lack of affordable housing for women and their families. Schneider had already taken individual action by handwriting forty-five letters to public officials about the housing problems she faced as a single mother. Tenants from second-stage housing had similar plans. Together they formed a group. The MUMS (Mothers United for Metro Shelter) first marched in protest through snow and freezing rain in downtown Halifax on November 3, 1984.

The MUMS subsequently organized public demonstrations, including a mock eviction of the "residents" of Province House, the elected members of the Nova Scotia government; two tent cities, where MUMS members risked arrest while constructing "Homeless Estates" on a patch of government-owned land; a ceremonial presentation to politicians of a booklet containing members' personal experiences with housing;[8] and a march and rally with other women on International Women's Day (1986). The MUMS helped to define housing as a public and political issue by their actions and ability to attract media attention and public support. It also acted as a support group for battered women, especially those in search of housing after leaving their husbands.

The MUMS example challenges traditional scholarly and public notions of organization and of "group success." For example, it is a convention to determine group membership by counting the number who have paid dues. The MUMS did not organize according to such rules. With no paid membership to count, a single numeric estimate was meaningless; at any given time one could have documented the membership at 2,000, 200, 20, or 2 individuals, depending on whether one was enumerating sympathizers and active supporters at demonstrations, those who received help and support from the group, those who attended weekly meetings, or the key organizers. In 1986, decision-making in the group was described as being made by the active membership who "throw ideas out at meetings and discuss them with all the women contributing what they can." Members also contributed by giving presentations and speeches to varied other groups about the MUMS and the housing crisis.

Although the organization's major goal was better, more affordable housing, other goals reflected the difficult life circumstances of its low-income, single-parent members. The MUMS wanted access to public housing that was clean, decent, and secure and also wanted tenants to be accepted without discrimination. Members described hardships they faced from landlords and employers because they were poor, because many of them received social assistance, or because they were single parents. They wanted to stop discrimination against poor people and violence against women and children. They demanded an end to blaming women for governmental and agency incompetence and for their partners' violence. The MUMS worked against discrimination, physical and mental abuse, woman abuse, child abuse, inadequate housing, social injustice, and government apathy toward the concerns of low-income families.

By 1986 the MUMS had been successful in raising poverty issues and in getting provincial and municipal governments to put housing on the public agenda. With an improved housing situation, the major problem had been solved; MUMS group activities subsided and eventually ceased. Thus this highly successful group was short-lived, a concept at odds with scholarly assumptions that equate group success with longevity.[9]

Although the group lost its energy, some members continued to give ongoing advice to government committees on housing and poverty issues. One member wrote a user's guide to welfare services, first for the city and later for the province. She also pursued her education at university and then graduate school. In the middle to late 1980s some former MUMS became key members of a provincial low-income network called LINC. In 1992 former MUMS continued to struggle with their material circumstances and to feel empowered by their political and personal accomplishments: one reported being pleased that the housing situation had improved and that single mothers "don't have to lie on the [housing] applications any more"; another recounted that she now "always voices her opinion about community activities."

WOMEN'S ISOLATION AND PANDORA: A FEMINIST NEWSPAPER

Pandora, a quarterly feminist newspaper published in Halifax, grew out of the frustration experienced by women and women's organizations with their isolation from one another and with silencing and distortions from mainstream media. Recurrent discussions among Halifax women identi-fied the need for a women's network, a women's center, a coalition, or a women's news service to coordinate efforts.

The initiative came in April 1985: several women attended the annual conference of the Women's Health Education Network (WHEN) because they had heard rumors that WHEN was planning a provincial network-ing paper. They were discouraged by discussions of feasibility studies and funding applications. On the return trip, as Betty-Ann Lloyd was express-ing disappointment that it seemed nothing would happen, Carol Millett pointed out, "It will happen if you make it happen." Lloyd had time and resources from unemployment insurance and experience as editor of a com-munity newspaper. She recruited Brenda Bryan, who had graphic design expertise and extensive contacts in the women's community. They made a personal commitment to put out four newspaper issues during the year and to build a continuing organization.

Pandora evolved and expanded as a working group and welcomed vol-unteers. As new skills were learned, production work became more evenly and widely distributed. By the third issue of the paper, some fifty women were identified as "Pandora women" either on the masthead or in pictures, or had become writers, distributors, or production workers; twenty-five of these were active members who attended semi-monthly meetings; and there was a wider number of supporters, including subscribers. Pandora women came from various economic and educational backgrounds and age groups, and represented a diversity of interests and orientations. Pandora was seen as a learning experience—for technical skills needed to produce a newspaper, for working cooperatively with diverse women, for forming networks, for creating news, and for political education in feminist praxis. Almost everyone said she joined Pandora partly to become involved with a women's or feminist organization.

In 1986 Pandora was organized into a number of functional working groups; these reported to regular meetings, where new policies and directions were formulated, usually by consensus. Pandora women described decision-making as "very democratic," "participatory," "collective," and "cooperative." Almost everyone felt involved with making decisions, at least "to the extent [she] want[s] to be." As part of its feminist praxis Pandora sought ways to counter hindrances to participation by diverse women. It created accessible language policies and an outreach committee with a mandate "to identify groups of women who might not automatically feel included by Pandora and encourage them to become involved." Efforts were made to reduce constraints to participation within group meetings. Pandora also established policies of funding child care and transportation for its low-income members. Pandora women offered rides to those for whom transportation was difficult, including a wheelchair user who lived outside the city.

In 1990 *Pandora* refused to publish a letter to the editor from a male. He filed a formal complaint of discrimination, and the Nova Scotia Human Rights Commission established a tribunal to hear the case. Pandora women received death threats for their principled stand for a women-only space. On March 17, 1992, with the help of a feminist lawyer, Pandora won its case—and the right for women-only organizations to advantage women. As member Debbie Mathers explained: "Pandora agreed from the beginning that she/we would not print a letter (or article) from a man. We believe that men (as a group) are advantaged, and women (as a group) are disadvantaged solely because of their/our sex. The Charter of Rights and Freedoms allows disadvantaged groups to band together providing their purpose is to remedy, or alleviate, their disadvantage. We based our defense on those principles."[10] Their feminist lawyer, Anne S. Derrick, praised "the courage and vision of Pandora women to construct the case exclusively in terms of women's equality interests" instead of relying on other legal arguments. As she points out, "Winning at any cost was not the strategy— winning a real victory for women was" (1992, 8).

ACADIAN WOMEN

Acadians are Francophones whose ancestors were Nova Scotia's first nonindigenous settlers. Their history has been one of expulsion and resettlement, and they fear losing their language and culture, as they now constitute only around 4 percent of the province's population. The Association des Acadiennes de la Nouvelle-Ecosse (AANE) is a provincial advocacy and support group of Acadian women; in 1992 approximately four hundred paid the $5.00 membership fee.[11]

AANE grew out of a concern within the mixed-gender group Fédération Acadienne de la Nouvelle-Ecosse (FANE) that the needs of Acadian women were not being adequately addressed. In 1981 FANE hired an organizer, Betty Dugas-LeBlanc, who began "by going and seeing what women were doing and what their needs were." AANE held its first annual meeting as a separate, independent organization in 1983. Its goals included the promotion of communication and cooperation among Acadian women, the provision of resources to groups in need, and the advancement and increased self-confidence of Acadian women generally. AANE has acted as a lobby group at the provincial level in order to enhance French services in Acadian communities.

AANE supports and encourages regionally based activities. In the one urban and five rural regions of Nova Scotia where Acadians live, members meet more or less regularly to organize conferences or to share information. For example, in 1986 the Clare members met only occasionally, whereas by 1992 they were convening regularly as a "circle," "La Société Madeleine LeBlanc," to organize workshops, work on health issues, and lobby local politicians. Members in the Richmond region gathered weekly as Femmes Acadiennes en Marche. Each region was active in different ways under its own name, and each elected a representative to a provincial executive council. AANE's constitution permitted three resource persons to sit on this board, together with a president and vice-president who were elected by members at the annual meeting.[12]

AANE members continued to have formal input into FANE through board membership, and the association has relied on the women's section of FANE to cover expenses for certain activities. AANE activities have focused on five areas: (1) the organization of conferences, workshops, and information sessions (dealing, for example, with law and with menopause); (2) the creation of training workshops on topics such as leadership, political action, and assertiveness training; (3) the provincial annual meeting; (4) the provision of preschools, daycare centers, and "play and learn groups" for parents with small children; and (5) the presentation of briefs to such committees as the Nova Scotia Select Committee on Health and the National Task Force on Prostitution and Pornography. In 1992 AANE was especially concerned about violence against women in Acadian communities and the fact that very few Acadian women actually do get the help they need. Other issues included promoting linguistic rights, accessing French instruction, and defending their voting strength in the province. One active member pointed out that in preparing for its tenth anniversary in 1993, AANE was in the process of reevaluating itself: "When we started we never expected to be around this long."

COMPARISON: GETTING THINGS DONE IN GROUPS

The three organizations exhibit striking similarities. All three are engaged in women's community work. All have arisen at a time of women's movement activity. They are all oriented to change. They all have multifaceted goals including service, support, public education, and advocacy. By my definition, all three are political because they are working toward what they consider important in community life. They hold a political orientation to changing community definitions of what is important: that is, the public agenda. Moreover, they have all planned and implemented actions designed to create change. In all three cases, they have achieved considerable success.

The political activities, structures, orientations, strategies, and tactics of the three groups differ considerably, however. The MUMS is oriented to changing the politicians' agenda and raising public awareness of housing and other poverty issues.[13] In its relatively short life it was highly successful in getting valued social resources and rights on the public agenda. Unlike that of the MUMS, Pandora's political orientation is not focused toward government or any other institution. Pandora embodies the feminist principle that the personal is political; thus all activities are potentially political. It works self-consciously within the feminist movement, believing that publishing women's news will help transform society. It also examines its own political and collective practices, asserting the importance of lived experience in creating a transformative politics. Although Pandora wanted nothing to do with government funding or regulations, the court case in which it was involved is evidence of the impossibility of escaping patriarchal institutions.

In its political orientation, AANE has goals that overlap those of the other two groups. Part of its political activity is to lobby and influence the government's agenda. Tactically, however, AANE differs from the MUMS in that its main approach to government is the presentation of briefs on the needs of Acadian women, based on research. Like Pandora, it directs some activities toward political education, but its workshops in leadership and political action are more oriented to existing political institutions. Like Pandora but with a different focus, AANE has identified needs of women and accordingly set up relevant services. AANE members established not a newspaper but preschools and day care centers in response to perceived educational gaps, especially in rural areas.

The three groups, whatever their differences, are all oriented to getting things done in the public arena in order to better the lives and conditions of women and their communities. According to the broad scholarly concept they are all political, but such a conception was not the majority viewpoint among members of these groups. I look next at how the sample of key group members in 1986 did conceive of "the political."

Three Conceptions of the Political

Why, in 1986, did a majority of the sample of group members say "no" in response to a question as to whether they saw their group as political when they first joined? The answer, as subsequent investigation revealed, is rooted in their individual views or internalized definitions of what politics is and of what "the political" entails. It is a major finding of this study that very different conceptual pictures of the political emerge from the individual-level data. Qualitative analysis of those data, performed in 1992, uncovered three fundamental variants in women's images of the political.

1. The first image is that of governments, political parties, and voting for politicians. This imagery refers to what might be called political institutions. It is the dominant societal definition of politics.

2. The second image is that of an unsavory world inhabited by a self-interested power elite. "Political" is perceived as a pejorative term describing the social arena of back-room deals. The imagery points to a hierar-

chical and patriarchal culture of power, controversy, aggressiveness, and competitive interaction. It is a world of unethical politics, beyond women's reach and control, where politics is a game played amorally and power used unjustly. Political institutions are relatively insignificant parts of the background to this social system of power.

3. The third image is one of women working together to articulate their diverse perspectives, situations, needs, and values more clearly and to participate in radically changing their worlds. This imagery resembles what Angela Miles (1981, 1984, forthcoming; Miles and Finn 1989) has called integrative feminism.[14] Its broad and full perspective challenges the shape and logic of current political definitions. It claims women's specificity and autonomy from male-based organizations as politically necessary for the conduct of feminist political affairs. Its transformative orientation leads to discussions of feminist ideals and of the diverse struggles necessary to reach ideals such as social justice, harmonious development, sustainable livelihoods, residential security, and peace.

I discovered that the first two conceptions of politics—the institutional and amoral power concepts—are reflected in contemporary definitions. This fact reveals the patriarchal origins and continuing construction of politics as fundamentally oriented in a male culture of patriarchal control. The third is a feminist concept, which may have far-reaching implications for the broadened view of politics introduced earlier. For now, I examine first the relationship between political imagery and group membership, and then the effects of these conceptualizations on members' understanding of their groups' activities.

Political Imagery and Group Membership

The three images of politics—as institutional involvement, as amoral power, and as social transformation—are strongly but not perfectly associated with specific group membership. Most Acadian interviewees held the institutional image; most members of the MUMS held the amoral and personalized image; most Pandora women held a feminist understanding of politics as social transformation.

These alternative images of politics highlight apparent contradictions between my definition of the political nature of these groups and the understandings of group members. The MUMS with their clear focus on making housing into a political issue were initially the least likely to define their group as political. The AANE members were oriented to lobbying politicians but almost equally unlikely to define their group as political. Pandora, on the other hand, avoided government and yet its members saw "a woman's paper—by women, for women, on women's issues" as highly political. These apparent contradictions are clarified when we focus on the dynamic interactions between individuals' political imagery and group orientations. The analysis also shows the impact of members' concepts on their groups. Since political conceptions shape and are shaped by the political reality in which individuals and groups find themselves, it is not surprising that group structures and priorities mirror these conceptions. What are the specific implications of these differing conceptions of politics?

AANE

Politics in the minds of AANE members was associated with partisanship, working in elections, and voting. Although only 17 percent were political party members, all reported always voting. The first reactions of all respondents was to view the political in terms of government and politicians (Dugas-LeBlanc 1986). A combination of their institutional conception of politics, their participation in the governmental arena, and the clear difference between that arena and their group combined in contemporary logic to shape their understanding of the political nature of AANE. Because of the dominant institutional conception of politics, some members described the "political" activity of the group as applying for and obtaining funds or grants from government. Since their group was not government, by definition it was not political.

Other Acadian respondents used the amoral power or transformative definition as well in their interpretation of the group as nonpolitical. One respondent, for example, defined partisan involvement as careerist. Holding a traditional view that politics is "about government," she saw her activities in AANE as "about helping people." To her, "a political person is active because he wants to go places in life . . . to get ahead. . . . I want to stay where I am." This view, that partisan involvement was about "getting ahead," while women's activities were about "getting things done" for people, was a classical statement of many women's perceptions of the careerist or "selfish" motivations of partisan activists as opposed to the service-oriented, caring, or "unselfish" motives of women in their communities (CRIAW 1987, 53). Another AANE member stressed "taking a stand on an issue" as the political element and therefore did not see her activities or those of the association as political. For her AANE was still about sharing information and not activist enough to meet her criteria for "political."

For most respondents in the Acadian group, the taken-for-granted concept of politics meant that the government, not the people or groups, was responsible for establishing goals and distributing resources. Voting, in this conception, provided the legitimate avenue for people to participate in the society. Political change thus was best accomplished by working for changes in government at times of election and influencing key members of political parties. Some members did not associate getting things done for people in the community—or even lobbying for day care—as politics; creative work for women in the community was seen as something outside of politics. As such, this activity had no name, no resources, and no prestige. The patriarchal world did not applaud this work, nor did it provide such groups with intellectual resources to understand their situation, its complexities, and the resistance to women's work that arises when traditional power relations are threatened and women's presence is felt in what men have assumed to be their territorial domains.

MUMS

When a majority of MUMS members were asked to describe their concept of the political, only one associated it with political institutions such as voting, elections, and political parties. The dominant image was the amoral one of a personalized and unsavory politics and of women's isolation or exclusion from it. Unlike members of the other two groups, MUMS members frequently named individual politicians, and words such as "aggressive" and "competitive" were common. Being political was perceived as negative or, at best, unknown. One said that she got "scared because I don't know anything about it," a comment echoed by another who felt the need for a political science course.

At first it seemed surprising that MUMS members stressed their own educational development the most, even though the group was the least self-conscious about education on its formal agenda. Unlike that of the Acadian group, which sponsored educational seminars, and Pandora, which held group retreats, the MUMS agenda articulated public education rather than self-education. Reflection, made it clear, however, that my expectations were distorted by scholarly formalism. The extraordinary experience of being in the MUMS and learning pragmatically offered more than formal courses and training programs. Involvement in the MUMS was itself considered a political education, and the majority retrospectively described their own perceptions as having changed quite dramatically. As one member said in 1992, "My life has changed entirely from being in that group."

Initially, all MUMS members saw their involvement in the group as *not* political. Even the leaders did not regard activities such as demonstrating in the streets as political. This perception was consistent with their concept of the political: the streets were not the arena of the power elites. Their original concept of the political also explains when and how they realized their political nature: namely, when they actually entered those "back rooms" and met face-to-face with politicians. As one of the leaders revealed: "Even up until we went to Province House, I didn't think it was political. It became political as soon as we went to Province House. We realized we [didn't] have a choice but to become political once we started dealing with politicians. We now think along the lines of politicians. We have become a very political group." The initial absence of a conception of political institutions and the presence of a personalizing conception of politicians helps explain the political activities and strategies of the MUMS in comparison with other groups.

Politically, the MUMS tried to change the minds and priorities of politicians in the state but activists realized that they would lack the power to change an individual politician's view unless they built their own community group and worked with others. Thus, they saw that the route to changing the government's agenda was to change politicians through group pressure. They wanted relatively quick and immediate responses. Once the agenda was changed to their liking, however, only those with feminist political resources saw their role as politically transformative. The rest lacked the political resources to see how their articulated insistence that housing was a right might become the basis for a sustained politics aimed at social transformation and a world where that right was taken for granted. As one member summed it up: "I didn't see how fighting for housing was political. I didn't see housing as a political thing. It is a right. . . . Since we have taken it to the streets, to government, it has become a political issue. I guess we are political, but I never realized it."

PANDORA

Pandora members held a broad, multifaceted, and multileveled conception of the political. Such a conception did not limit political behavior to political institutions, such as the party and voting, but included many "generative" components aimed at empowerment and social change. For Pandora, working through the state was only one of many potential ways to influence the future of the globe; Nova Scotian women, rather than politicians, were singled out as a focus of change-oriented energy. Although Pandora women voted, they actively pursued other forms of political contribution that they considered more relevant. They created the newspaper as a valuable community resource for moving the interests of poor women and children to the center of society's agenda, and they generated a feminist community. In contrast to the responses of the other two groups, two-thirds of the Pandora participants in the study recalled that they considered the group to be doing political work when they first joined, and the entire sample had come to see that political nature over time. Pandora's broad feminist conception of the political linked the personal with the political. As one woman explained: "Putting out a women's newspaper is a political act; maintaining it as women-only is a political act, and we do that very deliberately. Being women-positive is political; being lesbian-positive is political, and we are very clear on those."

From the beginning, a feminist political culture helped to shape Pandora and to develop its more sophisticated conception of the political. It was also an important political resource in Pandora's struggle with the Human Rights Tribunal. In fact, a feminist political culture helped members to understand their own situation by raising to the level of a principle the notion that one should act and make a difference in society. It helped them plan and win their case, but such a high level of political sophistication and political self-consciousness came about *before* the events surrounding the case had been labeled as political by others.

Women's Political Culture

These differing conceptions of politics shaped and limited group members' understanding of what they were doing. Especially for AANE and the MUMS, the members' conceptions of politics were initially not useful resources for their own group activities. But all these groups have accomplished things that are pro-woman, change-oriented, and political in the widest and fullest sense of the word. How did they succeed at politics despite initially lacking an articulated broad concept of the political? The explanation lies in the concept of a more or less closeted women's political culture.[15]

Women's political culture may be defined as a set of orientations, morals, values, and beliefs about the nature of a just and caring society, one that meets human needs. Women's political culture helps identify socially valuable goods and services, and strategies for maximizing women's goals. It has a material base, not a biological or essentialist one. This materialist base is rooted in the social organization of women's experience, which involves the nurturing of children, caring for people, and ensuring distributive justice. The institutional form it has taken has usually been relatively informal, interpersonal, small-scale, and communal. Its rootedness in multiplicity and its confidence in women's morality are two major features of women's political culture that are reflected in the actions and recollections of all three groups. Women's political culture as a political strategy was most strongly articulated by the MUMS:

> We decided earlier that in our group, we were going to treat our politicians the way we treat our children. The experience we have as mothers, we tend to think that is really important. What have we learned in our lives? Well, we have learned how to be mothers and raise children, learned to work with them so we can live comfortably and peaceably with them. So with our government we decided that what we should do is when they do something that hurts us, or disrupts our lives, we go at them, and we let them know and we let everyone know that our government is doing something that is hurting us. And we don't let them off easy. But when they do something good, we have to, we must, make a point of approving the good behaviour, because if we don't, we are not directing them; we're just creating a big fight. . . .
>
> Mothers have to be given credit for something. . . . Part of what we are doing is because we are mothers and what we have learned from being mothers. It does have effects on our society, and it shows in the treatment of our government and how we would like to be treated by our government.

The conception of women's culture as closeted is useful because it allows us to think of the continual, structurally generated orientation of a women's political culture while also recognizing its uneven appearance and articulation. It helps explain the consistent themes, such as peace and community well-being, that have been articulated by women not only in these three groups but in other groups over the centuries as well. It is no accident that it is women who initiate and organize urban reform movements involving housing, welfare, and the environment. Even when closeted, the latent power of women's political culture can be mobilized to act quickly with quite remarkable force. A closeted women's political culture allows one to understand short but effective public interventions by women such as the sudden brief flowering of political speech in Japan between 1882 and 1884 (see Sievers 1981), women's collective action in Barcelona between 1910 and 1918 (see Kaplan 1982), and women's constitutional gains in Canada (see Kome 1985). It also explains the significant but unrecognized contributions of Black women in Nova Scotia (see S. Hamilton 1993) and of community women in Labrador (see Christiansen-Ruffman 1980). It helps to account for the energy that all three groups brought to their specific projects and explains the remarkable political consistency of these community-based groups despite their differences.

When women's political culture is closeted and masked by the patriarchal structures of every institution in society, patricentric definitions of issues and political institutions dominate to such an extent that they are accepted by women as well as men. At some stages in patriarchal societies, the power of these definitions obscures women's realities to such an extent that most people are not even conscious of their existence. Under these conditions women are isolated, working in the dark, without benefit of a set of political ideals or strategies or even the words to name and communicate their diverse and common interests as women.

As part of the women's liberation movement, some of the treasures in the closet were discovered and their latent potential appreciated. Women's political culture began to emerge from the closet through the activities and analysis of women's organizations within the movement. When the three groups in Nova Scotia were founded in the 1980s, patricentric definitions were still dominant, but women's issues in Canada had emerged on the public agenda, and some features of women's political culture were becoming visible and audible around kitchen tables. By 1986, to a greater extent in the MUMS and to a lesser extent in AANE, the group process was bringing women's political culture out of the closet to provide members with a more complex conception of political activity. As women reacted with moral outrage, engaged in community work, organized group activities, discussed strategies, met with other groups, and became empowered, women's political culture in these groups was being articulated.

Although women's political culture provided the impetus for action, its relatively masked and closeted nature meant that it did not provide sufficient educational, strategic, or intellectual resources to be articulated fully. Women's political culture recognized needs and informed resourceful organizers, but it provided neither an adequate set of political concepts nor a flourishing environment to support women's community work. Because of this gap, it is not surprising that there was intense interest in education, in group process, and in changing conceptions of the political among members of all these groups. Members of all groups came to a fuller and more complex understanding of the nature of politics—and of different conceptions of politics—as part of their group involvement.

The case of Pandora illustrates how feminist political culture draws on women's political culture but also brings additional political resources. Its analysis seeks to understand and challenge patriarchy and other forms of dominating power, including racism, classism, homophobia, and colonialism. The explicit feminism of Pandora provided members with political wisdom developed as part of past struggles, visionary practices, and analysis within the women's movement. Its set of broad political concepts helped individuals to connect their personal lives and political issues and to challenge narrow and conventional political conceptions. Feminist politics encouraged the group to reach out to people of diverse backgrounds and varying abilities, to be "inclusive of women's different ideologies," and to practice a consensus-oriented decision-making process. Pandora's presence in the community demonstrated "that women as a group and as individuals have ideas worthy of publication," ideas that had been "actively ignored." It sought to change the way Nova Scotian women understood their own situation, perceived the world, and were active in it. Feminist political culture helped to articulate women's diverse material realities and strengths, women's oppression, and women's conscious commitment to social betterment.

But change is not easy. Feminists can imagine and foresee how contemporary patriarchal politics may distort women's political culture if its realm becomes appropriated. Feminists may wish to question seriously, as the MUMS did, whether it is desirable that all activities of the women's movement and women's community become labeled as political, as partisan, as open to manipulation in a patriarchal world. Perhaps community battles are best fought on the streets and in the kitchens rather than in patriarchal halls of politicians.

Although feminist political culture has made a contribution in terms of its scope and the possibilities in its vision, it is still in its infancy and in need of political development. Much of women's reality has not yet even been named. Its intellectual resources, important as they are, require refinement and elaboration. This knowledge will be developed from the wisdom of women working in groups who draw on their own realities, perspectives, and experiences; from feminist activists within the women's movement; and from feminist scholars who are grounded in these movements.

Conclusion

This comparative study of groups and individuals has uncovered several qualitatively different conceptions of the political. Recognition of these diverse but taken-for-granted scholarly and conceptual meanings is important for communication within and among groups. Clarity of communication and analysis should help feminists attain their goals of articulating women's experiences, eliminating discrimination and all forms of oppression against women, and creating an equitable world. It should be helpful to scholars, researchers, political activists, and community workers who must learn how to listen to the emerging voices of women. The task is made difficult, however, by overpowering patricentric intellectual resources and by the patriarchal "relations of ruling" (D. Smith 1987) that dominate all institutional spheres.

This analysis indicates that a broad, complex, and expanding concept of the political is crucial to understanding relations of ruling and women's struggles to change the agenda. Methodologically, this type of analysis—which discovers, recognizes, and uses the taken-for-granted alternative meanings of key concepts—has implications for future research. It provides a means by which the meanings and analysis of both group members and scholars are recognized as central. Thus, it is a way of fulfilling the feminist goal of treating women's experiences seriously on the one hand, while recognizing on the other hand that all those experiences and perceptions, as well as our scholarly concepts for approaching them, are still embedded in and shaped by patriarchy.[16]

Political wisdom is generated by groups around the world. Peggy Antrobus, for example, points to a similar discussion from a group of working-class women involved in the SISTREN Women's Theatre Collective of Jamaica. Its newsletter expressed the group's "frustrations with the 'narrow form of politics . . . defined by male political leadership'" and asserted: "Women need independent group-building and networking outside of the parties. . . . This is not party politics, but it is definitely politics. Women know that this kind of politics is their kind of politics. It is the kind of politics that has made national issues of rape, incest, domestic violence, conditions at the Free Zones, and the kind of politics that has shown us why women can be super-exploited in these ways. This is the kind of politics . . . that will make the road easier for Hannah the banana farmer, and . . . that influences women's movements around the world" (quoted in Antrobus 1989, 197). I join with Antrobus and others in recognizing how women's groups enable analysis to emerge from action, expand political horizons, redefine and challenge structures of oppression, and empower women to create a better, more just world for everyone.

Notes

Acknowledgments: This essay was facilitated by sabbatical leave and is based on research supported financially by Canada's Social Sciences and Humanities Research Council, by the Canadian Research Institute for the Advancement of Women, and by UNESCO. It has benefited intellectually from discussions with the members of MUMS, Pandora, and AANE; from the initial 1985–86 collaborative process of design, data collection, and analysis chaired by Jill Vickers; from research collaboration with Lois Corbett, Betty Dugas-LeBlanc, and Mary-Anne Finlayson; and from helpful comments on earlier drafts by Angela Miles, Jane Arscott, and the editors.

1. Empirical references and examples in this paper are selective and drawn mainly from the English Canadian literature, with which readers may not be familiar.

2. Conceptual portions of this analysis are from my widely circulated mimeographed paper, Christiansen-Ruffman 1983, which revised and combined two earlier papers: "Canadian Women and Political Action: Coming Out of the Closet?" (presented at a meeting jointly sponsored by the Society for the Study of Social Problems and Sociologists for Women in Society, Toronto, August 1981), and "Women's Political Culture and Feminist Political Culture" (presented at the Tenth World Congress of Sociology, sponsored by Research Committee 32 of the International Sociological Association and held in Mexico City, August 16–21, 1982). Those papers, in turn, were informed by research on women's organizations in Canada, especially in the provinces of Nova Scotia and Newfoundland/Labrador.

3. Berenice Carroll's (1979, 1980) useful review and critique of the biased nature of the literature was nevertheless grounded in the narrow conception of politics, prevalent in political science. Stacey and Price's (1981) adoption of the public/private dichotomy obscured women's community-based activities. Randall's book recognizes the contributions of feminist thought to a broader concept of politics and indeed starts with a discussion of the "politics of everyday life," but overall she writes that her book is "constrained by its intentions" of being "directed to political scientists" and of "attempting to show feminists that they can learn from mainstream political science" (1982, 10; 1987, 13–14).

4. An analysis of *Women's Studies Abstracts* in 1980–81, 1981–82, 1990–91,

and 1991–92 indicates that over 80 percent of the literature retains this narrow, institutionally based conception, with the remaining percentages distributed between "don't know" and a non-traditional, or broader, conception.

5. The conception of politics has begun to broaden as writers and scholars have collected articles focused on women's community and organizational activities and on what Bunch (1987) calls "passionate politics" (e.g., Fitzgerald, Guberman, and Wolfe 1982; Briṣkin and Yanz 1983; Kealey and Sangster 1989; Miles and Finn 1989; Wine and Ristock 1991), and even commissioned them (e.g., Roberts 1988). Case studies focus on grassroots ways of shaping the public agenda by specific Canadian women's organizations. See, e.g., Strong-Boag 1976 for a historical description of the National Council of Women, 1893–1929; Razack, 1991 for a description of LEAF, the Legal Education and Action Fund; Vickers, Rankin, and Appelle 1993 for a description of NAC, the National Action Committee for the Status of Women. Case studies of locally based groups in Newfoundland include Porter's (1985) description of rural Women's Institute activity; Pennell's (1987) analysis of a battered women's shelter in the province's capital city; and Neis's (1988) examination of women's support for the fishery. Some Canadian studies analyze interactions between community groups and institutional or state structures, including both state "appropriative practices" and the groups' "visionary practices" that result from this interaction (e.g., Christiansen-Ruffman and Catano 1986; Ng 1988; S. Burt 1990; Ng, Walker, and Muller 1990; Walker 1990; Kellough 1992), and Maticka-Tyndale and Drakich (1992) have used concepts from Adamson, Briskin, and McPhail 1988 and Briskin 1991 to describe the alternating nature of feminist organizational activities—between mainstreaming and disengagement—within the Women's Caucus of the Canadian Sociology and Anthropology Association.

6. CRIAW research collaborators had to resist pressures at the design stage to focus on a narrow concept of politics and, more persistently, to compare women with men. The study, commissioned by UNESCO and conducted by the Canadian Research Institute for the Advancement of Women, described the activities of nine groups in four provinces, based partly on in-depth interviews with women in these groups. One of the major findings is reflected in the title of our 1988 publication: *Getting Things Done: Women's Views of Their Involvement in Political Life.*

7. Fuller information on all three groups is available in CRIAW 1987.

8. The booklet, titled *Open More Doors: MUMS Speak about the Human Costs of the Housing Crisis. Case Histories, Mothers United for Metro Shelter*, was compiled, edited, and laid out by the International Women's Week Shelter Committee, Halifax, 1986. In the acknowledgments, the first major group of support listed was Pandora women. The MUMS and Pandora also had some overlapping membership in 1986.

9. The assumption that organizational longevity equals success was implicit in presentations at ARNOVA (Association for Research on Nonprofit Organizations and Voluntary Action) at Yale University, November 1992; it was made at the con-

ceptual, sampling, and analytic stages of the research process. Such an assumption does "make sense" from the perspectives of resource mobilization theories and functional theories concerned with the organizational need for survival.

10. Mathers 1992, 2–3. The September 1992 issue of *Pandora* contains details of the court case, letters to the editor supportive *and* critical of Pandora's position in the case, an explanation of why the position was taken, and personal recollections of Pandora witnesses and supporters. In addition to describing and celebrating the victory, the paper reports the patriarchal setting (a room lined with pictures of military leaders), and various articles discuss patriarchy's success at contesting feminist definitions of expertise, the apparent inability of the male lawyer for the Human Rights Commission to understand collective decision-making, and the silencing of lesbian witnesses.

11. Research on AANE throughout its history was conducted by Betty Dugas-LeBlanc, and significant parts of this section are presented in her words.

12. AANE was less structured and more informal than its mixed-gender counter-part, FANE. Nevertheless, as reported by CRIAW (1987, 41) and Vickers (1988), "the task-oriented collective mode of organization of . . . the MUMS and Pandora presents quite a different environment for political activity than [do] the more formally structured groups [such as AANE that] . . . clearly mobilize women more securely *over time*" (original emphasis).

13. Using Randall's (1987, 50–68) conceptualization, only the MUMS as a political protest group would be considered directly political.

14. Angela Miles (1984 and forthcoming) uses the term "integrative feminism" to name this full and transformative politics that cuts across many other categorizations of feminism and proposes alternatives to contemporary rationalities and values. She contrasts it with a more narrow pressure-group politics that focuses only on women's equality and treats this single issue as changeable in isolation from other features of patriarchal society.

15. Significant portions of this section are from Christiansen-Ruffman 1983 and its earlier versions (see note 3), where these ideas of a latent and more or less closeted women's political culture were first developed.

16. As I wrote this essay in fall 1992, Canada's constitutional discussions were again in full swing. The cries of outrage that greeted the call for gender parity in the senate indicate the deep-seated nature of patriarchal privilege under threat and of institutionalized misogyny. Almost no one considered it a violation of democracy to have a separate ballot in each province to elect an equal number of senators from large and small provinces alike, but the idea of a separate ballot to elect equal numbers of women and men per province generated a sputtering flurry of antidemocratic rhetoric. Even currently elected women members who have taken feminist stands on issues such as abortion have criticized proportional representation for men and women as antidemocratic on the grounds that they do not want to feel they were elected on "a second-rate ticket."

PART VII

Afterword

CHAPTER 25

From Seed to Harvest: Transformations of Feminist Organizations and Scholarship

■

JO FREEMAN

The essays in this book represent an extraordinary accomplishment. Approximately twenty-five years after the women's liberation movement first pushed its sprouts into the public consciousness, these authors have produced a bountiful crop of research, analysis, and knowledge. This harvest a quarter of a century later is extraordinary both for the length of the growing season and for the hardiness of its cultivators. To understand why, one must appreciate the barrenness of the soil and the lack of implements that researchers into feminism have had to face.

My education as a scholar and my early feminist activism coincided, so each was able to inform the other. I helped start one of the first new feminist groups in the fall of 1967 and entered the University of Chicago as a graduate student in political science in the fall of 1968. That winter a major student sit-in over the firing of a female professor, Marlene Dixon, created the opportunity for feminist ideas to become public on campus and, thanks to press coverage, off campus as well. While feminist ideas quickly spread, the feminist movement was devouring its own, hungrily trashing anyone who received the slightest acknowledgment from the outside world and many who were known only within it. Although I lived in Chicago when the Chicago Women's Liberation Union was formed in 1969, my only encounter with it was when I was informed that I had been censured in April 1970 for allowing my photo to appear in *Newsweek* without CWLU permission. By the time I graduated in 1973, activism and scholarly activity were bifurcated. Those who did one were distrusted by those who did the other.

Hostility made the women's movement hard to research and hard to write about. Most of the early activists came out of the New Left, where they had learned to be suspicious of anything remotely associated with "the establishment." Academia and anyone in it, even graduate students and junior faculty, were the establishment. This suspicion was compounded by an early feminist damnation of anyone who aspired to male-identified achievements and careers, such as getting a Ph.D. in order to teach college. In the fall of 1968 I brought to the first national women's liberation conference held outside Chicago a questionnaire I had drawn up asking how people became involved in the movement. I found it virtually impossible to get anyone to fill it out or even talk to me about her experience. Eventually, I heard the rumor that the information I was seeking would be used by the University of Chicago to screen applicants and eliminate radicals. Since no one confronted me with this accusation directly, I could not refute it. I had to research what became "The Origins of the Women's Liberation Movement" (Freeman 1973) as a "closet scholar." A decade later the covert hostility had become overt and spread to include all research on women. In 1978 I attended a conference in Washington, D.C., organized by the local movement. By then I had learned to keep quiet about my illicit intellectual interests, but not everyone else had. When a few academic women tried to talk about their interviews with lower-class women, which they hoped to publish, they were denounced for "making it off the backs of other women." Even NOW has been antagonistic to academic feminists, despite the fact that several were among its founders. Since insiders pay the price of ostracism for writing about the movement, its history will be written by outsiders without the insight that comes from participation.

The attitude of the academic world was more subtle. I was never told not to write on women or the women's movement. My own academic mentor, Ted Lowi, strongly encouraged me to do so; he said my work was original and creative, a contribution to the field. But when the time came to find a job, I found I didn't fit any of the available slots. The fact that I had published twenty articles was less important than that they were on such a narrow, uninteresting topic as women; what did that have to do with political science? This reaction did not surprise me; I had seen enough by then to know that such an attitude was not limited to my field. Junior female faculty at the University of Chicago who switched their research interests to women from whatever they had been doing when hired were denied contract renewals. They were openly told it was because their departments didn't want to support that kind of research. I learned that academic freedom is a luxury only those with tenure can afford. I also learned that the creation and production of knowledge is shaped not by the interests of the individuals who pursue it but by those who reward and punish the pursuers with jobs, promotions, and grants.

I finally got a job but not in a political science department. I taught for four years at two small state colleges in New York, schools so new that half the faculty were women and only a few had tenure. The first school I hated and eagerly left after a year. The second I loved until my immediate colleagues told me that they wanted to get rid of me. I fought this for two years (while also hunting for another job), but they won. After another two years of applying for academic jobs I gave up and went to law school. The most common response to my application had been "We don't need anyone to teach women and politics." Of course, I didn't teach women and politics. I taught courses in American government. I *wrote* about women and politics.

The authors in this book are to be admired for their perseverance in continuing their research despite hostile reactions from the feminist movement and the cold shoulder of the academic world. Frankly, the one-two punch silenced me. For over a decade after my exile from academia I did no original research; what little I wrote about feminism was either journalism or a rehash. When I returned to this topic, I did so as an ersatz historian, scouring archives and library collections wherever my travels took me. Libraries are not hostile; librarians are very supportive. Only some of this research has been written up, even though I find it easy to publish almost anything I write. It is the isolation and lack of reinformcement that makes the immediate tasks of everyday life so much more urgent than some future byline.

I found academic antipathy easier to understand than feminist hostility, perhaps because most academics are men. The values of the academic world extol merit, but the determination of what is and is not meritorious is highly subjective. In 1974 I wrote: "Contrary to popular belief, the academic establishment is not in business to pursue truth, promulgate knowledge, or even to package people. Its purpose is the production of prestige." As others before me had noted, women scholars were outside the prestige system. The study of women, the study of the feminist movement, and in particular the study of feminist organizations wasn't even sitting on the steps.

How women got inside the system—by pushing open the door or easing the camel's nose under the tent, supported by student demands and using the leverage of lawsuit and government action—is a long story best told in a long book. But it was not done quickly, easily, or evenly. The literature on women and on feminism grew despite many obstacles, somewhat like blades of grass that push their way up through the asphalt. It grew not because the academic world nourished it but because academic feminists truly believed the mandate "to pursue truth" and realized that "truth" was not what they were reading in the existing textbooks. The emergence of the study of women as an area of inquiry, or more accurately as a series of subfields within the different academic disciplines, varied enormously by field. It was easiest in the humanities, harder in the social sciences, hardest in the hard sciences.

Several factors affected the rate, and likelihood, of success. The most important was the number of women and the "percent female" in each discipline in the late 1960s when the feminist movement emerged, women became a hot topic in the popular press, and complaints were filed with the Department of Health, Education and Welfare demanding that government contracts be rescinded until sex discrimination was eliminated. Although women everywhere were concentrated at the lowest levels and in the lowest schools, sheer numbers made a difference. The curve of access was steepest in those fields that already had a critical mass of women, somewhere between 20 and 30 percent. Women begot more women. And more women fostered the study of women. Greater numbers of women in a field made the creation of specialty journals economically feasible and conferences on "women in ——" realistic. Many other scholarly phenomena—regular local meetings, research support, courses, the sharing of knowledge and interests—also require minimum numbers in order to exist and a critical mass in order to flourish.

Legitimation was further facilitated by the existence of compatible intellectual trends and hampered by incompatible ones. "Women's history" quickly became a respectable field in the historical profession because the rise of social history created a more receptive audience for the study of women. In such disciplines as political science and economics the growth fields were quantitative analysis of demographic, voting, and survey data in which women were merely degendered respondents. Indeed, it was the mid-1980s before any woman whose primary field of study was women got tenure in a department of political science. Before that some women political scientists who wrote on women got tenure by first writing on more "legitimate" topics; a few held joint appointments in women's studies so that their departure would mean loss of a line; and several others simply made their permanent homes in other departments.

As academic feminism grew, isolation became less of a problem. Community and discourse are characteristics often attributed to the academic world, but the reality is very different. This is compounded when one is writing about a topic that no one else knows or much cares about. It's not easy to find people to read a manuscript or even talk to about a topic that does not touch upon their own interests. By the time I started working on my dissertation, "The Politics of Women's Liberation," in the fall of 1972, my academic mentor had left for greener pastures, and the feminist women faculty (Marlene Dixon, Judith Long, Cathryn Adamsky, none in political science) with whom I had established talking relationships had all been expelled. Although I had a lot of material and had been a professional writer for several years, my intellectual block was not alleviated until I went to Berkeley in December to submerge myself in the Women's History Research Library, a collection of mostly contemporary feminist pamphlets and news clippings then lodged in the home of movement activist and archivist Laura X. That two-week immersion, and the stimulus of two long conversations with UC Berkeley political scientist Aaron Wildavsky and sociologist Jerome Skolnick, unlocked my mind. I returned to Chicago and finished my dissertation by June. In May, Maren Lockwood Carden sent me a draft of her book, *The New Feminist Movement* (published in 1974). Although we were working on cognate topics, I had not even known about her. I was thrilled to discover that although her research strategy and subjects were somewhat different from my own, we made similar observations when our topics coincided. This validated my work. How much our thinking and writing might have benefited had we been able to talk to each other while doing it, I'll never know. But I do know that the 1992 conference on feminist organizations organized by Myra Marx Ferree and Patricia Yancey Martin was immensely stimulating. This book is a product of that intellectual cross-fertilization.

Publishing has become easier because writing on women and the women's movement is now taken seriously. Previously, the academic journals would publish an occasional article on women, but if too many were submitted, they were rejected as repetitive. Most of the early work was published in "special issues"—usually at the instigation of a women's caucus in each discipline, or a female managing editor. It took the creation of topical journals on women, which provided a receptive audience, for research on women to flourish. Even book publishers, who—unlike journal editors—are guided by the anticipated volume of sales, were wary. *Women: A Feminist Perspective* was rejected by just about every publisher in New York and out of it, on the grounds that "this women's thing" was a temporary fad. It took a California publisher, where courses on women were proliferating, to see the sales potential in 1975. The book is now in its fifth edition (Freeman 1994).

Researching and writing about the women's movement was even harder than researching and writing on women. The pattern in the early years was for the feminist movement to attack research on it and for the scholarly disciplines to neglect it. Conversations with other scholars confirmed that the response to the 1975 publication of *The Politics of Women's Liberation* was not unique. The reviews fell clearly into four categories. The academic feminist journals (such as *Sex Roles*) gave the book raves. The nonacademic nonfeminist periodicals (*Boston Globe, New York Times*) gave it good but not rave reviews. The nonacademic feminist magazines (*Ms., off our backs*) universally panned it. And the nonfeminist academic journals ignored it. Although a few months after it was published the book won a special prize given by the American Political Science Association for the "Best Scholarly Work on Women and Politics," *Political Science Quarterly* was the only political science journal to review it. And although a prototype chapter from the book had been published by the *American Journal of Sociology* in 1973, not a single sociology journal reviewed it. That wouldn't happen today.

Research, like farming, is facilitated by specialized tools. Some of these implements, such as archives and special collections, had been forged by our feminist predecessors and were waiting to be used. Most of us didn't know they existed; it took a while for that knowledge to diffuse and a while longer before microfilm copies of the major papers became available. Other tools, such as bibliographies and specialized reference books, had to be created from scratch. Again, the difficulty of doing research varied by field. The historians had a head start, thanks to our predecessors, though a lot of important women died before anyone was interested in interviewing them or recognized that their papers were historically important. Scholars in disciplines for which survey research and quantitative analysis were the "in" methodologies had to persuade large, male-dominated organizations to include relevant topics in their questionnaires. Researchers who needed to do contemporary observation and interviews had to become moles or persuade their subjects to talk to them. Analysts of feminist organizations are in this category. Many of the papers in this book were written by participant observers; *how* they did their work would be an interesting story in itself.

What scholars write about reflects not only what interests us but what others have written about. We all build on the achievements of our fore-bears; none of us can do original research to fill every gap that touches on our concerns. When I was working on the first edition of *Women: A Feminist Perspective* I wanted something on minority women, so sometime in 1970–71 I burrowed into the University of Chicago library intending to read everything written on the topic. Today that would be a formidable task. Then, it wasn't. It took days of reviewing catalogues, indexes, and bibliographies to come up with a list, but the sources listed didn't take long to read. The bibliography was so short, and grew so slowly, that for several years I could recite it from memory. Although "The Tyranny of Structure-lessness" was written in 1970 for a feminist audience, I did try to turn it in as a term paper for a political science course. The professor rejected it because there were no citations to the literature; he didn't believe me when I said there was no literature to cite. Later, when there *was* some litera-ture to cite, I revised it in academic form and submitted it to social science journals. It was rejected on the grounds that it added nothing new to the literature. The article was published, and often reprinted, in its popular form (Freeman 1972), and has even been used in college courses—not bad for a rejected term paper!

This book makes a major contribution to the literature on feminist orga-nizations—a literature that has grown slowly and sporadically because of all the obstacles to this kind of research, only some of which I've discussed (I didn't even mention money, which is one of the biggest). But it does more than that. The questions raised by these authors have implications far beyond the specific groups they study. Several themes emerge from these essays which are important not only intellectually, for the under-standing of movements, but pragmatically, for understanding how to make change happen and how to sustain it. Some of the common themes concern socialization, institutionalization, encapsulation, identity, community, ac-countability, and empowerment.

I am one of those who believe that there is no such thing as a perma-nent social movement. Movements are inherently unstable. Even though they often develop complex organizational forms, they are essentially de-pendent on vast amounts of spontaneous volunteer energy to pursue their objectives and achieve their goals. The rewards for individual contribu-tions are limited; constant recruitment of new participants is necessary to replace those who burn out; these new members have to be socialized into the culture and history of the existing movement, or their energy will be dissipated or they will change it into something else; the very effort to do this creates barriers to new participants and undermines the common experiences and web of relationships that are among the few rewards for old ones. At the same time every movement, no matter how successful, encounters resistance, ranging from friendly institutions with their own agendas to those who would exploit the movement for their own ends to an antagonistic countermovement. A strong opposition is often better than no opposition, because it fosters solidarity and encourages commitment. And success is better than failure, because it validates one's actions. But whether manifested as apathy or antipathy, resistance is another source of instability, one which is unpredictable and for which coping strategies are not always transferable from person to person or group to group. The harassment of abortion clinics by Operation Rescue encouraged some clinic workers to translate their rage into radicalism but caused others to burn out. Reductions in governmental funding during the Reagan-Bush years affected those service centers that depended on it more than those that did not. New Right attacks caused greater changes in those movement activities involving nonmovement entities than in those that took place strictly within movement communities. The combination of internal instability and external resistance always takes its toll. At some point every social movement, successful or not, changes into something else. Often it changes into many other things.

Movements are not institutions, but to survive beyond the initial burst of spontaneity they must take on many of the characteristics of institutions. This means not just forming organizations but recruiting new participants and training them to work effectively in movement groups. Older members must socialize newer members into the history and culture of the movement to provide any kind of continuity. The Chicago Women's Liberation Union is one example of a feminist group that had to learn how to do this. The rapid expansion typical of a successful movement, however, often brings new recruits into it faster than they can be socialized. The changing types and levels of resistance also alter the experience of successive entrants. The micro-cohorts of the Columbus, Ohio, women's movement illuminate how these different experiences create different generations of movement participants. Rapid change internally and externally is one more cause of movement instability.

Institutionalization is what happens when a movement either penetrates existing institutions, capturing them sufficiently so that some of their resources can be used for movement goals, or movement organizations become routinized: that is, acquire stable sources of income, staff, and defined tasks. A movement does not institutionalize all at the same time; but when its identifiable components—whether people or organizations—are relatively stable from one year to the next, when participant behavior can be predicted, when adherents can be *relied* on to provide money, time, or other resources if called upon, institutionalization has occurred. This is one of the more desirable outcomes, but it has costs as well as benefits. Several chapters in this book describe the efforts of movement entities to institutionalize, and the consequences. *Ms.* magazine sought stable funding from advertisers for twenty years before concluding that this was not achievable without the loss of feminist values. Australian femocrats appear to have captured governmental institutions successfully—but are the first to warn activists that the price of doing so is loyalty to those institutions. Obtaining state funding helped women running battered women's shelters, feminist health clinics, and rape crisis centers to expand their services and take the feminist message to places it might not otherwise have gone; but the organizational requirements of the funding sources clashed with the more collective style favored by feminists, and when the funds declined, the organizations often did so as well. The women's policy network in Washington was the cutting edge for national policy changes benefiting women—while enduring accusations of elitism and co-optation by the movement.

Encapsulation is what happens when all or part of a movement loses its missionary impulse, when activity is directed inward rather than outward, and movement boundaries lose their fluidity to the point that they become barriers to new participants. Joining a new movement is like joining a street party: everyone's welcome; if you don't like what's happening, then do your own thing. Joining a mature movement, particularly one that's encapsulating, is more like rushing a sorority: you have to qualify, and the implicit, unspoken criteria are that you look, act, and think like those already there. When the Columbus, Ohio, Women's Action Coalition debated whether it should reach out to heterosexual women, the real topic was movement boundaries and the limits on entry. Homogeneity encourages encapsulation and vice versa. WAC never achieved the multicultural pluralism it coveted; it became increasingly White, middle class, and lesbian.

Institutionalization and encapsulation are *not* mutually exclusive; they may even coincide. But they are different responses to different aspects of a movement's environment. Encapsulation is a common reaction to hostility and rejection. Catholic women largely failed in their efforts to reform the patriarchal Church; they responded by creating their own religious world.

The institutional Church's resistance to change led them to challenge the values and assumptions on which that institution was based. These challenges may in the future provide a basis for institutional changes, but for the moment they provide a retreat.

One of a social movement's many tasks is to create a community that will provide shared experiences, reinforce values, foster relationships, and socialize new members. This community is the mobilizing base during times of movement expansion and makes survival possible during contractions. Movements may not last forever, but the communities they create can. Yet the creation of community itself creates boundaries. The very shared experiences and relationships that make a community viable and pleasurable also make it less permeable and, in turn, encourage encapsulation. When the environment is hostile, it is easy to retreat into a comforting community that reinforces one's identity and validates one's views. Encapsulated communities are rarely the source of new movement surges.

Identity, like community, is a basic need. The most committed of feminists internalize the movement as part, or even all, of their identity. For many women, participation in a *feminist* organization is part of their *feminist* identity. Yet some of the most heated debates are over what a *feminist* organization is, because the way in which one does things is as important for many as what they are done for. A feminist process is deemed essential to being a feminist organization. The debate over structure by the battered women's movement in St. Louis was about political identity. Yet the plethora of organizations calling themselves feminist and pursuing feminist goals question the proposition that collective decision-making and participatory democracy are prerequisites to being feminist. So does the fact that southern Black women organizing in the 1940s and 1950s used what is now called a feminist process without having a feminist identity.

Feminism as an identity is also complicated by the strong dedication to "hyphenated" feminism. Although most large movements have diverse and complicated ideologies, from the very beginning different feminists have sought to distinguish themselves from other feminists through labels. Such terms as "liberal feminist," "socialist feminist," "lesbian feminist," and "womanist" were adopted not to clarify ideas or policy positions but to identify oneself in relationship to both feminists and nonfeminists. Usually these labels are loaded; some are valued, some stigmatized. "Radical" in particular has been contended territory. The use of labels often tells us more about the identity of those who label than about the content of what they are labeling.

Feminism is a constructed identity. Contemporary activists aren't born into a feminist community—though future ones may be. The activists of the last twenty-five years have had to put together their own feminist identities as adults rather than inherit them from parents. Consequently, a feminist identity is both formed by prior experiences and buffeted by competing communities. Socialist feminists in particular were influenced by the New Left; even after they separated from it, many still felt the need to articulate their allegiance to its basic propositions. Minority women more than White women have felt the pressures of competing loyalties because their ethnicity is fundamental to their identities. Rather than choose between their birth community, which is often hostile to feminism, and a more ephemeral ideological one, the feminists among them have sought to fashion an identity that melds ethnicity and gender (and sometimes class).

Accountability is a fundamental and ancient issue in democratic theory. The American colonists rejected virtual representation in the British Parliament in favor of direct representation in their own. It is hard enough for states or organizations to design effective strategies of accountability; for movements, which grow and develop without design or deliberation, it is a constant challenge. The Chicago Women's Liberation Union created an elaborate organizational structure for demanding accountability through constant self-reports and criticism—so elaborate that it limited the number of people who had time to participate. But even without organizations, movement communities can serve a similar purpose—for those who are in them. Those who are not in movement communities may still be (or be held) accountable in the sense that they incorporate into their thinking the values of the movement and act on them without prompting or concern. But when there are cross-pressures, internalization is a slim reed. Most people reflect and articulate the concerns of the institutions of which they are a part. To articulate feminist ideas in a nonfeminist institution without support from a feminist community is very difficult. It is community that nourishes accountability. When one asks oneself not merely what is the right (feminist) thing to do, but what will other feminists think; when one has to explain one's action to other feminists, even in only social situations, one is more likely to do the right (feminist) thing. Accountability is particularly important for those movement entities that institutionalize, but it is easiest for those that encapsulate. Yet encapsulation creates boundaries that often exclude the women who most need to be accountable. This is one of the paradoxes of movement success.

The need for accountability is created by the possibility of empowerment. Empowerment of women is one of the few ideas on which feminists have agreed virtually from the beginning. Yet empowerment for what? Some believe that merely getting women into positions of power is sufficient; they will do the right thing. Others think that empowering women to take control over their lives is the primary goal. Yet empowering women by itself is not feminism, as the activities of the antifeminists clearly indicate. Nor is empowering women just to serve their communities; service to others is a traditional female function but does not necessarily make things better for women as a group. Still, the movement creates the possibility of empowering all women, even those who are opposed to its goals and those who are not conscious of those goals as relevant to their lives. The goal of feminism is to empower women as a group, not just individual women. That requires accountability.

The chapters in this book represent seeds planted at different times and places and cultivated in different ways. Harvesting them together illuminates patterns and themes that might not be apparent if they were read alone. Yet these early fruits merely whet our appetite for more. Each chapter can and should grow into a book of its own. With a little encouragement, perhaps all will do so. A bigger feast is yet to come.

Bibliography, About the Contributors, and Index

Bibliography

"Abortion: Right, Left." *Economist*, 1989. August 5, pp. 29–30.

Abramovitz, Mimi. 1982. "The Conservative Program Is a Woman's Issue." *Journal of Sociology and Social Welfare* 9:399–424.

Abramson, Jill. 1992. "Women's Anger about Hill-Thomas Hearings Has Brought Cast into Female Political Causes." *Wall Street Journal*, January 6.

Abu-Lughod, Lila, and Catherine Lutz. 1990. "Introduction: Emotion, Discourse, and the Politics of Everyday Life." In *Language and the Politics of Emotion*, ed. Catherine Lutz and Lila Abu-Lughod. Cambridge: Cambridge University Press.

Acker, Joan. 1990. "Hierarchies, Jobs, Bodies: A Theory of Gendered Organizations." *Gender & Society* 4:139–58.

———. 1992. "Gendered Institutions, From Sex Roles to Gendered Institutions." *Contemporary Sociology* 21 (September): 565–69.

———. 1994. "The Gender Regime in Swedish Banks." *Scandinavian Journal of Management*.

Adamson, Nancy, Linda Briskin, and Margaret McPhail. 1988. *Feminist Organizing for Change: The Contemporary Women's Movement in Canada*. Toronto: Oxford University Press.

Addelson, Katherine Pyne. 1988. "Moral Revolution." *Radical America* 22 (5): 36–43.

Aguirre, B. E., E. L. Quarantelli, and J. L. Mendoza. 1988. "The Collective Behavior of Fads." *American Sociological Review* 53:569–84.

Ahrens, Lois. 1980. "Battered Women's Refuges: Feminist Cooperatives vs. Social Service Institutions." *Radical America* 14 (3): 41–47.

Albrecht, Lisa, and Rose Brewer. 1990. *Bridges of Power: Women's Multicultural Alliances*. Philadelphia: New Society Publishers.

Alcoff, Linda. 1988. "Cultural Feminism versus Post-Structuralism: The Identity Crisis in Feminist Theory." *Signs* 13:405–36.

Alford, Robert R., and Roger Friedland. 1985. *Powers of Theory: Capitalism, the State, and Democracy*. New York: Cambridge University Press.

Allemang, John. 1989. "*Ms*. Gives It a Miss." *Toronto Globe and Mail*. November 3, p. C11.

Alvarez, Sonia E. 1990. *Engendering Democracy in Brazil: Women's Movements in Transition Politics*. Princeton, N.J.: Princeton University Press.

Andler, Judy, and Gail Sullivan. 1980. "The Price of Government Funding." *Aegis* (Winter–Spring): 10–15.

Antrobus, Peggy. 1989. "The Empowerment of Women." In *The Women and Inter-*

national Development Annual, ed. Rita S. Gallin, Marilyn Aronoff, and Anne Ferguson, 1:189–207. Boulder, Colo.: Westview Press.

Anzaldua, Gloria. 1987. *Borderlands: La Frontera.* San Francisco: Spinsters/Aunt Lute.

———, ed. 1990. *Making Face, Making Soul, Haciendo Cara: Creative and Critical Perspectives by Women of Color.* San Francisco: Aunt Lute Foundation Books.

Arnold, Mea. 1989. "The Metamorphosis of the Center for Women Policy Studies: From 1987–1989." Unpublished case study, Women's Studies Program, George Washington University, Washington, D.C.

———. 1991. "An Examination of National Organization for Women's Chapter Development Programs: National vs. State." Unpublished case study, Women's Studies Program, George Washington University, Washington, D.C.

Arnold, Roxanne, and M. Seiler. 1984. "State Prison, a Birthday Gift They'd Like to Pass." *Los Angeles Times,* February 17, p. B1.

Arscott, Jane. 1993. "Between the Rock and a Hard Place: Women in the Legislatures of Newfoundland and Nova Scotia." Paper presented to the Canadian Political Science Association, Ottawa.

"Asking for It?" *Time,* 1981. May 4, p. 29.

Atkinson, Ti Grace. 1974. *Amazon Odyssey.* New York: Link Books.

Baker, Andrea J. 1986. "The Problem of Authority in Radical Movement Groups: A Case Study of Lesbian-Feminist Organization." In *Leaders and Followers: Challenges for the Future,* ed. L. A. Zurcher, 135–55. Greenwich, Conn.: JAI Press.

Ball, Donald. 1967. "An Abortion Clinic Ethnography." *Social Problems* 14 (Winter): 293–301.

Barnett, Bernice McNair. 1989. "Southern Black Women of the Civil Rights Movement: The Unsung Heroes and Leaders." Paper presented at the annual meetings of Sociologists for Women in Society, San Francisco.

———. 1990. "Sharecroppers, Domestics, and the Club From Nowhere: Poor and Working Class Women Organizing for Indigenous Collective Action." Paper presented at the annual meetings of the Southern Sociological Society, Louisville, Ky.

———. 1991. "Career Patterns of Black Women Civil Rights Lawyers: A Case of Triple Advantage or Triple Jeopardy?" Paper presented at the annual meetings of Sociologists for Women in Society, Cincinnati, Ohio.

———. 1992. "The Rise and Demise of Participatory Democratic Organizations among Black Women Leaders of the Civil Rights Movement." Paper presented at the Annual Meetings of the American Sociological Association, Pittsburgh, Pa.

———. 1993. "Invisible Southern Black Women Leaders in the Civil Rights Movement: The Triple Constraints of Gender, Race, and Class." *Gender & Society* 7:162–82.

Barnett, Carol. 1987. "A Case Study: Displaced Homemakers, Inc." Unpublished case study, Women's Study Program, George Washington University, Washington, D.C.

Barrett, Michèle. 1980. *Women's Oppression Today*. London: Verso.

Barrios de Chungara, Dominila. 1978. *Let Me Speak!* London: Monthly Review Press.

Barry, Kathleen A. 1983. "Feminist Theory: The Meaning of Women's Liberation." In *The Women's Annual: The Year in Review, 1982–83*, ed. B. Haber, 55–78. Boston: G. K. Hall.

Bart, Pauline. 1987. "Seizing the Means of Reproduction: An Illegal Feminist Abortion Collective—How and Why it Worked." *Qualitative Sociology* 10 (4): 339–57.

Bashevkin, Sylvia B. 1993. *Toeing the Lines: Women and Party Politics in English Canada*. 2d ed. Toronto: Oxford University Press.

Batchelder, Jennifer. 1990. "Center for Women Policy Studies: Its Adaptation to a Changing Political Climate." Unpublished case study: Women's Studies Program, George Washington University, Washington, D.C.

Bates, Daisy. 1962. *The Long Shadow of Little Rock: Memoir*. New York: David McKay.

Bawden, D. Lee, and John L. Palmer. 1984. "Social Policy: Challenging the Welfare State." In *The Reagan Record*, John L. Palmer and I. V. Sawhill, 177–216. Washington, D.C.: Urban Institute.

Baxter, Libby. 1987. "A Case Study: Coalition of Labor Union Women and Public Policy." Unpublished case study: Women's Studies Program, George Washington University, Washington, D.C.

Beck, E. T., ed. 1980. *Nice Jewish Girls: A Lesbian Anthology*. Watertown, Mass.: Persephone.

"Bells Are Ringing for Me and My Gal." 1992. *Advocate*, July 30, p. 85.

Benson, Susan Porter. 1978. "The Clerking Sisterhood: Rationalization and Work Culture of Saleswomen in American Department Stores, 1890–1960." *Radical America* 12:41–55.

Berkebile, Candy. 1992. "RU-486: A Prescription for Death." *Family Voice*, March, pp. 4–13.

Bernardin, Joseph L. 1976. "The Ordination of Women." *Commonweal* 103 (January 16).

Berry, Mary F. 1993. *The Politics of Parenthood: A History of Childcare and Women's Rights*. New York: Viking/Penguin.

Beyer, Janice M. 1981. "Ideologies, Values, and Decision Making in Organizations." In *Handbook of Organizational Design*, ed. P. C. Nystrom and W. H. Starbuck, 166–98. New York: Oxford University Press.

Black, Naomi. 1989. *Social Feminism*. Ithaca, N.Y.: Cornell University Press.

Blakely, Mary Kay. 1990. "Remembering Jane." *New York Times Magazine*, September 23.

Blanchard, M. 1992. "Speaking the Plural: The Example of *Women: A Journal of Liberation.*" *NWSA Journal* 4 (1): 84–97.

Blonien, Rodney J. 1986. "The Los Angeles Crown Coach Prison Site—A Superior Location." *Americas 2001*, March, p. 2.

Blum, Linda. 1991. *Between Feminism and Labor: The Politics of the Comparable Worth Movement.* Berkeley: University of California Press.

Blumberg, Rhoda, and Guida West. 1990. *Women and Social Protest.* New York: Oxford University Press.

Blumer, Herbert. 1969. "Collective Behavior." In *Principles of Sociology,* ed. Alfred McClung Lee. New York: Barnes & Noble.

Boles, Janet K. 1979. *The Politics of the Equal Rights Amendment.* New York: Longman.

———. 1982. "Building Support for the ERA: A Case of 'Too Much, Too Late.' " *PS* 15: 572–77.

———, ed. 1991a. *American Feminism: New Issues for a Mature Movement.* Special issue, *AAPSS Annals* 515 (May).

———. 1991b. "Form Follows Function: The Evolution of Feminist Strategies." *AAPSS Annals* 515 (May): 38–49.

Boneparth, Ellen, ed. 1982. *Women, Power, and Policy.* New York: Pergamon Press.

Boneparth, Ellen, and Emily Stoper, eds. 1988. *Women, Power, and Policy: Toward the Year 2000.* 2d ed. New York: Pergamon Press.

Bookman, Ann. 1977. "The Process of Political Socialization among Women and Immigrant Workers: A Case Study of Unionization in the Electronics Industry." Ph.D. diss., Harvard University.

Bookman, Ann, and Sandra Morgen, eds. 1988. *Women and the Politics of Empowerment.* Philadelphia: Temple University Press.

Booth, Heather, Day Creamer, Susan Davis, Deb Dobbin, Robin Kaufman, and Tobey Klass. 1972. *Socialist Feminism: A Strategy for the Women's Movement.* Chicago: Chicago Women's Liberation Union.

Boris, Eileen. 1991. "Women and the Welfare State." *The Nation* 252: 526–29.

Boston Women's Health Book Collective. 1984. *The New Our Bodies, Ourselves.* New York: Simon & Schuster.

Bourque, Susan C., and Jean Grossholtz. 1974. "Politics as an Unnatural Practice: Political Science Looks at Female Participation." *Politics and Society* 4 (2): 225–66.

Bowleg, Lisa. 1990. "In and Out of Africa: Feminist Transitions. A Case Study of the Overseas Education Fund/Women, Law, and Development Project." Unpublished case study: Women's Studies Program, George Washington University, Washington, D.C.

Bradley, Rita Mary. 1960. *The Mind of the Church in the Formation of Sisters.* New York: Fordham University Press.

Braun, Rachel. 1984. "Equal Opportunity and the Law in the U.S." In *Sex Discrimination and Equal Opportunity*, ed. G. Schmid and R. Wertzel, 92–106. New York: St. Martin's Press.

Braungart, Richard G., and Margaret M. Braungart. 1984. "Life Course and Generational Politics." *Journal of Political and Military Sociology* 12 (1): 1–8.

Breasted, Mary. 1972. "Move Over, 'Cosmo,' Here Comes 'Ms.'!" *Saturday Review*, July 15, p. 12.

Breines, Wini. 1989. *Community and Organization in the New Left: The Great Refusal*. Rev. ed. New Brunswick, N.J.: Rutgers University Press.

Briskin, Linda. 1991. "Feminist Practice: A New Approach to Evaluating Feminist Strategy." In *Women and Social Change: Feminist Activism in Canada*, ed. Jeri D. Wine and Janice L. Ristock, 24–40. Toronto: James Lorimer.

Briskin, Linda, and Lynda Yanz. 1983. *Union Sisters: Women in the Labour Movement*. Toronto: Women's Press.

Brodie, Janine M. 1985. *Women and Politics in Canada*. Toronto: McGraw-Hill Ryerson.

Brodie, Janine M., and Jill M. Vickers. 1982. *Canadian Women in Politics: An Overview*. CRIAW Papers/Documents de l'ICREF no. 2. Ottawa: Canadian Research Institute for the Advancement of Women (151 Slater St.).

Brown, Elsa Barkley. 1990. "Womanist Consciousness: Maggie Lena Walker and the Independent Order of Saint Luke." In *Black Women in America*, ed. M. R. Malson et al., 173–96. Chicago: University of Chicago Press.

Buechler, Steven M. 1990a. "Conceptualizing Radicalism and Transformation in Social Movements: The Case of the Woman Suffrage Movement." *Perspectives on Social Problems* 2:105–18.

———. 1990b. *Women's Movements in the United States: Women's Suffrage, Equal Rights, and Beyond*. New Brunswick, N.J.: Rutgers University Press.

Bunch, Charlotte. 1987. *Passionate Politics: Feminist Theory in Action*. New York: St. Martin's Press.

Burgess, Ann Wolbert. 1985. *Rape and Sexual Assault: A Research Handbook*. New York: Garland.

Burgess, Ann Wolbert, and Linda Lytle Holmstrom. 1974. *Rape: Victims of Crisis*. Bowie, Md.: Brady.

Burgos-Debray, Elizabeth. 1983. *I, Rigoberta Menchu, an Indian Woman in Guatemala*. New York: Verso.

Burks, Mary Fair. 1990. "Trailblazers: Women in the Montgomery Bus Boycott." In *Women in the Civil Rights Movement: Trailblazers and Torchbearers*, ed. Vickie Crawford, Jacqueline Rouse, and Barbara Woods, 71–84. New York: Carlson.

Burstein, Paul, Rachel Einwohner, and Jocelyn Hollander. 1991. "Political Movements and Their Consequences: Lessons from the U.S. Experience." Paper presented at the annual meetings of the American Sociological Association, Cincinnati, Ohio.

Burt, Martha R., Janet Gornick, and Karen J. Pittman. 1984. "Feminism and Rape Crisis Centers." *Sexual Coercion and Assault* 2:8–13.

Burt, Sandra. 1990. "Organized Women's Groups and the State." In *Policy Communities and Public Policy in Canada*, ed. William D. Coleman and Grace Skogstad, 191–211. Toronto: Copp Clark Pitman.

Byington, Diane B., Patricia Yancey Martin, Diana M. DiNitto, and Sharon Maxwell. 1991. "Organizational Affiliation and Effectiveness: The Case of Rape Crisis Centers." *Administration in Social Work* 15:83–103.

Cancian, Francesca. 1975. *What Are Norms?* London: Cambridge University Press.

Carden, Maren Lockwood. 1974. *The New Feminist Movement*. New York: Russell Sage Foundation.

———. 1977. *Feminism in the Mid-1970's: The Non-Establishment, the Establishment, and the Future*. Report to the Ford Foundation. New York: Ford Foundation.

Carroll, Berenice A. 1979. "Political Science, Part I: American Politics and Political Behavior." *Signs* 5:289–306.

———. 1980. "Political Science, Part II: International Politics, Comparative Politics, and Feminist Radicals." *Signs* 5:449–58.

Cassell, Joan. 1977. *A Group Called Women: Sisterhood and Symbolism in the Feminist Movement*. Prospect Heights, Ill.: Waveland Press.

Chafe, William H. 1972. *The American Woman: Her Changing Social, Economic, and Political Roles, 1920–70*. New York: Oxford University Press.

Chafetz, Janet Saltzman, and Anthony Gary Dworkin. 1986. *Female Revolt: Women's Movements in World and Historical Perspective*. Totowa, N.J.: Rowman & Allanheld.

———. 1987. "In the Face of Threat: Organized Antifeminism in Comparative Perspective." *Gender & Society* 1:33–60.

Cherniss, Cary. 1980. *Staff Burnout: Job Stress in the Human Services*. Beverly Hills, Calif.: Sage.

Chittister, Joan. 1977. *Climb along the Cutting Edge: An Analysis of Change in Religious Life*. New York: Paulist Press.

"Choosing a National Lesbian Conference Steering Committee." 1989. *NWSA Lesbian Caucus Newsletter*, September, pp. 3–4.

Chow, Esther Ngan-Ling. 1987. "The Development of Feminist Consciousness among Asian American Women." *Gender & Society* 1:284–300.

Christiansen-Ruffman, Linda. 1980. "Women as Persons in Atlantic Canadian Communities." *Resources for Feminist Research*, spec. pub. no. 8, pp. 55–57.

———. 1982. "Comment on Lawson and Barton's 'Sex Roles in Social Movements: A Case Study of the Tenant Movement in New York City.'" *Signs* 8:382–86.

———. 1983. "Women's Political Culture and Feminism in Canada." Unpublished paper.

———. 1985. "Participation Theory and the Methodological Construction of Invisible Women: Feminism's Call for Appropriate Methodology." *Journal of Voluntary Action Research* 14 (2–3): 94–111.

———. 1987. *Wealth Re-examined: Toward a Feminist Reanalysis of Women's Development Projects in Canada and in the Third World.* Women in International Development working paper no. 140. East Lansing: Michigan State University.

———. 1989. "Inherited Biases within Feminism: The 'Patricentric Syndrome' and the 'Either/or Syndrome' in Sociology." In *Feminism: From Pressure to Politics*, ed. Angela Miles and Geraldine Finn, 123–46. Montreal: Black Rose Books.

Christiansen-Ruffman, Linda, and Janis Wood Catano. 1986. "Resistance to Consumer Participation among Health Planners: A Case Study of BONDING's Encounters with Entrenched Ideas and Structures." *Resources for Feminist Research* 15 (March): 21–23.

Christrup, Judy, and Robert Schaeffer. 1990. "Not in Anyone's Backyard." *Greenpeace* 15 (January–February): 14–19.

Cilik, Jean. 1988. "Displaced Homemakers Network: Reclaiming Its Grassroots." Unpublished case study, Women's Studies Program, George Washington University, Washington, D.C.

Ciolli, Rita. 1985. "Grant for Women's Shelter Attacked." *Newsday*, June 14, p. 14.

Clark, Septima Poinsette. 1962. *Echo in My Soul*. New York: Dutton.

———. 1986. *Ready from Within: Septima Clark and the Civil Rights Movement.* Navarro, Calif.: Wild Tree.

Cleverdon, Catherine L. 1950. *The Woman Suffrage Movement in Canada.* Toronto: University of Toronto Press.

Clifton, Jenny. 1985. "Refuges and Self-Help." In *Marital Violence*, ed. Norman Johnson, 40–59. London: Routledge & Kegan Paul.

Cohen, Jean L. 1985. "Strategy or Identity: New Theoretical Paradigms and Contemporary Social Movements." *Social Research* 52:663–716.

Coleman, James. 1957. *Community Conflict*. New York: Free Press.

Collier, Jane F. 1974. "Women in Politics." In *Woman, Culture, and Society*, ed. M. Z. Rosaldo and Louise Lamphere, 89–96. Stanford, Calif.: Stanford University Press.

Collins, Patricia Hill. 1990. *Black Feminist Thought: Knowledge, Consciousness, and the Politics of Empowerment.* Boston: Unwin Hyman.

Condit, Celeste Michelle. 1990. *Decoding Abortion Rhetoric.* Urbana: University of Illinois Press.

Conover, Pamela Johnston, and Virginia Gray. 1983. *Feminism and the New Right: Conflict over the American Family.* New York: Praeger.

Coser, Lewis A. 1956. *The Functions of Social Conflict.* New York: Free Press.

Costain, Anne N. 1982. "Representing Women: The Transition from Social Movement to Interest Group." In *Women, Power, and Policy*, ed. Ellen Boneparth, 24–67. New York: Pergamon Press.

———. 1988. "Representing Women: The Transition from Social Movement to

Interest Group" (revised). In *Women, Power, and Policy: Toward the Year 2000*, 2d ed., ed. Ellen Boneparth and Emily Stoper, 26–47. New York: Pergamon Press.

———. 1992. *Inviting Women's Rebellion*. Baltimore, Md.: Johns Hopkins University Press.

Cott, Nancy F. 1987. *The Grounding of Modern Feminism*. New Haven, Conn.: Yale University Press.

Crawford, Vickie, Jacqueline Rouse, and Barbara Woods, eds. 1990. *Women in the Civil Rights Movement: Trailblazers and Torchbearers*. New York: Carlson.

CRIAW (Canadian Research Institute for the Advancement of Women). 1987. *Women's Involvement in Political Life: A Pilot Study*. CRIAW Papers/Documents de l'ICREF no. 16/7. Ottawa: Canadian Research Institute for the Advancement of Women (151 Slater St.).

Crim, Susan. 1987. "The Public Policy Process Cycle at the American Association of University Women." Unpublished case study, Women's Studies Program, George Washington University, Washington, D.C.

CWA (Concerned Women for America). N.d. *Come Help Save America*. Washington, D.C. Leaflet.

Czitrom, Daniel. 1982. *Media and the American Mind: From Morse to McLuhan*. Chapel Hill: University of North Carolina Press.

Davis, Angela. 1981. *Women, Race, and Class*. New York: Random House.

Davis, Flora. 1991. *Moving the Mountain: The Women's Movement in America since 1960*. New York: Simon & Schuster.

Davis, Nanette. 1988. "Shelters for Battered Women: Social Policy Response to Interpersonal Violence." *Social Science Journal* 25 (4): 401–19.

Deacon, Desley. 1989. *Managing Gender: The State, the New Middle Class, and Women Workers, 1830–1930*. Melbourne: Oxford University Press.

Deckard, Barbara. 1975. *The Women's Movement*. New York: Harper & Row.

———. 1979. *The Women's Movement: Political, Socio-economic, and Psychological Issues*. New York: Harper & Row.

Dekkers, Onka. 1972. "Periodicals." *off our backs*, September, p. 19.

Derrick, Anne S. 1992. "To Get Back to What We Were Saying." *Pandora* 7 (2): 8.

Detlefs, Malinda. 1984. "Abortion Counseling: A Description of the Current Status of the Occupation Reported by Seventeen Abortion Counselors in Metropolitan New York." Master's thesis, City University of New York.

"Developing a Revolutionary Women's Culture." 1972. *Women: A Journal of Women's Liberation* 3 (2): 2–5.

Dobash, R. Emerson, and Russell P. Dobash. 1992. *Women, Violence, and Social Change*. London: Routledge.

Dodson, Debra, ed. 1991. *Gender and Policy Making: Studies of Women in Office*. New Brunswick, N.J.: Rutgers Center for the American Woman and Politics.

Donati, Paolo R. 1984. "Organization between Movement and Institution." *Social Science Information* 23 (4–5): 837–59.

Donnelly, Elaine. 1991. "The Unsung Victims of Operation Desert Storm." *Concerned Women for America*, March, pp. 1–14.

Dougherty, Philip H. 1975. "*Ms.* Publisher Spreads the Word." *New York Times*, November 20, p. 71.

Douglas, Carol Anne. 1990. Review of *Daring to Be Bad*, by Alice Echols. *off our backs*, April, pp. 16–17.

Downey, Gary L. 1986. "Ideology and the Clamshell Identity: Organizational Dilemmas in the Anti-Nuclear Power Movement." *Social Problems* 33 (5): 357–73.

Dowse, Sara. 1988. "The Women's Movement Fandango with the State." In *Women, Social Welfare, and the State*, rev. ed., ed. Cora Baldock and Bettina Cass, 205–66. Sydney: Allen & Unwin.

Dugas-LeBlanc, Betty. 1986. "The Participation of Women in Political Life." Paper prepared for the Canadian Research Institute for the Advancement of Women.

Ebaugh, Helen Rose. 1977. *Out of the Cloister*. Austin: University of Texas Press.

Echols, Alice. 1989. *Daring to Be Bad: Radical Feminism in America, 1967–1975*. Minneapolis: University of Minnesota Press.

———. 1990. Response to Carol Anne Douglas, review of *Daring to Be Bad*, by Alice Echols. *off our backs*, July, p. 26.

Eder, Donna, Suzanne Staggenborg, and Lori Sudderth. Forthcoming. "The National Women's Music Festival, Collective Identity and Diversity in a Lesbian-Feminist Community." *Journal of Contemporary Ethnography*.

Eder, Klaus. 1985. "The 'New Social Movements': Moral Crusades, Political Pressure Groups, or Social Movements?" *Social Research* 52:869–90.

Edwards, O. C. 1900. "The Political Position of Canadian Women." In *Women of Canada: Their Life and Work*, 51–56. Montreal: National Council of Women of Canada.

Eichenbaum, Luise, and Susie Orbach. 1987. *Between Women: Love, Envy, and Competition in Women's Friendships*. New York: Penguin Books.

Eichler, Margrit. 1983. *Sexism in Research and Its Policy Implications*. CRIAW Papers/Documents de l'ICREF no. 6. Ottawa: Canadian Research Institute for the Advancement of Women.

Eisenstein, Hester. 1983. *Contemporary Feminist Thought*. Boston: G. K. Hall.

———. 1991a. *Gender Shock: Practising Feminism on Two Continents*. Boston: Beacon Press.

———. 1991b. "Speaking for Women: Voices from the Australian Femocrat Experiment." *Australian Feminist Studies* 14 (Summer): 29–42.

Eisenstein, Zillah. 1993. *The Radical Future of Liberal Feminism*. Rev. ed. Boston: Northeastern University Press.

Elshtain, Jean Bethke. 1981. *Public Man, Private Woman: Women in Social and Political Thought*. Princeton, N.J. Princeton University Press.

Epstein, Barbara. 1991. *Political Protest and Cultural Revolution: Nonviolent Direct Action in the 1970s and 1980s.* Berkeley: University of California Press.

Epstein, Cynthia Fuchs. 1988. *Deceptive Distinctions: Sex, Gender, and the Social Order.* New York: Russell Sage Foundation.

Erie, Steven P., Martin Rein, and Barbara Wiget. 1983. "Women and the Reagan Revolution: Thermidor for the Social Welfare Economy." In *Families, Politics, and Public Policy,* ed. Irene Diamond, 94–119. New York: Longman.

Etzioni, Amitai. 1988. *The Moral Dimension: Toward a New Economics.* New York: Free Press.

Evans, K. 1980. "A Feminist Perspective on Ethics of Communication Explored in the Context of an On-going Group of Women with Decision-Making Responsibility." Paper presented at the conference of the National Coalition Against Domestic Violence.

Evans, Sara. 1979. *Personal Politics: The Roots of Women's Liberation in the Civil Rights Movement and the New Left.* New York: Random House.

———. 1992. "The Women's Movement in the United States in the 1960s." In *Challenging Times: The Women's Movement in Canada and the United States,* ed. Constance Backhouse and David Flaherty, 61–71. Montreal: McGill-Queens University Press.

Evans, Sara, and Harry Boyte. 1986. *Free Spaces: The Sources of Democratic Change in America.* New York: Harper & Row.

"Everything You Wanted to Know about Advertising and Were Not Afraid to Ask—Personal Report from *Ms.*" 1974. *Ms.,* November, p. 58.

Fabrikant, Geraldine. 1987. "Turnaround Sought at *Ms.* Magazine." *New York Times,* May 9, p. 37.

Faludi, Susan. 1991. *Backlash: The Undeclared War against American Women.* New York: Crown.

Farrell, Amy. 1991. "Feminism in the Mass Media: Ms. Magazine, 1972–1989." Ph.D. diss., University of Minnesota.

Farris, Buford. 1988. "Neighborhood Social Action Organizations and the Issue of 'Double Closure.'" *Quarterly Journal of Ideology* 12 (4): 17–30.

Feit, Rona F. 1979. "Organizing for Political Power: The National Women's Political Caucus." In *Women Organizing,* ed. B. Cummings and V. Schuck, 184–208. Metuchen, N.J.: Scarecrow Press.

Felsenthal, Carol. 1981. *The Sweetheart of the Silent Majority: The Biography of Phyllis Schlafly.* New York: Doubleday.

"Feminist Forum." 1971. *Newsweek,* November 8, p. 104.

Ferguson, Kathy E. 1984. *The Feminist Case against Bureaucracy.* Philadelphia: Temple University Press.

Ferraro, Kathleen. 1981. "Processing Battered Women." *Journal of Family Issues* 2 (4): 415–38.

———. 1983. "Negotiating Trouble in a Battered Women's Shelter." *Urban Life* 12 (3): 287–306.

Ferraro, Barbara, and Patricia Hussey with Jane O'Neill. 1990. *No Turning Back: Two Nuns' Battle with the Vatican over Women's Right to Choose*. New York: Poseidon.

Ferree, Myra Marx. 1987. "Equality and Autonomy: Feminist Politics in the United States and West Germany." In *The Women's Movements of the United States and Western Europe*, ed. Mary Fainsod Katzenstein and Carol McClurg Mueller, 172–95. Philadelphia: Temple University Press.

———. 1991–92. "Institutionalizing Gender Equality: Feminist Politics and Equality Offices." *German Politics and Society* 24 (Winter): 53–67.

———. 1992. "The Political Context of Rationality: Rational Choice Theory and Resource Mobilization." In *Frontiers in Social Movement Theory*, ed. Aldon Morris and Carol McClurg Mueller, 29–52. New Haven, Conn.: Yale University Press.

Ferree, Myra Marx, and Beth B. Hess. 1985. *Controversy and Coalition: The New Feminist Movement*. Boston: Twayne.

———. 1994. *Controversy and Coalition: The New Feminist Movement through Three Decades*. Rev. ed. New York: Twayne.

Ferree, Myra Marx, and Frederick D. Miller. 1985. "Mobilization and Meaning: Toward an Integration of Social Psychological and Resource Perspectives on Social Movements." *Sociological Inquiry* 55:38–61.

Fitzgerald, Maureen, Connie Guberman, and Margie Wolfe, eds. 1982. *Still Ain't Satisfied! Canadian Feminism Today*. Toronto: Women's Press.

Flexner, E. 1959. *Century of Struggle: The Women's Rights Movement in the United States*. Cambridge, Mass.: Harvard University Press.

Foley, Mary Jo. 1987. "Overseas Education Fund's International Third World Forum on Women, Law, and Development." Unpublished case study, Women's Studies Program, George Washington University, Washington, D.C.

Fonow, Mary Margaret. 1993. "Occupation/Steelworker: Sex/Female." In *Feminist Frontiers III*, ed. Laurel Richardson and Verta Taylor, 217–22. New York: McGraw-Hill.

"For the Liberated Female." 1971. *Time*, December 20, p. 52.

Franzway, Suzanne, Dianne Court, and R. W. Connell. 1989. *Staking a Claim: Feminism, Bureaucracy, and the State*. Boston: Unwin Hyman.

Fraser, Arvonne S. 1983. "Insiders and Outsiders: Women in the Political Arena." In *Women in Washington: Advocates for Public Policy*, ed. Irene Tinker, 120–39. Beverly Hills, Calif.: Sage.

Fraser, Nancy. 1989. *Unruly Practices: Power, Discourse, and Gender in Contemporary Social Theory*. Minneapolis: University of Minnesota Press.

———. 1990. "Rethinking the Public Sphere: A Contribution to the Critique of Actually Existing Democracy." *Social Text* 8 (3) and 9 (1): 56–79.

Freeman, Jo. 1972. "The Tyranny of Structurelessness." *The Second Wave* 2 (1): 20. Rpt. in *Berkeley Journal of Sociology* 17 (1972–73): 151–64; *Radical Feminism*, ed. Anne Koedt, Ellen Levine, and Anita Rapone (New York: Quadrangle Books, 1973), 285; *Women in Politics*, ed. Jane Jaquette (New York: Wiley, 1974), 202–14. Rev. in *Ms.*, July 1973, p. 76.

———. 1973. "The Origins of the Women's Liberation Movement." *American Journal of Sociology* 78 (4): 792–811.

———. 1974. "The Feminist Scholar." Speech, Montclair, N.J. Published in *QUEST: A Feminist Quarterly* 5 (Summer 1979): 26–36.

———. 1975. *The Politics of Women's Liberation: A Case Study of an Emerging Social Movement and Its Relation to the Policy Process.* New York: David McKay.

———. 1979. "Resource Mobilization and Strategy: A Model for Analyzing Social Movement Actions." In *The Dynamics of Social Movements*, ed. Mayer N. Zald and John D. McCarthy, 167–89. Cambridge, Mass.: Winthrop. Rev. as "A Model for Analyzing the Strategic Options of Social Movement Organizations," in *Social Movements of the Sixties and Seventies*, ed. Jo Freeman (New York: Longman, 1983), 193–210.

———, ed. 1983. *Social Movements of the Sixties and Seventies.* New York: Longman.

———. 1987. "Whom You Know vs. Whom You Represent: Feminist Influence in the Democratic and Republican Parties." In *The Women's Movements of the United States and Western Europe: Feminist Consciousness, Political Opportunity, and Public Policy*, ed. Mary Fainsod Katzenstein and Carol McClurg Mueller, 215–44. Philadelphia: Temple University Press.

———. 1993. "Feminism vs. Family Values: Women at the 1992 Democratic and Republican Conventions." *off our backs*, January, pp. 2–3, 10–17. Abridged in *P.S.: Political Science and Politics* 26 (March 1993): 21–28.

———, ed. 1994. *Women: A Feminist Perspective.* 5th ed. Mountain View, Calif.: Mayfield. Original publication 1975.

Freudenberger, Herbert. 1975. "The Staff Burn-out Syndrome in Alternative Institutions." *Psychotherapy: Theory, Research, and Practice* 12 (1): 73–82.

Friedan, Betty. 1963. *The Feminine Mystique.* New York: Norton.

———. 1981. *The Second Stage.* New York: Summit Books.

Friedland, Roger, and A. F. Robertson. 1990. "Beyond the Marketplace." In *Beyond the Marketplace: Rethinking Economy and Society*, ed. Roger Friedland and A. F. Robertson, 3–49. New York: Aldine de Gruyter.

Friedman, Debra, and Doug McAdam. 1992. "Collective Identity and Activism: Networks, Choices, and the Life of a Social Movement." In *Frontiers in Social Movement Theory*, ed. Aldon Morris and Carol McClurg Mueller, 156–73. New Haven: Yale University Press.

Frost, Jennifer, and Margaret Strobel. 1993. "JOIN and the CWLU: Women's Organizing in Chicago, 1964–1977." Unpublished paper.

Gabin, N. F. 1990. *Feminism in the Labor Movement: Women and the United Auto Workers, 1935–1975.* Ithaca, N.Y.: Cornell University Press.

Gale, Richard P. 1986. "Social Movements and the State: The Environmental Movement, Counter-Movement, and Governmental Agencies." *Sociological Perspectives* 29 (April): 202–40.

Gamson, William A. 1990. *The Strategy of Social Protest.* Homewood, Ill.: Dorsey Press, 1975; 2d ed., Belmont, Calif.: Wadsworth.

———. 1992. *Talking Politics.* New York: Cambridge University Press.

Garcia, A. 1989. "The Development of Chicana Feminist Discourse, 1970–1980." *Gender and Society* 3 (2): 217–39.

Garner, Roberta, and Mayer N. Zald. 1983. "The Political Economy of Social Movement Sectors." Center for Research on Social Organization Working Paper no. 303, University of Michigan, Ann Arbor.

Gaventa, John. 1980. *Power and Powerlessness: Quiescence and Rebellion in an Appalachian Valley.* Urbana: University of Illinois Press.

Gelb, Joyce. 1989. *Feminism and Politics: A Comparative Perspective.* Berkeley: University of California Press.

———. 1990. "Feminism and Political Action." In *Challenging the Political Order,* ed. Russell J. Dalton and Manfred Kuechler, 137–55. New York: Oxford University Press.

———. 1993. "Organizational Change: Survival, Transformation and Decline among Feminist Groups in the 1990's." Paper presented at the American Political Science Association, Washington, D.C., September 2–6.

Gelb, Joyce, and Marion Lief Palley, eds. 1982. *Women and Public Policies.* Princeton, N.J.: Princeton University Press.

———, eds. 1987. *Women and Public Policies.* Rev. ed. Princeton, N.J.: Princeton University Press.

Gerson, Judith M., and Kathy Peiss. 1985. "Boundaries, Negotiations, Consciousness: Reconceptualizing Gender Relations." *Social Problems* 32: 317–31.

Giddings, Paula. 1984. *When and Where I Enter: The Impact of Black Women on Race and Sex in America.* New York: Harper & Row.

Gilkes, Cheryl Townsend. 1980. "Holding Back the Ocean with a Broom: Black Women and Community Work." In *The Black Woman,* ed. La Frances Rodgers-Rose, 217–32. Beverly Hills, Calif.: Sage.

———. 1982. "Successful Rebellious Professionals: The Black Woman's Professional Identity and Community." *Psychology of Women Quarterly* 6 (3): 289–311.

———. 1988. "Building in Many Places: Multiple Commitments and Ideologies in Black Women's Community Work." In *Women and the Politics of Empower-*

ment, ed. Ann Bookman and Sandra Morgen, 53–76. Philadelphia: Temple University Press.

Gilligan, Carol. 1982. *In a Different Voice*. Cambridge, Mass.: Harvard University Press.

Ginsburg, Faye D. 1989. *Contested Lives: The Abortion Debate in an American Community*. Berkeley: University of California Press.

Gire, Cynthia. 1990. "Institute for Women's Policy Research: A Feminist Organization?" Unpublished case study, Women's Studies Program, George Washington University, Washington, D.C.

Gitlin, Todd. 1980. *The Whole World Is Watching*. Berkeley: University of California Press.

———. 1987. *The Sixties: Years of Hope, Days of Rage*. New York: Bantam.

Giveu, Dawn. 1986. "Mainline Church Women 'Empowered' by Gathering." *National Catholic Reporter* 23 (October 24): 1.

Glennon, Lynda. 1979. *Women and Dualism*. New York: Longman.

Goldman, Ari L. 1992. "Catholics Are at Odds with Bishops," *New York Times*, June 19, p. A16.

Goodman, Ellen. 1990. "*Ms.* Is Back, as a 'Magabook.'" *Star Tribune* (Minneapolis), August 10, p. 14A.

Gordon, Linda. 1990. "The New Feminist Scholarship on the Welfare State." In *Women, the State, and Welfare*, ed. Linda Gordon, 9–35. Madison: University of Wisconsin Press.

Gornick, Janet, Martha R. Burt, and Karen J. Pittman. 1985. "Structure and Activities of Rape Crisis Centers in the Early 1980s." *Crime and Delinquency* 31:247–68.

Gorz, Andre. 1967. *Strategy for Labor: A Radical Proposal*. Boston: Beacon Press.

Gottfreid, Heidi, and Penny Weiss. 1992. "Diversity in Feminist Organizations: Bringing Practice Back In." Paper presented at conference, "Feminist Organizations: Harvest of the New Women's Movement," Washington, D.C., February 14–16.

Gould, Meredith. 1979. "When Women Create Organizations: The Ideological Imperatives of Feminism." In *The International Yearbook of Organizational Studies*, ed. D. Dunkerley and G. Salaman, 237–52. London: Routledge & Kegan Paul.

Granovetter, Mark. 1990. "The Old and the New Economic Sociology: A History and an Agenda." In *Beyond the Marketplace: Rethinking Economy and Society*, ed. Roger Friedland and A. F. Robertson, 89–112. New York: Aldine de Gruyter.

Gundelach, Peter. 1984. "Social Transformation and New Forms of Voluntary Associations." *Social Science Information* 23 (6): 1049–81.

Gusfield, Joseph R. 1981. "Social Movements and Social Change: Perspectives of Linearity and Fluidity." *Social Movements, Conflict, and Change* 4:317–39.

Habermas, Jürgen. 1984. *The Theory of Communicative Action*, vol. 1, *Reason and the Rationalization of Society*. Boston: Beacon Press.

———. 1987. *The Theory of Communicative Action*, vol. 2, *Lifeworld and System: A Critique of Functionalist Reason*. Boston: Beacon Press.

Hainisch, Carol. 1970. "The Personal is Political." In *Notes from the Second Year: Women's Liberation, Major Writings of the Radical Feminists*, ed. Shulamith Firestone and Anne Koedt, 76–78. New York: Radical Feminists.

Hairston, Julie. 1990. "Killing Kittens, Bombing Clinics." *Southern Exposure* 18(2): 14–18.

Haller, Mary. 1984. "Decline of a Social Movement Organization: The Women's Action Collective." Class paper, Ohio State University, December 5.

Hamilton, Mildred. 1988. "New Blood for *Ms.* Magazine." *San Francisco Examiner*, February 7, p. E1.

Hamilton, Sylvia. 1993. "The Women at the Well: African Baptist Women Organize." In *And Still We Rise: Feminist Political Mobilizing in Contemporary Canada*, ed. Linda McCarty, 189–203. Toronto: Women's Press.

Hansen, Karen V. 1986. "The Women's Unions and the Search for a Political Identity." *Socialist Review* 16 (2): 67–95.

Hansen, Susan. 1987. "Catholic Women Citing 'Sexist' Church Call for 'Much Patience.'" *National Catholic Reporter* 24 (November 13): 1.

Harding, Sandra. 1986. *The Science Question in Feminism*. Ithaca, N.Y.: Cornell University Press.

———. 1991. *Whose Science? Whose Knowledge? Thinking from Women's Lives*. Ithaca, N.Y.: Cornell University Press.

Hart, Vivien. 1992. "Feminism and Bureaucracy: The Minimum Wage Experiment in the District of Columbia." *Journal of American Studies* 26 (1): 1–22.

Hartsock, Nancy C. 1979. "Feminism, Power, and Change: A Theoretical Analysis." In *Women Organizing: An Anthology*, ed. B. Cummings and V. Schuck. Metuchen, N.J.: Scarecrow Press.

———. 1983. *Money, Sex, and Power: Toward a Feminist Historical Materialism*. New York: Longman.

Harvey, Mary R. 1985. *Exemplary Rape Crisis Programs: A Cross-Site Analysis and Case Studies*. National Center for the Prevention and Control of Rape. Washington, D.C.: U.S. Government Printing Office.

Hays, Charlotte. 1984. "Feminists Rip Sexism, Patriarchal Structures at Chitown Conference." *National Catholic Register* 59 (November 27): 1.

Hernes, Helga. 1988. "The Welfare State Citizenship of Scandinavian Women." In *The Political Interests of Gender: Developing Theory and Research with a Feminist Face*, ed. Kathleen Jones and Anna G. Jonasdottir, 187–213. London: Sage.

Hertel, Bradley R., and Michael Hughes. 1987. "Religious Affiliation, Attendance, and Support for 'Pro-Family' Issues in the United States." *Social Forces* 65 (March): 858–82.

Hewlett, Sylvia Ann. 1986. *A Lesser Life: The Myth of Women's Liberation in America*. New York: William Morrow.

Higginbotham, Evelyn Brooks. 1992. "African-American Women's History and the Metalanguage of Race." *Signs* 17:251–74.

Hill, Samuel S., and Dennis E. Owen. 1982. *The New Religious Political Right in America*. Nashville, Tenn.: Abingdon Press.

Himmelstein, Jerome, and James A. McRae, Jr. 1984. "Social Conservatism, New Republicans, and the 1980 Election." *Public Opinion Quarterly* 48 (Fall): 592–605.

Hirsch, Marianne, and Evelyn Fox Keller. 1990. *Conflict in Feminism*. New York: Routledge.

Hixson, William B., Jr. 1992. *Search for the American Right Wing*. Princeton, N.J.: Princeton University Press.

Hochschild, Arlie. 1979. "Emotion Work, Feeling Rules, and Social Structure." *American Journal of Sociology* 85 (3): 551–75.

———. 1983. *The Managed Heart: Commercialization of Human Feeling*. Berkeley: University of California Press.

———. 1990. "Ideology and Emotion Management: A Perspective and Path for Future Research." In *Research Agendas in the Sociology of Emotions*, ed. Theodore D. Kemper, 117–32. Albany: State University of New York Press.

Hole, Judith, and Ellen Levine. 1971. *Rebirth of Feminism*. New York: Quadrangle Books.

hooks, bell. 1981. *Ain't I a Woman: Black Women and Feminism*. Boston: South End Press.

———. 1984. *Feminist Theory: From Margin to Center*. Boston: South End Press.

———. 1990. *Yearning: Race, Gender, and Cultural Politics*. Boston: South End Press.

———. 1992. "Out of the Academy and into the Streets." *Ms.* 3 (July–August): 80–82.

———. 1993. *Sisters of the Yam: Black Women and Self-Recovery*. Boston: South End Press.

Hordosch, Sylvia. 1987. "Project on Equal Education Rights of the NOW Legal Defense and Education Fund: A Case Study." Unpublished case study, Women's Studies Program, George Washington University, Washington, D.C.

Hughes, Everett C. 1971. *The Sociological Eye*. Chicago: Aldine.

Hull, Gloria T., Patricia Bell Scott, and Barbara Smith, eds. 1982. *All the Women Are White, All the Blacks Are Men, But Some of Us Are Brave*. Old Westbury, N.Y.: Feminist Press.

Hunter, Allen. 1981. "In the Wings: New Right Ideology and Organization." *Radical America* 15:113–38.

Hutchens, Trudy. 1992. "NOW Members Attack Religion." *Family Voice*, March, pp. 26–27.

Hyde, Cheryl. 1991. "Did the New Right Radicalize the Women's Movement? A Study of Change in Feminist Social Movement Organizations, 1977–1987." Ph.D. diss., University of Michigan.

———. 1992. "The Ideational System of Social Movement Agencies." In *Human Services as Complex Organizations*, ed. Y. Hasenfeld, 121–44. Newbury Park, Calif.: Sage.

Inglehart, Ronald. 1977. *The Silent Revolution: Changing Values and Political Styles among Western Publics*. Princeton, N.J.: Princeton University Press.

Isserman, Maurice. 1989. "The Not-So-Dark and Bloody Ground: New Works on the 1960s." *American Historical Review* 94:990–1010.

Jack, Dana Crowley. 1991. *Silencing the Self: Women and Depression*. Cambridge, Mass.: Harvard University Press.

Jaggar, Alison. 1983. *Feminist Politics and Human Nature*. Totowa, N.J.: Rowman & Allanheld.

———. 1989. "Love and Knowledge: Emotion in Feminist Epistemology." In *Gender/Body/Knowledge: Feminist Reconstructions of Being and Knowing*, ed. A. Jaggar and S. Bordo. New Brunswick: Rutgers University Press.

Jaggar, Alison, and Paula Rothenberg, eds. 1984. *Feminist Frameworks: Alternative Theoretical Accounts of the Relations between Women and Men*. 2d ed. New York: McGraw-Hill.

Jenkins, J. Craig. 1983. "Resource Mobilization Theory and the Study of Social Movements." *Annual Review of Sociology* 9:527–53.

Jenkins, Kelly. 1990. "Serving Women of Color at the Displaced Homemakers Network: A Case Study." Unpublished case study, Women's Studies Program, George Washington University, Washington, D.C.

Jennings, M. Kent. 1990. "Women in Party Politics." In *Women, Politics, and Change*, ed. Louise A. Tilly and Patricia Gurin, 221–48. New York: Russell Sage Foundation.

Joffe, Carole. 1986. *The Regulation of Sexuality: Experiences of Family Planning Workers*. Philadelphia: Temple University Press.

Johnson, John M. 1981. "Program Enterprise and Official Cooptation in the Battered Women's Shelter Movement." *American Behavioral Scientist* 24 (6): 827–42.

Johnson-Odim, Cheryl. 1991. "Common Themes, Different Contexts, Third World Women and Feminism." In *Third World Women and the Politics of Feminism*, ed. Chandra Mohanty. Bloomington: Indiana University Press.

Johnston, Jill. 1973. *Lesbian Nation: The Feminist Solution*. New York: Simon & Schuster.

Jones, Jacqueline. 1985. *Labor of Love, Labor of Sorrow: Black Women, Work, and the Family from Slavery to the Present*. New York: Basic Books.

Jones, Kathleen B. 1990. "Citizenship in a Woman-Friendly Polity." *Signs* 15 (4): 781–812.

Joseph, Gloria, and Jill Lewis. 1981. *Common Differences: Conflicts in Black and White Feminist Perspectives.* Garden City, N.Y.: Doubleday.

Judis, John. 1992. "The Pressure Elite: Inside the Narrow World of Advocacy Group Politics." *American Prospect* 9:15–29.

Kaminer, Wendy. 1990. *A Fearful Freedom: Women's Flight from Equality.* Reading, Mass.: Addison-Wesley.

———. 1992. *I'm Dysfunctional, You're Dysfunctional.* Reading, Mass.: Addison-Wesley.

Kanuha, Valli. 1987. "Sexual Assault in Southeast Asian Communities: Issues in Intervention." *Response* 10:4–6.

Kaplan, Temma. 1982. "Female Consciousness and Collective Action: The Case of Barcelona, 1910–1918." *Signs* 7:545–66.

Katzenstein, Mary Fainsod. 1987. "Comparing the Feminist Movements of the United States and Western Europe: An Overview." In *The Women's Movements of the United States and Western Europe: Consciousness, Political Opportunity, and Public Policy,* ed. Mary Fainsod Katzenstein and Carol McClurg Mueller, 3–20. Philadelphia: Temple University Press.

———. 1990. "Feminism within American Institutions: Unobtrusive Mobilization in the 1980s." *Signs* 16:27–54.

Katzenstein, Mary Fainsod, and Carol McClurg Mueller, eds. 1987. *The Women's Movements of the United States and Western Europe: Consciousness, Political Opportunity, and Public Policy.* Philadelphia: Temple University Press.

Kealey, Linda, and Joan Sangster, eds. 1989. *Beyond the Vote: Canadian Women and Politics.* Toronto: University of Toronto Press.

Keller, Evelyn Fox. 1985. *Reflections on Gender and Science.* New Haven, Conn.: Yale University Press.

Kelley, Siok-Hian Tay. 1988. "Alhambra Heeds Protest against Parole Office Site." *Los Angeles Times,* September 4, p. 11.

Kellough, Gail D. 1992. "Pro-Choice Politics and Postmodernist Theory." In *Organizing Dissent: Contemporary Social Movements in Theory and Practice,* ed. William Carroll, 81–100. Toronto: Garamond Press.

Kemper, Theodore D. 1978. *A Social Interactional Theory of Emotions.* New York: Wiley.

———. 1981. "Social Constructionist and Positivist Approaches to the Sociology of Emotions." *American Journal of Sociology* 87 (2): 336–62.

———. 1990. "Themes and Variations in the Sociology of Emotions." In *Research Agendas in the Sociology of Emotions,* ed. Theodore D. Kemper, 3–23. Albany: State University of New York Press.

King, Deborah. 1988. "Multiple Jeopardy, Multiple Consciousness: The Context of a Black Feminist Ideology." *Signs* 14 (1): 42–72.

King, Martin Luther, Jr. 1958. *Stride towards Freedom: The Montgomery Story.* New York: Harper.

Kitschelt, Herbert P. 1986. "Political Opportunity Structures and Political Protest: Anti-Nuclear Movements in Four Democracies." *British Journal of Political Science* 16:57–85.

Klandermans, Bert. 1984. "Mobilization and Participation: Social-Psychological Expansions of Resource Mobilization Theory." *American Sociological Review* 49:583–600.

———. 1989. "Introduction: Social Movement Organizations and the Study of Social Movements." In *International Social Movement Research*, ed. Bert Klandermans, 2:1–17. Greenwich, Conn.: JAI Press.

Klandermans, Bert, and Sidney Tarrow. 1988. "Mobilization into Social Movements: Synthesizing European and American Approaches." In *From Structure to Action: Comparing Movement Participation across Cultures, International Social Movement Research*, ed. Bert Klandermans, Hanspeter Kriesi, and Sidney Tarrow, 1:1–38. Greenwich, Conn.: JAI Press.

Klatch, Rebecca. 1987. *Women of the New Right*. Philadelphia: Temple University Press.

Klein, Ethel. 1987. "The Diffusion of Consciousness in the United States and Western Europe." In *The Women's Movements of the United States and Western Europe*, ed. Mary Fainsod Katzenstein and Carol McClurg Mueller, 23–43. Philadelphia: Temple University Press.

Kome, Penney. 1985. *The Taking of Twenty-Eight: Women Challenge the Constitution*. Toronto: Women's Press.

Koss, Mary P., and Mary R. Harvey. 1991. *The Rape Victim: Clinical and Community Interventions*. 2d ed. Newbury Park, Calif.: Sage.

Kriesberg, Louis. 1973. *The Sociology of Social Conflict*. New York: Free Press.

LaGanga, Maria L. 1990. "Revised *Ms.* to Publish, but without Ads." *Los Angeles Times*, March 5, p. D7.

Lamphere, Louise. 1987. *From Working Daughters to Working Mothers: Immigrant Women in a New England Industrial Community*. Ithaca: Cornell University Press.

Langevin, Liane. 1977. *Missing Persons: Women in Canadian Federal Politics*. Ottawa: Advisory Council on the Status of Women.

Largen, Mary Ann. 1981. "Grassroots Centers and National Task Forces: A History of the Anti-Rape Movement." *Aegis*, Summer, pp. 46–52.

Lathrop, Jan. 1989. "The Demographic Dilemma: *Ms.* Sells Out." *Feminist Voices: A Madison Area News Journal* 2 (6): 13–15.

LeBon, Gustave. 1960. *The Crowd: A Study of the Popular Mind*. New York: Viking Press.

Leckey, Dolores. 1988. "Women in Society and Church: Measuring the Progress, Charting the Future." Keynote address to the Conference on Representatives of Diocesan Commissions on Women, Tampa, Fla.

Leidner, Robin. 1991. "Stretching the Boundaries of Liberalism: Democratic Innovation in a Feminist Organization." *Signs* 16:263–89.

———. 1993. "Constituency, Accountability, and Deliberation: Reshaping Democracy in the National Women's Studies Association." *NWSA Journal* 5 (Spring): 4–27.

"Letters." 1987. *Ms.*, May, p. 8.

Levine, Judith. 1992. *My Enemy, My Love: Man-Hating and Ambivalence in Women's Lives*. New York: Doubleday.

Levine, Suzanne Braun. 1987. "New Words, New Understanding." *Ms.*, February, p. 35.

Lipsitz, George. 1988. " 'This Ain't No Sideshow': Historians and Media Studies." *Critical Studies in Mass Communication* 5:147–61.

Lipsky, Michael. 1980. *Street-Level Bureaucracy: Dilemmas of the Individual in Public Services*. New York: Russell Sage Foundation.

Lo, Clarence Y. H. 1982. "Countermovements and Conservative Movements in the Contemporary U.S." *Annual Review of Sociology* 8:107–34.

———. 1992. "Communities of Challengers in Social Movement Theory." In *Frontiers in Social Movement Theory*, ed. Aldon Morris and Carol McClurg Mueller, 224–37. New Haven, Conn.: Yale University Press.

Lobel, Kerry, ed. 1986. *Naming the Violence: Speaking Out about Lesbian Battering*. Seattle, Wash.: Seal Feminist Press.

Lofland, John. 1982. "Crowd Joys." *Urban Life* 10:356–81.

———. 1985. *Protest: Studies of Collective Behavior and Social Movements*. New Brunswick, N.J.: Transaction Books.

———. 1989. "Consensus Movements." *Research in Social Movements, Conflict, and Change* 11:163–96.

Lorde, Audre. 1984. *Sister Outsider*. Trumansburg, N.Y.: Crossing Press.

Lugones, Maria C., and E. Spelman. 1983. "Have We Got a Theory for You! Feminist Theory, Cultural Imperialism, and the Demand for 'The Woman's Voice.' " *Women's Studies International Forum* 6 (6): 573–82.

Luker, Kristin. 1984. *Abortion and the Politics of Motherhood*. Berkeley: University of California Press.

Lum, Joan. 1988. "Battered Asian Women." *Rice*, March, pp. 50–52.

Lutz, Catherine. 1988. *Unnatural Emotions: Everyday Sentiments on a Micronesian Atoll and Their Challenges to Western Theory*. Chicago: University of Chicago Press.

Lutz, Catherine, and G. White. 1986. "The Anthropology of Emotions." *American Review of Anthropology* 15:405–36.

McAdam, Doug. 1982. *Political Process and the Development of Black Insurgency*. Chicago: University of Chicago Press.

———. 1988. *Freedom Summer*. New York: Oxford University Press.

————. 1989. "The Biographical Consequences of Activism." *American Sociological Review* 54 (October): 744–60.

McAdam, Doug, John D. McCarthy, and Mayer N. Zald. 1988. "Social Movements." In *Handbook of Sociology*, ed. N. J. Smelser, 567–80. Beverly Hills, Calif.: Sage.

McCarthy, Abigail. 1978. "Sanity & Sister Says." *Commonweal* 105 (December 24): 773–75.

McCarthy, John D. 1987. "Pro-Life and Pro-Choice Mobilization: Infrastructure Deficits and New Technologies." In *Social Movements in Organizational Society*, ed. Mayer N. Zald and John D. McCarthy, 49–66. New Brunswick, N.J.: Transaction Books.

McCarthy, John D., and Mark Wolfson. 1992. "Consensus Movements, Conflict Movements, and the Cooptation of Civic and State Infrastructures." In *Frontiers in Social Movement Theory*; ed. Aldon Morris and Carol McClurg Mueller, 273–97. New Haven, Conn.: Yale University Press.

McCarthy, John D., and Mayer N. Zald. 1973. *The Trend of Social Movements in America: Professionalization and Resource Mobilization*. Morristown, N.J.: General Learning Press.

————. 1977. "Resource Mobilization and Social Movements: A Partial Theory." *American Journal of Sociology* 82 (6): 1212–41.

McCormack, Thelma. 1975. "Toward a Nonsexist Perspective on Social and Political Change." In *Another Voice: Feminist Perspectives on Social Life and Social Science*, ed. Marcia Millman and Rosabeth Moss Kanter, 1–33. New York: Anchor Books.

McCracken, Ellen. 1993. *Decoding Women's Magazines: From Mademoiselle to Ms.* New York: St. Martin's Press.

McDonald, Sharon, and Robert McGarvey. 1988. "The Most Beautiful Women in L.A." *L.A. Style*, September, p. 245.

McGrath, Ellen, Gwendolyn Puryear Keita, Bonnie R. Strickland, and Nancy Felipe Russo. 1990. *Women and Depression*. Washington, D.C.: American Psychological Association.

McIntosh, Mary. 1978. "The State and the Oppression of Women." In *Feminism and Materialism*, ed. A. Kuhn and A. M. Wolpe, 254–89. London: Routledge & Kegan Paul.

MacKinnon, Catherine. 1982. "Feminism, Marxism, Method, and the State: Toward Feminist Jurisprudence." *Signs* 7:515–44.

————. 1983. "The Male Ideology of Privacy: A Feminist Perspective on the Right to Abortion." *Radical America* 17 (4): 23–35.

————. 1989. *Toward a Feminist Theory of the State*. Cambridge, Mass.: Harvard University Press.

Mackle, Nancy, Deanne Pernell, Jan Shirchild, Consuelo Baratta, and Gail Groves.

1982. "Dear Aegis: Letter from Santa Cruz Women against Rape." *Aegis* 35:28–30.

Maille, Chantal. 1990. *Primed for Power: Women in Canadian Politics*. Ottawa: Canadian Advisory Council for the Status of Women.

Mannheim, Karl. 1952. "The Problem of Generations." In *Essays on the Sociology of Knowledge*, ed. P. Kecskemeti, 276–332. London: Routledge & Kegan Paul.

Mansbridge, Jane J. 1973. "Time, Emotion, and Inequality: Three Problems of Participatory Groups." *Journal of Applied Behavioral Science* 9:351–68.

———. 1980. *Beyond Adversary Democracy*. New York: Basic Books; rpt. Chicago: University of Chicago Press, 1983.

———. 1982. "Fears of Conflict in Face-to-Face Democracies." In F. Lindenfeld and J. Rothschild-Whitt, eds., *Workplace Democracy and Social Change*. Boston: Porter Sargent Publishers.

———. 1986. *Why We Lost the ERA*. Chicago: University of Chicago Press.

———. 1990. *Beyond Self-Interest*. Chicago: University of Chicago Press.

———. 1993. "The Role of Discourse in the Feminist Movement." Paper presented at the annual meeting of the American Political Science Association, Washington, D.C.

Marc, David. 1984. *Demographic Vistas: Television in American Culture*. Philadelphia: University of Pennsylvania Press.

Marshall, Susan E. 1985. "Ladies against Women: Mobilization Dilemmas of Anti-feminist Movements." *Social Problems* 32 (April): 348–62.

———. 1989. "Keep Us on a Pedestal: Women against Feminism in Twentieth-Century America." In *Women: A Feminist Perspective*, 4th ed., ed. Jo Freeman, 567–80. Mountain View, Calif.: Mayfield.

———. 1991. "Who Speaks for American Women? The Future of Antifeminism." *AAPSS Annals* 515 (May): 50–62.

Martin, Biddy, and Chandra Mohanty. 1986. "Feminist Politics: What's Home Got to Do with It?" In *Feminist Studies/Critical Studies*, ed. T. de Lauretis, 191–212. Bloomington: Indiana University Press.

Martin, Patricia Yancey. 1987. "A Commentary on *The Feminist Case against Bureaucracy* by Kathy Ferguson." *Women's Studies International Forum* 10 (5): 543–48.

———. 1989. "The Moral Politics of Organizations: Reflections of an Unlikely Feminist." *Journal of Applied Behavioral Science* 25 (4): 451–70.

———. 1990a. "The Implications of Feminism for Organizations." Paper presented at the Eastern Sociological Society meetings, Boston, March.

———. 1990b. "Rethinking Feminist Organizations." *Gender & Society* 4:182–206.

———. 1993. "Rape Crisis Centers, Feminism, and the Politics of Rape Processing in the Community." Paper presented at the annual meeting of the American Sociological Association, Miami, Fla.

————. 1994. "The Local Politics of Rape Processing." Unpublished paper, Department of Sociology, Florida State University.

Martin, Patricia Yancey, Diana DiNitto, Diane Byington, and M. Sharon Maxwell. 1992. "Organizational and Community Transformation: The Case of a Rape Crisis Center." *Administration in Social Work* 16 (3–4): 123–45.

Martin, Patricia Yancey, Kenneth R. Wilson, and Caroline M. Dillman. 1991. "Southern-Style Gender: Trends in Relations between Men and Women." In *The South Moves into Its Future: Studies in the Analysis and Prediction of Social Change*, ed. J. S. Himes, 103–48. Tuscaloosa: University of Alabama Press.

Martin, Patty. 1989. "Case Study of the Women's Equity Action League." Unpublished case study, Women's Studies Program, George Washington University, Washington, D.C.

Mather, Anne. 1974. "A History of Feminist Periodicals." *Journalism History* 1 (3): 82–85.

Mathers, Debbie. 1992. "Pandora's Human Rights Inquiry: The Whole Story." *Pandora* 7 (2): 2–3.

Mathews, Donald G., and Jane S. DeHart. 1990. *Sex, Gender, and the Politics of ERA: A State and the Nation.* New York: Oxford University Press.

Maticka-Tyndale, Eleanor, and Janice Drakich. 1992. "Striking a Balance: Women Organizing for Change in the CSAA." In *Fragile Truths: Twenty-five Years of Sociology and Anthropology in Canada*, ed. William K. Carroll, Linda Christiansen-Ruffman, Raymond F. Currie, and Deborah Harrison, 43–55. Ottawa: Carleton University Press.

Matthews, Nancy A. 1989. "Surmounting a Legacy: The Expansion of Racial Diversity in a Local Anti-Rape Movement." *Gender & Society* 3 : 519–33.

————. 1994. *Confronting Rape: The Feminist Anti-Rape Movement and the State.* London: Routledge.

Megyery, Kathy, ed. 1991. *Women in Canadian Politics: Toward Equity in Representation.* Research Studies of the Royal Commission on Electoral Reform and Party Financing, vol. 6. Toronto: Dundurn Press for Supply and Services Canada.

Melosh, Barbara. 1982. *The Physician's Hand: Nurses and Nursing in the Twentieth Century.* Philadelphia: Temple University Press.

Melucci, Alberto. 1985. "The Symbolic Challenge of Contemporary Movements." *Social Research* 52 : 781–816.

————. 1989. *Nomads of the Present: Social Movements and Individual Needs in Contemporary Society.* Trans. J. Keane and P. Mier. Philadelphia: Temple University Press.

Meyer, Alan D. 1982. "How Ideologies Supplant Formal Structures and Shape Responses to Environments." *Journal of Management Studies* 19 : 45–61.

Meyer, David S., and Nancy Whittier. 1994. "Social Movement Spillover." *Social Problems* 41(2):277–98.

Michels, Robert. 1959. *Political Parties: A Sociological Study of the Oligarchical*

Tendencies of Modern Democracy. Trans. Eden Paul and Cedar Paul. 1915; rpt. New York: Dover.

Miles, Angela. 1981. "The Integrative Feminine Principle in North American Feminist Radicalism: Value Basis of a New Feminism." *Women's Studies International Quarterly* 4 (4): 481–95.

———. 1984. "Integrative Feminism." *Fireweed: A Feminist Quarterly,* Summer–Fall, pp. 55–81.

———. Forthcoming. *Integrative Feminisms: Building Global Visions, 1960s to 1990s.* New York: Routledge.

Miles, Angela, and Geraldine Finn, eds. 1989. *Feminism: From Pressure to Politics.* Montreal: Black Rose Books.

Milhaven, Annie Lally. 1987. *The Inside Stories: 13 Valiant Women Challenging the Church.* Mystic, Conn.: Twenty-Third Publications.

Miller, James. 1987. *"Democracy Is in the Streets": From Port Huron to the Seige of Chicago.* New York: Simon & Schuster.

Minkoff, Deborah. 1992. "Bending with the Wind: Organizational Change in American Women's and Minority Organizations." Paper presented at the meetings of the American Sociological Association, Pittsburgh, Pa.

Mirowsky, John, and Catherine E. Ross. 1989. *Social Causes of Distress.* New York: Aldine de Gruyter.

Moan, Frank S. J. 1978. "Growing Pains." *America* 139 (19): 433.

Monaghan, Brigid E. 1990. "Agonizing, It's Agonizing, I'm Agonized, Are Y'all? A Case Study of a Radical Organization Operating within the U.S. Policy Process." Unpublished case study, Women's Studies Program, George Washington University, Washington, D.C.

Moraga, Cherrie, and Gloria Anzaldua, eds. 1981. *This Bridge Called My Back: Writings by Radical Women of Color.* Watertown, Mass.: Persephone.

Moran, Barbara, and Karen Schwarz. 1987. "Living on the Edge: Women and Catholics." *Probe* 15 (3).

Morgan, Patricia. 1981. "From Battered Wife to Program Client: The State's Shaping of Social Problems." *Kapitalistate* 9:17–39.

Morgen, Sandra. 1983. "Towards a Politics of 'Feelings': Beyond the Dialectic of Thought and Action." *Women's Studies* 10:203–23.

———. 1986. "The Dynamics of Cooptation in a Feminist Health Clinic." *Social Science and Medicine* 23 (2): 201–10.

———. 1988. "The Dream of Diversity, the Dilemmas of Difference: Race and Class Contradictions in a Feminist Health Clinic." In *Anthropology for the Nineties,* ed. J. Sole. New York: Free Press.

———. 1990a. "Two Faces of the State: Women, Social Control and Empowerment." In *Uncertain Terms: Negotiating Gender in America,* ed. F. Ginsburg and A. Tsing. Boston: Beacon Press.

———. 1990b. "Contradictions in Feminist Practice: Individualism and Collectivism in a Feminist Health Center." *Comparative Social Research* Supplement 1:9–59.

Morgen, Sandra, and Alice Julier. 1991. "Women's Health Movement Organizations: Two Decades of Struggle and Change." Unpublished report.

Morris, Aldon. 1984. *The Origins of the Civil Rights Movement: Black Communities Organizing for Change.* New York: Free Press.

———. 1992. "Political Consciousness and Collective Action." In *Frontiers in Social Movement Theory,* ed. Aldon Morris and Carol McClurg Mueller, 351–73. New Haven, Conn.: Yale University Press.

Morris, Aldon, and Carol McClung Mueller, eds. 1992. *Frontiers in Social Movement Theory.* New Haven, Conn.: Yale University Press.

Mottl, Tahi L. 1980. "The Analysis of Countermovements." *Social Problems* 27 (June): 620–35.

Ms. Collection. Sophia Smith Archives, Smith College, Northampton, Mass.

Ms. Letters Collection. Schlesinger Library, Radcliffe College, Cambridge, Mass.

"*Ms.* Makes It." 1972. *Time,* December 25, p. 51.

Mueller, Carol McClurg. 1987. "Collective Consciousness, Identity Transformation, and the Rise of Women in Public Office in the United States." In *The Women's Movements in the United States and Western Europe: Consciousness, Political Opportunity, and Public Policy,* ed. Mary Fainsod Katzenstein and Carol McClurg Mueller, 89–108. Philadelphia: Temple University Press.

———, ed. 1988. *The Politics of the Gender Gap: The Social Construction of Political Influence.* Newbury Park, Calif.: Sage.

———. 1990. "Ella Baker and the Origins of Participatory Democracy." In *Women in the Civil Rights Movement: Trailblazers and Torchbearers,* ed. Vickie Crawford, Jacqueline Rouse, and Barbara Woods, 51–70. New York: Carlson.

———. 1992. "Building Social Movement Theory." In *Frontiers of Social Movement Theory,* ed. Aldon Morris and Carol McClurg Mueller, 3–25. New Haven, Conn.: Yale University Press.

———. 1993. "Factionalism and Cultural Innovation in Radical Feminism." Unpublished manuscript.

Mulligan, Ann. 1987. "Business and Professional Women's Foundation." Unpublished case study, Women's Studies Program, George Washington University, Washington, D.C.

Murray, Susan B. 1988. "The Unhappy Marriage of Theory and Practice: An Analysis of a Battered Women's Shelter." *National Women's Studies Association Journal* 1 (1): 75–92.

Myron, Nancy, and Charlotte Bunch. 1975. *Lesbianism and the Women's Movement.* Baltimore, Md.: Diana Press.

Nadel, Laura. 1991. "Interviews and Organizational Data Collected from the National Council of Jewish Women." Unpublished case study, Women's Studies Program, George Washington University, Washington, D.C.

Neal, Marie Augusta. 1990. *From Nuns to Sisters: An Expanding Vocation.* Mystic, Conn.: Twenty-Third Publications.

Neis, Barbara. 1988. "Doin' Time on the Protest Line: Women's Political Culture, Politics, and Collective Action in Outport Newfoundland." In *A Question of Survival: The Fisheries and Newfoundland Society,* ed. Peter R. Sinclair, 133–53. Saint John's: ISER (Institute for Social and Economic Research).

Newman, Kathleen. 1980. "Incipient Bureaucracy: The Development of Hierarchies in Egalitarian Organizations." In *Hierarchy and Society: Anthropological Perspectives on Bureaucracy,* ed. G. Britain and A. Cohen. Philadelphia: Institute for the Study of Social Issues.

New York Radical Feminists. 1974. *Rape: The First Sourcebook for Women.* Ed. Noreen Connell and Cassandra Wilson. New York: Plume/New American Library.

Ng, Roxana. 1988. *The Politics of Community Services, Immigrant Women, Class, and State.* Toronto: Garamond Press.

Ng, Roxana, Gillian Walker, and Jacob Muller, eds. 1990. *Community Organization and the Canadian State.* Toronto: Garamond Press.

Noble, Barbara Presley. 1992. "Economics As If Women Mattered." *New York Times* December 13, p. F25.

Oberschall, Anthony. 1973. *Social Conflict and Social Movements.* Englewood Cliffs, N.J.: Prentice-Hall.

Offe, Claus. 1985. "New Social Movements: Challenging the Boundaries of Institutional Politics." *Social Research* 52:817–68.

Okin, Susan M. 1979. *Women in Western Political Thought.* Princeton, N.J.: Princeton University Press.

Olson, Mancur. 1965. *The Logic of Collective Action.* Cambridge, Mass.: Harvard University Press.

"One in Christ Jesus: A Pastoral Response to the Concerns of Women for Church and Society." 1990. *Origins* 19 (4): 717–40.

"On the Bias." 1986. *Affilia: Journal of Women and Social Work* 1 (2): 53–56.

O'Reilly, Jane. 1972. "The Housewife's Moment of Truth." *Ms.,* Spring, pp. 54–59.

———. 1980. *The Girl I Left behind Me.* New York: Macmillan.

Paige, Connie. 1983. *The Right to Lifers: Who They Are, How They Operate, Where They Get Their Money.* New York: Summit Books.

———. 1987. "The Amazing Rise of Beverly LaHaye." *Ms.,* February, pp. 24–28.

Papa, Mary. 1978. "Women Mix Social Change, Ordinational Aims." *National Catholic Reporter* 15 (November 24): 1.

Payne, Charles. 1990. "Men Led, But Women Organized: Movement Participation of Women in the Mississippi Delta." In *Women in the Civil Rights Movement: Trailblazers and Torchbearers,* ed. Vickie Crawford, Jaqueline Rouse, and Barbara Woods, 1–12. New York: Carlson.

Pennell, Joan. 1987. "Ideology at a Canadian Shelter for Battered Women: A Reconstruction." *Women's Studies International Forum* 10 (2): 113–23.

Perrow, Charles. 1986. *Complex Organizations: A Critical Essay.* 3d ed. New York: McGraw-Hill.

"Personal Report from *Ms.*" 1972. *Ms.*, July, p. 7.

"Personal Report from *Ms.*: Everything You Have Always Wanted to Know About Advertising—and Haven't Been Afraid to Ask." 1974. *Ms.* November, p. 56.

"Personal Report: Reader Alert." 1978. *Ms.*, July.

"Personal Report: What Is a New *Ms.*?" 1979. *Ms.* November, pp. 4–13.

Petchesky, Rosalind Pollack. 1982. "Antiabortion, Antifeminism, and the Rise of the New Right." *Feminist Studies* 7: 206–46.

———. 1987. "Fetal Images: The Power of Visual Culture in the Politics of Reproduction." *Feminist Studies* 13 (Summer): 263–92.

Phyllis Schlafly Report. 1984. "New Weapons in the Battle against Pornography." June.

———. 1989a. "The Feminization of the U.S. Military." September.

———. 1989b. "The Teaching of Values in the Public Schools." October.

———. 1989c. "Insights into Feminist Ideology." December.

———. 1990. "Time to Tell the Feminists Bye-Bye." December.

———. 1991a. "Sending Mothers to the Gulf War!" March.

———. 1991b. "What's Wrong with Women in Combat." June.

———. 1991c. "Feminist Falsehoods, Follies, and Funding." July.

———. 1991d. "NEA Disrespect for Home and Parents." August.

———. 1991e. "Feminism Falls on Its Face." November.

———. 1991f. "The Radical Goals of the Feminists." December.

———. 1992. "Feminist Goals vs. Fairness and Truth." April.

Piven, Frances Fox, and Richard A. Cloward. 1977. *Poor People's Movements.* New York: Pantheon.

———. 1992. "Normalizing Collective Protest." In *Frontiers in Social Movement Theory,* ed. Aldon Morris and Carol McClurg Mueller, 301–25. New Haven, Conn.: Yale University Press.

Pizzorno, Alessandro. 1978. "Political Science and Collective Identity in Industrial Conflict." In *The Resurgence of Class Conflict in Western Europe since 1968,* ed. C. Crouch and Alessandro Pizzorno, 277–98. New York: Holmes & Meier.

Popkin, Ann Hunter. 1978. "Bread and Roses: An Early Moment in the Development of Socialist-Feminism." Ph.D. diss., Brandeis University.

———. 1979. "The Personal Is Political: The Women's Liberation Movement." In *They Should Have Served That Cup of Coffee,* ed. Dick Cluster, 181–222. Boston: South End Press.

Porter, Marilyn. 1985. "The Tangly Bunch: The Political Culture of Newfoundland Women." *Newfoundland Studies* 1 (1): 77–91.

Powell, Walter W. 1991. "Expanding the Scope of Institutional Analysis." In *The New Institutionalism in Organizational Analysis*, ed. W. W. Powell and P. J. DiMaggio. Chicago: University of Chicago Press.

Pringle, Rosemary, and Sophie Watson. 1990. "Fathers, Brothers, Mates: The Fraternal State in Australia." In *Playing the State: Australian Feminist Interventions*, ed. Sophie Watson, 229–43. London: Verso.

Quinn, Liz. 1986. "Pay Equity and Workers of Color: A Case Study of the National Committee on Pay Equity and Its Coalition Building." Unpublished case study, Women's Studies Program, George Washington University, Washington, D.C.

Quinney, Valerie. 1990. "Hera: A Woman's Cooperative Art Gallery." Paper presented at the Berkshire Conference on Women's History, Rutgers University, New Brunswick, N.J.

Quinonez, Lora Ann, and Mary Daniel Turner. 1992. *The Transformation of American Catholic Sisters*. Philadelphia: Temple University Press.

Radicalesbians. 1973. "The Woman Identified Woman." In *Radical Feminism*, ed. Anne Koedt, Ellen Levine, and Anita Rapone, 240–45. New York: Quadrangle.

Randall, Vicky. 1982. *Women and Politics*. London: Macmillan.

———. 1987. *Women and Politics: An International Perspective*. Chicago: University of Chicago Press.

Rawls, John. 1993. *Political Liberalism*. New York: Columbia University Press.

Razack, Sherene. 1991. *Canadian Feminism and the Law: The Women's Legal Education and Action Fund and the Pursuit of Equality*. Toronto: Second Story Press.

Redstockings. 1975. "Redstockings Challenge." *off our backs*, July, p. 32.

Reilly, Patrick M. 1989. "*Ms*. to Be Published without Ads in Attempt to Save the Magazine." *Wall Street Journal*, October 13, p. B3.

Reiner, Renee. 1988. "National Coalition Against Domestic Violence: The Complicated Issue of Funding." Unpublished case study: Women's Studies Program, George Washington University, Washington, D.C.

Remington, Judy. 1990. "Running with the Brakes On." Paper presented at the meeting of the National Network of Women's Funds, Boston.

———. 1991. *The Need to Thrive: Women's Organizations in the Twin Cities*. St. Paul: Minnesota Women's Press.

Ridington, Jillian. 1977–78. "The Transition Process: A Feminist Environment as Reconstitutive Milieu." *Victimology: An International Journal* 2 (3–4): 563–75.

Riger, Stephanie. 1984. "Vehicles for Empowerment: The Case of Feminist Movement Organizations." In *Studies in Empowerment: Steps toward Understanding and Action*, ed. J. Rappaport, C. Smith, and R. Hess, 99–117. New York: Haworth Press.

———. 1994. "Challenges of Success: Stages of Growth in Feminist Organizations." *Feminist Studies* 20 (1).

Rimonte, Nilda. N.d. "Pacific Asian Survivors." *Los Angeles County Protocol on Rape*.

Ristock, Janice. 1990. "Canadian Feminist Social Service Collectives: Caring and Contradictions." In *Bridges of Power*, ed. Lisa Albrecht and Rose Brewer, 172–81. Philadelphia: New Society.

Roberts, Barbara. 1988. *Smooth Sailing or Storm Warning? Canadian and Quebec Women's Groups and the Meech Lake Accord*. Ottawa: Canadian Research Institute for the Advancement of Women (CRIAW, 151 Slater St.).

Robinson, JoAnn Gibson. 1987. *The Montgomery Bus Boycott and the Women Who Started It*. Knoxville: University of Tennessee Press.

Rodriguez, Noelie M. 1988. "Transcending Bureaucracy: Feminist Politics at a Shelter for Battered Women." *Gender & Society* 2:214–27.

Rothman, Barbara Katz. 1986. *The Tentative Pregnancy: Prenatal Diagnosis and the Future of Motherhood*. New York: Viking.

———. 1989. *Recreating Motherhood: Ideology and Technology in a Patriarchal Society*. New York: Norton.

Rothschild, Mathew. 1989. "Third Party Time?" *The Progressive* 53 (10): 20–25.

Rothschild-Whitt, Joyce. 1976. "Conditions Facilitating Participatory Democratic Organizations." *Sociological Inquiry* 46:75–86.

———. 1979. "The Collectivist Organization: An Alternative to Rational-Bureaucratic Models." *American Sociological Review* 44 (August): 509–27.

———. 1982. "The Collectivist Organization: An Alternative to Bureaucratic Models." In *Workplace Democracy and Social Change*, ed. F. Lindenfeld and Joyce Rothschild-Whitt. Boston: Porter Sargent.

Rothschild-Whitt, Joyce, and J. A. Whitt. 1986. *The Cooperative Workplace*. Cambridge: Cambridge University Press.

Rothstein, Vivian, and Naomi Weisstein. 1972. "Chicago Women's Liberation Union." *Women: A Journal of Liberation* 2 (4): 2–9.

Ruby, Jennie, and Carol A. Douglas. 1992. "NWSA: Working to Survive." *off our backs*, August–September, pp. 1–15.

Rucht, Dieter. 1988. "Themes, Logics and Arenas of Social Movements: A Structural Approach." In *International Social Movement Research*, ed. Bert Klandermans, Hanspeter Kriesi, and Sidney Tarrow, 1:305–29. Greenwich, Conn.: JAI Press.

Ruddick, Sara. 1989. *Maternal Thinking: Toward a Politics of Peace*. New York: Ballantine Books.

Ruether, Rosemary Radford. 1986. *Women-Church: Theology and Practice*. San Francisco: Harper & Row.

Rupp, Leila J. 1980. "'Imagine My Surprise': Women's Relationships in Historical Perspective." *Frontiers* 5:61–70.

Rupp, Leila J., and Verta Taylor. 1987. *Survival in the Doldrums: The American Women's Rights Movement, 1945 to the 1960s*. New York: Oxford University Press.

Rusher, William A. 1984. *The Rise of the Right*. New York: William Morrow.

Russ, Joanna. 1985. *Magic Mommas, Trembling Sisters, Puritans, and Perverts: Feminist Essays.* Trumansburg, N.Y.: Crossing Press.

Russell, Dick. 1989. "The Air We Breathe: Viva Las Madres!" *Parenting,* November, pp. 127–28.

Ruzek, Sheryl. 1978. *The Women's Health Movement.* New York: Praeger.

Ryan, Barbara. 1989. "Ideological Purity and Feminism: The U.S. Women's Movement from 1966 to 1975." *Gender & Society* 3:239–57.

——. 1992. *Feminism and the Women's Movement.* New York: Routledge.

Ryan, William. 1976. *Blaming the Victim.* Rev. ed. New York: Random House.

Sachs, Karen. 1988a. *Caring by the Hour: Women, Work, and Organizing at Duke Medical Center.* Urbana: University of Illinois Press.

——. 1988b. "Gender and Grassroots Leadership." In *Women and the Politics of Empowerment,* ed. Ann Bookman and Sandra Morgen, 77–94. Philadelphia: Temple University Press.

Saldivar-Hull, Sonia. 1991. "Feminism on the Border: From Gender Politics to Geopolitics." In *Criticism in the Borderlands: Studies in Chicano Literature, Culture, and Ideology,* ed. Hector Calderon and Jose Saldivar. Durham, N.C.: Duke University Press.

Sandoval, Chela. 1990. "Feminism and Racism: A Report on the 1981 National Women's Studies Association Conference." In *Making Face, Making Soul, Haciendo Caras,* ed. Gloria Anzaldua, 55–71. San Francisco: Aunt Lute Foundation Books.

Sapiro, Virginia. 1987. "What Research on the Political Socialization of Women Can Tell Us about the Political Socialization of People." In *The Impact of Feminist Research in the Academy,* ed. C. Farnham. Bloomington: Indiana University Press.

——. 1991. "The Gender Gap and Women's Political Influence." *AAPSS Annals* 515 (May): 23–37.

Satake, Kazue. 1990. "Case Study of the National Committee on Pay Equity." Unpublished case study: Women's Studies Program, George Washington University, Washington, D.C.

Sawer, Marian. 1990. *Sisters in Suits: Women and Public Policy in Australia.* Sydney: Allen & Unwin.

Schechter, Susan. 1981. "Speaking to the Battered Women's Movement." *Aegis* 32:41–45.

——. 1982. *Women and Male Violence: The Visions and Struggles of the Battered Women's Movement.* Boston: South End Press.

Scheff, Thomas J. 1990. *Microsociology: Discourse, Emotion, and Social Structure.* Chicago: University of Chicago Press.

Schlafly, Phyllis. 1977. *The Power of the Positive Woman.* New Rochelle, N.Y.: Arlington House.

Schlesinger, Melinda Bart, and Pauline B. Bart. 1983. "Collective Work and Self-

Identity: The Effect of Working in a Feminist Illegal Abortion Clinic." In *Feminist Frontiers: Rethinking Sex, Gender, and Society*, ed. Laurel Richardson and Verta Taylor, 337–44. Reading, Mass.: Addison-Wesley.

Schlozman, Kay Lehman. 1990. "Representing Women in Washington: Sisterhood and Pressure Politics." In *Women, Politics, and Change*, ed. Louise A. Tilly and Patricia Gurin, 339–82. New York: Russell Sage Foundation.

Schmitt, Fredericka. 1994. "Seeking Justice: A Local Center's National Campaign to Eradicate Campus Rape." Master's thesis, Department of Sociology, University of Delaware.

Schneider, Beth. 1988. "Political Generations in the Contemporary Women's Movement." *Sociological Inquiry* 58:4–21.

Schreader, Alicia. 1990. "The State Funded Women's Movement: A Case of Two Political Agendas." In *Community Organizing and the Canadian State*, ed. Roxanna Ng, Gillian Walker, and Jacob Muller. Toronto: Garamond Press.

Schreiber, Ronnee. 1986. "Case Study: National Coalition Against Domestic Violence." Unpublished case study: Women's Studies Program, George Washington University, Washington, D.C.

Schumaker, Paul. 1975. "Policy Responsiveness to Protest Group Demands." *Journal of Politics* 37:488–521.

Schwartz, Michael, and Shuva Paul. 1992. "Resource Mobilization versus the Mobilization of People." In *Frontiers in Social Movement Theory*, ed. Aldon Morris and Carol McClurg Mueller, 205–23. New Haven, Conn.: Yale University Press.

Scott, Charlene. 1988. "Bishops' Draft of Pastoral on Women Stirs Reaction." *National Catholic Reporter*, November 25, p. 33.

Scott, James. 1985. *Weapons of the Weak: Everyday Forms of Peasant Resistance*. New Haven: Yale University Press.

Sealander, J., and D. Smith. 1986. "The Rise and Fall of Feminist Organizations in the 1970's: Dayton as a Case Study." *Feminist Studies* 12:321–42.

Sekulow, Jay. 1991. "A Sense of Urgency Unites CWA and CASE Legal Teams." *Concerned Women for America*, March, p. 5.

Shuit, Douglas, and Jerry Gilam. 1986. "Governor Meets Top Lawmakers on Prison Issue." *Los Angeles Times*, September 3, p. 13.

Sievers, Sharon L. 1981. "Feminist Criticism in Japanese Politics in the 1880's: The Experience of Kishida Toshiko." *Signs* 6:602–16.

Sigelman, Lee, Clyde Wilcox, and Emmett H. Buell, Jr. 1987. "An Unchanging Minority: Popular Support for the Moral Majority, 1980 and 1984." *Social Science Quarterly* 68 (December): 876–84.

Simmons, Ruth, Bonnie Kay, and Carol Reagan. 1984. "Women's Health Groups: Alternatives to the Health Care System." *International Journal of Health and Services* 14 (4): 619–34.

Simon, Barbara Levy. 1982. "In Defense of Institutionalization: A Rape Crisis Center as a Case Study." *Journal of Sociology and Social Welfare* 9:485–502.

Simonds, Wendy. 1991. "At an Impasse: Inside an Abortion Clinic." *Current Research on Occupations and Professions* 6:99–115.

———. 1992. *Women and Self-Help Culture: Reading between the Lines.* New Brunswick, N.J.: Rutgers University Press.

Sirianni, Carmen. 1993. "Learning Pluralism: Democracy and Diversity in Feminist Organizations." In *Democratic Community: NOMOS XXXV,* ed. John Chapman and Ian Shapiro, 283–312. New York: New York University Press.

Smelser, Neil. 1962. *Theory of Collective Behavior.* New York: Free Press.

Smith, Barbara, ed. 1983. *Home Girls: A Black Feminist Anthology.* New York: Kitchen Table Press.

Smith, Dorothy E. 1974. "Women's Perspective as a Radical Critique of Sociology." *Sociological Inquiry* 44 (1): 7–13.

———. 1979. "A Sociology for Women." In *The Prism of Sex: Essays in the Sociology of Knowledge,* ed. Julia Sherman and Evelyn Beck, 135–87. Madison: University of Wisconsin Press.

———. 1987. *The Everyday World as Problematic: A Feminist Sociology.* Boston: Northeastern University Press.

Snow, David A., and Robert D. Benford. 1992. "Master Frames and Cycles of Protest." In *Frontiers in Social Movement Theory,* ed. Aldon D. Morris and Carol McClurg Mueller, 133–55. New Haven, Conn.: Yale University Press.

Snow, David A., E. Burke Rochford, Jr., Steven K. Worden, and Robert D. Benford. 1986. "Frame Alignment Processes, Micromobilization, and Movement Participation." *American Sociological Review* 52 (August): 464–81.

Snyder, David, and William R. Kelly. 1979. "Strategies for Investigating Violence and Social Change." In *The Dynamics of Social Movements,* ed. Mayer N. Zald and John D. McCarthy, 212–37. Cambridge, Mass.: Winthrop.

Solomon, Alisa. 1991. "From C-R to PR: Feminist Theatre in America." In *Contemporary American Theatre,* ed. Bruce King, 227–42. New York: St. Martin's Press.

Sonosky, Colleen. 1988. "National Association of Commissions for Women." Unpublished case study, Women's Studies Program, George Washington University, Washington, D.C.

Sottile, Stephanie. 1985. "The Center for Women Policy Studies: A Story of Survival as Success." Unpublished case study, Women's Studies Program, George Washington University, Washington, D.C.

Spalter-Roth, Roberta M., and Heidi I. Hartmann. 1990. "Science and Politics: The Dual Vision of Feminist Policy Analysis; The Case of Family and Medical Leave." In *Parental Leave and Child Care: Setting a Policy and Research Agenda,* ed. J. S. Hyde and M. Essex, 41–65. Philadelphia: Temple University Press.

Spelman, Elizabeth. 1988. *Inessential Woman: Problems of Exclusion in Feminist Thought.* Boston: Beacon Press.

Stacey, Judith. 1983. "The New Conservative Feminism." *Feminist Studies* 9 (Fall): 559–83.

————. 1990. *Brave New Families: Stories of Domestic Upheaval in Late Twentieth Century America.* New York: Basic Books.

Stacey, Margaret, and Marion Price. 1981. *Women, Power, and Politics.* London: Tavistock.

Staggenborg, Suzanne. 1986. "Coalition Work in the Pro-Choice Movement: Organizational and Environmental Opportunities and Obstacles." *Social Problems* 33 (5): 374–90.

————. 1987. "Life-Style Preferences and Social Movement Recruitment: Illustrations from the Abortion Conflict." *Social Science Quarterly* 68:779–97.

————. 1988. "The Consequences of Professionalization and Formalization in the Pro-Choice Movement." *American Sociological Review* 53:585–606.

————. 1989a. "Organizational and Environmental Influences on the Development of the Pro-Choice Movement." *Social Forces* 68 (1): 204–40.

————. 1989b. "Stability and Innovation in the Women's Movement: A Comparison of Two Movement Organizations." *Social Problems* 36 (1): 75–92.

————. 1991. *The Pro-Choice Movement: Organization and Activism in the Abortion Conflict.* New York: Oxford University Press.

Staggenborg, Suzanne, Donna Eder, and Lori Sudderth. 1993. "Women's Culture and Social Change: Evidence from the National Women's Music Festival." *Berkeley Journal of Sociology* 38.

Stamiris, Eleni. 1988. "The Women's Movement in Greece." In *Women, Power, and Policy: Toward the Year 2000*, ed. Ellen Boneparth and Emily Stoper, 247–62. New York: Pergamon Press.

Starr, Paul. 1979. "The Phantom Community." In *Co-ops, Communes and Collectives: Experiments in Social Change in the 1960s and 1970s*, ed. John Case and Rosemary C. R. Taylor, 245–73. New York: Pantheon.

Stearns, Peter. 1988. "Anger and American Work: A Twentieth Century Turning Point." In *Emotion and Social Change: Towards a New Psychohistory*, ed. C. Stearns and Peter Stearns. New York: Holmes & Meier.

Steinem, Gloria. 1979. "What Is a New *Ms.*?" *Ms.*, November, pp. 4–19.

————. 1990. "Sex, Lies, and Advertising." *Ms.*, July–August, pp. 18–28.

Steiner, Linda. 1988. "Oppositional Decoding as an Act of Resistance." *Critical Studies in Mass Communication* 5:1–15.

Steinfels, Peter. 1992. "Pastoral Letter on Women's Role Fails in Vote of Catholic Bishops." *New York Times*, November 19, p. 1.

Stevens, Robin. 1992. "Eating Our Own." *Advocate*, August 13, pp. 33–41.

Stone, Gregory. 1962. "Appearance and the Self." In *Human Behavior and Social Processes*, ed. A. Rose. Boston: Houghton Mifflin.

Stoneback, Sharon. 1989. "Developing Feminist Strategies for Policy Change: The Women's Legal Defense Fund and the Family and Medical Leave Act." Unpublished case study, Women's Studies Program, George Washington University, Washington, D.C.

Stoper, Emily. 1989. *The Student Nonviolent Coordinating Committee.* Brooklyn: Carlson.

Strobel, Margaret. 1990. "Women's Liberation Unions." In *Encyclopedia of the American Left,* ed. Mari Jo Buhle, Paul Buhle, and Dan Georgakas, 841–42. New York: Garland.

———. 1995. "Consciousness and Action: Historical Agency in the Chicago Women's Liberation Union." In *Provoking Agents: Gender and Agency in Theory and Practice,* ed. Judith Kegan Gardiner. Urbana: University of Illinois Press.

Strong-Boag, Veronica J. 1976. *The Parliament of Women: The National Council of Women of Canada, 1893–1929.* Mercury Series. Ottawa: National Museum of Man.

Sullivan, Gail. 1982a. "Cooptation of Alternative Services: The Battered Women's Movement as a Case Study." *Catalyst* 14:39–56.

———. 1982b. "Funny Things Happen on Our Way to Revolution." *Aegis* 34:12–32.

Summers, Anne. 1986. "Mandarins or Missionaries: Women in the Federal Bureaucracy." In *Australian Women: New Feminist Perspectives,* ed. Norma Grieve and Ailsa Burns, 59–67. Melbourne: Oxford University Press.

———. 1991. "Speaking for Women? Comments on Paper by Hester Eisenstein." *Australian Feminist Studies* 14 (Spring): 43–46.

Susser, Ida. 1982. *Norman Street.* New York: Oxford University Press.

Suttles, Gerald D. 1972. *The Social Construction of Communities.* Chicago: University of Chicago Press.

Tarrow, Sidney. 1983. "Struggling to Reform: Social Movements and Policy Change during Cycles of Protest." Occasional paper no. 15, Western Societies Program, Center for International Studies, Cornell University.

Tax, Meredith. 1988. "The Sound of One Hand Clapping: Women's Liberation and the Left." *Dissent,* Fall, pp. 456–62.

Taylor, Verta. 1983. "The Future of Feminism in the 1980s: A Social Movement Analysis." In *Feminist Frontiers: Rethinking Sex, Gender, and Society,* ed. Laurel Richardson and Verta Taylor, 434–51. Reading, Mass.: Addison-Wesley.

———. 1986. "Breaking the Emotional Rules of Motherhood: The Experience and Treatment of Postpartum Depression." Ohio State University Research Foundation Final Report to the Ohio Department of Mental Health.

———. 1989a. "The Future of Feminism: A Social Movement Analysis." In *Feminist Frontiers II,* ed. Laurel Richardson and Verta Taylor, 473–90. New York: Random House.

———. 1989b. "Social Movement Continuity: The Women's Movement in Abeyance." *American Sociological Review* 54:761–75.

Taylor, Verta, and Leila J. Rupp. 1993. "Women's Culture and Lesbian Feminist Activism: A Reconsideration of Cultural Feminism." *Signs* 19:32–61.

Taylor, Verta, and Nancy Whittier. 1992. "Collective Identity and Lesbian Feminist Mobilization." In *Frontiers of Social Movement Theory*, ed. Aldon Morris and Carol McClurg Mueller, 104–29. New Haven, Conn.: Yale University Press.

——. 1993. "The New Feminist Movement." In *Feminist Frontiers III*, ed. Laurel Richardson and Verta Taylor, 533–48. New York: McGraw-Hill.

——. 1995. "Frameworks for the Analysis of Social Movement Culture: The Culture of the Women's Movement." In *Culture and Social Movements*, ed. Hank Johnston and Bert Klandermans. Minneapolis: University of Minnesota Press.

Terborg-Penn, Rosalyn. 1978. "Discrimination against Afro-American Women in the Woman's Movement, 1830–1920." In *The Afro American Woman: Struggles and Images*, ed. Sharon Harley and Rosalyn Terborg-Penn, 17–27. Port Washington, N.Y.: Kennihat Press.

Terrelonge, Pauline. 1984. "Feminist Consciousness and Black Women." In *Women: A Feminist Perspective*, 3d ed., ed. J. Freeman, 557–67. Palo Alto, Calif.: Mayfield.

Texas Council on Family Violence. 1990. "1990 Grants and Contracts Enhance TCFV Services to Family Violence Service Providers." *The River*, January, p. 1.

Thiele, Beverly. 1986. "Vanishing Acts in Social and Political Thought: Tricks of the Trade." In *Feminist Challenges, Social and Political Theory*, ed. C. Patemen and E. Gross. Boston: Allen & Unwin.

Thoits, Peggy A. 1990. "Emotional Deviance: Research Agendas." In *Research Agendas in the Sociology of Emotions*, ed. Theodore Kemper, 180–203. Albany: State University of New York Press.

Thom, Mary. 1987. *Letters to Ms.* New York: Henry Holt.

Thomas, Jan. 1993. "Feminist Women's Health Centers: Internal Structures and External Forces." Paper presented at the annual meeting of the American Sociological Association, Miami, Fla.

Thompson, E. P. 1963. *The Making of the English Working Class*. London: Gollancz.

Tierney, Kathleen. 1982. "The Battered Women Movement and the Creation of the Wife Beating Problem." *Social Problems* 29 (3): 207–20.

Tilly, Charles. 1978. *From Mobilization to Revolution*. Reading, Mass.: Addison-Wesley.

Tilly, Louise A., and Patricia Gurin, eds. 1990. *Women, Politics, and Change*. New York: Russell Sage Foundation.

Tinker, Irene, ed. 1983. *Women in Washington*. Beverly Hills, Calif.: Sage.

Tom, Allison. 1986. "To Make a Life for Myself: An Ethnography of a Job Training Program." Ph.D. diss., Stanford University.

——. 1987. "High Hopes and Small Chances: Explaining Conflict in a Women's Job Training Program." In *Women and Education: A Canadian Perspective*, ed. J. S. Gaskell and A. T. McLaren, 371–88. Calgary, Alberta: Detselig.

Tong, Rosemary. 1989. *Feminist Thought*. Boulder, Colo.: Westview Press.

Touraine, Alain. 1981. *The Voice and the Eye: An Analysis of Social Movements*. New York: Cambridge University Press.

————. 1985. "An Introduction to the Study of Social Movements." *Social Research* 52:749–87.

Travis, Nancy. 1989. "A Case Study of the National Institute for Women of Color." Unpublished case study, Women's Studies Program, George Washington University, Washington, D.C.

Tudiver, Sari. 1986. "The Strength of Links: International Women's Health Networks in the Eighties." In *Adverse Effects: Women and the Pharmaceutical Industry*, ed. Kathleen McDonnell, 187–214. Toronto: Women's Press.

Tuite, Marjorie. 1986. "Let's Talk: Women-Church, Its Struggle and Its Vision." *Probe* 14 (4): 3.

Turner, Ralph H., and Lewis M. Killian. 1987. *Collective Behavior*. 3d ed. Englewood Cliffs, N.J.: Prentice-Hall.

United Nations. 1991. *The World's Women, 1970–1990: Trends and Statistics*. New York: United Nations.

U.S. Department of Justice. 1975. *Rape and Its Victims: A Report for Citizens, Health Facilities, and Criminal Justice Agencies*, by Lisa Brodyaga, Margaret Gates, Susan Singer, Marna Tucker, and Richardson White. Washington, D.C.: U.S. Government Printing Office.

Van Gelder, Lindsy. 1991. "The Jane Collective: Seizing Control." *Ms.*, September–October, pp. 83–85.

Vickers, Jill M. 1988. *Getting Things Done: Women's Views of Their Involvement in Political Life*. Ottawa: UNESCO, Division of Human Rights and Peace, and Canadian Research Institute for the Advancement of Women.

Vickers, Jill M., with M. Janine Brodie. 1978. "Where Are the Women in Canadian Politics?" *Atlantis* 3(2) Part II (Special issue of papers presented at the CRIAW meeting): 40–51.

Vickers, Jill M., Pauline Rankin, and Christine Appelle. 1993. *Politics as If Women Mattered: A Political Analysis of the National Action Committee on the Status of Women*. Toronto: University of Toronto Press.

Viguerie, Richard. 1981. *The New Right: We're Ready to Lead*. Falls Church, Va.: Viguerie Company.

Vobejda, Barbara. 1992. "At 25, NOW Still Defining Feminism, Deflecting Critics." *Washington Post*, January 11, p. A3.

Walker, Gillian A. 1990. *Family Violence and the Women's Movement: The Conceptual Politics of Struggle*. Toronto: University of Toronto Press.

Wallace, Ruth A. 1992. *They Call Her Pastor*. Albany: State University of New York Press.

Walls, Jennifer. 1990. "Examining the Queen Bee Syndrome: The Fund for the

Feminist Majority." Unpublished case study, Women's Studies Program, George Washington University, Washington, D.C.

Walsh, Edward. 1974. "Garbage Collecting: Stigmatized Work and Self-Esteem." In *Humanizing the Workplace*, ed. R. Fairfield, 181–94. New York: Prometheus Books.

Ware, Ann Patrick, ed. 1985. *Midwives of the Future: American Sisters Tell Their Story*. Kansas City, Mo.: Leaven Press.

Warrior, Betsy. 1978. *Working on Wife Abuse*. 6th ed. Cambridge, Mass.: Warrior Press.

Wasielewski, Patricia. 1991. "A Feminist Perspective on Emotion and Collective Action." Unpublished manuscript.

Watson, Jennifer. 1988. "Case Study: Wider Opportunities for Women." Unpublished case study, Women's Studies Program, George Washington University, Washington, D.C.

Watson, Sophie, ed. 1990. *Playing the State: Australian Feminist Interventions*. London: Verso.

Wattleton, Faye. 1990. "Teenage Pregnancies and the Recriminalization of Abortions." *American Journal of Public Health* 80 (March): 269–70.

Wayne, Leslie. 1988. "*Ms.* Magazine Is Being Sold for 2d Time in 6 Months." *New York Times*, March 18, p. D1.

Weaver, Mary Jo. 1986. *New Catholic Women: A Contemporary Challenge to Traditional Church Authority*. New York: Harper & Row.

Weil, Marie. 1986. "Women, Community, and Organizing." In *Feminist Visions of Social Work*, ed. N. Van Den Bergh and L. Cooper. Silver Springs, Md.: NASW (National Association of Social Workers).

Wharton, Carol. 1987. "Establishing Shelters for Battered Women: Local Manifestations of a Social Movement." *Qualitative Sociology* 10 (2): 146–63.

White, Evelyn C. 1985. *Chain, Chain, Change: For Black Women Dealing with Physical and Emotional Abuse*. Seattle, Wash.: Seal Feminist Press.

———. 1990. *The Black Woman's Health Book*. Seattle, Wash.: Seal Press.

Whittier, Nancy. 1991. "Collective Identity and Social Movement Continuity: The Impact of the Women's Movement on Social Movements of the 1980s." Ph.D. diss., Ohio State University.

———. 1995. *Feminist Generations: The Persistence of the Radical Women's Movement*. Philadelphia: Temple University Press.

Wilcox, Clyde. 1987. "Religious Orientations and Political Attitudes: Variations within the New Christian Right." *American Politics Quarterly* 15 (April): 274–96.

Wilenski, Peter. 1986. *Public Power and Public Administration*. Sydney: Hale & Iremonger/RAIPA.

Wilkey, Cindy. N.d. "The Role of Women in Local Radical Organizations." Unpublished paper, Ohio State University.

Wilson, Elizabeth. 1977. *Women and the Welfare State.* London: Tavistock.

Wine, Jeri D., and Janice L. Ristock, eds. 1991. *Women and Social Change: Feminist Activism in Canada.* Toronto: James Lorimer.

Winegar, Karin. 1988. "New *Ms.* Appears Slicker: Some Say It's Less Militant." *Star Tribune* (Minneapolis), April 2, p. 1E.

Wolf, Dagny. 1990. "Case Study: Wider Opportunities for Women." Unpublished case study, Women's Studies Program, George Washington University, Washington, D.C.

"Women's Free Press." 1973. *Know News Bulletin,* January, p. 1.

Yeatman, Anna. 1990. *Bureaucrats, Technocrats, Femocrats: Essays on the Contemporary Australian State.* Sydney: Allen & Unwin.

Young, Stacey J. 1992. "Post-Modern Feminism: Discourse Politics and Political Science Research on the Women's Movement" Ph.D. diss., Cornell University.

Zald, Mayer N. 1988. "The Trajectory of Social Movements in America." In *Research in Social Movements, Conflicts, and Change,* ed. Louis Kriesberg, 10:29. Greenwich, Conn.: JAI Press.

Zald, Mayer N., and Roberta Ash. 1965. "Social Movement Organizations: Growth, Decay, and Change." *Social Forces* 44:327–41.

Zald, Mayer N., and John D. McCarthy. 1980. "Social Movement Industries: Competition and Cooperation among Movement Organizations." In *Research in Social Movements, Conflicts, and Change,* ed. Louis Kriesberg, 3:1–20. Greenwich, Conn.: JAI Press.

———. 1987. "Social Movement Industries: Competition and Conflict among SMOs." In *Frontiers in Social Movement Theory,* ed. Aldon Morris and Carol McClurg Mueller, 161–80. New Haven, Conn.: Yale University Press.

Zald, Mayer N., and Bert Useem. 1987. "Movement and Countermovement Interaction: Mobilization, Tactics, and State Involvement." In *Social Movements in an Organizational Society,* ed. Mayer N. Zald and John D. McCarthy, 247–72. New Brunswick, N.J.: Transaction Books.

Zambrano, M. M. 1985. *Mejor sola que mal acompanada: Para la mujer golpeada/ For the Latina in an Abusive Relationship.* Seattle, Wash.: Seal Feminist Press.

Zavella, Patricia. 1987. *Women's Work and Chicano Families: Cannery Workers of the Santa Clara Valley.* Ithaca, N.Y.: Cornell University Press.

———. 1991. "Reflections on Diversity among Chicanas." *Frontiers* 12:73–85.

Zinn, Howard. 1965. *SNCC: The New Abolitionists.* Boston: Beacon Press.

Zuckerman, Laurence. 1988. "From Upstart to Mainstream." *Time,* December 12, p. 72.

About the Contributors

JOAN ACKER is a professor of sociology at the University of Oregon, a consultant to feminist researchers in Scandinavia, the author of articles on gender and organizations, and a survivor of feminist organizing.

GRETCHEN ARNOLD recently completed her Ph.D. in sociology at Boston University and is currently teaching at the University of Missouri, St. Louis. She wrote her dissertation on the battered women's movement and is now investigating how women's movements bring about normative change.

BERNICE MCNAIR BARNETT is an assistant professor in the Departments of Educational Policy Studies and Sociology at the University of Illinois, Urbana-Champaign, and a former American Sociological Association Minority Fellow. Refocusing attention on issues of leadership in social movements and challenging traditional conceptualizations that limit women's opportunities and recognition, she is writing a book on Black women civil rights leaders.

LINDA CHRISTIANSEN-RUFFMAN seeks new ways of working, knowing, and creating a better world, locally and globally. She has researched and led a variety of feminist groups and professional associations, including Atlantic Women's Fish Net, the Canadian Sociology and Anthropology Association, the Canadian Research Institute for the Advancement of Women, and the International Research Committee on Women in Society. She cofounded the Women's Studies Programme at Saint Mary's University (Halifax, Nova Scotia), where she is a professor of sociology.

HESTER EISENSTEIN, a professor of American studies at the State University of New York at Buffalo, is the author of *Gender Shock: Practicing Feminism on Two Continents*, *Contemporary Feminist Thought*, and a forthcoming book on the Australian femocrats. She is interested in feminist theory; the comparative history of the women's movement and the welfare state; and race, class, and gender in public policy.

AMY FARRELL is an assistant professor of American studies and coordinator of women's studies at Dickenson College. She is currently finishing her book *Yours in Sisterhood??? Ms. Magazine and the Promise of Popular Feminism*.

MYRA MARX FERREE is a professor of sociology and women's studies at the University of Connecticut and the coauthor, with Beth Hess, of *Controversy and Coalition: The New Feminist Movement through Three Decades*. Her current projects include a book in progress on varieties of feminism in the now united Germany, and a collaborative study of mass media and movement discourse about abortion in the United States and Germany.

Jo Freeman is the author of *The Politics of Women's Liberation* (winner of a 1975 American Political Science Association prize as the best scholarly work on women and politics) and editor of *Social Movements of the Sixties and Seventies* and *Women: A Feminist Perspective* (now in its fifth edition). She has a Ph.D. in political science from the University of Chicago (1973) and a J.D. from New York University School of Law (1982). She has published widely in the areas of feminism, social movements, law, public policy, party politics, and organizational theory.

Joyce Gelb, the author of *Feminism and Politics* and coeditor of *Women and Public Policies*, has recently coedited a volume titled *Women of Japan and Korea: Continuity and Change*, with Marian Lief Palley. She is a professor of political science and director of the Graduate Center Program in Women's Studies and Center for the Study of Women and Society at the City University of New York.

Cheryl Hyde is an assistant professor at the Boston University School of Social Work and editor of the *Journal of Progressive Human Services*. She is currently working on a book about grassroots feminism in the 1980s. Her interests include multiculturalism and oppression in social work praxis, organizational culture and transformation, progressive models of social change, and the women's movement and the New Right.

Mary Fainsod Katzenstein is an associate professor of Government and Women's Studies, Cornell University. She is the author or coauthor of two books on ethnic politics in India and is coeditor (with Carol McClurg Mueller) of *The Women's Movements of the United States and Western Europe: Consciousness, Political Opportunity, and Public Policy*. She is completing a book on feminist organizing in the U.S. armed forces and the American Catholic Church, to be called *Liberating the Mainstream*.

Jane Mansbridge is Jane W. Long Professor of the Arts and Sciences in the Department of Political Science at Northwestern University, and a Faculty Fellow of the Center for Urban Affairs and Policy Research. She is the author of *Beyond Adversary Democracy* and *Why We Lost the ERA*, and editor of *Beyond Self-interest*. She is currently working on *Becoming a Feminist*, an interview-based analysis of the effects of social movements on nonactivists.

Susan Marshall is an associate professor of sociology and former director of the women's studies program at the University of Texas at Austin. She is the author of numerous articles on U.S. antifeminist movements, women's right-wing political organizations, and gender and race differences in political attitudes.

PATRICIA YANCEY MARTIN is Daisy Parker Flory Alumni Professor and a professor of sociology at Florida State University. She studies gender and organizations and is completing a monograph on 130 organizations (including twenty-five rape crisis centers) that process rape victims. Her current research, funded by a National Science Foundation grant, is on gender in large for-profit corporations.

NANCY MATTHEWS teaches sociology at Oberlin College and writes about social movements, power, bureaucracy, and inequality. Her recent book *Confronting Rape: The Feminist Anti-Rape Movement and the State* develops those connections in the social history of a local anti-rape movement.

SANDRA MORGEN is director of the Center for the Study of Women in Society and an anthropologist in the Department of Sociology at the University of Oregon. She is writing a book on the women's health movement and has been involved in feminist organizations in the community or in universities since 1974.

CAROL MUELLER is the coordinator of the social and behavioral sciences at the new West Campus of Arizona State University. She has edited *The Women's Movements of the United States and Western Europe: Consciousness, Political Opportunity, and Public Policy* (with MARY KATZENSTEIN), *The Politics of the Gender Gap: The Social Construction of Political Influence*, and *Frontiers in Social Movement Theory* (with Aldon Morris).

MARY PARDO teaches in the Department of Chicano Studies at California State University, Northridge. She is currently working on a book about Mexican American women and grassroots activism.

CLAIRE REINELT is a Ph.D. candidate in sociology at Brandeis University. She is working as a consultant with the Lincoln Filene Center at Tufts University on a project to build the self-evaluation capacity of nonprofit feminist organizations.

RONNEE SCHREIBER is pursuing her Ph.D. in political science at Rutgers University, where she also works for the Center for American Women and Politics. Before returning to school, she was a lobbyist and political organizer for the American Association of University Women and the National Coalition Against Domestic Violence.

WENDY SIMONDS is an assistant professor of women's studies at Emory University. She is the author of *Women and Self-Help Culture: Reading between the Lines* and coauthor, with Barbara Katz Rothman, of *Centuries of Solace: Expressions of Maternal Grief in Popular Literature*. She is currently writing a book about abortion workers.

ROBERTA SPALTER-ROTH is research director at the Institute for Women's Policy Research in Washington, D.C., and teaches in American University's Department of Sociology, where she is building a feminist-oriented master's program in social policy. She is currently involved in researching income packaging strategies of low-income families and in using this research to prevent draconian "welfare reform" policies.

SUZANNE STAGGENBORG is an associate professor of sociology at McGill University. Her work includes *The Pro-Choice Movement: Organization and Activism in the Abortion Conflict*, the recipient of the 1993 Scholarly Achievement Award of the North Central Sociological Association. She is currently studying the development of the U.S. women's movement and movement-countermovement dynamics.

MARGARET STROBEL, a professor of women's studies and history at the University of Illinois at Chicago, is currently researching the Chicago Women's Liberation Union. For many years she was active in the socialist feminist New American Movement in Los Angeles and Chicago. Her first book, *Muslim Women in Mombasa, 1890–1975*, was co-winner in 1980 of the Herskovits Prize awarded by the African Studies Association. Her most recent book, *Restoring Women to History: Africa, Asia, Latin America and the Caribbean, and the Middle East* (coedited with Cheryl Johnson-Odim), is forthcoming.

VERTA TAYLOR is an associate professor of sociology and member of the graduate faculty of women's studies at Ohio State University. She is coauthor (with Leila J. Rupp) of *Survival in the Doldrums*, coeditor (with Laurel Richardson) of *Feminist Frontiers III*, and an associate editor of *Gender & Society*. Her research is on women's movements and the gay and lesbian movement. She is currently writing a book on gender and the contradictions of women's self-help, based on the postpartum depression movement.

ALLISON TOM is an assistant professor in the Department of Administrative, Adult, and Higher Education at the University of British Columbia. She teaches courses on women in education and on ethnographic research. Her primary research interest is women's relationship with their work.

NANCY WHITTIER is an assistant professor of sociology at Smith College. Her current book, *Feminist Generations: The Persistence of the Radical Women's Movement*, examines generational dynamics and feminist culture in the radical feminist movement since the 1960s.

Index